PRISONERS OF WAR
in British Hands during WWI

A study of their history, the camps and their mails

Upper: an unusual registered cover from a British soldier in France to an internee at Knockaloe.
Middle: a letter from August Rhein, in the Privilege Section of Frith Hill Camp, September 1915.
Lower: an early letter from Albert Hardt, at Dorchester, 24 September 1914, to America.

PRISONERS OF WAR
in British Hands during WWI

A study of their history, the camps and their mails

by

Graham Mark

The Postal History Society

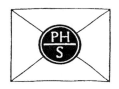

2007

By the same author
Imperial & Foreign Mails - Sea Conveyance During War 1914-1918
(a survey of lost and damaged mails during the Great War)
published by The Postal History Society 1997
British Censorship of Civil Mails during World War I, 1914-1919
published by The Stuart Rossiter Trust Fund, 2000

—o0o—

First published in Great Britain by The Postal History Society in 2007

Copyright © Graham Mark 2007

The moral right of Graham Mark to be identified as the author of this work has been asserted in accordance with the Copyright, Designs and Patents Act of 1988

All rights reserved. No part of this publication may be reproduced, stored in a retrieval system, or transmitted in any form or by any means, electronic, mechanical, photocopying, recording, or otherwise, without the prior permission of both the copyright owner and the above publisher of this book.

ISBN 978 0 85377 029 9

Obtainable from:
Graham Mark, Oast House West, Golden Hill, Wiveliscombe, Somerset, TA4 2NT

Printed in Great Britain by
Short Run Press Limited
Bittern Road, Sowton Industrial Estate
Exeter EX2 7LW

Contents

Acknowledgements	vi
Preface	vii
Notes and Abbreviation	viii
1. Prisoners of War, Historical background	1
2. Prisoners of War, Military and Naval in WWI	5
3. Internees, Civilians of enemy nationality	9
4. Correspondence and parcels of Prisoners of War and censorship considerations	13
5. The work of the P/W Branch of the Postal Censorship M.I.9 (C)2	23
6. Conduct, Discipline, Facilities, etc	31
7. PoW Stationery and Labels and handstamps used on mail	33

The major camps

Alexandra Palace, London N	41	Lewisham, London SE	135
Aylesbury, Buckinghamshire	46	Libury Hall, Ware, Hertfordshire	136
Beachley, Gloucestershire	48	Lofthouse Park, Wakefield, Yorks WR	139
Beech Abbey, Alton, Hampshire	51	Margate, Kent	145
Belmont Hospital, Sutton, Surrey	53	Newbury, Berkshire	146
Blandford, Dorset	55	Oldcastle, Co Meath, Ireland	148
Bramley, near Basingstoke, Hampshire	56	Olympia, London W	150
Brocton, Staffordshire	57	Oswestry, Shropshire	151
Catterick, Yorkshire, North Riding	61	Pattishall, Northamptonshire (previously named Eastcote)	154
Colsterdale, Masham, Yorkshire, NR	62	Queen's Ferry, Flintshire	158
The German Hospital, Dalston, London N	65	Isle of Raasay, Inverness-shire	161
Dartford War Hospital, Dartford, Kent	67	Ramsgate, Kent	163
Donington Hall, near Derby	70	Redmires, Sheffield, Yorkshire WR	164
Dorchester, Dorset	73	Ripon, Yorkshire NR	165
Douglas, Isle of Man	78	Sandhill Park, Taunton, Somerset	166
Dyffryn Aled, Llansannan, Denbighshire	84	Scapa Flow, Orkney Isles	170
Eastcote (see Pattishall)		Ships used as places of detention	172
Edinburgh	88	Shrewsbury, Shropshire	184
Feltham, Middlesex	89	Skipton, Yorkshire WR	187
Frith Hill, Frimley, Surrey	92	Slough, Buckinghamshire	189
Frongoch, Bala, Merionethshire	95	Southampton, Hampshire	191
Hackney Wick, London E	99	Southend-on-Sea, Essex	194
Handforth, Cheshire	101	Stobs, Hawick, Roxburghshire	195
Holyport, near Maidenhead, Berkshire	106	Stratford, London E	200
Horsham, Sussex	111	Stratford-by-Bow, London E	204
Islington, London N	112	Templemore, Co Tipperary, Ireland	205
Jersey, Channel Islands	117	York	206
Kegworth, near Derby	119	Other places of Internment and Prisons	208
Knockaloe, Isle of Man	121	PoW Labour Companies in France	213
Lancaster, Lancashire	130		
Leigh, Lancashire	132		

Appendices:	Camp list	217
	Escapes	235
	Bibliography	249
Index		253

Acknowledgements

Without the assistance and encouragement of friends, collectors, researchers and correspondents, a study of this topic would be much more difficult to compile than it has, in fact, proved. My thanks grateful are extended to:

Richard Arthurs	Alan Green	Frank Quast
Andrew Brooks	James Grimwood Taylor	Fergus Read
Peter Burrows	Julius Harstein	Charles Sacconaghi
Barry Chinchen	Ted Huggins	Derrick Slate
John Coltman	Prof. Barrie Jay †	Derek Smeathers
Patrick Codron	Alan Jeffreys	Donald Somerville
David Cornelius †	Les Jobbins	John Thiesen
Mike Cox	Alistair Kennedy	Peter and Jenny Towey
Terry Crawford	Kenneth Killeen	Hal Vogel
Frank Daniel †	John Leathes	John Walling
Rudolf Ehfrank	Charles Leonard	Eddie Weeks
Martin Evans	Martin Lynes	Mike White
Richard Farman	Konrad Morenweiser	Alan Wishart
Myron Fox	Hans Moxter	Kenneth Wright
Patrick Frost	Nic Nicol	Argyll Etkin Ltd
Pat Gale	Tony Osmond	Cavendish Philatelic
Reg Gleave	John Peart	Auctions Ltd
Michael Goodman	Bill Pipe	The Imperial War Museum

I hope that any person whose name has been omitted will forgive me for missing them from this list, but I trust I have not overlooked their contribution.

I must also thank the librarians and curators in many towns and cities around the country and the staff in the National Archives both at Kew and Washington DC. All have helped with locating material and answered my questions. I also acknowledge the freedom I have been allowed, to browse among the shelves and use the copier, by Mervyn Todd at the House of Antiquity.

A very sincere thank you is due to Prue Henderson who read the draft script and pointed out my inconsistencies, errors of grammar and syntax and she made many valuable comments which I have incorporated into this work. Any remaining errors of fact or opinion are entirely my own.

I also thank the President and Council of The Postal History Society for allowing this book to be published under their imprint.

Preface

I began work on this study some six years ago, but I was diverted into another project and only returned to this topic in early 2006. The patience of a number of friends with an interest in this project has been commendable and I thank them for their forbearance.

My interest in this subject developed from a collection of PoW mail. However the letters themselves rarely tells many stories, for the restrictions on what the prisoners were allowed to write about, and the limit of two letter-sheets per week, severely curtailed their opportunities to tell of their day-to-day experiences. Few books have been published in English about life in the camps in Britain, and not a large number in German. My imperfect knowledge of the language has restricted my use of German resources very considerably.

Previous writers on this topic, and there have not been many of them, have focussed on particular aspects, or locations. Other than John Bird, in his thesis, none have appeared to have considered the subject as widely as I hope I have been able to do. Whilst there must be many individuals worth researching, and work camps with interesting histories, the time, travel, costs and other aspects required to research them would prove very great and the resulting book would be of almost encyclopaedic length. A colleague has been focussing his research on the Scottish work camps and his data will be sufficient to fill a substantial volume on its own, when he is able to get it into print.

Official records have been examined, but with over 500 boxes in the FO383 series at the National Archives at Kew and the scattered files in the HO45 series, plus Admiralty, Board of Trade, Ministry of Munitions and many other Government departments involved, it is inevitable that I have missed a fair amount of valuable information which might have been incorporated into this work. I hope that others with the inclination to research a family member or a local camp will be able to use this study as a starting point and in due course publish their work.

The illustrations used in this book come from my own collection of material and from friends and colleagues. Some collectors prefer their names not to be shown as the owner of a particular item so, for consistency, no names are used in connection with illustrations, but I trust I have remembered to include then in the list of acknowledgements.

Graham Mark
Wiveliscombe
16 August 2007

Notes and Abbreviations

Footnotes, or references within the text in the style:

763.27114/..	USA, National Archives, Records of the Department of State, film rolls M367, Nos. 283 to 303. In these micro-films the documents are numbered continuously from 1, which is the extension to the basic reference number.
ADM...	Admiralty files in British National Archives
CAB...	Cabinet Office files in British National Archives
FO 383/...	Foreign Office files in British National Archives concerning PoWs and Internees
HO 45/...	Home Office files in British National Archives concerning Internees
MT...	Transport Departments' files in British National Archives
OS...	Ordnance Survey
POST...	Post Office files in the British Postal Museum and Archive
Cd.., or Cmd..	British Parliamentary Papers published by command. Cd. was the prefix used until 1918, Cmd. was used from 1919. Other British Government papers have more complicated index references so are usually referred to in this work by a short title; the full title and publishing details are given in the bibliography.

Abbreviations used:

Orders and decorations after an officer's name are abbreviated according to standard practice.

ACI	Army Council Instructions
BEF	British Expeditionary Force
C-in-C	Commander in Chief
Grid Ref	Grid Reference as used by the Ordnance Survey in the United Kingdom
HC Branch	Hostile Countries Branch of the Postal Censorship, became P/W Branch in Dec 1914.
M.I.9	The Postal Censorship, a division of Military Intelligence from January 1916. In 1914 it was M.O.5 (H) and from April 1915 it was designated M.O.9
NCO(s)	Non-Commissioned Officer(s)
ORs	Other Ranks
PoW(s)	Prisoner(s) of War
POW Dept	A department of the Foreign Office
POWIB	Prisoner of War Information Bureau
P/W Branch	Prisoner of War Branch of the Postal Censorship (this abbreviation was used by them)
WW1	World War I (1914-1919)
RAMC	Royal Army Medical Corps

1. PRISONERS OF WAR
Historical background

Until the 16th century, prisoners of war were an accepted form of booty, from which a successful army could profit by ransoming their captives. The families of the common soldiers could not raise money to buy back their relations, so such poor unfortunates were either butchered on the spot or sold into servitude or slavery. The more affluent a captive, the higher was his price, so there was an active trade in this human 'commodity' with all participating, from the lowly archers right up to their Lords, Princes and Kings. Probably the highest price for a PoW was 3 million gold écus, demanded by King Edward III, of England, for King John of France, after he was captured at the Battle of Poitiers in 1356. King Edward received about half of this sum, which was raised from the French people by taxes on salt, wine and other goods, but the balance remained unpaid when King John died in 1364, still in captivity. Soldiers of lesser rank, on both sides, profited from the trade and a number of family fortunes were made at this time, which resulted in the building of mansions and castles, some of which survive today, along with their titled descendants. Two good examples are Knowle, in Kent, and Herstmonceaux, in Sussex, built by the Fiennes brothers, Sir James and Sir Roger respectively, partly with their profits from the Agincourt campaign of 1415.

The Treaty of Westphalia (1648), which ended the Thirty-Years' War, reduced the powers of the Holy Roman Empire and enhanced the standing of the German Princely States. That treaty also released prisoners of war without ransom and is now accepted to be the end of the era of widespread enslavement of PoWs.

The French philosopher Montesquieu, in *L'Espirit des Lois* (1748), stated that the only right in war was to prevent a captive from doing harm. No longer was a prisoner to be treated as a piece of property. Others followed his thoughts and developed them, but in subsequent wars the treatment of PoWs left much to be desired, especially during the Napoleonic Wars (1803-15), the American Civil War (1861-65) and the Franco-Prussian War (1870-71).

In Britain the welfare of Prisoners of War was vested in the Admiralty, initially with *The Commissioners for Taking Care of Sick and Wounded Seamen and for Exchanging Prisoners of War*, colloquially known as 'The Sick and Hurt Office'. At the end of 1799 The Transport Office took over responsibility until 1819, when this duty was transferred to the Victualling Office, still within the Admiralty.[1]

The Seven Years War (1756-63) had presented Britain with a problem of accommodating some 26,000 PoWs during the last year of that conflict. Only Milbay Prison at Plymouth was purpose built, so other premises were taken over. These included the castles at Edinburgh, Porchester (Hants) and Sissinghurst (Kent), local gaols, country houses, farms etc., and of course the notorious hulks (disused and dismasted naval vessels). Britain and France agreed conventions on the treatment of the sick and wounded, of PoWs and deserters. Prisoners were to be exchanged or ransomed, a tariff being agreed, while certain non-combatant functionaries were exempt from capture. However, the apparent good intentions of these agreements were nullified to some extent by a combination of the politicians and their creatures, also the merchants who had personal greed to satisfy from the commissariat contracts, and disciplinarians among the prison governors and naval commanders of the hulks.[2]

---

[1] Abell F (1914) and *Postal History* #199 (1977) pp18-20, #217 (1981) pp8-9. For a copy of the 1798 agreement, called a Cartel, between France and Britain for the exchange of prisoners, see *Postal History* #289 (1999) pp24-25.

[2] Abell *ob cit* and Firebrace J in *Postal History* #273 (1995) p19

The American War of Independence (1775-83) was fought between a professional British Army plus mercenaries on one side, which were poorly accommodated, and a hastily organised volunteer force of secessionists. Neither side had the facilities for holding any number of PoWs and on the British side hulks, disused warehouses, churches and gaols were used. None of them satisfactory by any stretch of the imagination.

The Napoleonic Wars created a greater need for accommodation for PoWs in Britain. 122,000 were brought to this country between 1803 and 1814 and the largest number held at one time was 72,000 in 1814. Many 'other rank' prisoners, and some officers, were held on the hulks moored in naval dockyards and it was the proximity of those hulks to the naval arsenals at Plymouth that prompted the Admiralty to seek alternative sites. New prisons were therefore built in England, at Dartmoor (Devon) and Norman Cross (Huntingdonshire), and in Scotland, at Valleyfield (Midlothian) and Perth. A number of existing gaols were also used, as well as buildings requisitioned and adapted by the Admiralty Transport Office. Officers were usually confined to a particular town and they had to give their parole to stay within defined limits, but if they broke their parole they were imprisoned.

The wars of the mid and later 19th century, which involved Britain, did not require PoW facilities in the home country. The Crimean, Indian and South African wars all resulted in captures of enemy soldiers but almost all of them were held in places abroad. It was not until the South African wars that civilian populations were held in places of confinement; this was the first usage of the term Concentration Camps. Until that time civilians were allowed to continue their own life and business, providing they did not interfere with the military or naval activities. Espionage was undertaken by both sides, but they were small scale operations, and any captured spies were held as PoWs or criminals. In any event, the three wars mentioned all took place in distant parts, so there was little danger to British troops in the Crimea from, say, a Russian emigrant pursuing his trade in London even if he was writing home and referring to military or naval matters.

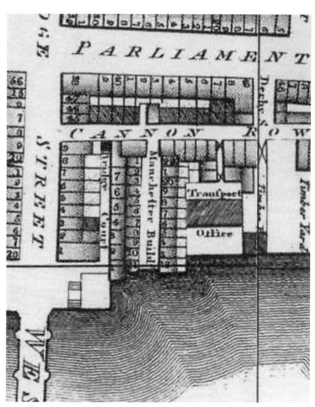
The Transport Office of the Admiralty, near to Westminster Bridge in London. (North is to the right on this map by Horwood & Faden 1813.)

Letter dated 13 July 1815, from Dartimorh (*sic*) Prison to Morlaix, from one of 1,879 French soldiers captured at Waterloo. The letter includes (in translation):
... I was made prisoner on June 18, at 9 pm at the Mountain of Iron near Brussels [Waterloo] *by the English Army and immediately brought to England*

Until the 17th century it is unlikely that many 'other rank' prisoners of war would have been active letter writers but, with the increase in literacy, steps were needed to supervise the correspondence of captives. From the period of the Napoleonic Wars, prisoners' letters become more frequent. In Britain it was a duty of the Agents of the Admiralty, local officials supervising the prisoners on parole, to ensure that the prisoners' letters were sent to the Admiralty where they were censored by the department responsible for PoWs. Prison Governors and Commanders of the hulks also had to send any letters written by their charges to the Admiralty for censorship.

During the Crimean war the mails between Britain and Russia were not affected: the Post Offices in London and St Petersburg continued to exchange mails with each other, via Germany. It was only with the South African wars that international mail services were interrupted by one side, the British, to inconvenience their enemy. As Britain had command of the seas around Southern Africa, this was a relatively easy step to take. Censorship of the mails by British officials was first carried out on a substantial scale during the South African wars, and pretty well all prisoners' mail was examined on the British side.

The Brussels Conference of 1874, was called to codify rules of warfare in the light of the Franco-Prussian war. *Inter alia*, it discussed treatment of PoWs, but none of the Conventions drawn up and agreed between the delegates were ever ratified by the participating Governments. More successfully the Hague Conventions of 1899 and 1907 laid down rules for warfare and treatment of prisoners.

However, the numbers of PoWs taken during WWI overwhelmed the rules. In addition, the 1906 Geneva Convention dealt with medical personnel and chaplains taken prisoner, and again, circumstances or deliberate evasion of these rules, were common during WWI.

It should be noted that a precondition of the Hague Conventions was that all the combatant nations should ratify and adopt them for the rules to become effective. Although some belligerents had not ratified the 1907 Conventions, therefore they were technically inoperative, most nations involved in WWI sought to adhere to the principles, and they even negotiated agreements which exceeded the Hague Rules. An example of such an agreement would be the transfer of sick and wounded to internment in Switzerland. The Geneva Convention of 1929 improved the rules, which were generally accepted, but not always applied by the belligerents, during WWII. For example the transfer of the sick and wounded to neutral countries was not repeated. The rules were further strengthened by a 1949 Convention and by protocols agreed in 1977.

Token coinage, issued to PoWs in camps in Britain in WWI (enlarged). The 2s/6d, 1s/- and 6d were similar in size to, but not the same as, the official coinage, but much lighter. There was no design on the reverse side. The metal used appears to have been susceptible to corrosion.
(Courtesy The Imperial War Museum)
Token coins were also issued to PoWs held by the British Army in France. Those were 1 franc, 50 centimes and 10 centimes (see p.214). No examples of the French currency tokens have been seen by the current author.

2. PRISONERS OF WAR
Military and Naval in WWI

The 1907 Hague Rules required each belligerent state to set up a PoW Enquiry Bureau upon the outbreak of hostilities. In Britain, the Prisoner of War Information Bureau (POWIB) was established in August 1914, at 49 Wellington Street, London WC [3] (near the Aldwych), under Sir Paul Harvey KCMG CB (1869-1948), a civil servant who had extensive foreign experience, but since 1912 he had been Chief Auditor of the National Health Insurance Scheme. Harvey was succeeded, in November 1915, by Sir John David Rees Bt KCIE CVO MP (1854-1922), previously a civil servant in India, then Member of Parliament from 1906, first for Montgomery and later for Nottingham. One duty of the POWIB was to maintain registers of prisoners and internees held anywhere in the Empire. Camp Commandants had to provide lists of new prisoners immediately they arrived, and these brief data were expanded with more detailed returns compiled on Red Cross information cards. Reports of transfers and hospitalisations were also provided, when appropriate, for transmission to the prisoner's family in his home country. Another duty of the POWIB was to keep records of British and Empire prisoners held by the enemies.

PoW Welfare Committees were set up in Britain, and the Empire countries, by regimental organisations, municipal associations, large employers etc., and they sent parcels to prisoners held in Germany, Austria, Turkey and Bulgaria. A lack of co-ordination between these bodies in Britain prompted the formation of a Central Committee, but this lacked official backing. Therefore the War Office took over responsibility in September 1916, and thereafter it was run by a Committee, which included members of the Red Cross and the Order of St John of Jerusalem. The first Chairman was Sir Starr Jameson Bt CB (1853-1917) and on 3 January 1918 *The Times* reported that Lord Sandwich would chair the Central Committee. The organisation operated from Thurloe Place, London SW7, where 750 people were employed.

In 1914 Britain was quite unprepared to accommodate PoWs. The War Office sent out a telegram to all Commands in Britain:-

---

[3] *The Times* 15 August 1914 p4d

Make temporary arrangements at once to accommodate guard and ration prisoners of war in your district. Buildings may be requisitioned or camps formed but not in vicinity of defended ports. Wire places selected where prisoners can be sent. Report as soon as possible what permanent arrangements you propose. Attention is called to page 248 Manual of Military Law. Copy of rules for discipline and treatment of prisoners of war will be sent to you today. Admiralty have arranged for prisoners to be landed at following ports Sheerness Dover Portsmouth Plymouth Southampton Queenstown and Rosyth. (HO45/10729/255193)

In the early weeks of the war, because of the great retreat of the Allies to the Marne, few prisoners were taken by the British Army. Of those who were captured, many were Uhlans from scouting parties. The first report of prisoners being moved to Britain, published in *The Times*, was on 22 August 1914. It stated that 18 officers and 432 men were en route from Bruges. At sea, the Battle of Heligoland, 28 August 1914, resulted in the capture of 348 Germans, rescued from the sea and sinking ships. There were no prepared Camps, so improvisation had to be the order of the day. Some older military camps were converted but, at the same time, the Army needed all its barracks as it was on an energetic drive to recruit, equip and train large numbers of volunteers who had joined the colours in response to Lord Kitchener's appeals. Therefore PoW camps were created from disused industrial buildings, schools, a racecourse and in addition tented camps were opened.

Responsibility for PoWs within the War Office was at first vested in a section of the Adjutant General's Department, AG3, under Lt General Sir Herbert Belfield KCB DSO (1857-1934). In February 1915 a new Directorate of Prisoners of War was formed, with Belfield still its Director, and it continued to be part of the AG's Department. From a Director and an Assistant, shown in the March 1915 Army List, the staff grew so that by November 1918 there was a Director, still Belfield (by then with a KCMG, and in 1919 a KBE), a Deputy Director and two Assistant Directors (all three got CBEs in 1919), three Deputy Assistant Directors, seven Staff Captains, two Staff Lieutenants and five other officers. No doubt there were also a fairly large number of NCOs and clerks, both civilian and military.

At the outbreak of war the Embassy of the United States of America took on responsibility for protecting the interests of Germans and Austrians in the UK, as well as for the interests of British citizens in Germany and Austria; this included both interned civilians and PoWs. However instructions from Robert Lansing, the US Secretary of State, dated 23 June 1915 to Mr Gerrard, their Ambassador in Berlin, made it clear that the American Government was willing to undertake relief work and inspections, but only at the request of the belligerent powers, and clearly on the basis that neither the United States nor their representatives assumed responsibilities of any kind. (763.72114/498)

Reports by the US Embassy officials on the PoW camps in UK refer to Lowry and Markel Committees. Edward G Lowry was an official of the US Embassy who was specifically charged with the task of looking after the welfare of Germans in the UK. He had special facilities for the distribution of money, parcels and gifts, sent by the German government or individuals, to prisoners and internees (Cd.7817, p42). Dr Markel, a chemist, was a German immigrant who had taken British nationality in the 1880s, and lived in London. He organised welfare schemes from an office at 20 Queen's Gate Terrace, London SW, distributing money and articles to PoW and internee camps, rather than to individuals, and he was allowed to visit the camps, until his pass was withdrawn in July 1916. In the House of Commons it was stated that his pass was withdrawn because he had used it infrequently.[4] However, a report of visits made by Dr Markel's agency to six camps in early 1916 (in FO 383/162), shows that the pass was used, so maybe there was another reason for cancelling his pass.

On 4 March 1915 the German submarine *U8* was sunk in the English Channel. 29 officers and seamen were rescued, but the Admiralty did not consider they should be treated as other prisoners of war, because German submarines had attacked and sunk un-armed merchant ships, thereby endangering non-combatants, neutral citizens, women and children. These PoWs were therefore held in the Royal Naval Detention Barracks at Chatham, but otherwise their conditions were similar to other PoWs in Britain. A further ten from *U12*, destroyed in the North Sea on 12 March 1915, were held at Devonport Detention Barracks. Following publicity of this in the British press, the German Government lodged a protest, and the Foreign Office replied robustly (*The Times* 9 March 1915). Nevertheless, Germany segregated a number of British officer PoWs, 7 Captains and 32 Lieutenants, all titled or from well-connected families, in reprisal. In early May, Mr Lowry visited Chatham and Devonport and found conditions and food quite satisfactory, the only complaint by the PoWs was that they were not in regular PoW camps. (763.72114/442 and 457)

On 5 June *U14* was rammed and sunk off Peterhead and 6 officers and 21 men of the crew were captured. However, on 9 June 1915 it was announced in the House of Commons, by Arthur Balfour (recently appointed First Lord of the Admiralty) that the policy of segregating submarine PoWs had ended.[5] As *The Times* stated next day ... *it was futile to pursue a course which appeared to compete with the Germans in the matter of reprisals*. The officers were moved to Dyffryn Aled, Donington Hall and Holyport, while the seamen were transferred to Shrewsbury, Frith Hill and Dorchester (763.72114/565). The Admiralty expressed strong misgivings over this new arrangement, for they considered the submarine officers to be higher security risks. Some PoW officers had been repatriated and the Admiralty feared that before being released they had been able to mix with the submariners, so that information would get back to Germany on British methods of detecting and capturing submarines. As a result of subsequent discussions it was decided, with the War Office that the submarine officers would be concentrated at Dyffryn Aled. (ADM 1/8445/15)

The Cabinet discussed the complex administration of PoWs in September 1916. The Admiralty, War Office, Foreign Office and Home Office all had responsibilities in this field and no doubt a smoother administration could have been achieved if only one or two departments were involved. Lord Robert Cecil (of the Foreign Office), supported by Viscount Grey, proposed that the Foreign Office should be in overall control. An alternative, that the Admiralty and War Office should have joint responsibility, was discussed but difficulties were foreseen. A third option of creating an entirely new department was

---

[4] *Hansard HC* 29 June 16, vol.83, col.1064: 17 July 16, vol.84, col.649: 25 July 18, vol.108, col.2022

[5] *Hansard HC* vol.72, col.267. However, papers in CAB 37/129/9 include a letter from Prime Minister Asquith, 5 June 1915, which stated that there was then no intention to change the separate treatment.

offered but not taken up. Papers in CAB37/155/36 do not make clear any results from these discussions but, other later papers indicate that these four principal departments, and others, continued to be active in administering the PoWs and Alien Internees.

By December 1916 there were 38 camps in England, eight in Scotland, two on the Isle of Man, Oldcastle in Ireland, and a camp in Jersey. There were also two large camps in France under British control. Some civil prison accommodation was taken over to hold PoWs where camps lacked facilities for punishment cells. For example, parts of Chelmsford gaol and Woking Military Detention Barracks became prisons for army PoWs, officers and soldiers respectively, and Bodmin gaol became a naval prison. Other detention centres for PoWs were arranged within existing military establishments.

The proposal to employ PoWs with the British Army in France was first put to General Haig in early1916. He was not in favour of the scheme as he feared escapes and expenses, and he expected a poor performance from such labour. However, he was persuaded to try out the plan and 3,000 were transferred from Britain to France, in April and May 1916. They were put to work in the ports, forests and quarries. With the demands on manpower for the Battle of the Somme, PoW labour was more extensively employed, and by the end of hostilities large numbers of prisoners were held by the British in France (see Table 1), where the Army employed over 150,000 of them in nearly 350 labour companies. This topic is more fully covered at pages 213-216.

The employment of PoWs in Britain also began in early 1916 but the growth was much slower than with the BEF. In March 1917 only 7,000 were being employed outside the camps, but by the end of the war this figure had risen to 65,000. A large proportion of these were engaged in agricultural work. A 1919 *List of Places of Internment* gave the locations of 190 agricultural camps and depots where the PoWs were based. From these bases they went out to work on local farms. There were also 267 work camps listed where the occupations included road-making, quarrying, tree-felling and sawmills. Jackson (p140) suggested that the harvests of grain and potatoes would not have been possible, in 1917, without the PoW labour gangs, in view of the departure of farm workers conscripted into the Army.

When the USA joined the war in April 1917, the responsibilities their Ambassadors had carried out in Britain, Germany and Austria, in terms of protecting the interests of PoWs and internees, were taken over by Swiss and Swedish diplomats. The Swiss became responsible for German PoWs and internees in the United Kingdom and British persons in Germany while the Swedish looked after the interests of Austrians, Hungarians and Turkish in this country and the British subjects in those countries.

On 24 January 1917 the German Government issued a demand, that German PoWs employed in France and Belgium, by the British Army, should be withdrawn from the battle zone and housed as least 30km from the lines and in accommodation suitable to the weather conditions. 'In view of the evil conditions' suffered by the German prisoners, a reply was demanded by 1 February and, in the absence of such a reply, they threatened to move British PoWs into the operations area of the Western Front (763.72114/2456).

In early 1918, when it had been irrefutably established that the Germans were moving British PoWs into areas liable to attack from the Allies, the British Government bowed to public agitation and moved German officer prisoners into requisitioned buildings in Margate, Ramsgate and Southend, south-east coastal towns that had been bombed by the Germans, and also in two suburbs of London. These were termed Reprisals Camps in some official documents, but the Government denied that description in a letter of 26 July 1918, to the Swiss Minister (FO 383/440).

Articles in the various Armistice Agreements in 1918 provided for all Allied PoWs and internees to be handed over unconditionally and without reciprocity. Cox & Co's *List of British Officers taken Prisoner* indicates that most British officer PoWs held by the enemy got home for Christmas 1918 but some were delayed until January 1919. *The Times*, 13 January 1919, p5c, reported that 153,372 PoWs had returned from Germany and a further 4,081 were awaiting passage in the Netherlands.

In January 1919 British forces held over half-a-million prisoners, of whom 43,308 were civilians (see Table 1, overleaf). Britain released some 6,000 Polish men of German nationality in January 1919.

Articles 214-224 of the Treaty of Versailles, signed on 28 June 1919, dealt with the release and repatriation of German PoWs. Article 214 provided for repatriation 'as soon as possible after the coming into force of the present Treaty', and Article 217 stated that the whole cost of repatriation, and

held in	German	Austrian & Hungarian	Turkish	Bulgarian	Others *	Total
UK	122,121	5,644	97	23	158	128,043
France	199,840					199,840
Italy		6,600				6,600
elsewhere †	21,551	3,122	119,062	7,049	21,948	172,732
Total	343,512	15,366	119,159	7,072	22,106	507,215

Table 1: PoWs held by Britain and Empire countries in January 1919.
* includes friendly nationalities, e.g. Poles, Czechs, Arabs, Syrians etc
† includes Salonika, Egypt, the Dominions and Colonies

provision of the necessary transport, would be for account of the German Government. Similar articles featured in the treaties with other countries. The British and American Governments wanted to proceed with the return of German PoWs, as promptly as possible, but France preferred to retain her prisoners so that they could be used as labourers to assist in reconstruction schemes. France even offered to 'borrow' the PoWs held by the UK and USA, but the British and American governments considered such a step illegal.

Britain decided not to await the ratification of the Treaty and, with the consent of the Supreme Council in Paris, began repatriating German PoWs on 30 August 1919. By the end of September 120,000 had been returned to Germany, with most of the remainder going during October and November. Although the treaty required Germany to provide the necessary shipping, that country was in fact not in a position to do so because the Allies had sequestrated many German ships. Hence only about half the repatriations were carried by German ships. (*The Times* 1 Dec 1919)

The other peace treaties [6] had similar provisions, but only that with Austria was signed before the PoWs were repatriated. The Bulgarians and Czechs were released in October, and the Austrians by November 1919. Some difficulty was found in selecting a suitable route for the return of prisoners to the landlocked states of central Europe, but in the event most were moved first to France then on by train to Germany. At Cologne they were handed over to their respective national representatives who arranged onward transport with the German Government.

By the end of November 1919 there were some 1,400 German officers and some orderlies in this country, who were released about Christmas time. In addition, the crews from the scuttled German fleet at Scapa Flow, 144 officers and 1,600 ratings, were not released until January 1920.

Brief press reports in April 1920 [7] stated that the last German PoW had left Oswestry, under escort for Scotland, but there was no explanation for the delay, nor his destination. Belfield, p79, reported that in December 1919, 4 officers and 9 other ranks, against whom charges had been laid, were held in Britain, but did not state when or whether they were released.

In 1926 there was a move to have the remains of all Germans who died as prisoners or internees in Britain, or whose bodies were brought to Britain, re-interred at one place, but it appears that negotiations were protracted and no agreement was reached. However, in 1959 an agreement was made between the British and the Federal German Governments to move the remains, from both world wars, to a new cemetery at Cannock Chase. The work was completed by 1962. Now under the care of the German War Graves Commission, there are 2,143 graves belonging to WWI soldiers, sailors, airmen and civilians, and nearly 2,800 from WWII. A further 263 dead remain buried elsewhere in Britain. In Ireland a similar move has brought all the remains to one location at Glencree, Co Wicklow, 11 miles south of Dublin.

---

[6] Treaty of St. Germain, signed with Austria 10 September 1919; Articles 160-170. Treaty of Neuilly, signed with Bulgaria, 27 November 1919; Articles 105-115. Treaty of Trianon, signed with Hungary, 4 June 1920; Articles 144-154. Treaty of Sevres, signed with Turkey 10 August 1920; Articles 208-217.

[7] *The Times*, 17 April 1920, p11f and *Border Counties Advertiser* 21 April 1920, p7

3. INTERNEES
Civilians of enemy nationality during WWI

The Home Office was responsible for civilian internees. During the war about 30,000 men, and a very few women, were detained under Defence of the Realm Regulations. Initially this restricted the movement, or residence, of an alien, and in breach of such regulations the alien was liable to be interned or confined, in a similar manner to prisoners of war. Later the regulations were extended and public agitation resulted in the large numbers being detained.

The Aliens Restriction Act [4&5 Geo V, Cap.12], passed 5 August 1914, provided a framework of powers to restrict the movement of non-British people within, into or out of the country, permitting deportation, requiring aliens to reside and remain within certain districts, and obliging them to register. On 7 August, the War Office sent instructions to all military Commands in the country to arrest, as prisoners of war, all Germans and Austrians aged between 17 and 42 years, but that telegram was cancelled by a further message on 9 August. Significantly the instruction included Austrians, but war against that country was not declared until 12 August.

Following the second message it was explained to military commanders that the Police, subject to some caveats, were to be responsible for arresting aliens and that they would be handed over to the military authorities for custody. Hence men of enemy nationality of military age, or if suspect or destitute, were arrested, many of them in the early days of the war at ports as they tried to leave for the Continent. So internment began in early August 1914, and the first camps were at Olympia, Frith Hill and Horsham. War Office instructions dated 31 August 1914 (in HO45/10729/255193) listed places which had been selected as 'places for internment'.

Permanent camps
Dorchester   Frith Hill   Queen's Ferry
Dyffryn Aled   Lancaster   Templemore
Edinburgh   Newbury

Temporary camps
Dublin   Horsham   Olympia   and   York

Not all the sites came into use immediately, but the list does show that some plans were being made, although in the early weeks of the war other places were used. Local newspapers from around the country mention schools, ships in harbour, workhouses etc, being pressed into use pending arrangements to move the internees to the formal camps. (See p.208)

Meanwhile, on 20 August 1914, the Destitute Aliens Committee was formed with Sir William Byrne KCVO CB, Chairman of the Board of Control [for mental institutions], in the chair. Other members were: John Pedder, an Assistant Secretary at the Home Office; Arthur Belmore Lowry, Chief Inspector, Local Government Board; Hon. Frank Trevor Bigham, Assistant Commissioner, Metropolitan Police; Colonel John William Gascoigne Roy, an Assistant-Adjutant-General at the War Office, and Edgar Seligman (not traced). Edmund Sebag-Montefiore was appointed Secretary on 24 August and Miss L Burton joined as clerk and shorthand typist.

This Committee was formed to arrange for the repatriation of destitute aliens, to cooperate with and guide charitable societies relieving destitute aliens and organise their accommodation and maintenance.[8] In November 1916 this body changed its name to the Civilian Internment Camps Committee. Also in August 1914, The Religious Society of Friends appealed for funds to aid innocent alien enemies in Britain rendered destitute by the war, and the United Alien Relief Societies launched a similar appeal. This latter body was chaired by Frederick Huth Jackson PC (1862-1921), a partner in Huth & Co and a Director of the Bank of England. Other members included Countess Benckendorff, wife of the Russian Ambassador; Mrs Garrett Fawcett, widow of Henry Fawcett MP, the blind Postmaster General; Baron Bruno von Schröder, the senior partner of the banking family; and Mr Geoffrey Drage who, from his *Who's Who* entry, appears to have been a professional committee member.

Circulars were sent to the Police in September and October directing them to arrest male enemy subjects of military age. In a paper dated 4 October 1914, the Foreign Office stated that some 10,000 had been

---

[8] *The Times* 2 September 1914, p5e

arrested and were detained in 'concentration camps'. 8,600 of them were Germans and 1,400 Austro-Hungarians, but these were less than one third of the enemy-alien male population, of military age, then residing in the UK. A Cabinet sub-committee reported, on 17 October 1914, that it was of the opinion that all aliens of military age should be interned and those not of military age should be sent to Germany or Austria-Hungary (CAB 38/28/49). As the accommodation for those arrested proved insufficient, Chief Constables asked the government to amend their policy and this resulted in a series of 'stop-go' orders from the Home Office.

By the end of October 20,000 had been interned and they were held camps in all parts of the UK, including two in Ireland, two in Scotland, one in Wales and nine in England. Many of these camps were mixed, *ie* they held both military PoWs and civilian internees, but at the end of November the Government announced a policy of separating combatant PoWs from civilian internees.[9] By then large numbers of relatives and friends were applying for the release of internees on grounds of harmlessness, ill-health or for business reasons. To handle these cases a PoW Branch had been formed in the Home Office on 4 November 1914, but Lord Kitchener did not agree with the Home Office running it, so the responsibility for this Branch was transferred to the War Office, although physically it remained in Home Office buildings (HO45/11025/410118/2). Further instructions were issued to the Police requiring them to make recommendations for release where they considered it appropriate and, through the winter of 1914-15, nearly 3,000 men were liberated, and further releases were made in the Spring.

The big increase in numbers interned during the Autumn of 1914, combined with the poor conditions in some camps, particularly those under canvas, resulted in the Admiralty chartering passenger liners on which civilian and combatant prisoners were held. These were a temporary measure until permanent camps could be built on land. By April 1915 the prisoners were being moved ashore, to purpose built camps, and the ships were being released one-by-one.

On 8 May 1915 a German submarine sank the Cunard liner SS *Lusitania* off the south cost of Ireland. This provoked wide-scale ill feeling in Britain against people of German origin and those with German names. Demonstrations and riots took place in many cities and towns, resulting in damage to the property of those perceived as enemies. Some victims of the riots simply moved away, others voluntarily surrendered for internment, and many were arrested and interned. In Hull, for example, the shops and homes of a number of pork butchers were attacked but there was no looting; on the other hand much more damage was done in Liverpool.

On 13 May Mr Asquith announced that all male enemy subjects of military age would be interned and those over or under military age, together with women, would be deported.[10] Three weeks after SS *Lusitania* was sunk, an air-raid on Hull, by Zeppelin *L9*, killed 24 and injured a considerable number. In the aftermath of that raid, more serious civil disturbances took place in that city. Many more German shops were attacked, and this time they were ransacked. As a result of these incidents, and similar disturbances in many other places, more German men were placed into internment (see Woodhouse).

By mid-1915, some of the early camps had been closed as unsuitable, or had been taken over for other uses, and the ships used as prisons had been released. But the number of internees then being rounded up continued to provide a considerable problem for the Home Office. It was at this point that a major expansion of Knockaloe was decided upon (eventually it held over 23,000). Following the first stages of this enlargement, there were three camps for civilians in London; at Alexandra Palace, Islington and Stratford: three elsewhere in England; Eastcote, Libury Hall and Lofthouse Park: one on Scotland, half of the Stobs camp: one in Ireland, Oldcastle: plus Douglas and Knockaloe on the Isle of Man.

In June 1915 a committee, of two High Court Judges and several MPs, began to examine cases for exemption from internment or repatriation, and at the same time the responsibility for the PoW Branch of the Home Office was transferred back from the War Office. Nearly 16,500 cases for repatriation were examined and, of those, nearly 15,000 were allowed to remain in the country. Of a similar number of cases for exemption from internment, 7,500 cases were recommended and, of those, half were Polish, Czech or Italian, or from Alsace or Schleswig who, although technically enemy subjects, were considered friendly to the Allies (HO45/11025/410118/2). All the cases had been examined, and recommendations

---

[9] *Hansard HC*, 23 Nov 1914, vol 68, col 787

[10] *The Times* 14 May 1915, p9b and 9f

made, by the end of October 1915, so the committee was then wound up.

In the Autumn of 1915 an agreement was made with Germany for the mutual repatriation of invalid civilian internees and in December 1915 another agreement provided for the repatriation of merchant seamen under the age of 17 or over 55 (HO45/11025/410118/2). A further agreement of 2 January 1917 extended the arrangement for mutual repatriations to those over the age of 45. Up to February 1917 nearly 3,200 internees were repatriated to Germany under these various arrangements. At that point the Dutch, whose ships had been used to transfer the repatriated internees, refused to allow their vessels to be used, because German submarines had recently sunk six of their freighters in one day off West Cornwall. (See *Lloyd's War Losses* 22 February 1917)

During 1916 the PoW Branch of the Home Office had responsibility for Irish prisoners held after the Easter Rising. Those who had been convicted by the Courts were held in English prisons while others were interned at Frongoch. Meanwhile, the number of alien internees remained about the same; although some were released or repatriated during that year, others were arrested.

In June 1917 agreements were reached with the German Government to release some internees to the Netherlands.[11] 1,600 Germans were released from Britain, in exchange for 400 Britons from Germany. This imbalance was because Germany held far fewer civilians than did Britain. Not many of these internees were disabled, in the way that released PoWs were, but they were selected on medical and mental grounds, such as 'barbed-wire disease'. The Dutch were persuaded to permit their ships to be used once more, but from this date they bore the distinctive markings of hospital ships. Between October 1917 and the Armistice, a further 3,600 civilians were transferred to the Netherlands, under this agreement.

However, on 6 June 1918, the Germans sank the Dutch paddle steamer *Koningin Regentes*, en route from Boston, Lincolnshire, to Rotterdam, while carrying men being repatriated. Seven lives were lost in this incident and understandably the Dutch again suspended sailing on this route. Newspaper reports at the time were contradictory, for some said no prisoners were on board, but an Admiralty statement (in *The Times* 17 June 1918) confirmed that 67 PoWs were on the ship, en route to Holland. Sailing with the *Koningin Regentes*, was another Dutch ship, SS *Sindoro*, which picked up many of the crew and passengers of the sunken vessel.

Travelling on board the *Sindoro*, that day, was a diplomatic mission which was to meet with German representatives at The Hague. Their conference drew up a further agreement in July 1918, which would have provided for a much larger scale repatriation of civilians, but the Armistice was signed before the agreement was ratified and implemented. Meanwhile, the Dutch steamers resumed sailing in October, but repatriations were stopped upon the signing of the Armistice.

By the end of December 1918, the War Office considered the military position in Germany sufficiently stable to permit the general repatriation of civilians. Steps were immediately taken to secure shipping and by the end of April 1919 some 21,000 had departed. Almost all went willingly. A few others had been released and allowed to remain in Britain, but about 5,000, who did not want to leave the country, remained in five camps. In May a committee was set up to consider applications, by these internees, for leave to remain in this country, consequently voluntary departures ceased for a while.

Between May and November 1919 a further 1,000 men were repatriated of which 600 were voluntary and 400 were deportees. The remainder, about 4,000, were released, but a proportion of them were in the 'friendly aliens' category, vouched for by the diplomatic representatives of their nations, and many of them then travelled willingly to their newly emerging countries (HO45/11025/410118/3).

Throughout these notes on civilian internees reference has been made to German nationals, but Austrians, Bulgarians and Turks were also covered by various agreements and their nationals were sent over to the Netherlands along with the Germans being repatriated. However, in the case of Bulgarians and Turks there were very few. Four Bulgarians and two Turks were repatriated prior to the Armistices, and 23 and 100, respectively, during 1919.

---

[11] Miscellaneous No.12 (1917) Cd. 8590

A section of the P/W Branch of the Postal Censorship, on the top floor of Strand House, Carey Street, London.

4. CORRESPONDENCE AND PARCELS OF PRISONERS OF WAR,
AND CENSORSHIP CONSIDERATIONS.

This chapter covers:
Military and naval PoWs, Internees, ie civilians held in camps, and some Detainees, *ie* aliens not held in camps but living in the community, subject to parole and/or restricted movements.

Free postage.
PoW mails were free of cost to the sender and addressee, to and from belligerent countries, in terms of The Hague Convention 1907, Chapter II, Article XVI, and were carried in special mail bags. That Article was based on principles contained in the 1785 treaty between Prussia and USA, which had become widely recognised, and established that PoWs had to be granted the facilities of life, provided those facilities did not endanger the State according them. Such rights included the opportunity to write to, and receive letters from, home and family. From the evidence of the letters of both Germans held in Britain and British prisoners in Germany, it was clear that correspondence with home was an essential tonic helping them to keep a healthy mental state.

The Universal Postal Union Convention at Rome in 1906, also agreed that such letter- and parcel-posts were free in the countries of origin, transit and destination. This was a financial, rather than a humanitarian arrangement, but the burden of it did not fall on the Post Office accounts in Britain. In October 1914 the Post Office and War Office agreed between them that the War Office would be charged for PoW and internee letters at the bulk rates applicable to official correspondence and parcels, both inland and foreign, which was 25% less than the public rates. This arrangement was approved by the Treasury on 16 December 1914 (POST 29/1361, packet 25/1919). Internees' mail was not specifically covered by either the Hague or UPU Conventions but during the war they were accorded the same privileges as combatant PoWs.

Despite the principle of free postage, from November 1915 inland parcels and packets over 2oz, to and from PoWs and internees held in the UK, were no longer free of postage, but there was still no charge for re-direction of parcels. This step was taken in response to a German rule that parcels and packets posted in Germany, addressed to PoWs in that country, were not free of postage, while letters and postcards were only free if they did not exceed 50 grammes in weight.[12]

Defensive aspects of censorship.
No arrangements had been made in the preparations for war (the War Books) for the censorship of PoW correspondence and difficulties arose when the intelligence services tried to define the limits of such correspondence. There were problems in the early part of the war due to the perceived, or actual, steps taken by the Central Powers against prisoners they held, and the consequent reprisals taken by the Allied side. In turn, these lead to further reprisals by the enemy. Such steps affected the correspondence of PoWs, resulting in the rationing of letters and the use of complaints, or plaudits, for propaganda purposes. Letters from prisoners held in this country which praised their treatment were photographed and used as propaganda.

Secret inks were an early problem and it was believed that the Germans had trained their men in their use. However, Farquharson pointed out that knowledge of such modes of secret writing needed to be brought to a camp by only one prisoner and soon that knowledge would become widely known among his fellow inmates.

The fact that PoW correspondence went direct, and in bulk, to and from an enemy country was a consideration for the censors. For example: it was possible for a letter to be despatched, addressed to a fictional prisoner or internee in Germany and, upon receipt in Germany, the letter so addressed could be picked out by sorters and passed to the intelligence service. Using a pre-arranged disguise or code, an

---

[12] Post Office Circular 2264, 23 November 1915, and POST 29/1273, packet 124/15. This file has a copy of the German instructions in this matter, dated Berlin, 8 December 1914, reference 1128/11.14.U.3.

enemy agent's messages could be transmitted in this way. Red Cross correspondence was another area of potential danger. Enquiries were made through the Red Cross organisations about casualties and missing persons. By phrasing the enquiry in a certain way it was possible for the enemy to elicit facts about the units serving on a particular sector of the front.

Internees' correspondence with their friends and families in Britain caused some problems, largely on account of the numbers held and consequently the sheer volume of letters. On the other hand, internees were allowed visitors which negated any efforts to control the written word. In the light of this the percentage of internees' inland mail examined was significantly reduced.

Objects of censorship
outward correspondence
- to stop leakage of news to the enemy
- to detect complaints so that remedial steps could be taken
- to prevent false complaints reaching the enemy
- to detect breaches of discipline, escape plots, etc.

inward correspondence
- to gather intelligence of military, economic and social nature
- to get news of British men taken PoW
- to intercept letters seeking information on behalf of the enemy

Information gained from censorship
There was little appreciation of this potential early in the war. Letters from families in enemy countries addressed to prisoners gave a good impression on the economic and social conditions being experienced. Systematic cross referencing of snippets of information led to the piecing together of useful military information. Parcels received from the continent were examined (outside the censorship) to evaluate the state of the food supply in different areas of enemy countries.

History
Initially in 1914, prisoners' mail, both British and enemy, was examined in London by the Hostile Countries Branch of the Postal Censorship. However, inland letters and parcels, addressed direct to some camps in Britain was censored at the camps (see Table 2 below). It also appears that foreign mail arriving at those camps was also censored locally. As this latter category grew, the camp staff found they could not cope and, rather than engage more interpreter staff at the camps, it was decided to centralise the censorship of foreign mails in London. There, both inward and outward letters could be dealt with. Each table handled a section of the alphabet, thereby improving the intelligence gathering aspects. Laboratory resources were available in London, which could not easily be duplicated in each of the camps. Lastly, the facilities for co-ordinating and using the information gleaned from the letters were available in a centralised operation.

However, when the moves to have all the foreign letters examined in London were taken, the camp interpreter staff continued to examine inland letters from the prisoners, providing the prisoner paid the postage. This meant that such letters got into the postal stream more quickly than if they had been sent to London for censorship. If money was being sent, to purchase some goods, it is likely the PoWs and Internees preferred to have the letter dealt with at the camp as they could see it being closed after inspection. If the letter went off to London for censorship, the prisoners might suspect the censors there of having sticky fingers. Camp interpreters also examined inland letters addressed to the camps.

A letter from the Postal Censor, 3 March 1915, to the Post Office, in POST 29/1238, requested that inland correspondence for PoW camps and ships should be circulated as in the table overleaf. This list was handwritten, but it was repeated as a duplicated memo in November 1915, by when it was obsolete to the extent that the ships and a number of the early camps had been cleared.

Mail to be sent direct to camps, where it would be censored	Mail to be sent to P/W Branch, Salisbury House, for censorship
Donnington Hall *(sic)*	Alton Abbey
Dorchester	Bull Point
Douglas	Cork
Dyffryn Aled	Dublin
Handforth	Eastcote
Holyport	Frongoeli *(sic)*
Knockaloe	Jersey
Lancaster	Leigh
Lofthouse Park	Queensferry
Oldcastle	Queenstown
Ships at Ryde	Ships at Southend
Ships at Portsmouth	Stratford
Shrewsbury	Templemore
Southampton, Bevois Mount and Shirley	Wakefield
Stobs	

Table 2. Instructions 3 March 1915, for censorship of mails to PoW camps. How the Post Office coped with the dichotomy of Lofthouse Park in one list, and Wakefield in the other, when they were one and the same place, has not been discovered.

Regulations for letters sent from the UK by PoWs and Internees were drawn up by the Postal Censorship and promulgated as Army Council Instructions (ACIs). They were usually subject to the concurrence of the hostile governments, but if decided unilaterally, the hostile governments were informed. ACI 359 of 1916 and 305 of 1917 were earlier versions, and ACI 49, dated 16 January 1918, was the final form.

Based on this author's collection, it appears that the letter-sheet format was introduced in the second half of 1916. From then, the rules allowed only this highly glazed paper to be used by prisoners in this country for their letters to enemy countries. This special paper was developed for the Censorship to guard against the use of secret inks. The format was useful to the censors for it dispensed with the need for an envelope (which would have to be examined and then re-sealed) and it restricted the length of the letters, so easing their work-load. Some German Commands adopted a similar format of letter sheet, and that imitation was considered a flattery by the censorship in Britain (Farquharson, p210).

In January 1917 the US Ambassador was requested, by the German Government, to present a *Note Verbale*, dated Berlin 9 December 1916, which complained about the letter sheets restricting correspondence to 20 lines (there were 23). A Whitehall official wrote on the file, *this is a very trivial complaint* (FO 383/276). Ruled paper had been in use for two years, but the letter-sheet was stated to have been introduced some six months previously and that the style expedited censorship.

Photographs and drawings were generally forbidden but, under certain conditions, specially taken photographs were permitted along with approved printed matter. Theatre and concert programmes, printed menus and the like, from the camps provided problems for the censors. The proposed matter had to scrutinised and approved, then individual items had to examined for hidden messages. The usual method for dealing with such items was for the censorship to obtain an adequate supply from the printer, outside the influence of the camp inmates, and to substitute fresh copies for the items sent by the prisoners. Camp newspapers, such as *Stobsiade* and *Knockaloe Lager Zeitung*, were submitted to the censors in proof form and once approved they had to be printed outside the camps. Crosswords, puzzles and chess problems were forbidden as it was too easy to conceal secret messages within them. Once printed the despatch by post was undertaken by the camp staff; the prisoners were not allowed access to this operation.

Beginning in 1916, PoWs were employed in labour groups which presented further difficulties to the censors. Mail from the PoW Companies in France required special measures to be taken, including the employment of a specialised section, under an officer with censorship experience in France. For PoWs employed in this country care had to be taken to ensure that references to their work was not included in their letters. Uncommon languages and dialects also caused problems for the censors and delay was inevitable. Prisoners were instructed to write on the obverse of the letter the name of the language used in order to reduce the delays.

Mail from captured U-boat and Zeppelin crews was deliberately delayed and special measures were taken to try to obtain as much useful information as possible from those letters. It was unfortunate that in the early days, a systematic approach was not achieved but over time the handling of this mail was improved, particularly by ensuring that all mail from these prisoners was sent in a special bag to the censorship and once there it could all be treated in a uniform manner (Farquharson p.211). There was an overlap with the censorship of civil mails in connection with Zeppelins and enemy aircraft brought down. Besides the systematic examination of the crew mails, the censors kept a special watch on civilian mails from the area to see that sensitive information was not leaked. An example of the censor deleting part of a letter, referring to a Zeppelin raid, is shown below:

To prevent conspiracies, correspondence between prisoners in different camps within Britain was not normally allowed. Neither was mail allowed from PoWs in Britain to PoW labour companies in the British Sector of France, nor between different labour companies in France. However, correspondence was permitted between PoWs in Britain and those in French hands.

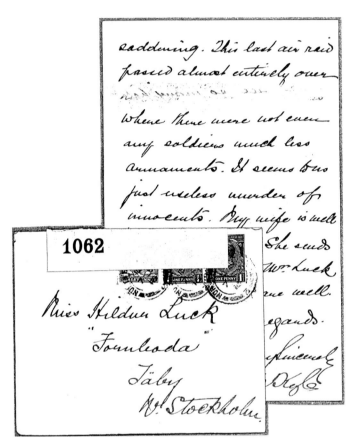

Letter written 5 February 1915, posted at Church End, Finchley, 7 February, to Sweden. Part of the message was deleted by the censor using a hard 'ink-rubber'. The passage referred to the first Zeppelin raid over Britain on the night of 19-20 January, in which 4 were killed and 17 injured in Norfolk.

The Despatch of parcels was permitted, under very strict supervision. Farquharson (p.212) considered that, in the light of the intelligence sent back to Britain in parcels, by British PoWs in Germany, such a facility should be denied in any future war.

The Philatelic Magazine of 1 August 1919, stated that the censorship of PoW correspondence had been moved to Cologne:

> ' ... owing to the large number of German Prisoners who have been sent to work in Northern France. The entire staff of examiners is now in Cologne, where the prisoners' mail to and from Germany will be dealt with until they are released.'

This statement has not been corroborated from official sources, but from personal correspondence with the daughter of a lady censor in the P/W Branch, this author can confirm that some censors were transferred to Germany in 1919.

Inward correspondence
No limit was put on the number of letters received. Two per week was considered in the early part of the war, but fear of reprisals of a similar nature by the German side, lead to this suggestion being abandoned. Prisoners were advised to notify their correspondents that in order to minimise the delays letters should not be over long, obscurely written nor illegible. It was proposed that inward letters should be passed uncensored, but that was never done in any systematic way because of the value of examining both sides of any correspondence, and because it was appreciated that useful information was available in the letters. When, on occasions, the workload became too great, batches of inward letters were released to the camps uncensored, but with a note to the Commandants explaining the matter, and those officers were then at liberty to examine the letters themselves.

Books about the war were not permitted, nor enemy newspapers or propaganda, whether sent from abroad or from an address in Britain. The undesirability of the prisoners having access to enemy publications were the reasons for these two prohibitions. Books and other publications, which were on the permitted list, were examined in the censorship to ensure that secret messages were not being transmitted and, if the books were passed, they were stamped with the common PC marking. Sheet music was also prohibited, except under special precautions, but Farquharson (p.212) considered this particular rule somewhat excessive.

Parcels were sent to PoWs by their families or by welfare organisations. These were opened at the camp, normally in the presence of the prisoner. The wrappings were destroyed and any prohibited articles confiscated. These steps were taken as much to control the contents as to prevent charges of pilfering. Any written communication contained in a parcel was sent to London for censorship before being delivered to the prisoner.

Statistics of mail received at, and sent from, camps in the Isle of Man are found in FO 383/359 as an annex to a report of inspection by the Swedish Legation. Statistics of mail from Germany in the period December 1918 to April 1919 can be found in FO 383/515. Summaries of these reports appear as Tables 6 and 8 on pp 30 and 81.

Inland letters
With up to 30,000 aliens interned, it was natural that they would generate considerable correspondence with their families, friends and businesses. Outgoing letters, on which postage was paid, were censored in the camps by the interpreter staff and incoming letters were also censored at the camps. Of inland mail passing through the London censorship, ie on which postage was not prepaid, the examination was reduced to 50% from November 1915. In May 1916 an officer from the censorship in London visited the camps to see that their censoring arrangements were satisfactory. In his report he observed that personal interviews were permitted between visitors and internees, without close surveillance, so it was concluded that postal censorship was near valueless in most cases. Therefore the examination of the remaining letters was gradually reduced further as more important work needed to be tackled. However, unpaid letters still passed through the censorship and the rules required them to be submitted unsealed. As a courtesy to the correspondents' privacy the letters were sealed with a special label [type 17], see p.38.

Correspondence with Embassies and Legations
Until the USA joined the war, in April 1917, their diplomats looked after the interests of British subjects in Germany, and enemy nationals in the United Kingdom. From April 1917, the Germans were looked after by the Swiss, while the Austrians and Hungarian came under Swedish care. Special facilities were granted to prisoners so that they could correspond with the mission which undertook their protection. Such letters were free of censorship, but that did not mean the letters were not examined. They were read, either at the camp or in London, and where they contained false statements they were returned to the prisoner for re-writing. If the letter was addressed to a diplomatic mission or person, other than the one officially charged with the protection, it was returned for re-addressing. Many letters complained of delays to correspondence to and from the prisoners' homes on the Continent. The censorship investigated these complains and found that most of the delays occurred in the enemy countries and in transit via the Netherlands or Switzerland.

Telegrams
Telegrams addressed to prisoners were not prohibited. Upon receipt at the Cable Censorship they were sent to the Postal Censors for examination. If passed, they were forwarded by post. Only in very exceptional circumstances were prisoners allowed to send telegrams. They were examined by the Postal Censors and, if passed, were transmitted through the diplomatic mission which had charge of that prisoner's interests.

Reprisals on PoW correspondence
Between 14 February and 10 July 1915 German prisoners in Britain were not allowed to receive any books. This measure was taken in response to a similar prohibition imposed by Germany, but upon the Germans relaxing the measure, the ban imposed by Britain was lifted.

During 1916 the correspondence of Turkish prisoners was restricted in reprisal for the Turks announcing a limit upon the communications of British PoWs they held to four lines of writing only. At first a similar four-line limit was applied by ACI 94 of January 1916, but on 27 April the restrictions were modified so that Turkish prisoners could write one letter a week, but they could still only receive four-line messages. On establishing that the Turks were no longer applying the four-line limit, ACI 1535 of 6 August 1916 cancelled the restrictions.

> **Postal Censorship.**
>
> This letter is returned because the Turkish Authorities refuse to deliver any communication which is of greater length than a few lines.
>
> W 15287--251 5000 1/16 H W V(P 151)

Censor's slip inserted into a cover sent on 13 November 1915, to a British PoW of 8th Hampshire Regt, (Isle of Wight Rifles), taken prisoner at Suvla.

On 22 February 1917 the British government announced their intention to withdraw facilities for communications, between the occupied former German colonies and Germany, as a reprisal for the Germans imposing restrictions on the correspondence of Belgians in the occupied portion of their country. No response was received from the Germans until August 1918, and then only to deny the allegation. Meanwhile the Colonial Office was requested to notify overseas administrations and, because of a mistake in London, some Colonial Governments applied the withdrawal more widely than intended by including PoW correspondence. These restrictions remained in force until October 1918, when they were abandoned at the specific request of the Belgian Government when the Germans threatened to stop all Belgian correspondence entirely.

Prisoners of War Information Bureau (POWIB)
Britain established a POWIB, under the terms of the 1907 Hague Convention, chapter II, Article XIV, on 14 August 1914. This office enjoyed the privilege of free postage. Until 1917 the Bureau decided what, if any, of its outgoing correspondence should be censored, but questions were then raised and subsequently all of its international mail was sent to the censors in London.

Incoming mail to the Bureau was subject to censorship from the beginning. The censorship also examined and stamped, as passed, the personal effects, other than clothing, of a prisoner who died, and returned them to the Bureau for disposal. Letters addressed to a deceased PoW were received from the Bureau, suitably marked, and were returned to the senders through the censorship. Inward letters addressed to prisoners, c/o the POWIB, or c/o GPO, or otherwise insufficiently addressed, were censored and sent to the Bureau for forwarding to the correct camps. Letters to enemy prisoners who had been released to the Netherlands or Switzerland, and re-addressed by the Bureau, were censored before being released to the Post Office. Any item marked "Return to Sender" by the Bureau was also censored before despatch.

Detained persons - ie aliens not interned
The question was raised as to whether such persons in the UK, and those detained in the Central Powers, could enjoy the privilege of the PoW mail bags. In Autumn 1915 it was decided that only interned people could use the free mail system, but an exception was made for un-interned indigent enemy aliens; for example, the German community at Libury Hall. Persons detained under Defence of the Realm Regulation 14B (which allowed the restriction or detention of anyone with a hostile origin, association or intent) had no right to use the PoW bags. Their mail was subject to double examination: outward mail, first by Military Intelligence (MI5), and then by the Postal Censorship (MI9), inward mail in the reverse order. The inland correspondence of detainees was not subject to censorship, unless they were committed to prison, however MI5 held a brief to watch over their activities.

PoWs held in Empire countries overseas.
Letters both to and from PoWs in four countries were normally examined in London:

Bermuda, Gibraltar, India and Malta

Letters to PoWs in much of the rest of the British Empire (as follows), and passing through London, were examined there, principally to ensure that information of a military character was properly collated.

Australia	Egypt	Singapore
Barbados	Hong Kong	South Africa
Burma	Jamaica	Trinidad
Canada	Mesopotamia	West Indies
Ceylon	New Guinea	West Africa
East Africa	New Zealand	

Letters from PoWs in the Dominions and colonies in this second list were censored at the camps locally and were not re-examined in London. A good reason for that was that the censors in London had no knowledge of local conditions, so were unable to judge whether any comment in a letter was justified or not.

Remittances to PoWs in the United Kingdom
Early in the war Dr Markel (see p.6) set up an agency which dealt with remittances for PoW welfare in general terms, hence he dealt with camps or compounds to provide facilities, rather than individuals. The London office of the Deutsche Bank handled remittances from Germany for named prisoners. With the closure of the German banks in London, a PoW Relief Committee was formed in December 1917 to continue that work. The postal censorship monitored these payments and kept records.

Remittances were also made from USA and the American Government suggested a limit of US$25 per month. That figure was not formally approved by the British Government, but payments at that level were tolerated until June 1918. At that point it was realised, with the prospect of prisoners being released one day, that they would be able to take their accumulated balances with them, and in aggregate that could amount to a considerable sum. It would also relieve the Germans of providing similar remittances, so such payments from USA were, accordingly, stopped.

Registered letters to PoWs and Internees are frequently found marked on the outside with a manuscript note of the amount enclosed in the cover. This was done by the camp censor/interpreter. Money, in excess of the amount a prisoner was permitted to hold, was credited to his account with the camp purser. The American Embassy report on visits to the camps in February 1915 included the rules for Knockaloe where internees were not allowed to keep more than five shillings. Cash in excess of this and money sent to them by post was credited to the prisoners account. The illustration below shows an example of a cover which contained money. The report of the inspection of Alexandra Park on 21 May 1915 included the Standing Orders which stated that money on deposit could be withdrawn at the rate of £1 per week, on Tuesdays at 9am (763.72114/556). Later, token coins were issued in PoW camps to prevent prisoners putting aside money for use in an escape attempt (see p.4).

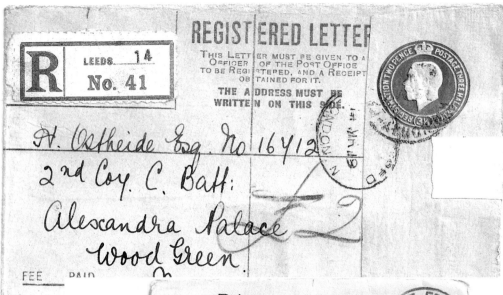

Registered cover to an internee at Alexandra Palace in March 1919, inspected by the camp staff, sealed with plain gummed paper and marked in blue pencil to show the contents £2.

Cover and contents dated 8 July 1915, from Curt Wollheim at Handforth, marked **Business Letter**, addressed to USA. Postage 1d was paid for censorship at the camp, and the initials *CH*, at lower left of the cover, were probably the censor's. The letter itself was not marked. As it was addressed to USA it had to pass through the PW branch of the censorship in London, where it was merely marked with the circular POST FREE P.C. handstamp. The cover is marked on the back *Received Aug 3rd*.

Business letters of internees
These were permitted, and indeed there were cases during the first year of the war where an internee continued to manage his business from a camp rather than from his usual office. However business with enemy countries or with names on the statutory lists ("Black Lists") was not allowed, but transactions with others, in allied or neutral countries, were permitted, providing there was no enemy interest in the matter.

Loans between PoWs in camps in Britain.
This was a practice which came to the notice of the censorship when debtors wrote to their family, or a friend, in Germany instructing them to pay their creditor's family. This practice contravened the terms of the Trading with the Enemy Laws and was therefore banned. However, the senior German officer at Donington Hall, Oberst Leibrock, submitted a request that such loans between officers be permitted as newly captured officers frequently arrived with only the clothes they stood up in, and no money to obtain necessities. After discussions, loans up to £10 were authorised and letters instructing repayment of such loans in Germany were permitted to pass. Similar, but much more serious abuses occurred in the civilian camps. Any letters concerning such repayments were therefore stopped and returned to the Camp Commandants. By this action it was believed that the practice was ended. There was considerable correspondence on this subject, between January and August 1918 (in FO383/436).

–o0o–

For the sake of completion and reference the following paragraphs are included, although they do not strictly fall within the scope of this study.

Letters from British PoWs held abroad.
With the increase in scope of the censorship in the spring of 1915, leading to a greater workload, it was proposed to dispense with the examination of this category of mail. The Director of PoWs objected to this plan, claiming that the information gathered from such letters provided news of the real situation of the British soldiers in captivity. Examination of these inward letters continued therefore until December 1918. However, there were times when pressure of work meant that large quantities of letters were released unexamined. When that was allowed the letters of anyone under special observation, for any reason, were picked out and censored.

In general the censorship was able;
- to obtain information about the conditions and treatment of prisoners and occasionally about the situation in enemy countries
- to intercept letters from enemy intelligence seeking information from a soldier's family or friends in Britain
- to assist in the compilation and correction of casualty lists.

From such letters it was learned in 1918 that the Germans were using PoWs as labourers close to the front line, and even under Allied shell-fire. The first news of the appalling conditions which prisoners from the Siege of Kut experienced also came from PoW letters.

Letters to British PoWs in enemy countries
Farquharson pointed out (p.221) the difficulties faced by the censorship in dealing with the British public. He wrote that the public appeared to delight in ignoring, or attempting to circumvent, or were completely oblivious to, the regulations formulated to ensure the unfortunate PoWs actually received their mail, and to prevent the enemy profiting from items or information sent contrary to the rules.

The regulations were first laid down by the Post Office, purely for postal reasons, *vide* PO Circulars 2187 of 29 September, and 2192 of 20 October 1914. Later instructions included paragraphs concerning the postal censorship and the Press Bureau. In 1915, a summary of the rules under which letters and parcels could be sent, including via the Red Cross, was incorporated in Postmasters notice No 599, which ran to a number of editions. The first essentials were, that written matter had to pass by letter or postcard, nothing else could be sent by letter post and no written matter could be included in any parcel. Letters could not be sent through an intermediary to a PoW, nor to a PoW for forwarding to a third party.

The censors' objectives in handling this mail were:
- to prevent the passing of any information or matter which might be of use to the enemy for propaganda purposes
- to interdict anything sent to assist in escape plans of PoWs, the discovery of which in Germany tended to lead to reprisals against the mails of the whole camp
- to prevent the despatch of certain goods, of which the enemy was in serious need, for example: soap, leather and rubber.

The requirement of a permit to send printed matter out of the country by post began in July 1915. At first, the permit system was confined to printed matter in bulk, but by October private individuals could no longer send newspapers to neutral Europe. Incrementally, permits were extended to second hand books, picture postcards, postage stamps and illustrated matter. The geographical limits were also extended, in June 1916, to include the Americas and also to PoW mails. Many books were sent to PoWs in breach of the regulations. These were stopped and passed to an organisation called the 'British Prisoner of War Book Scheme'. That office was licensed to despatch books, provided they were for educational purposes and did not deal with the war. It distributed books to camps, rather than to individual prisoners, so any danger of passing messages via the books was minimised. A similar, reciprocal scheme was offered to Germany for the benefit of their nationals in Britain, but the offer was never taken up.

Parcels to British PoWs in enemy countries

For the first year of the war there was little control over parcels to PoWs and few were censored owing to lack of staff and accommodation. Enemy agents discovered this loophole and were prompt in exploiting it - sending their reports in parcels to fictitious prisoners. In May 1915, the censorship realised the inadequacy of their arrangements, and proposed a scheme whereby a central body would pack and despatch parcels to PoWs. The plan was supported by the PoW Help Committee but it was shelved because the War Office feared a risk of offending the Germans, by having the parcels made up by an official agency, and the likely unpopularity with the British public.

In October 1915 a PoW Parcels Branch was set up in north London by the censorship. It was, at first, housed in Islington (precise location was not stated) but soon it had to move to larger premises, nearby, at Gilbey Hall (part of the Royal Agricultural Society premises between Liverpool Road and Upper Street, London N1). The parcel censors moved again in December 1916, to a large wooden building in Regents Park.[13] That building also served the Army Post Office and was reported to be the largest wooden building (in terms of floor area).

The centralised packing scheme was revived and brought into operation in late 1916 under the Central Prisoners of War Committee of the British Red Cross. This was partly in response to a survey of parcels sent to prisoners which demonstrated that some men received too little food, while others received an abundance. It was also found that prohibited items, and information, were being sent in the parcels. The Central PoW Committee appointed supplier firms as authorised packers and the censorship inspected the premises, work and staff of those firms.

The families of rank and file prisoners could also send their own parcels once a quarter, but the contents were strictly controlled, and the censors examined them. The number and frequency of those parcels was controlled by the Central Committee who issued coupons which had to be stuck onto the parcel. Officers' families could also send parcels, with a more generous allowance as to numbers, and these were also examined in the censorship.

---

[13] Farquharson, pp 137 and 229. For pictures of the Regents Park building see *Journal of The Friends of BPMA*, vol.11, No.3, Autumn 2006.

5. THE WORK OF THE P/W BRANCH OF THE POSTAL CENSORSHIP - M.I.9 (C) 2.

This Branch was originally called the Hostile Countries Branch of the Postal Censorship, but at Christmas 1914 the name was changed to the Prisoner of War Branch, and was usually referred to, within the censorship organisation, as the P/W Branch.

PoW correspondence fell into two large, broad divisions:
- (a) British PoWs in enemy and neutral countries
- (b) Enemy PoWs in Britain and elsewhere

and two lesser ones:
- Red Cross correspondence
- POWIB correspondence

division (a) was sub-divided into:
- letter mail
- parcel mail

and (b) was sub-divided:
- letter mail to and from UK,
- letter mail to and from PoWs in the zones of the British Armies in the field
- books and other printed matter to enemy PoWs.

Standing Orders, covering methods of examination, submission etc, were basically similar to those for civilian mail. Blacklists were kept, and a watch-list for PoWs (British & enemy) whose mail was subject to special monitoring. Letters concerning PoWs found in the Private Branch, or Trade Branch, were always transferred to the P/W Branch and were returned after examination with "No further interest" or a request for deletion or condemning.

Mail to British and Allied PoWs
Mail was received from the GPO. Letters were then sorted alphabetically and groups of examiners dealt with small sections of the alphabet. Hence they needed to remember only small portions of the P/W Black List and watch-list. Post Office notice 'Postmasters No 559', which gave instruction to the public, was inserted into any letter returned for an infringement. Remittances and any other items of value were recorded in a register. Unmounted personal photographs were permitted, unless emanating from the BEF, but picture postcards, Christmas cards and similar enclosures were removed and condemned. Picture postcards with messages were returned to sender, if there was a sender's address. Press cuttings were treated on their merits. Printed matter was referred to the appropriate section of the censorship, M.I.9 (C)4.

The War Bond Slogan postmarks, introduced in 1917, caused problems as the censors considered those markings would cause trouble for the British PoWs. After censorship the letters were put into fresh envelopes by Post Office staff. Mail to PoWs released to Switzerland and the Netherlands was treated more leniently than letters to enemy countries: for example, comments upon current events were allowed. Letters addressed care of the General Officer i/c Interned PoWs were transferred to the Private Branch. Letters to PoWs or internees, intended for forwarding by the first addressee, were returned to sender. This class of mail was usually from Belgians in the UK, to their countrymen interned in the Netherlands, for forwarding to Belgium.

Mail from British & Allied PoWs
This mail was read in order to discover the situation of the prisoners. Watch was kept for news of casualties, attempted escapes etc. Mail from PoWs in neutral counties was not read after a short while, due to shortage of staff and the fact that the PoWs were under British supervision.

Red Cross Mail
'Red Cross' was the name applied to all correspondence of Red Cross Societies, as well as 'Comforts Funds' organisations, PoW Committees, etc. Outward letters were generally enquiries about casualties and care was taken to ensure that the Battalion number, and other detail identifying higher formations were not mentioned, unless the enquiry concerned a man already known to be a PoW. Enclosures for a PoW were examined at the appropriate table for that prisoner's name. Incoming 'Red Cross' letters were almost entirely replies about casualties and Prisoners. Records were kept of the news about such men.

Registered mail
The Registration room examined all registered letters, and recorded: any contents of value, orders for food and tobacco etc, and any letter concerning the transfer, or disposal, of funds or property in the UK

or British Empire. They also dealt with incoming remittances to enemy PoWs or internees. In addition, from 20 March 1918, they cyphered all bank notes sent abroad. (This author believes this was marking the notes in some way, so that they could be identified if/when they came back into circulation in Britain.) All financial transactions of, or remittances to, PoWs were recorded and compared with the licence lists. Excesses, or remittances without licences, were referred to M.I.9 (C)1c. A registered mail service to enemy countries was not available (merely on postal, not censorship, grounds). Anything posted in the UK as a registered item had the registration cancelled, while transit mail was forwarded as registered. No example of the registration fee being refunded has been observed.

Parcels
In the early days there was no special staff but inspections were made at Post Office parcel depots. In October 1915 a parcel censorship section was set up in Islington with 100 soldiers as assistants. In June-July 1916 a census of parcels was done and, as a result, a new scheme of the Central PoW Committee was set up in October 1916.[14]

Enemy PoWs
Correspondence to and from Enemy PoWs was examined by the P/W Branch, M.I.9 (C)2b. Most mail came from Germany, via the Netherlands, and contained all classes of mail. These mails arrived irregularly, usually about once a fortnight but, from mid 1918 about every ten days. From other parts, mail arrived daily. Outgoing mail usually came twice a week. Letters from working camps came mainly through the parent camps. Quantities of mail rose quickly towards the end of the war and immediately after the armistice (see Tables 4 and 6 on pp 28 and 30)

Regulations
Army Council Instructions (ACIs) were the basis of instructions to the P/W Branch and Camp censors (eg ACI 49 of 1918). Many of these instructions were agreed with, or simply sent to, hostile governments. PoWs were permitted to write twice per week (unless special permission was granted by the Camp Commandant). For letters going abroad a glazed paper was developed, to show up attempts to write in secret inks, and introduced in 1916 as a folded letter sheet with 23 ruled lines. Letters were not allowed to exceed this and inter-line writing was not permitted. Sometimes working groups, outside the main camps, did not have the glazed letter sheets (Farquharson, p.381). Inter-camp correspondence was not allowed without permission, but mail between parent camp and working camps, and between working camps under the same parent camp, was allowed, as were letters to PoWs in hospital. PoWs were permitted to use the Thomas Cook & Son's mail service. (See p.212)

Outward mail
Letters containing passages about poor treatment, insufficient food etc, were returned to the Commandant, with a covering form, for action. Letters containing more serious objectionable matter were first submitted to higher levels within the censorship. Letters of complaint to neutral diplomatic mission were referred back to the camp for the Commandant's information and comment before being sent on.

Mail from camps arrived in bundles, labelled to show the origin. On arrival the mail was picked over to extract items to or from prisoners on the watch lists, which were sent to a special section. Nine other sections of examiners (about 30 on average), each under a Deputy Assistant Censor (DAC), dealt with the remaining enemy PoW correspondence. Each section dealt with a camp, or group of camps, according to the numbers of PoWs, and within the sections each examiner dealt with a specific compound or group of working camps. In this way the examiners became familiar with the PoWs' interests and friends, so that suspicious or 'interesting' passages were more easily detected.

Once read and passed the examiner refolded the letter sheet and stuck her, or occasionally his, gummed OPENED BY CENSOR (OBC) label on the back. If the letter was going to a hostile country, the label was placed clear of the slot to facilitate the enemy censorship. If it was addressed to a neutral country the label was placed over the slot, to secure the tuck-in flap, as the item would not be subject to further examination. Postcards could be sent, but only using Army Form types (see illustrations on p26)

Inland letters from PoWs and Internees were closed with the GR labels [type 17] if they had not been read. The earliest recorded printing date, for this style of label, is July 1916, which gives a good indication of when this practice began. These labels did not carry a number as, in this situation, it was not

---

[14] War Office communique 21 October 1916, GPO leaflets of December 1916, October 1917 and July 1918 and PO Circulars 2324 of 28 Nov 1916, 2376 of 30 Oct 1917 and 2415 of 16 July 1918.

necessary to be able to identify the examiner. (For example of these labels see p.38)

Personal photographs could be sent by the PoWs, but they had to be sent to the censors by the photographers with lists of addresses of the recipients. Greetings cards for Christmas, New Year, Easter etc, had to be approved for design by the Censorship, and then they were printed outside the camp. The envelopes had to be pre-addressed by the PoWs, and the cards were put into the envelopes by the camp staff. Bundles were sent to the censorship and had to be accompanied by a certificate that the PoWs had not had access to the printed cards. In 1918, because of the pressure of work PoWs were limited to two greetings cards each. These regulations, as described by Farquharson, appear to have been interpreted rather loosely for examples can be found of group photographs signed by each of the group, and others despatched as postcards, addressed by a PoW, to his home.

Anything where codes or secret writing was suspected was sent to the Testing Department. Once code or secret writing had been discovered, all mail of that PoW was sent for testing. If the first noted secret message was harmless, the letter was allowed to pass in the hope of discovering further, more important, messages later.

Business letters were normally referred to the Trade Branch. Farquharson stated that letters concerning Powers of Attorney and Powers of Agency gave the censorship much trouble (but he was not explicit as to the nature of the 'trouble').

PoW Companies in France.
Letters were censored in London on the same lines as other PoW correspondence. However they were also subject to Field Regulations (see SS 468) and many have a handstamp showing BEF censorship. A monthly report was sent by the P/W Branch to the Chief Field Censor in France.

Inward mail
There was no restriction on the number of letters a PoW might receive. Naturally no regulation was possible on the nature of the paper used, length or language, but PoWs were told to instruct their correspondents to write clearly and not at great length. Harmless letters were sealed with an OBC label. Illegible letters were condemned. Long or poorly written letters gave difficulties but were dealt with, and slip 6 ('Letters should be short & clear') was inserted (see overleaf).

Letters with deletions by the enemy censor were sent to the laboratory to restore the deleted passages - in this way economic intelligence was often revealed. If the item was mutilated by the enemy censor, slip 24, which explained that the mutilation was not done by the British authorities, was inserted. Some letters were found in parcels when opened at the camps. These were confiscated and sent up to the censors, and, if they were passed, they were returned to the Commandant for delivery to the addressee. Postage stamps on incoming letters were removed to detect any hidden message. Postcards were stamped with the 'PC' stamp as passed.

Mail addressed to camps in Salonika, Egypt and Malta, which were examined in the P/W Branch, frequently had to be submitted to the Uncommon Languages Department of the censorship. Letters to enemy PoWs released to internment were also handled in the P/W Branch.

POWIB of the Censorship
This dealt with the correspondence of the Prisoners of War Information Bureau (POWIB), mail to prisoners c/o POWIB, or c/o GPO, and also Red Cross or Prisoners' Aid Societies' mail relating to enemy PoWs or personnel missing in action. Any correspondence to, or about, a deceased prisoner or internee and letters to PoWs that were insufficiently addressed were handled in this section. The domestic correspondence of the POWIB was also censored, but not in the first half of the war, when it was passed direct to the Post Office by the Bureau.

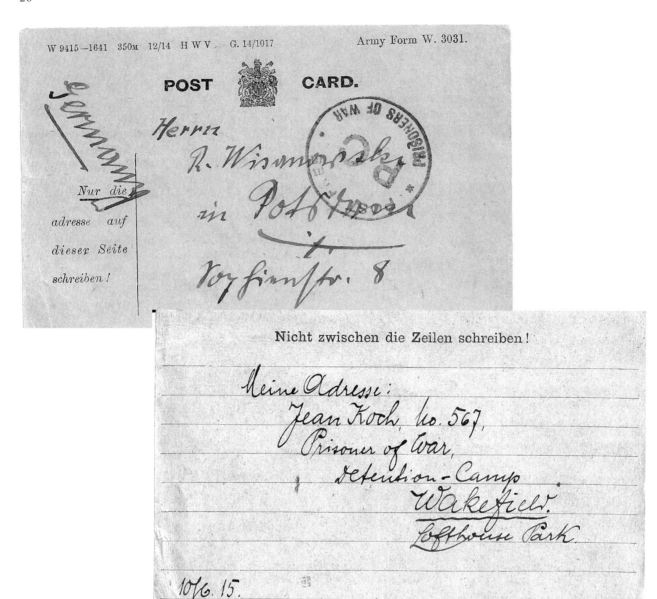

Printed postcards, Army Form W.3031 (Burrows type 4.5) for PoW use. The upper example was written 22 April 1915 to Potsdam, the lower one to Berlin, W8. Both sent from Lofthouse Park, Wakefield, and both struck with the circular P.C. marking of the postal censorship in London.

Censor's slip 6, an English/French version. No doubt, a similar slip was provided with a German text for PoW letters, but such a slip has not been seen by this author.

Non-Terminal correspondence
Transit mail addressed to real or fictitious PoWs was transferred from the Transit Section to the P/W Branch. Much of this was from the USA to PoWs in Russia seeking to open trade, and all was condemned. Similarly, when enemy PoWs were transferred to the Netherlands or Switzerland, Americans tried to establish trade, or use them as intermediaries. Once the American censorship was set up in 1917, such mail was transferred to them in New York. Mail from enemy ships detained in neutral ports was examined. Mail from camps in the USA (after April 1917) was censored in London up to the end of that year, when the US censors took over. Mail to US camps was still examined in London. Mail from Japanese camps was examined in London to intercept harmful communications, but the Foreign Office considered the matter to be a Japanese responsibility and was loathe to interfere.

Irish Prisoners
The P/W Branch examined the mail of the Irish prisoners in 1916, but after 20 March 1917, the Home Office censored the mail of convicted Irishmen still in prison. In 1918, when further arrests were made, their mail was handled by the Private Branch of the Postal Censorship.

Staff and premises of P/W Branch
Throughout the Great War the examination of PoW mail by the Postal Censorship was done in London, at various locations. The Postal Censorship began on 4 August 1914 with one retired officer, Lt Colonel P.J. Bellamy, with no staff and no premises. Soon he gathered a team, mostly volunteers, who worked in Post Office premises at Mount Pleasant. By the end of August the decision was taken to censor neutral mails and at that point the censorship was divided into two sections: Hostile Countries Branch (HCB) and Neutral Countries Branch (NCB).

The NCB moved to Salisbury House, on London Wall, on 14 September, and the HCB followed them on 17 November. At that date the HCB consisted of 32 men but the NCB was much larger with nearly 190 staff. During the Autumn of 1914 the HCB was mainly concerned with formulating instructions for handling PoW mails. Meanwhile they dealt with PoW and Internee mail and the small amount of private and commercial mail which came to hand from enemy countries. Mail from Britain to enemy countries was simply returned to sender.

On 24 December 1914, the HCB was re-named P/W Branch and from that date it confined itself to PoW and Internee mails only. Ladies joined the P/W Branch as examiners in November 1915, although female staff had been employed in other sections of the censorship more than a year earlier.

In May 1916 the P/W Branch moved to Strand House, at the junction of Carey Street and Portugal Street, where they joined most of the other staff of the Postal Censorship, who had moved there during the previous month. Strand House had been built as the distribution depot for the newsagents W H Smith & Sons Ltd. Today it is the British Library of Political and Economic Science at London University. The P/W Branch occupied the top floor of this building.

In August 1916 the establishment of the P/W Branch was put on a formula basis of 1 Deputy Assistant Censor (DAC) to 25 examiners, and 1 examiner to every 360 prisoners. This resulted in automatic increases in staff throughout the following months.

The Parcels Branch was set up in January 1917, and it took over 3 examiners and 80 parcel packers. In April of that year it was decided that the P/W Branch in London would examine correspondence from PoW Labour Companies in France. Four officers were brought in from GHQ in France but two, of junior grade, were dispensed with when found to be surplus to the requirements. Seven examiners were appointed Travelling DACs in December 1917. They visited the camps to review procedures.

Also during December 1917/January 1918, the Central PoW Committee took over parcel work, and January 1918 saw the staffing formula amended, to one examiner for every 300 prisoners. With increasing numbers of prisoners taken by both sides (particularly during the German Spring Offensive), the volumes of mail being handled grew, so that conditions in Strand House became over-crowded, sufficient to cause a breach of the Local Authority Regulations. Therefore in July 1918 the P/W Branch was moved to the, then incomplete, Science Museum building in South Kensington.

In view of the armistice of 11 November 1918, the Postal Censorship ceased examining the mail of British and Allied PoWs in enemy hands and in neutral countries. This allowed for a reduction in staff of 700 examiners by the end of the year, and the remaining P/W Branch staff moved back to Strand House. Although GHQ in France wanted all enemy PoW mail to be censored, it was appreciated in London that, other than to watch for seditious material in the post, there was little point in the detailed examination of everything in this category of mail. Therefore the percentage of outgoing mail which was censored was reduced to 15% in January 1919, allowing further staff to be released.

On 29 May 1919 the Colonial Office was requested to inform the overseas censorships that, other than enemy PoW mails, censorship could cease. In Britain this policy came into effect on 21 June. PoW mails continued to be examined in London until 21 September 1919.

Farquharson (p.334) gave statistics for an unspecified month of 1918 for British and Allied PoW mail handled and the percentages examined:

	Letters	examined
to prisoners	631,130	95%
from prisoners	716,500	78%
parcels to officers	16,759	100%
parcels to other ranks	7,536	100%

Table 3: PoW mail, British and Allied, during one month of 1918

At p.378, Farquharson quoted statistics for enemy PoW mail for 1918:

1918	Incoming		Outgoing	
	UK Camps	BEF Companies	UK Camps	BEF Companies
January	364,800	299,500	550,830	421,360
February	262,000	187,000	510,030	422,320
March	334,700	312,000	511,480	406,110
April	237,500	219,800	558,830	301,230
May	583,300	389,500	647,690	346,680
June	218,000	146,200	588,860	365,530
July	457,550	327,660	637,180	359,490
August	328,710	93,470	598,270	436,390
September	317,800	205,600	655,300	623,620
October	257,730	123,200	735,220	868,890
November	518,000	279,600	753,820	861,790
December	834,000	628,000	* 802,840	728,130
Total	4,714,090	3,211,530	7,550,350	6,141,540

Table 4: Statistics of enemy PoW mail handled by the Postal Censorship
* includes 77,800 items from the German fleet at Scapa Flow

The figures in this table show a significant increase in incoming letters after the armistice. The grand total, of over 21½ million for the year, compares with 3¼ million for the second six months of 1916, and 13¼ million for the year 1917.

Date	Deputy Chief Censor	Asst. Chief Censorr	Censor	Military Officers	Asst Censor	Deputy Assistant Censor	Examiners	Others
4 Aug 1914			1					
17 November: HC Branch moved to Salisbury House, with a staff of 32. 24 Dec: HC Branch renamed P/W Branch								
March 1915	1				1	5	100	
May	1				1	6	120	
July	-		1		-			
Oct			1			8	165	
Nov			1			9	165	
18 November: Women examiners introduced								
February 1916			1			10	190	80 parcel packers
April			1			10	200	80
May: P/W Branch moved to Strand House								
July			1			10	225	80
August: Staff put onto a formula basis: 1 DAC to 25 examiners, and 1 examiner for every 360 prisoners lost and taken								
August			1			13	287	80
September			1			13	300	80
November			1			14	340	80
January 1917			1			15	361	80
January			Transfers to parcels branch			15	358	-
April: 4 officers from GHQ in France (2 soon released) to supervise mail from PoW Working Companies in France								
May			1	2		18	390	
June			1	2		18	417	
July			1	2		18	438	
August			1	2		21	462	
September			1	2		22	491	
October			1	2		24	531	
November			1	2		25	562	
December			1	2		25	568	
December: 7 examiners made travelling DACs							32	561	
December			1 (1)	3 (1)	(1)	31 (27)	575 (562)	
January 1918: Staffing formula adjusted to 1 examiner per 300 prisoners								
January			1	3	1	29	631	
February			1	3	2	29	649	
April			1	3	2	35	799	
July: P/W Branch moved to Science Museum Building in South Kensington.								
11Nov 1918		1 (1)	2 (2)	1 (1)	2 (2)	71 (47)	1607 (1153)	2 typists (2)

Table 5: Staff numbers of the P/W Branch 1914-1918.

This table of the staff establishment, with *actual numbers in brackets,* of the HCB - P/W Branch of the Postal Censorship, was extracted from Farquharson pp.321-329. It demonstrates that in the last months of the war the actual staff numbers fell short of the requirements. In consequence a backlog of mail built up.

Statistics of mail received from Germany, December 1918 to April 1919			
	to UK camps	to PoW Companies in France	transit times of mail
			longest/shortest/bulk of mail
December 1918*	834,000	628,000	99 days/6 days/4-8 weeks
January 1919	835,000	843,100	90 days/7 days/3-4 weeks
February	763,000	592,500	60 days/4 days/ 3 weeks
March	608,200	765,800	45 days †/7 days/3 weeks
April	544,000	638,500	32 days/6 days/3 weeks

Table 6: PoW Mail received from Germany, drawn from FO 383/515
* most mail received between 14 and 31 December was released uncensored so the transit times of those mails were not recorded for these statistics.
† one bundle, dated 26 December, was received in the last week of March; 90 days in transit.

6. CONDUCT, DISCIPLINE, FACILITIES ETC

Prisoners of War were, under Article 8 of the Annex to the 1907 Hague Convention, subject to the laws, regulations and orders of the Army which held them. Standing Orders were published by the War Office as Army Council Instructions (ACIs). These covered such topics as discipline, restricting access to alcohol, forbidding gambling, forbidding conversations with employees of the camps or outsiders without permission, forbidding the possession of certain articles, the issue of cash or tokens, and dress regulations. These Standing Orders also, briefly, mentioned that PoWs should strictly adhere to the lengthy regulations regarding correspondence, which were published separately.

Correspondence of PoWs and Internees, summarised from ACI 49, dated 16 January 1918.

- Two letters were permitted per week. They could not be sent on the same day.
- Postcards and acknowledgements for parcels etc, providing there was no message on them, could be sent in addition to the two letters.
- Commandants could approve additional letters under certain conditions.
- Correspondence had to be on the approved stationery.
- Letters should be written in Latin characters if possible.
- Plain language had to be used. Letters other than in English, French or German had to have the name of the language written on the cover to expedite censorship and despatch.
- Letters had to be written in ink, but pencil was allowed for patients in hospital and prisoners at working camps.
- Interline writing and cross-writing was forbidden
- Outward correspondence had to show the writer's name, number and place of internment on the outside, and letters had to be unsealed.
- If an envelope was used, writing on the inside of the envelope was prohibited
- Inland letters had to be addressed to an individual by name, not by initials alone, nor could they be addressed care of a Post Office, or to an accommodation address.
- Letters had to be about private and family matters only, but for newly arrived prisoners this requirement could be relaxed.
- Ciphers, codes, signs and shorthand were forbidden, as were mere references to published books, but verbatim quotations were permitted.
- Letters were not allowed if they contained pictures, drawings or other embellishments.
- Photos of PoWs, singly or in groups, were permitted
- Christmas and Easter cards were allowed, subject to regulation from time to time
- PoWs were not allowed postage stamps. Where the postage was paid by the PoW on inland letters the stamp was affixed by the camp authorities.
- Business letters were permitted providing they did not infringe any law, or regulation.
- Remittances by PoWs were closely circumscribed, and all had to be referred to the Postal Censor.
- Correspondence with other PoW Camps was not allowed, but between a parent camp and a PoW in hospital, or in a working camp, was permitted
- PoWs in civil hospitals and asylums were subject to the same rules. Commandants of camps, from which they were transferred, supplied the stationery, explained the rules, and all letters had to be sent from the hospital or asylum to the camp for censorship.

The instructions continued with clauses directed at the censor/interpreter officer.

- Letters mentioning political, naval or military matters had to be sent to the Postal Censor, along with any letters likely to encourage the enemy, which disclosed routes for hostile trade, or which appeared to conceal secret writing.

Attention was drawn to potential methods for evading the censors.

- Writing on the inside of envelopes or wrappers, or under the postage stamp
- apparently harmless but unintelligible marks or signs
- faint pencil writing obscured by writing in ink
- use of invisible ink: 'oils, scents, chemicals and other substances' were mentioned as capable of being used for this purpose
- underlining, or other methods, to highlight words or letters to form a hidden message
- the use of veiled or obscure language

- the use of drawings, shorthand, Morse or other codes, musical notation, chess or mathematical problems
- insertion of messages between the layers of a postcard etc
- concealment of forbidden items in incoming parcels, in false bottom boxes, in double linings, inside otherwise innocent items (like a cake or sausage) or beneath the lining of clothes.

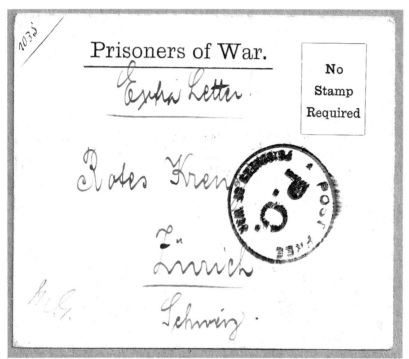

Extra Letter from Obermaschinist W Schulz at Stobs Camp, initialled *MG* signifying it was approved, sent unsealed and received at Zurich 9 April 1916.

Captain's Letter from H Voss in Hut 71 at Stobs, posted at Hawick 17 November 1915, after censorship at the camp and received in London next day.

7. PoW STATIONERY AND THE LABELS AND HANDSTAMPS USED ON THEIR MAIL

Stationery for the use of PoWs and Internees
At the beginning of the war the PoWs and internees used whatever stationery was available for their letters. No pre-printed envelopes have been seen used during 1914 from the early camps such as Frith Hill, Lancaster, Olympia, Queen's Ferry etc.

Envelopes with the heading Prisoners of War. and a boxed note at the top-right 'No Stamp Required' were introduced by early 1915. They were not regarded as a secure form of stationery so there was no consistency in the size of the heading. The overall length from 'P' to the stop varies between 49 and 56mm and the underlining is between 2 and 3mm below the lettering. The envelopes were a standard size, 5x4 inches (125x102mm).

Printed letter paper with the camp address is known from a few camps, and envelopes printed with the camp name are also known.(see pp 79 and 127)

Folded letter-sheets with printed lines were introduced in 1916, at the behest of the censorship. They were printed on glazed paper to make the detection of secret writing easier and the absence of an envelope meant that did not have to be examined as well, saving time and effort. Again the size of the printed heading varies by a few millimetres, between 56 and 61mm. However, these new forms could not be made mandatory for prisoners were allowed to send enclosures, subject to certain rules.

The patent style of folded letter-sheets appear to have been introduced in early autumn of 1918, but the previous pattern of letter-sheets continued in use well into 1919 at some camps. The patented style of letter-sheets has two varieties. The two slots or cuts either side of the heading Prisoners of War, which were used to close the item, are either vertical or diagonal. The same patent number, 2333/15, appears on both styles.

For PoWs employed in labour companies in France a special printing of the letter-sheet and a postcard were also provided.

Peter Burrows has published a comprehensive, illustrated listing of the officially printed postcards with printers' references S.S. or A.F.W. Among these, were cards which provided a printed message to the addressee informing them that the writer had been captured, others had a lined reverse side for general messages. (See p.26)

Registered envelopes, as sold by the Post Office, with embossed postage and registration fee stamps, were also used by PoWs and Internees when sending cash with orders for goods from major London stores such as Gamages and Harrods.

Prisoner of War Information Bureau stationery
The Prisoner of War Information Bureau had a whole series of forms numbered I.B. xx.. Form I.B.1 recorded the full details of a prisoner. This had to be completed immediately upon arrival at his first place of internment. Other forms recorded the movement of prisoners between camps, returns of prisoners admitted to or discharged from hospital, and returns from the camp medical officers. Enquiry and reply forms were also printed.

Postcards were also used by the POWIB with part-preprinted messages to respond to enquiries from enemy countries. These were numbered I.B.34, with suffixes.

POWIB Handstamps and labels
Three types of handstamps used to authenticate Bureau mail and certify the post free status of early PoW mail sent in plain envelopes were shown by Brown[15] and a selection of other markings. He also showed one re-addressing label, but now others are known.

Note: the illustrations overleaf are not true to size, but the captions give the correct measurements taken from real examples where possible. Too few original examples of some markings have been seen by this author and many are too poorly struck to use as illustrations, so scans of Alan Brown's illustrations and examples from other collectors have been use.

---

[15] Brown A: 'British Prisoner of War Camp Markings' a series or articles in *Forces Postal History Society Newsletters*, ISSN 9051 7561, between Sept 1970 and July 1973.

Type 1 was a simple domicile handstamp, seen used in conjunction with a 'released' marking in November 1914.

Types 2, A, B and C are office stamps, usually found in shades of grey. 2A was used on early PoW and internee mail to certify the right to free postage. Types 2B and 2C have been seen on official mail later in the war.

Types 3-12 were used on returned mail, the reasons for uses are self-evident. They have been recorded in green, black/grey and red ink.

Type 4: appears to be a type 3 marking with the word 'UNDELIVERABLE' removed.

Type 6: Brown reported that this marking usually has some manuscript addition in the blank space, such as 'Gone away' or 'Repatriated'.

Type 2B: POWIB cachet, 49 x 30mm. A group of four dots at each side. (Brown type 2)

Type 2C: POWIB cachet, 50 x 33mm. Eight-pointed stars at each side, and taller lettering. (Brown type 3)

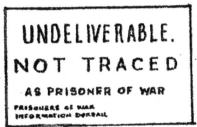

Type 3: 'Undeliverable' cachet, 53 x 33mm. (Carter type 14, Brown type 6)

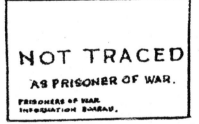

Type 4: 'Not Traced' cachet, 53 x 33mm, (Brown type 7). This appears to be type 3 with the word 'undeliverable' removed.

Type 1: Simple departmental name cachet, 31 + 38 x 9mm, seen used in red on a cover to Newbury, November 1914, together with a 'Released' marking.

Type 2A, POWIB cachet, 50 x 28mm, Six-pointed stars at each side. (Carter type 15, Brown type 1)

Type 5: 'Place not traced' cachet, 55 x 13mm (Brown type 9)

Type 7: similar to type 6, but has the word 'UNDELIVERABLE.' in the space at the top. This has been seen, in green, on a cover to Dorchester in April 1915.

Type 6: 'Released' cachet, 83 x 55mm. (Carter type 1, Brown type 4). A manuscript addition, such as *Repatriated* is often found written in the space at the top.

Type 8: 'Released' cachet, 57 x 33mm   Type 9: 'Repatriated' cachet, 56 x 36mm.

Type 10: 'Liberated'   Type 11: 'Unknown'   Type 12: 'Repatriated'

These three types have been copied from Alan Brown's drawings (published at different times). The only example seen by this author is type 12, which was also illustrated by Carter as type 2 on his plate 2. Carter's illustration and the actual examples were 43 x 39mm, and it seems likely that types 10 and 11 were of the same dimensions.

Overleaf POWIB forwarding labels are illustrated.

Label I.B./92, applied to PoW mail when the man had been transferred under the Anglo-German agreement. Varieties are recorded in the imprints of HWV (Hazell, Watson & Viney Ltd of Long Acre, London) even for printings of the same month.

A different version of I.B./92, printed in February 1918. Note the line across the label. Label sizes are not regular, but most are approximately 70 x 40mm. This version was described by Brown, but not illustrated.

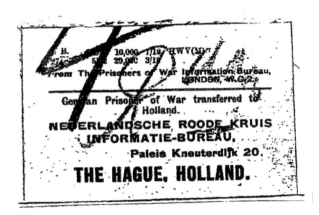

Label I.B./274, (number obscured, so it might be wrong) illustrated by Brown and numbered type 6 by him.

Censorship labels

The labels used by the censors in London on PoW and internee mail, during the first two years of the war, were Mark type 11, a pale pink label with a Coat-of-Arms over the wording (in a single line) **OPENED BY CENSOR** - this comes in two varieties, with a full stop and without. In mid-1916 white labels, without the coat-of-arms but with the same wording (now in two lines) and a PW number were introduced. Three different fonts (Mark types 14, 15 and 16) suggest three different printers were used. These white labels were used through to the end of censorship in 1919. As with the envelopes and letter sheets these items of stationery were not considered high security so variations in the print sizes are found, and odd mixtures of fonts have been noted in the numbers, particularly in type 15, but not in the wording.

The lowest and highest printed censor numbers, recorded to date, on PW labels are 4 and 1632, but some higher numbers in manuscript have been seen, which appear to be language specialists on loan from other departments.

If a PoW's letter passed through the censorship which was not subject to examination, but in accordance with the regulations it was unsealed, the censors placed a seal on the cover as a courtesy. Such labels were white, with the Coat-of-Arms and the initials G.R. (Mark type 17) These labels usually carry a contractor's imprint, the earliest seen being for July 1916, but in 1919 they are usually without an imprint date.

When the work of the P/W Branch was reduced in 1919, and the staff moved back to Strand House, some P/W censors went to the trade and private mail branches. When not examining PoW mail these censors deleted the P/W prefix from their censor labels, often using a blue pencil.

Pale pink label, Mark type 11a (with stop) used by the Hostile Countries Branch of the Postal Censorship, which became the PW Branch. Overall length of printing, O to stop, 69mm. Recorded use August 1914 to April 1916.

Pale pink label (Mark type 11b) recorded used in the HCB/PW Branch from August 1914 until June 1916. Length O-R 67mm.

OBC labels, Mark types 14, 15 and 16 used in the PW Branch of the censorship from mid-1916.

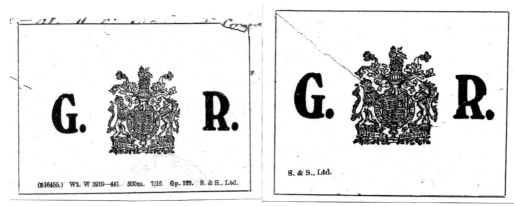

These labels (Mark type 17) were used to close PoW mail that had been submitted open, in accordance with the rules, but had been passed unread (see Farquharson pp 213 and 381. The left hand version (type 17A) is known with printers' dates from July 1916. The right hand version (type 17B) is only known used in 1919 and has no date in the contractor's imprint.

Censorship Handstamps

Previous illustrations of camp and other markings by F J Carter, who published his own book [16] and wrote for *Philatelic Adviser* in the 1930s, and by Alan Brown, who wrote for *The Forces Postal History Society Newsletter* in the 1970s, can now be enlarged upon. The former was seriously incomplete as Carter would have had no access to official records when he wrote, and even Brown's more recent records have obvious gaps, some of which are filled, but many camp and censor markings remain to be discovered.

Illustrations of generic markings applied at the HC, later P/W Branch, in London follow opposite and overleaf. Carter showed seven circular types which Brown extended to eight. Recently two more types have been noted and a cut-down version of one of these is known. Of the previous eight types, it should be noted that some of them have been seen with missing full stops, missing asterisks, and cuts in the outer rim which were not mentioned by either of the earlier authors.

It is clear that each camp had some form of handstamp used as a domiciliary marking for forms, returns etc, but few of them have been recorded. Some of these were used as censor markings. Camp censor handstruck markings have been recorded, but not from every camp, indicating more gaps in the present knowledge. Some of the censoring officers used handstamps showing their initials, but this author has not had much success in matching such sets of initials, even when printed, with the indexes of the contemporary Army Lists. Illustrations of camp markings and censors' handstamps, where known, will be found in the chapters on each camp.

Boxed marking 42 x 24mm, used in the early months of the War on PoW and other mail.

M.O.5 (H) was the abbreviation of the Postal Censorship, a division of Military Operations, until April 1915. This cachet, 40 x 20mm, is found on early PoW and internee mail.

---

[16] Carter FJ: *The Post and Censor and other marks from Prisoners of War letters 1914-1919*, (undated) published privately, in parts 1930s.

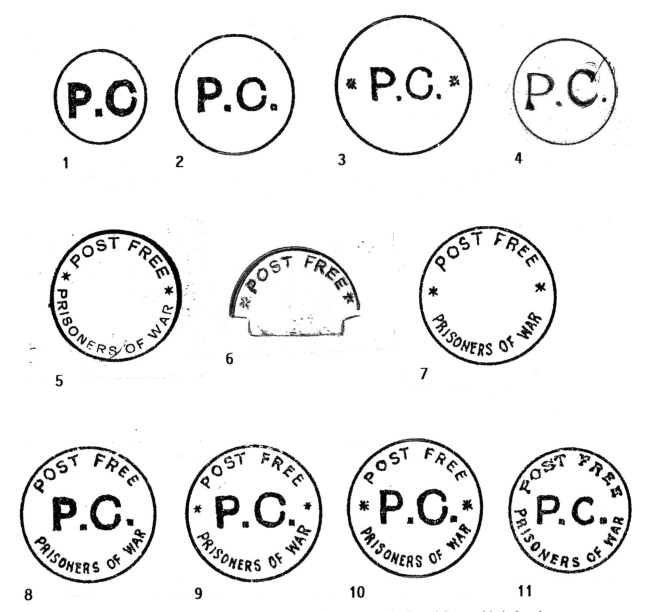

Generic censor markings, believed to have been used in the Postal Censorship in London.
(See notes below)

Type 1:	(Carter type 1, Brown type 1)	25mm circle, one square stop only. Known used in 1914 and 1915.
2:	(Carter type 2, Brown type 2)	31mm circle, square stops. May have also been used at camps.
3:	(Carter type 7, Brown type 7)	34mm circle, eight-point stars.
4:	(not listed by Carter or Brown)	26mm circle, P.C. in serif font. Only known used in 1919.
5:	(not listed by Carter or Brown)	33mm circle, wider font for PRISONERS OF WAR, stars higher.
6:	(not listed by Carter or Brown)	cut down version of type 5, known used in 1914.
7:	(Carter type 4, Brown type 6)	34mm circle, in early months often used with type 2
8:	(Carter type 5, Brown type 3)	34mm circle, without stars at the sides.
9:	(Carter type 3, Brown type 4)	similar to type 8 but with six-point stars. The most common type.
10:	(Carter type 6, Brown type 5)	similar to type 8 but with eight-point stars.
11:	(not in Carter, Brown type 8)	31mm circle, serif font for POST FREE.

Types 8, 9 and 10 are known with broken rims, missing stops and missing stars. Some handstamps in this group are a millimetre or so larger or smaller than the sizes quoted above, possibly due to wear, or they could be different instruments made at different dates. In view of the large staff of the P/W Branch it is likely there were quite a number of handstamps available at any one time. Type 11 has not been seen used by this author.

Blue and purple inks were used in the early months of the war. Then red ink becomes common, but shades of grey to black are the most usual colours.

PARCEL
FOR
PRISONER OF WAR
OPENED BY CENSOR
AND OFFICIALLY RE-CLOSED.

This is a label, illustrated by Brown (as type 7). No example of this has been seen by the present author.

Lastly a special postmark seen on early PoW and Internee mail. This has only seen, in red ink, on mail with dates in September 1914. After that the more common 'London Official Paid' postmark, handstruck or machine, is found on mail passing through the POWIB or the Postal Censorship.

Postage Paid P.O.W. datestamp only known used early in the war.

An aspect of PoW mail which the British Government sought to exploit was the use of facsimile messages, which were supposed to have been written by prisoners in Britain, giving reassuring messages as to good treatment and food. It is said that these were dropped over enemy territory from aircraft and probably others were sent through postal system. Examples seen were printed on the glazed letter sheets.

Alexandra Palace, London N

Civilian internee camp.

Grid Ref TQ 295 901

This large edifice was built on high ground, between Muswell Hill and Wood Green, in north London as an entertainment venue, a competitor to Crystal Palace which had been re-erected in the southern suburbs. Alexandra Palace was first opened in 1873 but was burnt down a fortnight later. It was rebuilt and opened afresh in 1875 but, under an Act of Parliament, 63 & 64 Vict cap.259 of August 1900, it was purchased by a consortium of Local Authorities in the area in 1901, after "a chequered career". Its finances were just getting into surplus when war was declared.

Immediately upon the outbreak of war the Palace and grounds were closed to the public and parts of the building were used by the Army as a barracks for King Edward's Horse. Their horses were picketed on the tennis courts. This Reserve Cavalry Regiment only stayed a fortnight and then the park and buildings were re-opened to the public. However this amenity did not last long, for early in September 1914 the Metropolitan Asylums Board took over the buildings for the use of Belgian refugees. The *Hornsey Journal* 12 September 1914 reported that 400 Belgians had arrived on Monday 7th, with a further 800 since then, and that there was accommodation for 3,000. It was used as temporary accommodation while more permanent homes were found for the refugees. In all some 38,000 passed through before the last batch of 300-400 moved out at the end of March 1915 and were taken to Olympia.

Almost immediately the building was taken over for use as an alien's camp, and a labour squad set to work erecting fences and sentry towers. This squad was from the 18th (Service) Battalion, Middlesex Regiment, a pioneer unit, and pictures of them at work were published in the *Daily Express* and *Liverpool Post*. The first arrivals were a party from Queen Ferry on 7 May, and others came from the ships, *qv*, which were being cleared at this time. *Hornsey Journal* 28 May 1915, regretted the loss of the public amenity, but trusted that knowledge of the presence of German internees would deter the enemy from dropping bombs on the place. The first Commandant was Lt Colonel Robert Sandilands Frowd Walker CMG (1850-1917) late Commandant of the Malay State Guides.

On 21 May 1915 the first visit of inspection by the US Embassy took place, when there were 1,386 internees present, of which about 100 were Austrians, all others were German. The report noted that there was accommodation for up to 3,000, and a plan of the building was given. This plan showed space for 900 in the Bazaar Department and adjoining galleries (Battalion 'A'), 1,045 in the Great Central Hall (Battalion 'B'), 500 in the Concert Room, and 480 in various rooms in the south-west area of the building (Battalion 'C'). Areas adjacent to the West Entrance were devoted to hospital wards and their connected facilities. The cookhouse was behind the orchestra and organ of the Great Hall where furnaces, which were installed to provide steam to drive the pumps for the organ, were adapted to heat the ovens. While officers of the guard and staff were noted to occupy rooms in the south-east corner of the building, accommodation for NCOs and men was not identified (FO 383/33). Presumably the soldiers were in huts, out in the park. From James, it seems likely that in 1915 the guards may have been provided by the 26th Battalion, The Middlesex Regiment.

The German Government complained about the conditions, but the Foreign Office rebutted almost all their allegations. In their reply dated 10 August 1915, (in FO 383/33) the numbers were stated:

Battalion	'A'	'B'	'C'	Total
	956	1,268	530	2,754
in hospital	13	7	6	26

It is notable that these actual numbers for A and B Battalions exceed, by some margin, the figures given on the plan sent with the US Embassy inspection report less than three months previously.

A 'neutral writer' visited the camp and his report appeared in *The Times* of 21 December 1915. There were then 2,115 internees and he explained that they were divided into three battalions, each made up of companies of 100. Each company comprised four sections of 25 men. He gave the daily routine of the

Two International Red Cross postcards showing civilian internees.

internees and complimented both the food and the postal arrangements. He mentioned dramatic performances on Fridays and music on Sundays, and he noted the respect given to the Commandant. A similar report by Ella Hepworth Dixon was published in the *Daily Mail* of 13 January 1916. It is evident from these reports, the figures given by the Foreign Office and by the US Embassy inspectors, that the population of internees fluctuated considerably.

During its four-year period of operation about 17,000 men passed through, and though the accommodation was stated to be for about 3,000, *The Times* of 20 September 1915, reported about 4,000 held, of which 75% were Germans. This total seems an exaggeration. To some extent this camp was used as a short term holding and sorting point, for many held there were soon moved to the Isle of Man as accommodation became available at Knockaloe. This provoked complaints from the families who lived in London as they could not then easily visit their menfolk. Therefore many internees, who had previously lived in London, were sent back to Alexandra Palace, so their families could more easily stay in touch by making visits.

A later inspection by US Embassy officials noted, in May 1916, that there were 2,334 internees, of which 1,598 were Germans, 695 Austrians, 17 Turkish and 27 others. There were six rooms for privileged men, in one of which some consular officers were awaiting exchange. The report also mentioned two hospital wards and an observation ward, staffed by three British doctors, eight RAMC orderlies and two German attendants. There were 37 in-patients on that day, but none in the isolation wards, which were separate. Two deaths were recorded in the year since opening as an internee camp. That report highlighted the work upon which men were engaged: carpentry,

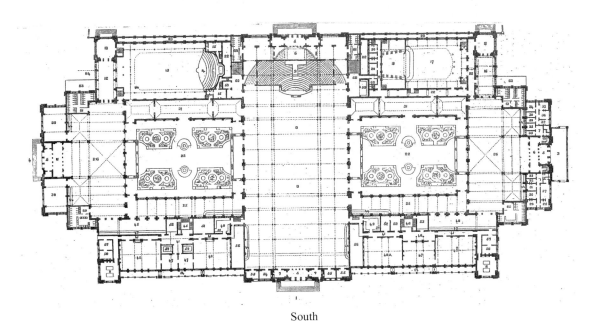

South

Plan of Alexandra Palace. B Battalion (nominally 1,045 men) occupied the Great Central Hall (180 x 290 feet); A Battalion (900 men) occupied the central area to the right (east) with staff offices in the south-east; C Battalion occupied the Concert Hall in the northwest (500 men) and the ground and upper floor in the south-west (240 men in each). The hospital facilities were at the west end. The large room at the northeast was a recreation room. The cook-house was behind, and below the orchestra steps and organ at the north end of the Great Central Hall.

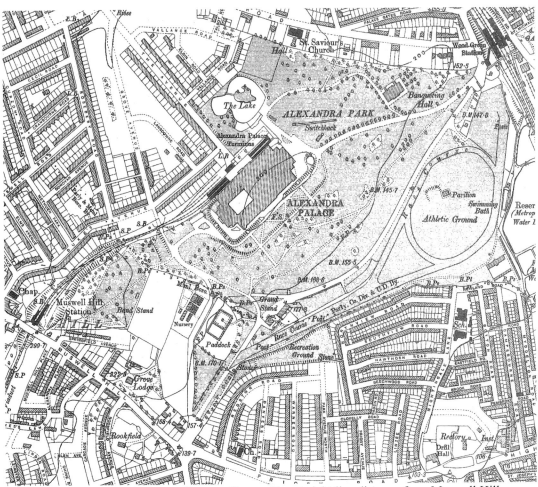

Reproduced from 1919 Ordnance Survey 6"map. The straight line distance from Muswell Hill station to Wood Green station is approximately one mile.

shoe-making, tailoring, glass engraving and model building. Pictures of these various activities, and the rows of truckle-beds, can be found in Noschke and Rocker[1]. In addition to 200 allotment gardens, which provided regular occupation to gardeners, a poultry farm was started, and the lake was used for sailing model boats. The horse-racing course, at the foot of the hill below the Palace, was used as an exercise ground; the oval track with spurs provided a route-march of about one mile.

Notable among the escapes from this camp was Johannes Schmidt, a ship's captain, age 39, who had been taken from SS *Chirlos* at Plymouth on 10 October 1914. He got away on 2 September 1915, the fifth man to get out of Alexandra Palace, but the earlier four had been recaptured. *The Times* of 5 October and *Tottenham & Edmonton Weekly Herald* 8 October, carried items from German newspapers reporting Schmidt's successful return to Germany. He was one of five who managed to get out of the UK during the war, but not all of those got back to Germany.

Konstantin Maglic, alias Petrovitch *The Dandy Hun* was less successful. He was a Hungarian pilot of the Austrian Air Force, shot down over the Adriatic in July 1915. He and his observer were captured by the Italians, but he escaped and took passage to the USA on a Greek steamer from Genoa. In trying to get back to Germany from New York, posing as a Serbian with a ticket to St Petersburg on a Danish liner, he was arrested at Kirkwall when the ship, SS *Frederick VIII*, was examined. On 23 March 1916 he found himself as No.9082 at Alexandra Palace.

On 18 May he got out and stowed away on SS *Gerona*, a Norwegian ship, which sailed from Gravesend on 12 June, but the next day he was found and handed over to a Customs Patrol off Great Yarmouth. A Court Martial sentenced him to 12 months at Chelmsford gaol.[2]

The Commandant, Lt Col Frowd Walker died on 16 May 1917 and the following month he was succeeded by Major, temporary Lt Colonel, G A Luscombe who moved from Stratford when that camp was cleared.

Richard Noschke, an internee who wrote of his experiences, had a poor opinion of Luscombe when they were both at Stratford but made no comment about him after they moved, separately, to Alexandra Palace.

In September 1917, 54 Austro-Hungarian internees at Radford, Nottinghamshire, who had volunteered and been sent from Alexandra Palace, refused to work on an aircraft assembly building, pending instructions from the Swedish Legation. They questioned whether the work was too closely involved with munitions of war and they claimed that they had expected to work merely as carpenters, bricklayers and labourers for 1½d per hour. They were sent to Knockaloe. All these men were married to British born wives residing in London. On 12 October the Home Office wrote to the POW Department that the men were to be returned to Alexandra Palace and that their transfer to Knockaloe had not been intended as a punishment. (FO383/247)

At the end of the war, civilian internees were repatriated or released before the military PoWs. Alexandra Palace was used as a collecting and holding centre for dealing with the internees, but at the end of May 1919, the Government decided to take over the building for use as offices for the Ministry of Munitions and other departments. The loss of this accommodation resulted in delays to the repatriation programme. The internees who were still at Alexandra Palace, at that time, were moved to Frith Hill Camp, which was inconvenient for their families and for the authorities, moreover, being a tented camp, it was quite unsuitable for many of the older men and lead to protests.

During the war 51 internees died at Alexandra Palace. A memorial to them was placed at the entrance to The Great Northern Cemetery at Southgate, 1½ miles to the north of the Palace.

The Park was re-opened to the public in 1920 and the Palace in 1922, but there was considerable delay before the Trustees obtained compensation from the Treasury for the war-time occupation.

---

[1] Noschke R & Rocker R: *An Insight into Civilian Internment in Britain during WWI.*

[2] Maglic, K: *The Dandy Hun.*

ALEXANDRA PALACE CENSOR MARKINGS

1. Camp censor cachet

O. H. M. S.
Prisoners of War,
Alexandra Palace, N.

2. Camp cachet for certifying official mail

LT. INT., FOR COMMANDANT
ALEXANDRA PALACE

3. Camp censor cachet;
'Lt. Int.,' stands for Lieutenant, Interpreter

4. Handstamp of censor's initials

Type 1: 40mm double circle, recorded in black/grey (May 1916) and purple (August 1917).
Alan Brown also recorded a larger version, about 48mm diameter, and Myron Fox has one 51mm across. An even larger example has been recorded, on the back of a Post Office registered cover, to an internee. That has a diameter of 55mm, but it is a poor strike on a dark cover, so will not copy well.

2: The three lines are 22mm, 40mm and 46mm (over stops/comma). The initials are in manuscript.
Recorded in red on an inland cover from an internee postmarked 13 April 1916

3: The two lines are 72mm and 55mm long. Recorded in grey on inland covers, with AP.4 alongside. A very similar handstamp with a hyphen, instead of a stop, after LT has also been recorded.
3a: The same as AP.3 but "LT. INT.," removed.
Recorded in purple on inland covers, with the same censor's initials in manuscript.
Note types 3 and 3a have precisely the same alignment of letters so it is assumed it was a proper handstamp, not loose type in a frame, and was cut down at some date, or there were two handstamps in use at the same time.

4: The initials of the censor. Overall width 23mm. Recorded used from late 1916 on inland mail. It has not been possible to identify the censor from these initials.

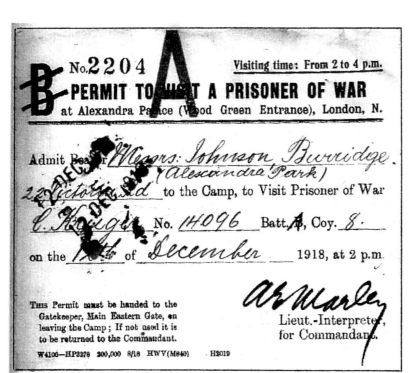

"Permit to visit a Prisoner of War", issued to two men, from North London, to visit Mr C Kruger, 14096, at Alexandra Palace, on the afternoon of 12 December 1918. It was posted to Mr Johnson the day before..
The signatory, Lt A E Marley, was gazetted Temporary Lieutenant and Interpreter on 20 June 1916.

Aylesbury, Buckinghamshire

Women internees

Grid Ref SP 826 143

In 1845-47 a new prison was built on Bierton Road (later called Cambridge Road), to the north-east of the town. This provided 256 cells. By 1902 this accommodation was divided into 16 cells for men and 253 for women. The men were only brought to this gaol for appearances at the assizes.[3] In 1905 a State Inebriates' Reformatory was built as a separate unit at the east corner of the prison estate, approached by a narrow lane. This Reformatory had room for 118 female inmates in three, one-sided blocks of three stories, aligned NE/SW, plus a block of quarters for the staff outside the main yard (Alford, p56). Contemporary maps of the town do not show the layout of buildings within the prison estate. In 1915 both the Governor, William Henry Winder, and his lady Superintendent, Miss Selina Fitzherbert Fox, were medical doctors (*Kelly's Directory* 1915).

In January 1916 the Prison Commission wrote to the Home Office stating there were only 14 inmates in the Inebriates Reformatory at Aylesbury and suggested that the institution be declared, formally, a Place of Internment. On 4 February, The Home Secretary (Sir Herbert Samuel) approved Block B being set aside *as a place on internment for persons awaiting expulsion or deportation, or who were interned as hostile persons under Defence of the Realm Regulations*. The internal rules to be applied to such internees were annexed to that order. (HO45/10785/291742)

After the 1916 Easter Rising in Dublin, Constance Markievicz was sentenced to life imprisonment, and was held at Aylesbury. She was released in June 1917 as part of the amnesties leading up to the Irish Convention, in Dublin, which began the following month. *Hansard* also made reference to Irish women prisoners at Aylesbury in November and December 1916,[4] and from Townshend's account there were five in addition to Markievicz.[5] However it is not clear whether these Irish women were held in the prison or the reformatory.

By June 1917, problems arose from communications between the internees, borstal girls and convicts. At first, the occupants of the reformatory were either internees or inebriates, and although association between these groups was permitted, it was generally shunned by each side. Later borstal and convict inmates were also held there, so continued association facilitated messages and information to pass too readily. Two proposals to deal with this problem were laid before the Home Office:
    a) transfer one or more groups elsewhere, or
    b) confine the internees to a portion of the grounds. The first option was not practical, so the second was adopted.

In October 1917 the Home Office stated that two internees were under consideration for release under restrictions. Miss Howsin, a British born subject who had been interned in September 1915, and Mrs Hatton, a German by birth, but British by marriage, interned since November 1915 (HO45/11522/287235). As these two were detained before Aylesbury was declared a Place of Internment, one can speculate where they were held until February 1916.

The numbers of internees held at Aylesbury are not clear, but Panayi (p112) stated that in February 1918 there were only five women, of German nationality, interned there. Rudolf Rocker, who was held at Alexandra Palace, wrote that his wife Milly was held at Aylesbury from September 1916 and remained there well into 1918.[6] He was repatriated to Germany in March 1918, and it would be a reasonable assumption that his wife would have been allowed to accompany him or be repatriated within a short time. However no information on this point has been discovered.

---

[3] Gibbs R: *A History of Aylesbury*, p503, and Alford RG: *Notes on the Building of English Prisons*, p48

[4] *Hansard HC*, vol.88, cols. 345, 470 and 1813.

[5] Townshend C: *Easter 1916, The Irish Rebellion*, p285

[6] "An Essay by Rudolf Rocker" in *An Insight into Civilian Internment in Britain during WWI*

In February 1918 the Swiss Minister forwarded a *Note Verbale* from the German Government requesting that he be allowed to visit Aylesbury. The Foreign Office replied that the place was not a PoW camp in the usual sense as British and alien women were held there, but the Swiss Minister was invited to apply to the Home Office if he wished to inspect the place. No report of inspection by the Swiss representatives has been traced by this author, indeed on 11 October 1918 a further *Note Verbale* from Berlin was presented which complained that the Swiss Minister had not been allowed to visit the women at Aylesbury. (HO45/10785/291742)

No mail has been recorded from any internees at Aylesbury, and no camp or censor cachets have been seen.

Beachley, Gloucestershire

Other Ranks

Grid Ref ST 547 911

This camp was established in December 1917 in connection with a Government scheme to build ships on the lower reaches of the River Wye, at Chepstow and Beachley. The whole project became a major scandal, because no ships were completed under the scheme during the war and large amounts of taxpayers' money was wasted. *The Times* carried articles on the project in its columns from mid-1916, but particularly large numbers of reports, comments and correspondence throughout 1919.

In 1848 Edward Finch came from Liverpool to build Brunel's railway bridge, over the River Wye, for the Great Western Railway. After completing the bridge, of a most unusual design, Finch stayed on and changed his business to building ships. His yard, on the Chepstow side of the river, near the railway station, was called The Bridge Works. In 1915, Lord Inchcape (Chairman of P&O) and other men with shipping interests, started a second yard, next to Finch's, which would be able to build vessels up to 600 feet long on eight slipways. This second yard became the Standard Shipbuilding and Engineering Co, intended to build ships rapidly, to simple standard designs, as replacements for war losses.

Chepstow, a small town with a population less than 3,000, was quite unable to provide labour in the numbers required to operate such a venture. Therefore, a 'garden city' of new houses was planned for the additional workers. Little progress had been made by the autumn of 1916 because of the shortage of labour, both for building the houses and the ships. 3 vessels had been started by early 1917 and 30 cottages were built.

The two shipyards, Finch's and Standard, were requisitioned by the Admiralty in September 1917. Henceforward these Chepstow yards became National Shipyard No.1 while a new yard to be built on the Beachley shore of the Wye was to be National Shipyard No.2. A third yard at Portbury, on the Bristol side of the Severn, was planned but it was abandoned in 1919 after being 'on hold' for over a year. A large labour force of soldiers was moved in, and more were expected. *The Times* of 17 September 1917, reported that 40 of the 240 planned houses had been built and that 10,000 men were expected to be employed in the neighbourhood. Skilled men would have to be brought in from the Clyde and Tyneside.

It was not until December 1917 that the first ship built under wartime conditions was launched. This was *Petworth*, 2,012 tons gross, built by Finch's to a pre-nationalisation order. Meanwhile, extensive construction work was in progress down-river at the Standard yard. It was at this point that the PoWs were brought in as labourers and the camp at Beachley was opened with huts for 4,000 men. The following month, the Admiralty announced that they would concentrate on Chepstow and Beachley and that 33 slipways would be built. Railway sidings were available at Chepstow, but new ones were laid from Tidenham to the yard on the east bank.

A second vessel *Tutshill*, sister to the *Petworth*, was launched in March 1918. At this time it was stated that the War Office had agreed to release 20,000 men from the Army, and they were being taken on at the yards at the rate of 1,000 per month. In view of the soldier-labour being used the War Office appointed Major General Wulff Henry Grey CB (late Royal Engineers) to head the executive. *Hansard HC*, 11 April 1918, reported that the War Office had taken over the land from the Admiralty, and that only two berths had been completed, but eight were planned by the following October. A further statement in the House of Commons, on 17 April, said the slipways were being built by the PoWs, and *The Times* reported, on 23 April, that the first keel had been laid. By July though, Ministers were saying that the PoWs would be used more for the housing project.

Also in July 1918, the Fourth Report of The Select Committee on National Expenditure criticised the shipyard policy, saying:

The Admiralty were mainly influenced ... by the fact that it would be possible to utilize unskilled labour and prisoners of war, first in the construction of the yards and afterwards in assembling the standardised ships ... Nevertheless, the policy of employing military unskilled labour had to be abandoned owing to the hostility of organised labour.

By then 35 of 130 houses were completed and in occupation and, of further schemes for 2,080 houses, 220 were practically complete. When some of the houses were finished there was an outcry; *pigsties* and *dog-kennels* were terms used to describe their small size. The Admiralty did agree to modify about half the smaller types. The houses that were eventually completed stand today in The Garden City and The Bulwark, at Chepstow, and to the east of the river at Sedbury.

The Government decided to abandon the project and, at the end of January 1919, announced that the yards were for sale, but meanwhile the housing schemes were progressing. Between 400 and 500 PoWs had been engaged in building the houses, but in March they were making the concrete blocks for the houses. This upset local Trade Unionists who complained that British workers were being denied jobs. Reports and letters in *The Times* during March 1919, spoke of little activity.

> *Gangs of German prisoners, well fed, cheerful and well supplied with tobacco, moved about in batches, apparently marking time.*

There was much further critical comment and a searching enquiry was demanded. £4 million had been spent up to January 1919, 12 berths had been completed, six keels laid, but no new ships launched. The houses, estimated at £450 each had actually cost double that figure. All this despite conscript and PoW labour.

In an effort to deal with the problems the Office of Works took over the construction work in March 1919, but the Ministry of Shipping continued to be responsible for the policy. This provoked further criticism of muddle, mismanagement and lack of qualified staff. 4,000 soldiers at the site were asked if they would remain as civilian workers. Initially, only 36 agreed, but later this number rose to just over 100. Comment was also made that, when some official visitors came to the site, the German prisoners were instructed to make as much noise as possible 'clanging iron upon iron' to give the impression of work.

> *Unfortunately, as the party of visitors left, the prisoners all stopped together, thereby somewhat spoiling the effect.*

On 31 March 1919 the Swiss Legation inspected the PoW camp. The Commandant was Lt Colonel William Edward Comber Hood, late Bedford Regiment (born 1867, appointed with temporary rank in the previous June). There were 3,394 Germans in four compounds and 22 in the hospital, of whom three were in isolation. Nine were in detention and 67 were awaiting repatriation. It was expected that the work would not last much longer, that the camp would soon close and that the PoWs would be transferred to Little Fern Hill Camp at Oswestry. In April the Admiralty issued an order authorising the withdrawal of the PoW labour from the shipyards. However, from later newspaper and *Hansard* reports it appears that PoWs remained at Beachley for some time.

By June the muddle and mismanagement had not been sorted out and it was reported that there was still a critical shortage of civilian labour. The PoWs had been employed in road making. One keel had been laid at Beachley (which was never finished), while there were three vessels on the stocks at Finch's and four in the adjacent Standard yard.

By November 1919 the PoWs had been repatriated. Of the large number of houses planned only 209 had been built and 253 more were in course of construction. There were then 1,328 employees and management on the shipbuilding side and a further 1,985 engaged on house building, site clearance, sorting and stacking materials for disposal, and maintenance. Expenditure to date totalled £5 million, while three ships had been launched during the year: *War Forest* 3,103 tons, *War Apple* 2,492 tons, and *War Trench* 3,080 tons gross.

Nine more ships were launched during 1920, six of 6,500 tons gross and three of 2,500 tons. Only one vessel was launched in 1921 and three more in 1922. In 1923 the shipyard was taken over by Fairfield Shipbuilding and Engineering Co., of Glasgow. They continued to build ships on the Clyde, but the Chepstow site was converted to general engineering, structural work, bridges, cranes etc.

The Town Council of Chepstow purchased two wooden huts from the PoW camp, which were re-erected as a public hall for dances, concerts, whist drives and other social functions. In 1919 the War Office proposed a central training school for apprentices and in 1923 they 'found' an ideal, ready-made camp at Beachley. The Army Apprentices' School opened in 1924. Today the site is overlooked by the Severn Bridge.

Information from Chepstow Museum indicates that four PoWs died at the camp and were buried at Beachley.

Photocard of German PoWs at Beachley, sent by Franz Richwein, PoW 1000, to Frau Marie Richwein at Bückenburg (near Minden). The sign held up reads *Ein Erinnerung der Lustigen Acht, PoW 1918*, (A memory of the jolly eight).

Beech Abbey, Alton, Hampshire

Civilian seamen

Grid Ref SU 675 378

Charles Plomer Hopkins (1861-1922) who was born in America, a descendant of a *Mayflower* family, was ordained an Anglican priest in 1885, and became Port-Chaplain in Rangoon. In 1889 he moved to Calcutta as River-Chaplain. His work among the merchant seamen, prompted him to found establishments in India where seamen could rest and be diverted from baser forms of recreation. In 1893, one of his colleagues came to Britain to assist distressed and lonely seamen, and he founded a Priory at Barry, in South Wales. In 1894 Father Hopkins returned to Britain and joined the community at Barry which took the name of "The Order of St Paul". In 1899 the rule of St Benedict was adopted, but the order remained Anglican.

In 1895 Father Hopkins moved to Hampshire where 100 acres of land had been acquired at Beech, 2 miles west of Alton. He began by cutting trees, clearing land and erecting first a tent, then a wattle hut, followed by a wattle church. One of the reasons for choosing Beech was that it was some distance from the sea, and in a peaceful part of the country. Soon sailors, and other travellers moving between south-coast ports and London were welcomed with food and shelter. By 1903 the first permanent buildings had been erected and building continued over the years. The church is described in Pevsner's *Buildings of England*. Father Hopkins became a Trustee of the National Sailors' and Firemen's Union, served as a member of the National Maritime Board and also on the Council at Alton. He was involved in settling the great seamen's strike of 1911-12.

At the outbreak of WWI there were many German seamen employed on British merchant ships. These men were put ashore by the shipping companies, so they had neither jobs nor income, and many had nowhere to go. Father Hopkins offered the services of the Alton community to provide for some of these destitute seamen and boys. The first of them arrived on 10 August. Up to 200 alien sailors were housed at Beech; the seamen lived in tents, officers in the nave of the church building (at that time not consecrated), and the boys in a corrugated iron building. There was no special guard, but Boy Scouts, armed with their customary staves, were reported to be on duty (*Hampshire Herald* 22 August 1914). This local paper also commented upon the 'entertainment' provided to their readers in Alton, almost every evening, by the arrival of groups of Germans destined for the Abbey.

On 23 August a party of officials from the Admiralty, War Office and Home Office visited the camp. *The Times*, 28 August, reported less than 200 German seamen, previously on British ships, were confined to the precincts, watched by the local police. At the end of September and subsequently there were occasional incidents when seamen became insubordinate or obstreperous. In each case the offenders were taken away to more formal camps. Frith Hill was alluded to, but not specifically mentioned, in the reports of incidents in September and October.

Local people became concerned about the lack of formal guard and in October a meeting was planned to air views. However, it was pointed out that such a public meeting would contravene the Defence of the Realm Act, as they had not obtained permission. The meeting was therefore called off. On 20 October 1914 the Home Office approved "Rules and Regulations for Alton Abbey Concentration Camp", which were printed in the Abbey's journal *The Messenger* in 1915.

Another 50 or so seamen were at a daughter house, 38 Hyde Vale, Greenwich, in south-east London, (Grid Ref TQ 386 771) which was run by Sister Frances. This accommodation was temporary, for there the men were documented and sorted according to where they were to be interned. The cost of feeding and clothing the internees at both sites, 10s/- per man, per week, was borne by the British Government, but Father Hopkins would have been happier if the seamen's previous shipping company employers had funded his work. There was no report of any escape attempt.

In the early morning of 15 April 1915 the War Office sent a troop of 11th Hussars, accompanied by fifty policemen, to Beech, to arrest the sailors whilst they were at breakfast. This matter was badly handled by the War Office and Home Office, neither of which had the good manners to tell the Abbey staff what was going on, nor apologise afterwards. The local paper reported 'over 80' sailors being taken away. They were marched to Medstead station, their hastily packed baggage following in a cart, and were taken away by train towards London, but their actual destination has not been discovered. It was stated that the reason for sending the men to Medstead station, was because the authorities feared a demonstration by the people of Alton if the interned sailors had marched through the town.

The following day a Home Office memo (in HO45/10946/266042) stated that it was hoped the War Office would recognise the good work done by Father Hopkins. A manuscript addition reads:

> *Father Hopkins has been very badly treated by the WO. The Destitute Aliens Committee will try to smooth him with thanks etc, but ex-post facto.*

Two interned men died at Beech; Ewald Stelter (42) died on 30 December 1914 of heart failure, and Josef Wighard (21) died on 23 September 1915. The reason this second death was so long after the other internees had been moved away was because the man was already sick in April. He died of consumption five months later. Both were buried in the Abbey graveyard, but their remains were removed to the German War Cemetery at Cannock Chase in 1966.

Father Hopkins was awarded a CBE for his war work. He died at St Mawes, Cornwall in 1922, and was buried at Beech Abbey. An obituary notice appeared in *The Times* of 27 March 1922, p4, and a small portrait photo on p16.

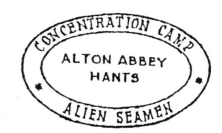

Cachet 50 x 30mm, used at Alton Abbey

Beech Abbey, near Alton (a recent photograph).

Belmont Hospital, Sutton, Surrey

PoW Hospital, ½ mile south of Sutton

Grid Ref TQ 255 624

This was originally an Industrial School, built in 1852, for a thousand orphaned and poor children from parishes in south London. In 1902 the school closed as, with rising standards of living, the number of children needing admission had dropped dramatically, and the site was sold to the Metropolitan Asylums Board. Parts of the buildings were used from 1905 as a home for mental patients, but from 1908 it became Belmont Workhouse under the Fulham Board of Guardians. It was an overflow institution to which a number of Boards of Guardians could send men they could not accommodate in their own workhouses.

Edwards[7] wrote that the workhouse was closed in 1915 to become a hospital for PoWs and internees. However, a postcard is illustrated, date-lined *Belmont Workhouse 9/9.14*, sent by a German seaman, to a Captain W Lorenz, c/o the German Sailors Home in Limehouse. In his message the writer mentioned colleagues who had been moved to Frith Hill on 29 August. This suggests an earlier use, of at least part of the premises, for internees, although it is not recorded as a place of internment in any of the early lists seen. It seems possible that indigent German seamen were placed in Belmont Workhouse as a temporary measure. See illustration overleaf.

The Swiss Legation inspected Belmont on 11 July 1917. The report noted that the hospital had been opened for internees and PoWs on 9 May 1917 and that there were then 875 beds with 342 military patients, of which 22 were officers. There were 48 wards in blocks 1 and 3, while block 2 was used for staff accommodation. The total area was five acres and it was enclosed by a wire fence. Lt Colonel Butler RAMC was the Commandant.

At subsequent inspection, on 3 October 1917, the Commandant was Major Robert Lyall Guthrie MA MD (previously at Fulham Military Hospital). At this visit there were 1,069 patients, all German, of which 45 were officers. They were mostly surgical cases.

Female masseuses were employed originally, but they were replaced with men by 20 July 1918.[8] 35 German orderlies were employed no doubt assisting patients and overcoming language barriers.

The Times recorded only one escape from Belmont, that of Alfred Voigt on 13 January 1919. No report of his recapture has been traced.

In May 1919, when Alexandra Palace was taken over for other government uses, the internees were moved to Frith Hill, a tented camp. After objections from all sides the older and weaker men, unfit to live under canvas, were brought to Belmont, until there was room for them at Islington, which at that time was being used as a clearing house.

After the war Belmont Hospital reverted to being a workhouse, despite furious opposition from socialist MPs, but under a new name, Belmont Institution. In 1929 the Poor Law Guardians came to an end and the London County Council took over, again changing the name, this time to Sutton Training Centre. During WWII it became Belmont Hospital again, specialising in neurosis cases, and after that war it continued that valuable work, gaining a high reputation.

---

[7] Edwards G: "The Story of Belmont Hospital", in *Surrey County Journal*, vol.5 #2 (1958)

[8] *Hansard HC* 18 November 1918, vol.110, c3221 and 20 November 1918, vol.110, c3445

A postcard from W Holtz at Belmont Workhouse, 29 September 1914, sent to a ship's Captain at the German Sailors' Home near London Docks. This suggests that Belmont was used for internees well before the May 1917 date given by the Swiss inspectors.

Blandford, Dorset

Two Other Ranks' camps   Grid Refs ST 930 082 and ST 882 075

The area occupied by Blandford Naval Camp was noted as "Blandford Race Course (Disused)" on the 1902 Ordnance Survey maps. The Naval Camp was set up in the Autumn of 1914 and the first arrivals were Nelson Battalion of the Royal Naval Division on 27 November, followed shortly by Drake Battalion. Other naval and Royal Marine battalions arrived during the Spring and when the Royal Naval Division went to Gallipoli, Blandford became their home depot.

There were construction difficulties as the lanes, along which materials had to be carried, were not suitable for use by traction engines in winter weather. The chalk, below a thin clay soil, was rapidly eroded by the heavy traffic. So much of the timber brought to the railway station, intended for construction, was laid in these lanes to improve the surface. In 1918 a railway line was laid out to the camp.

The PoW camp was established on the eastern side of the Naval Camp, adjacent to a wooded area called Cuckoo Clump, ¾ mile SW of Tarrant Monkton. The date of opening is not precisely known, but was probably in the Spring of 1916. The first inspection visit traced was by the Swiss Legation on 30 March 1917 and it was commented in the report that there had been twenty escape attempts in the past twelve months, which gives some indication of when the camp was opened.. The Commandant was Lt Colonel John Hall, late Lancashire Fusiliers, who had previously commanded Frith Hill. The camp then held 1,378 soldiers and 17 sailors. There were 34 dormitory huts, some still empty, two hospital wards of 20 beds, with ten in-patients, and about 50 out-patients, mostly with wounds. About 680 men were employed in motor repairs, electrical shops, blacksmiths, plumbers, sawmill etc and 200 in agriculture. Two work camps under the control of Blandford were mentioned: Yatesbury, near Calne, with 795 men and Castle Bromwich with 174. Later, both these camps came under the administration of Dorchester.

At a second inspection by the Swiss Legation, on 5 October 1917, 555 were in employment out of 1,204 PoWs, including 333 NCOs. The 1917 rates of pay have been recorded as 4d per hour for labourers hired out to farmers and 9d per day for the cook. In 1918 those rates were 5d per hour and 9d per day. Blandford ceased to be a parent camp on 22 September 1918 when it became a working camp under Dorchester (Home Office list of October 1918).

In mid-1918 the RAF took over the previous Naval Camp and on 19 October the Air Ministry wrote to the War Office to say that the RAF men, then under canvas, were to be moved into the huts occupied by the PoWs and they in turn would go into the tents. It appeared unjust to the Air Ministry that their men should have poorer conditions than the prisoners. It is not known how long the PoWs were under canvas but War Office policy, stated in a letter to the Foreign Office (in FO383/164), was that PoWs should be in hutted camps during the winter months. During the influenza epidemics four died at the camp, and were buried at Tarrant Monkton, but their names were not recorded.

The Times 13 February 1919, reported a prosecution for forged banknotes. The case was brought against prisoners from Bramley, but it was stated that the forgeries emanated from Blandford.

In 1919 the RAF moved out. The railway line up from Blandford station was then closed to traffic but it was re-opened in 1920 to remove materials and stores as the camp was dismantled. The railway was lifted in 1928. Today a military camp occupies the site again, the home of the Royal Corps of Signals.

A second camp was established alongside the Somerset & Dorset Railway at Milldown, 1,100 yards north-west of Blandford station, where a siding was installed. Milldown was a work camp, under the control of Dorchester, where timber was cut and sectional buildings and bridge trusses were made. The Swiss Legation visited the camp on 5 October 1917 and reported that the camp had opened on 10 June 1917, under the command of Lt Cuthbert. There were 199 prisoners, including three naval ratings. Huts were in course of erection and the work was described as timber felling and a sawmill. Two PoWs died at Milldown, Karl Jager on 21 May and Max Heinitz on 4 November 1918. They were buried in the military section of the town cemetery.

Bramley, Nr Basingstoke, Hants

An other ranks camp   Grid Ref SU 665 570

MacPherson stated that this camp was opened in March 1917, in timber and brick-built huts. However, Toogood wrote that it was not until May 1917 that the War Office requisitioned 1,000 acres of farmland for a munitions depot in the parishes of Bramley, Sherfield and Old Basing. Toogood stated that PoWs had arrived by August and at the end of the year there were 3,500 of them in an area called South Camp. British troops and the guards lived in North Camp. The PoWs were employed on the site constructing the early buildings. It is questionable whether the use of PoW labour to build a munitions depot was within the Hague Rules, but no doubt the War Office would not have admitted to any outside enquirer the true intention of the building programme.

Bramley opened as a working camp under Dorchester, and when that parent camp was inspected by the Swiss Legation on 29 and 30 March 1917, Bramley was one of the work camps listed in the report. This backs up MacPherson's date. From the evidence of the sender's address on the back of a PoW letter-sheet written 18 March 1918, Bramley was still a work camp under the control of Dorchester at that date. However, the January 1919 list by the POWIB shows it as an independent camp.

Although Toogood wrote that there were few escapes there were in fact eleven incidents reported in the *Hants and Berks Gazette* and in *The Times*. These involved 23 different prisoners (not all named), some were mere attempts, but most got away from the camp, at least for a short period. Among these press reports, an early escape was that of Otto Hanke, 22, a sailor who got out on 2 September 1917, but he was recaptured after boarding a ship in the Thames. On 19 November Karl Buchgeister, 25, of the Prussian Guard, attempted to escape, but was shot by the guard, and died in hospital at Reading. In June 1918 an un-named prisoner was recaptured after three months on the run. It was stated in the newspaper reports that this particular prisoner had been in every PoW camp in Britain, and escaped from them all.

In addition to the escapes, the two newspapers mentioned carried a number of reports of civilians appearing in court charged with supplying tobacco and other articles to PoWs. One accused man was discharged but others were fined, and two received sentences of imprisonment with hard labour, two months and three months respectively.

One of the more interesting court cases involving PoWs concerned forged £5 and 10 shilling notes. It was reported in *Hants & Berks Gazette* of 2 and 9 November 1918 and 15 February 1919, and by *The Times* on 13 February 1919. Four men faced a total of 21 charges of uttering forged notes. One was an Englishman the other three were PoWs. The former, Herbert Warrington, was jailed for six months by the magistrates, but the Germans, Fritz Meusel, Paul Hans and Josof Heutz, were committed to the Assizes, where in February 1919, Heutz was acquitted but the other two were sentenced to three months in prison with hard labour. During the case it was said that the forgeries had some link to Blandford PoW Camp. The reports stated that the Court could not understand why the three PoWs had been committed to the Assize while the British citizen had been sentenced by the magistrates.

The Times Monday 3 November 1919, reported that there were 3,500 PoWs at Bramley and that they were to be repatriated in three batches, via Dover, during that week. On 10 November that paper confirmed that the last prisoners had departed.

Subsequently the site remained a major munitions store but maps of the area never showed any buildings, nor the railway sidings which served the depot. More recently the US Air Force had use of the depot, but today parts of the area have been redeveloped as a housing estate.

Brocton, Staffordshire

Other Ranks camp and hospital

Grid Ref SJ 976 195

Brocton village is 4 miles southeast of Stafford, on the edge of Cannock Chase. The Chase is south of Shughborough, the home of the Earls of Litchfield, who owned large tracts of the area. From the late 19th century parts of the Chase were used for military exercises and training camps. There were plans in 1891 to create a 'Northern Aldershot' in the area, but that did not materialise. However, two large camps, Brocton and Rugeley, were built in 1914-15, either side of the central ridge of the Chase, at about 500 ft above sea level. Each camp could accommodate 20,000 men (a Division, complete with artillery and ancillary units), but in practice they were only used for transit and later training camps. Railways were laid to serve the camps.

MacPherson wrote that the PoW camp opened in April 1917 with hutted accommodation for 7,000 and a hospital. The exact location of the PoW camp is not certain but Whitehouse believe it was in the north-east of the army camp. Letter-sheets, written from Brocton Camp to Germany in October 1918, and others in 1919, give the sender's address as 'F Camp, Hutte E22'. Map 2 in Whitehouse shows the F Lines in the north of the camp, to the west of the railway to Midford (on the LNWR main line). Official inspection reports give further clues as to the location - see below.

Little information has been found in the contemporary local newspapers of Stafford. *The Times* carried reports of four escapes. Large scale Ordnance Survey maps of the 1920s show nothing of the Army Camp above Brocton, and only minor traces of the railway alignment. Whitehouse, p10, referred to a tunnel being discovered when the huts were dismantled.

The Swiss Legation visited the PoW hospital on 9 June 1917. It was stated to be adjacent to the PoW camp and commanded by Lt Colonel Michael O'Halloran RAMC (b1861) who had two specialist surgeons on the staff. The site covered 11 acres, which included 4 acres of recreation ground. There were 43 wards containing 1,000 beds and kitchen facilities for 1,250. 639 patients were present comprised two officers, three sailors and 634 soldiers. There had been four deaths since opening. No complaints were recorded and the inspectors' report was full of praise. They stated *the hospital could not be better run*. Port Clarence, Middlesborough, was mentioned as one of the work camps under Brocton. The work there was reported to be road-making and quarrying. (FO 383/277)

At the next visit, on 16 January 1918, Major Henry Edward Howley RAMC (b1873) was in command of the hospital. It was reported that the average number of patients was 800, of which 95% were surgical cases. At this date the officers' ward had been enlarged, but no details were given of the numbers of patients present. No complaints were recorded. The PoW Camp, which was under the command of Lt Colonel Sir Alfred Grant Bt, DSO (b1879) late 12th Lancers, was also inspected. 4,715 were present, all German, of which 292 were naval ratings, the others were soldiers (these figures included the hospital patients). There were then four compounds; A and B were the original PoW camp, E and F had been added. E compound was for the disabled awaiting repatriation, while F was for officers and NCOs awaiting transfer to a neutral country (FO 383/431).

If the PoW compounds A, B, E and F equate to the designations of the Lines shown in Whitehouse, E was next to and north of F, while A and B were close by, but on the other side (east) of the railway to Midford.

A War Office inspection was undertaken by Major Wright (previously Commandant at Leigh and Frongoch) on 16 March 1918. His report confirmed the opening date of 11 April 1917 and stated there were 3,791 PoWs present, including 181 sailors, 12 Zeppelin crew, and 411 in the hospital. His report went on to detail the numbers in each of the five compounds:

    A   521   NCOs and convalescents
    B   1,181 who did various work
    C   411   the Hospital
    E   562   mostly medical men due for repatriation
    F   1,116 NCOs awaiting transfer to the Netherlands.

A list of working parties was annexed to the report. (FO 383/432)

A further visit by the Swiss Legation, on 6 January 1919, reported in much the same terms as before but they noted that those in E and F compounds, expecting to be transferred to a neutral country, were disappointed as the move had been cancelled. There were 4,470 in the camp and a further 6,100 in work camps under the control of Brocton. There were no complaints. The menu included horseflesh once or twice a week. There had been 80 to 90 cases of influenza resulting in a few deaths. 150 deaths had occurred since the camp was opened. The hospital had then 1,800 beds of which 1,500 were occupied, many with serious wounds. 30 officers were in a separate ward. (FO 383/505)

On 27 February 1919, a prisoner named Kobbellick was found outside the camp and was shot by a sentry, but it is not clear from the report whether he was killed or just wounded. Four reports of escapes have been found in *The Times* between February 1918 and September 1919.

On 23 March 1919 the Swiss Legation made another visit when 4,955 prisoners were present. This included 22 Austrians who were about to depart for Frith Hill. 111 prisoners were out at work on farms without escort, and 142 worked in migratory gangs. Another 5,800 were employed in dependant working camps. In the hospital, where 43 German orderlies were employed, there were 43 officer and 1,499 soldier patients. The officers had been brought from their camps when they needed treatment. 173 patients were due to return to Germany.

No report has been found of clearing this camp.

Nearby, the German Military Cemetery, open to the public since 1967, contains 2,143 graves from WWI and 2,796 from WWII. A further 263 German WWI casualties remain buried elsewhere in the United Kingdom. The first proposals to bring all the German dead to a single cemetery were made in the 1920s, and discussions continued into the 1930s, but nothing was settled at that time. The subject was re-opened in the 1950s and agreement was reached in 1959.

The PoW football team at Brocton. An undated postcard sent by Sanitary Gefreiter Seyfert to a young lady in Merseburg, Saxony.

Cover from Sauerland (southern Westphalia) 22 October 1917, sent via the Red Cross in Geneva, to an infantry Gefreiter at Brocton War Hospital. After censorship (PW 529 label on the back) it was delivered but marked *Transferred left PW Hosp Brocton* and dated *4.12.17*. Label I.B./93 was affixed at the POWIB and the letter was sent to Switzerland, where is was directed to *Oberalp, Ledrun*.

Camp cachet 49 x 28mm. Note there is a word cut out - in this style the word 'Officers' or 'Hospital' would be expected, but there was no officers' camp at Brocton.

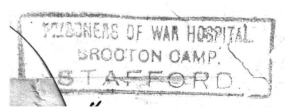

Frame 66x19mm, lettering 55, 36 and 46mm, not including stops. Struck in purple on a letter-sheet to Stettin, written 24 September 1918. Also recorded in red in July 1917, when the frame was 64x19mm.

*Prisoners of War Camp Ashbourne. Date 7 FEB 1919

To Mr J. Garland
Pilstones Farm.
Swynnerton. Stone.

Work done by Prisoners of War.

Date. Week ending	No. of Men.	Total Hours Worked.	Rate. per hour.	Amount. £ s. d.	Remarks.
3/1/19	6	36	5½	16 6	

Accounts rendered up to and for last Friday in each month.

Cheques to be made payable to Commandant P/W Camp Ashbourne.

Y.P.C.—5,000—15/3/1918

P. of War Camp, Ashbourne.

Army Book 57.

Station .... Date 11/2/ 19 19

RECEIVED of* Mrs A. Garland & R. Garland
the sum of sixteen shillings and six pence
in respect of Work done by Prisoners of War

£ —: 16: 6   [signature] Capt. for Commandant
                  P. of War Camp, Ashbourne.

An Agricultural Depot operated at Ashbourne, under the control of Brocton, in 1919. From there PoWs went out to work for local farmers when requested. This bill and receipt to a farm at Swynnerton, 3 miles west of Stone, could be for one day's work for six men, or one man for six days. Note the two Ashbourne Camp handstamps, straight line (57mm long) and circular (33mm diameter) used on the forms.

Catterick, Yorkshire, North Riding

Other Ranks   Grid Ref: SE 180 974

The War Office established a new camp, which they called Richmond Camp, at the outbreak of WWI. The site had been recommended in 1908 by Lt General Robert Baden-Powell CB (later Lord Baden-Powell), when he was General Officer Commanding, Northumbrian Territorial Division. The camp was planned for 40,000 men, *ie* two Divisions, complete with artillery and all ancillary units.

MacPherson recorded that the PoW camp opened on 12 April 1917, with accommodation for 4,000 men in concrete huts. The site was either side of the Scotton Road, just south of the branch railway line which served the camp area. It began as a working camp under Brocton, presumably when prisoners were sent from there to erect the fencing, watch-towers etc, and possibly the huts themselves if sections of existing lines were not taken over. The January 1918 List of Camps, compiled by the Home Office, shows it had become a parent camp by that date and the January 1919 POWIB list of camps entry was 'Catterick (formerly a Working Camp under Brocton)'. At this later date it then controlled its own group of 20 working and agricultural camps.

In common with other late opened camps, and particularly those built within an existing military complex (Brocton and Ripon are other examples), very little news of them got into the national newspapers. Four escapes have been found recorded in the columns of *The Times*. On 11 March 1918, 59 German NCOs were tried by a Military Court for stealing from the Quarter-Master's stores and all were sentenced to six months with hard labour. This was commuted to 84 days military confinement, which was served at Stafford Detention Barracks. (FO383/440)

The *Northern Echo* 22 and 23 August 1918, reported that Sergeant-Major Karl Pliefke, was shot by a sentry when he approached the perimeter fence and disregarded shouted warnings. An inquest jury found that the prisoner was shot while disobeying lawful orders, and the guard was commended for doing his duty. The German prisoners complained to the Swiss Legation.

The Swedish Legation inspected the camp on 30 January 1919 when the Commandant was Lt Colonel G Cawston (not traced). The report stated that the camp was erected in June 1917; that it consisted of three compounds, each had its own kitchen, with accommodation for 4,000 in concrete huts, similar to those in the British barracks adjacent, and that the camp was nearly full. The Swedish diplomats looked after the interest of the Austro-Hungarians, so only their numbers, 77, were stated. All the fit men worked making a new road from the camp to Richmond, which required cuttings, bridges etc. The camp was described as *well commanded and directed and the prisoners well treated and cared for*. (FO383/478)

The Catterick Garrison web-site states that in addition to making the new road towards Richmond the PoWs also built the Officers' Club at Catterick.

No reports of closure of this camp have been found. After the war the Bapaume, Piave and Perrone Lines were built on the site of the PoW camp compounds.

Camp cachet (54 x 27mm) used on letter-sheets.

This man was an Offizier-Stellvertreter writing to his family in Munich. He numbered his letters, and #66, written 25 April 1918, indicates (at two per week) that he had probably been captured in mid-1917, possibly in the 3rd Battle of Ypres, which began on 31 July 1917. On that day 5,000 German prisoners were taken.

Colsterdale, Masham, Yorkshire North Riding

Officers' camp   Grid Ref SE 155 801

This camp was originally built to house workers constructing the Leighton Dam for Leeds Corporation Water Works. The initial plans had been to build a reservoir in the Colsterdale Valley but the geology proved unsuitable so a new site, below the Roundhill Reservoir, was selected.

When the Roundhill dam was being built, in 1901, a light railway was laid to carry men and materials to the site. The line was extended to Masham in 1906, and when the Leeds Corporation selected their site they purchased the railway. Work began on the Leighton site in 1908 and the labourers camp was erected on the hillside at Breary Banks. This comprised fifty wooden buildings and included a hospital, a mission hut, recreation rooms and married quarters.

At the outbreak of war in 1914 the dam was not complete and work was halted. The camp was handed over to the Army and the first military occupants were the 15th Battalion, West Yorkshire Regiment, a Leeds Pals battalion, who arrived by train at Masham, on 22 and 25 September 1914, and marched the five miles to Breary Banks. The War Office named the camp Colsterdale. On arrival, these recruits had three rows of tents and three rows of huts, but more huts were built in the following month. A temporary Post Office was opened for the camp (Post Office Circular 2193, of 27 October 1914). Leeds Corporation ran the power plant providing electricity. The Leeds Pals occupied the camp until June 1915, when they moved to Ripon. Other units followed until the end of 1916.

The camp opened for PoWs in April 1917, (but Macpherson gave a later date) with huts for 700 officers and 200 orderlies, approximately the numbers of a British infantry battalion. So, other than the obvious adaptations for a PoW camp, and possibly some additional accommodation for the guards, little work would have been required to change the nature of the camp. There were 46 huts, of which 24 were dormitories, over an area of 75 acres. The War Office took over the running of the power house.

The Swiss Legation visited the camp on 16 June 1917. Their report gave the date of opening as April and named the Commandant as Colonel H A Johnstone (not traced). There were 370 officers present, 342 army and 28 navy, with 105 servants. The report was very positive:

> we do not hesitate to name Colsterdale as the best camp for officer prisoners of war in Great Britain.

On 26 June 1917, a question in the House of Commons asked about officers at this camp being allowed out for exercise with only two escorts. It was confirmed that this was allowed with an officer and one other escort, both armed, but not with rifles.

In July the Swiss Minister presented a *Note Verbale* from Berlin, of 22 June 1917, in which the German Government pressed for the transfer to Switzerland of thirty officers, from South West Africa, then at Colsterdale. (FO 383/276)

On 24 August 1917, *The Times* reported that four German officers, Thomas von Grota and Heinrich Emil Matthies, both navy, with Fritz Laue and Willi Brossmann, both army, had escaped and on 29th that they were recaptured at Whitby. Von Grota had previously been caught trying to tunnel his way out of Holyport in March 1916, for which he was sentenced to nine months in Chelmsford, but his sentence had been commuted in September 1916.

Heinz Justus, who was captured at Langemark on 31 July 1917, wrote that he escaped from Colsterdale (date not given) disguised as the Canteen Manager, Mr Budd. Once clear of the camp, he changed into a long skirt and a hat with a veil, but he was apprehended quickly and marched back to the camp, much to the amusement of the guard. Following a Court Martial, he was sentenced to 35 days at Chelmsford, and after serving his time he was sent to Holyport.

Sachsse & Cossmann wrote that 150 officers, mostly the more recent arrivals from Cambrai (November 1917), were moved from Colsterdale to Skipton in January 1918. There was no mention in that account of soldier servants being moved with the officers. German documents mention a visit by Swiss inspectors in October 1917, when the prisoners complained of the cold and wet conditions at Colsterdale, which is fairly exposed, and they sought a move. It could be a result of that complaint, as well as more officers being captured, that the new camp was built at Skipton.

The weather conditions were not much different the following winter, for a German *Note Verbale*, dated 8 February 1919, complained that the climate at Colsterdale was not suitable and that unfit orderlies had been selected to work there. (FO 383/506)

The camp was cleared in October 1919 and the Leeds Corporation regained possession of the site the next month. Work recommenced on the construction of Leighton dam in 1920 and it was completed in 1924. The light railway was removed in 1926.

Today traces of the camp can be seen on the hillside and there is a memorial to the Leeds Pals, unveiled in 1935, as a tribute to over 500 of the Battalion who were killed on 1st July 1916, the opening day of the Battle of the Somme.

Christmas 1918 greetings card from Colsterdale.

Postmark COLSTERDALE CAMP / YORKS while this camp was exclusively a PoW Officers' camp.

Camp cachet (47 x 31mm) applied (faintly) in purple to a brown OHMS cover, addressed to the Assistant Director of Medical Services at Ripon. The postmark is shown at left.

Another card for Christmas 1918, with allusions to cold weather.

The German Hospital, Dalston, London N

Hospital for PoWs and Internees

Grid Ref TQ 334 851

The proposal to establish a hospital for the German-speaking population of London was first floated in 1843. Among the first committee members were the Prussian Ambassador, two prominent German merchants (one was Frederick Huth, well-known to postal historians), two German doctors and two German churchmen. The Schröder family also became involved from an early date.

The hospital was opened in 1845 in premises on Graham Road, Dalston, which had previously been an orphanage. That institution had moved out to Wanstead, in Essex. The first nursing staff were deaconesses from a protestant order based at Kaiserwerth (on the Rhine 10km north of Dusseldorf). In 1864 new buildings were erected to replace and expand the original accommodation.

The hospital gained a very high reputation for medical and surgical standards and its humanitarian treatment of needy patients, be they German-speaking, native English, or others, who came to their doors. In 1894 the Kaiserwerth sisters were replaced by Sarepta Sisters from Bielefeld. Sarepta Sisters provided a substantial proportion of the nurses in German hospitals, both in Germany and in other countries where German hospitals had been established.

Upon the outbreak of war in August 1914 the Hospital Committee resolved to continue the work of the hospital so long as sufficient medical and nursing staff could be maintained. The British Government did not attempt to interfere with the running of the hospital, nor did they arrest any of the staff, except later when one or two were indiscrete in their letters. The Mother-house of the Deaconesses allowed the nurses in England to remain, but some were on holiday in Germany upon the outbreak of war so could not return. Hence, additional German-speaking staff had to be recruited in London to replace them. Some of the doctors returned to Germany, to serve in the army or navy, so a dispensary in Whitechapel was closed and the Out-patients Department had to restrict admissions to urgent and serious cases.

During the war civilian internees and PoWs were sent to the hospital for treatment:

375 were admitted during 1915
180 during 1916
52 during 1917
24 during 1918 (all civilian internees).

The reducing numbers were due to a two major factors. In September 1915, Dartford PoW Hospital was opened and early in 1917 the War Office decided to use military hospitals for PoWs, providing beds were available.

In 1918 the Metropolitan Police were asked for their reaction to an official German request for some concessions for the nursing sisters to be allowed to travel to Germany. Scotland Yard reported, on 13 March 1918, that there were then 14 sisters on the staff at Dalston, while there had been 20 at the beginning of the war. Two members of the order ran a baby home at Clapham Common and another lived in retirement at Clapton. No precise reaction was indicated in the file (FO 383/436), but it would seem impractical to have allowed an exchange of sisters at that time.

Financing the hospital had always been on a voluntary basis with wealthy Germans, particularly the Schröder family, coming to the rescue on a number of occasions. With large numbers of Germans being interned, who therefore could not maintain their subscriptions, and with no money coming from Germany, the hospital ran up a substantial deficit of over £12,000 during the war. This was very largely covered by a generous grant from the (British) National Relief Fund.

After the war it took time to re-establish the hospital's pre-war position and it was 1920 before the staff could obtain permission from the authorities to go to Germany for holidays and before the British government would allow any new staff to come from Germany.

In the Second World War the attitude of the British Government was rather different for the nursing sisters were all arrested on 28 May 1940 and interned at Port Erin, on the Isle of Man. Nurses from The London Hospital provided cover for those taken away.

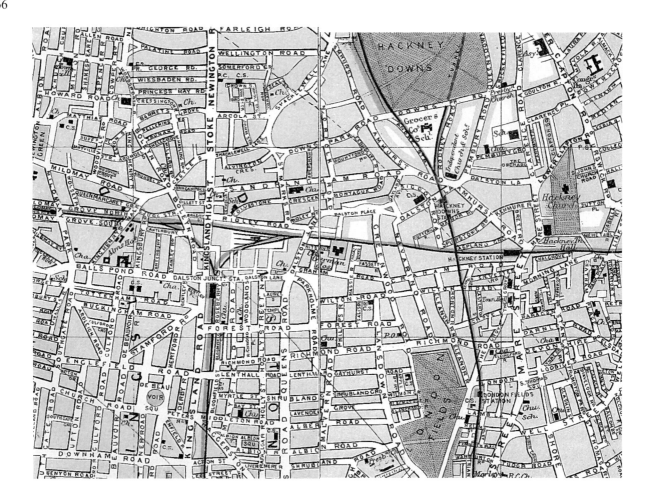

The German Hospital is in the centre of the map, south of the railway line and north of Graham Road.
(Extracted from Bacon's Atlas and Guide to London, 1908)

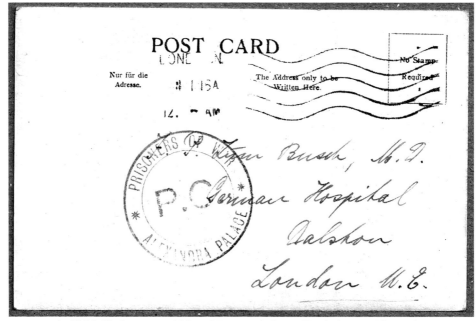

A 1915 Christmas and New Year card from FJ Plotke, at Alexandra Palace, to Dr zum Busch, the senior surgeon at The German Hospital. In 1916, Dr zum Busch was forced to resign and he moved to Switzerland.

Dartford War Hospital, Dartford, Kent

Hospital for PoWs and Internees

Grid Ref TQ 566 723

In 1876 the Metropolitan Asylums Board began building at Darenth, 2 miles south-east of Dartford, in Kent. The first buildings were a school for 580 handicapped children which opened in November 1878. Two years later an asylum for 1,000 adults was built. In 1884 a smallpox camp was opened on a site which had been part of Gore Farm, and in 1888-89 Gore Farm Upper and Lower Hospitals were built. In 1903 these two units became a fever and a convalescent hospital and in 1911 they were renamed Southern Upper and Southern Lower Hospitals. From photographs in Payne[1] it appears both were entirely hutted complexes, which was confirmed in the reports of inspections by the American Embassy and others during the war.

In May 1915 Southern Lower Hospital was handed over to the War Office and it opened as a PoW Hospital on 9 September 1915, with 1,242 beds. Macpherson, p139, wrote:
> A hospital was opened ... in which proper precautions to prevent escape ... to ensure the censorship of correspondence ... and other special conditions could be enforced.

The Commandant was Lt Colonel Richard Pratt Bond RAMC, b1856, who came out of retirement in 1914 and was graded an Assistant Director of Medical Services.

On 16 February 1916 when American officials visited the hospital there were 156 patients: twelve army officers, 128 soldiers, five naval officers, four seamen and six civilians (all Germans) and one Austrian. The report stated: *The German prisoners are treated precisely in every respect as English wounded are treated*, and explained that the German wards were on higher ground than the British, and that the two wards occupied by the German officers were the highest and most desirable. The cooks were all English, their kitchens and the diet were praised. A dry path, about 200 yards long, where invalids could walk, and a field of 2 to 3 acres for more rigorous exercise in warm weather, were mentioned. The hospital clothing was the same as that issued to British wounded and invalids. The patients looked contented and were making good progress.

At the next inspection in June 1916 there were 198 patients: seven army officers, 143 soldiers, six sailors and 42 civilians, comprising 193 Germans, four Austrians and one Turk. Three officers and 37 men were awaiting transfer to Switzerland under an agreement, of April 1916, between the British and German governments. Sixteen deaths were reported, mostly of heart or lung disease or wounds.

In September 1916 a further inspection was made and the preamble to that report is enlightening.
> 'These reports were made with reference to a *Note Verbale* from the German Foreign Office, No. III b 25825, dated July 25, 1916, in which attention is called to complaints ... with regard to the surgical treatment ... for Prisoners of War at Dartford'.

Mr Lowry, of the American Embassy, was accompanied by two American doctors, A.E.Taylor and F.L.Pleadwell, and it was the doctors who wrote the reports. Dr Taylor examined matters relating to rations, subsistence and nutrition. There were no complaints by the soldier patients about the quality, but some wanted more bread, and desire was expressed for greater variety. Dr Taylor assessed the food values for the normal diet, and he suggested an extra 4oz of bread per day, which would increase the calories to 2,500 from 2,200. The officers had no complaints of either quality or quantity. Dr Pleadwell, a US Navy surgeon, inspected the medical and surgical side of the hospital and neither he, nor any of the patients to whom he spoke, found any fault with the facilities or treatment. He wrote:
> *The care and consideration shown patients by the nursing staff appears all that could be desired* (763.70114/2091).

At the date of this visit, 11 September 1916, the number of patients was much higher than in June. There were 816 German soldiers, 26 German officers and 18 English privates, casualties from the Battle of the Somme, which had opened on 1 July.

---

[1] Payne F: *A History of the Darenth Hospitals*

An outbreak of gastro-enteritis occurred on 31 October 1916; 22 cases were reported that day and by 4 November, when the US Embassy visited, the total had reached 61. Three had died by that date and two cases were considered serious. All the others were improving and were expected to make full recoveries. The outbreak appeared to have originated in one dining room, but the specific source was not traced.

In January 1917, when a further visit was made, there were 462 patients: 22 officers, 434 soldiers, one sailor and five civilians. By nationality they were all Germans, except one Austrian and one Turkish man. That report also detailed the accommodation:

surgical: 5 wards with 46 beds = 230
           11 with 40 beds   440
            9 with 32 beds   288
            2 with 24 beds   48
                       total   1,006 beds
infectious: 2 wards with 12 beds   24
            1 with 6 beds   6
           30 wards   1,036 beds

Ten wards were not in use at that date. There were two operating theatres. The staff included 16 doctors, 2 matrons, 45 nurses, 2 masseuses and 152 British orderlies. A British dentist attended twice a week. 4 Austrians and 70 Germans had died at the hospital, mostly of wounds. The kitchens were run by 13 women cooks. Some statistics of mail received were reported:

	Letters	Parcels
Nov 1916	4,368	972
Dec 1916	6,375	756
1-26 Jan 1917	10,236	1,059

The Swiss Legation visited the hospital on 17 July 1917 and they reported 819 patients present. Among these were 53 civilians in wards separate from the PoWs. Some of these civilians had been transferred from Dalston when that hospital was closed to internees a few months previously. Up to 31 March 1917, 3,726 patients had been admitted, of whom 79 had died. A further 1,170 had been admitted since 1 April and 45 had died. The reason for the recent higher mortality rate was that one transport had brought in many seriously wounded cases.

In March 1918 when Swiss officials made another inspection there were 504 patients. Their official report entirely refuted allegations of ill treatment made in a complaint from the German Foreign Office, of 29 January, and they dismissed a further, ridiculous allegation that American medical students had replaced the British doctors.

On 27 October 1918 the Swedish Legation visited and reported 1,082 patients present, which meant the accommodation was full, and that further wards were being erected for 240 more patients. No doubt heavier streams of casualties were arriving from France and Flanders, due to the Allied 'Final Advance' which had begun in August. There had been some reorganisation since January 1917, for this report described the hospital as 37 huts, of which 29 were 36-bed wards, 3 wards for officers and 26 for NCOs and soldiers, plus two dining halls, two operating theatres and a guard room. Separate from these were two isolation wards and a pathology laboratory.

Payne wrote that the PoW patients who died were buried in the hospital cemetery. 285 graves were later exhumed and the remains re-interred at the German War Cemetery on Cannock Chase. The registers for the hospital cemetery have been lost.

Parts of the Dartford War Hospital site are now lost under recent road developments.

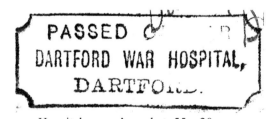

Hospital censor's cachet, 55 x 20mm.
The indistinct word is CENSOR.

Macpherson stated that eventually there were 8,800 beds available to treat PoWs and internees. The January 1919 *List of Places of Internment* included over 60 hospitals throughout the United Kingdom. Among them, Brocton, Oswestry and Stobs, were part of PoW camps. There were also a number of purely military hospitals and many civilian hospitals that were taken over by the War Office for military use.

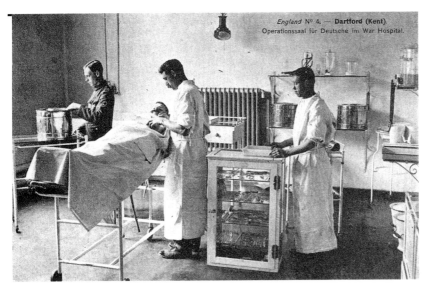

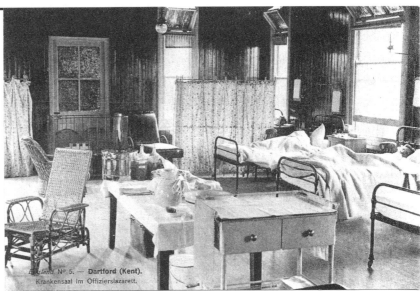

Views of Dartford War Hospital from International Red Cross postcards. The lower picture shows German patients wearing 'hospital blues' the British Army hospital uniform.

Donington Hall, Castle Donington, Nr Derby

Officers' Camp   Grid Ref SK 421 269

Note the correct spelling with single 'Ns', but Donnington with a 'double N' was, and is still, frequently found, especially in Post Office use. However, there are other places in the country where the 'double n' is the correct spelling.

Donington Hall, a stately mansion, had been the residence of Francis Rawdon Hastings KG GCB (1754-1826), 2nd Earl of Moira, created Marquis of Hastings in 1816. He was Governor General of Bengal and C-in-C India (1812-21) and C-in-C Malta (1824-26). The house was surrounded by 10,000 acres of parkland. The direct line of the Hastings family died out in 1858, and in the late 19th century the estate was bankrupt, so it was put up for sale in 1901. It was purchased by Frederic Gretton (of one of the Bass Brewery families), but he never lived at the house, as his marriage plans came to nought. He was Sheriff of Leicestershire in 1908. His elder brother was an MP and Chairman of Bass. The Grettons only used the estate for hunting and shooting.

The mansion and 20 acres of the park were taken over by the War Office in 1914 and work was put in hand to make a PoW officers' camp. *The Times*, 4 February 1915, commented on the costs of £20,000 for fittings, fencing and huts for PoWs and guards, but an answer in the House of Commons on 24 February gave the figure as £13,000, of which £4,000 was spent on furniture. The initial camp capacity was 174 prisoners, who all lived in the house. Barrack huts were built later, but full capacity, 410 officers and 121 servants, was not achieved until late in the war.

The first Commandant was Captain Charles Powlett Aldridge (b.1866, late Sussex Regiment, retired 1906). His first 'guests' were 20 German officers, said to have come from Wakefield, who arrived on 9 February 1915, and 15 German civilians, previously hotel employees, who were sent to act as servants.[2] However Mr Jackson, the American representative who inspected the camp the following week, reported that this first batch had come from Southampton and that a further party was expected from Holyport. He also mentioned a gymnasium being arranged in a former coach-house, that a good size recreation field, enclosed with wire, was available and that part of the woods were being fenced (HO45/10760/269116).

The arrival of a party of 65 officers shortly afterwards prompted a question in the House of Commons on 24 February 1915. The patriotic questioner wanted to know why German officers were taken by car from the railway station to the camp, while their guard, of National Reservists, had to march.

In early 1915 rumours circulated, that the German officers enjoyed luxury conditions, whilst bad reports were then currently circulating about the conditions in German camps for British PoWs. In March a Parliamentary Committee inspected this camp and reported that all was as prescribed by the War Office and that exceptional conditions did not prevail. On Sunday afternoon 14 March, the park was opened for public inspection, but almost immediately the War Office issued instructions that the public was not to be admitted to the park (*Derby Mercury*, 19 March 1915). In April, Berlin newspapers commented favourably on the conditions at Donington but it was said in *The Times* (19 April 1915) that the Berlin reports were exaggerated.

Gunter Plüschow, a German pilot who had flown out of Kiao-Chow before the German garrison capitulated, was arrested on a ship at Gibraltar when trying to return to Germany and arrived at Donington Hall on 1 May 1915. He came from Holyport, in a group of 50 which had been selected and sent by the Commandant at Holyport when none had volunteered for the move. With that arrival, Plüschow stated there were then 120 officers at the camp. Plüschow and Ober-Lt Trefftz, a naval officer, were the first to escape from Donington; during the night 4-5 July 1915, they got away over the fence, which ripped the seat out of Plüschow's trousers. Trefftz was apprehended at Millwall Docks in London, but Plüschow got back to Germany, via Flushing, and received an Iron Cross for his exploit. *The Times* 5 October, carried a report from a German newspaper of his return. Plüschow's account was published as *My Escape from Donington Hall*.

---

[2] *Derby Mercury* 12 February 1915, and similar report in the *Derby Evening Telegraph*

When the American Embassy made their second visit, on 9 August 1915, there were 118 officers and three civilians, plus 40 German soldier servants. Of the total, five were Austrians and all the others were Germans. One of the civilians was Frederick von Bülow, brother of Prince von Bülow, the former Imperial Chancellor. At this visit all the PoWs were living in the mansion. Huts had been erected but they were not then occupied. The Commandant was then Lt Colonel Francis Slater Picot, b1859.[3] The Senior German Officer, Korvettenkapitan John Ross, ex SMS *Blücher*, made some mild complaints, including the suspension of newspapers, following the escape of the previous month. One man was held in a locked room, awaiting Court Martial; he was not named, but it was probably Trefftz. (763.72114/734)

In August 1915, another prominent name, von Rintelen, appeared at the roll call. He was suspected of being responsible for sabotage in USA, so was arrested on a Dutch ship at The Downs, and sent to Donington Hall. In April 1917 he was taken to Liverpool and put on a ship for New York, where he stood trial with ten others. He was convicted and sentenced to 18 months with hard labour and fined $2,000. The judge said he would have preferred to give a longer sentence.

Another escape attempt was made on 17 September 1915. Lt Otto Thelan (Air Force) and Lt Hans Keilbach (Navy) got away after digging a 50 yard tunnel from the library cellar. A reward of £100 was offered for their recapture. They were caught six days later at Chatham and then faced a Court Martial. Thelan became an habitual escaper.

The American Embassy made a further visit on 9 June 1916, when 195 were present, comprising 102 army officers, 39 naval officers, 50 army orderlies, one naval orderly and three civilians. Four of the army officers were Austrians and one of the naval officers was Turkish; the remainder were German. The civilians were probably a hairdresser, tailor, shoemaker, or cooks. The report spoke of a recent innovation in that parties of 25 officers were permitted to go out for country walks for one to two hours, escorted by an officer and a soldier of the guard. (Cd.8324)

The Times correspondent, the following month, reported 247 officers and 'about sixty' soldier servants present, and by October, when the next American inspection took place there were 391 on the roll, of which 90 were orderlies. This visit was reported to be 'for the purpose of inspecting the wooden huts referred to in the *Note Verbale* of the German Foreign Office dated September 30, 1916'. The huts were described as regulation army huts 60 feet by 15 feet, well built and insulated. Each hut was occupied by 16 or 17 officers, with the usual bedding, chests-of-drawers, wash-stands and chairs. Previously, officers had created cubicles for themselves with hangings, but these had been taken down because they presented a fire risk. There were eleven patients in the infirmary, including three cases of tuberculosis which were to be submitted to the medical referees, and one case of tertiary syphilis in isolation. (763.72114/2150)

In July 1917 it was stated in the House of Commons that there were 389 officers, 115 servants and 173 guards at Donington Hall. This would have included three who had escaped the previous week. Karl Spindler and Max Ernst Winkelmann, both of the German Navy, were arrested at Nottingham and the third, an Austrian named Arped Horn, was recaptured in London. The *Derby Mercury* 3 August 1917 reported that two sets of uniform were found close to the camp and the third man still had his uniform with him when arrested.

Lt Colonel Picot, Commandant of both Donington Hall and Kegworth, had his office at Kegworth. When Kegworth camp was closed in February 1919, he moved too, and became Commandant at Oswestry. Lt Colonel Phillip J.R. Nunnerley (retired, late RAMC), who had been the sub-commandant at Donington was appointed Commandant.

After the German Fleet had been sunk at Scapa Flow in June 1919, the crews were landed and taken to PoW camps. The officers were split between Lofthouse Park and Oswestry, but Admiral von Reuter and his Flag Lieutenant were soon transferred from Oswestry to Donington Hall. When the Admiral arrived he found Graf Kageneck was the Senior German Officer. Most PoWs were released during the Autumn of 1919, but not the crews of the German Fleet. When others had been repatriated, leaving space at Donington, the naval officers at Lofthouse Park and Oswestry, about 150 in all, were brought together at Donington Hall in

---

[3] Late Wiltshire Regt, and Commandant of Detention Barracks. In October 1916, when Kegworth camp was opened, he was also appointed Commandant of that camp. In 1917 he received a CMG. His older brother, Lt.Col Henry P Picot, CBE, was Military Attaché at Berne, and took charge of British PoWs released to internment in Switzerland from May 1916.

early November, where they had the company of two airmen and a submarine commander. These three un-named officers had been threatened with charges of war-crimes, but it never came to that, and they were released with the Scapa Flow prisoners.

On 19 January 1920 the War Office announced to the Scapa Flow officers that they should be ready to depart. That was followed by orders and counter-orders until departure was eventually fixed for 4 am on 29 January. They were taken by train to Hull, where they met up with the crews who came from Oswestry. They sailed at midday in two German steamers for Wilhelmshaven.

At the opening of a Soldiers and Sailors Club at Castle Donington after the war, one of the speakers remarked that the presence of the PoWs had saved the town from visits by the Zeppelins (*Derby Mercury*, 6 February 1920). Three months later the sale of huts and building materials from the camp was advertised (*The Times*, 8 May 1920).

A game of football at Donington Hall

Two German officer PoWs at Donington Hall, from an International Red Cross postcard.

After WWI a motor-racing circuit was laid in the park, which during WWII became an RAOC driving and vehicle maintenance depot. The RAF also had an establishment, presumably the airfield (now East Midlands Airport). After WWII the park reverted to motor racing and in 1956 the Hall housed Hungarian refugees. In 1980, the mansion (then unused for some years) and the immediate grounds were acquired by British Midland Airways, and converted to be their company headquarters.

Camp cachet 50 x 30mm

Dorchester, Dorset

Mixed, but mostly civilians until December 1914,
Other Ranks from December 1914

Grid Ref: SY 686 908

This was a barracks for the Royal Horse Artillery (but not in use in 1914), and an adjacent open area, on the north-west edge of the town. Jackson (p135) wrote that this was the first camp to be opened, but Horsham and Olympia both appear to predate Dorchester by a few days..

The weekly *Dorset County Chronicle*, Thursday 13 August 1914, reported that four Companies of the 3rd Battalion, Royal Scots, had arrived from Edinburgh for duty at the Artillery Barracks where German prisoners would have to be guarded.[4] The first Commandant was Colonel Block, but he has not been positively identified as there were two retired officers of that surname in the 1914 Army List, both had been in the Artillery.

The first batch of prisoners, 18 from Falmouth, arrived on 10 August and later the same day a larger group came from the direction of Southampton and London. More arrived during that month so that on 27 August *Dorset County Chronicle* was able to state that there were about 1,000 held at the Barracks. It is likely that most of them were either taken off ships at British ports, or were German and Austrian reservists unable to leave the country. Also on this date *The Times* mentioned that prisoners at Dorchester were assisting with the harvest, but that report has not been corroborated from local sources. On 24th, there was a story about a carrier pigeon being shot at Dorchester and found to be carrying a German message.

During the early months the internees lived in the barrack buildings and in tents on the green, but by December huts were being erected on the green. At that time, it was stated in the local paper that the civilian internees, about 1,000, were about to be dispersed and double that number of military PoWs were to come in their place.

The Times 14 December 1914 carried the story of the "German in the Box". Otto Koehn, who had been taken off the German ship SS *Potsdam* at Falmouth on 25 August, had himself shut in a box with water, some provisions and a blanket, and was taken along as baggage with a group of 58 older men from Dorchester, who were being repatriated via Rotterdam. When their train reached Tilbury, on Saturday morning, 12 December, their baggage was unloaded and sent down a chute into the lighter which was to take them out to the Dutch ferry *Batavier V*, at anchor in the river. On loading the baggage from the lighter to the ferry-boat, the porters found one box too heavy and awkward to carry, so they rolled it over and over. This was too much for the occupant who pushed off the lid and disclosed himself. On 21 January 1915, the local paper reported that Koehn had been transferred to SS *Canada* off Ryde. He did not, it seems, face a Court Martial and the US Embassy report in February stated that Koehn was back at Dorchester, indicating that his military status had been established..

While Koehn was in his box, the other civilians, not being repatriated, were moved out of Dorchester. 352 went to Handforth, in Cheshire, on Friday 11th and a further batch, about 300, followed them on Sunday. Also on Sunday, 300 'officers and better class' were moved to SS *Canada*. When the US Embassy visited that ship in early February, these men were reported to be displeased with their new accommodation. Following the departure of the civilians, the first 500 military PoWs arrived from Frith Hill on 15 December, and a new Commandant was appointed, Colonel Henry O'Brien Owen, b1854, late Royal Field Artillery, retired 1905.

Mr Jackson, of the American Embassy, visited on 4 February 1915, and noted that the camp, previously a mixed establishment, was then an exclusively combatant PoW camp holding 909 soldiers and 25 sailors, but there were also 25 German boys, brought from a reformatory in Belgium. Huts were being erected which would increase the capacity to 2,500. British labour was being employed to put up the huts as trade unionists objected to the use of PoWs for these jobs. New toilet and wash-house facilities were being installed and a large recreation field was being prepared. Meantime, the men were taken on escorted

---

[4] The paper named the regiment as Royal Scots Fusiliers, but that appears incorrect. 3 postcards in this writer's collection indicate by their captions or message, *The Royal Scots*. The officer of the guard, Viscount Newport, was a Captain in that regiment.

An unused postcard view of Dorchester Camp. This must be an early date for the tents on the green were being replaced by huts from December 1914.

marches in the local area. There were no complaints about the food, which was prepared by German cooks. NCOs had separate rooms, while the men were housed in converted stables, lofts and other rooms. (HO45/10760/269116)

A Danish report of a similar date considered conditions and treatment 'splendid'. Major Henry Charles Bulkeley DSO, b1858, late 4th West Yorks Regt., was said to be particularly popular (later he was appointed Commandant of the camp). Around this time Gunter Plüschow, a German pilot arrested at Gibraltar, was brought to Dorchester. In his book Plüschow mentioned Captain Mitchell and 'Major' Owen (the Commandant?) of the camp staff. Plüschow did not stay long as he was transferred to Holyport at the end of March and from there he went on to Donington Hall, escaped, and got back to Germany, a hero.

Five escaped in September 1915; Joseph Strautmann and Walther Iven were caught at Southampton, on a train for Waterloo, while Edwin Bergmann and Hans Heym were recaptured at West Hartlepool and sentenced to six months hard labour. The recapture of the fifth man, surname Valker, has not been traced, nor any punishment for the first two named.

When Mr Lowry of the American Embassy visited on 1 December 1915, there were 3,447 present, all from the German Army. He described the accommodation as the barracks plus 113 wooden huts, each for 30 men. In the original buildings there were 45 sleeping rooms, with between two and thirty men per room, and two lofts for 100 men each. There were twenty men in the infirmary which had beds for 60. The isolation ward had no patients. The Commandant at this time was Major Bulkeley (promoted to temporary Lt Colonel 16 December 1915) in succession to Colonel Owen who had resigned.

In *Dorset Evening Echo*, 26 August 1976, a report of a riot in the camp in 1915 was mentioned, during which a young electrician got locked inside with the PoWs. No further details have been found of this incident.

Another escape on 2 February 1916 was reported in the *Police Gazette*. Fahnrich Ernst von Schweinichen, age 22, and another named Gohmer got away and their recapture was recorded in that paper on 11 February. The following August, the US Embassy, having been asked by the German Foreign Office to interview von Schweinichen, went to see him at Woking prison, but he had been sent back to Dorchester on 24 June, having received five months remission of sentence.

In early April 1916, 750 prisoners were sent to Rouen as the first PoW Labour Companies, after General Haig, the British Commander-in-Chief, had been persuaded to employ them. A further 750 were sent over to France on 10 May, thirty of the first batch having been returned as unfit for work. The Battle of the Somme, in the summer of 1916, meant that every able-bodied British soldier was needed in the lines rather then on the docks unloading supplies, making roads or cutting timber, so the usefulness of PoW labour was firmly established.

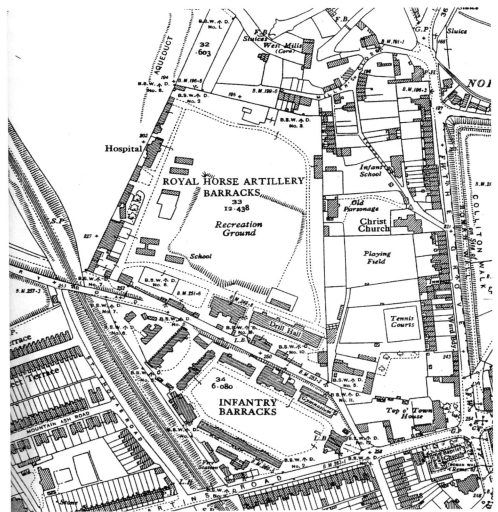

The northwest part of the town of Dorchester. The Royal Horse Artillery Barracks became the PoW camp. Reproduced from 6" OS map (c1910) Crown Copyright

The departure of nearly 1,500 men to France was reflected in the numbers present at the next American inspection on 1 June 1916. The contents page of booklet of reports referred to this camp as 'Prince of Wales Camp' (Misc No.30 (1916) Cd.8324). There were then only 1,779 present, all Germans, of which seven were sailors and one a civilian. This report also mentioned two camps, amounting to a total of about 25 acres. No.1 camp was the barracks itself, and No.2 camp was a fenced off area on Poundbury Hill, adjacent to the barracks. Mail bags were reported to form the principal occupation of the men; 37,000 had been made, but some PoWs were employed outside the camp on road-making, quarrying and agriculture. Belfield mentioned thermometers (mostly for the dairy industry) were made at Dorchester by PoWs with an output averaging 300 per week, but he gave no further details of this industry (HO 45/11025/68577).

The day after this American visit to Dorchester, Frongoch Camp, in North Wales, was cleared of military PoWs (there were nearly 1,000) and local reports spoke of them being moved to 'southern England'. Following the departure of PoWs to France, Dorchester had space for them and it was the only camp, at the time, in southern England. However, a report of an inspection in July, of a camp at Le Havre, stated that those PoWs had come from Frongoch and Handforth. So it is not entirely clear what the moves were.

Another visit by the US Embassy took place on 31 July 1916 when there were 3,073 prisoners, all German. 581 of them were wounded and awaiting transfer to Switzerland of which 319 were expected to leave on 2 August and the rest a week later. 100 huts were then in use with a maximum of 40 men per hut, but few of them were full. There were 21 patients in the hospital and 40 to 60 out-patients each day. Four deaths were recorded since the camp opened: two cases of appendicitis, one of gas-poisoning and one of carbolic acid poisoning. (763.72114/1746)

The following month a survey was carried out, by Dr Taylor of the American Embassy, on the diet of the PoWs at Dorchester. Out of 2,450 there, about 600 were reported as going out to work daily. The diet was found to be satisfactory and the food properly prepared, but those engaged on heavy labour sought an increase. Additional vegetables were suggested by Dr Taylor, who also commented on the monotony of the diet. (763.72114/2089)

Between 17 September and 8 October 1916 certain privileges were suspended because of escapes. The War Office wrote to the Foreign Office on 3 January 1917, explaining that newspapers were withheld during the whole period, while outgoing letters were delayed only until 27 September.

The first visit by the Swiss Legation (after USA declared war) was on 29 and 30 March 1917. The report (in FO 383/276) gave comparative figures: 3,409 at the camp on 1 January 1916, 3,543 on 1 January 1917 and only 1,575 on the day of the visit. The accommodation was described as three barrack blocks and 112 huts, each for twenty men. 200 worked in a carpenter's shop making sections for huts. 65,000 mailbags had been made but that work was now stopped. The hospital was in a brick building plus three hutted wards, providing 112 beds. 377 cases were treated in 1916, many severely wounded. Seven deaths and one lunacy were reported. 10 working camps, employing 2,355 men were listed. These included Sandhill Park and Bramley (*qv*). This large number of PoWs in the working camps explains the dramatic reduction in the population of the parent camp.

In the spring of 1917 the use of PoWs as labour in this country, particularly on the land, was increasing but at Dorchester, it was reported that while most of the men were available for work, lack of accommodation outside the camp meant that they could only be employed locally, on a week-to-week basis. For example, five PoWs were working at a cabinet maker's shop in the town, guarded by two soldiers, which prompted a question in Parliament.[5] These reports do not tally with the Swiss report a few days before.

In October 1917 the prisoner numbers were 2,431, but by March 1919 it had risen to 4,407. At that later date there were 130 working camps under Dorchester.

A German prisoner's gallantry was rewarded at a ceremonial parade held in Dorchester at the end of July 1919. Private Bruckmann was presented with a silver watch and a gift of money in recognition of the gallantry he displayed in extricating a British officer from a crashed and burning aeroplane on Salisbury Plain. He also earned early repatriation, leaving on Sunday 3 August, with a free passage to his home.[6]

The PoWs departed in early November 1919. *Dorset County Chronicle* of 20 November, remarked that the departures were not generally known to the public as the prisoners had left in batches during the night. The plateau used by the PoWs as a recreation ground, on Poundbury Hill, was again open to the public.

In 1937 the same paper carried a long report of a visit by German ex-PoWs. That article mentioned 48 deaths at the camp.

---

[5] *Hansard HC* 2 April 1917, vol..92, col..959, also *The Times* 3 April.

[6] *Western Gazette* 8Aug19 4b: also reported in *Northampton Mercury* 8Aug19.

Souvenir postcard with names of passengers, or crew, from SS *Lapland*, Red Star Line (a Belgian company), held at Dorchester in 1914.

This town mark (43mm over the stop) is the only cached recorded used at Dorchester camp.

A label for Dorchester Camp (on blue paper). Similar labels have been seen for most of the major camps in this country.

Douglas, Isle of Man

A Home Office camp for civilians   Grid Ref: SC 388 773

This was the Cunningham's Holiday Camp, between Douglas and Onchan, which had first been set up in 1894 at Howstrake and moved to Victoria Road in 1904. Joseph and Elizabeth Cunningham, had come from Liverpool and ran the camp on strict presbyterian lines. The sleeping accommodation was provided for up to 1,500 in bell tents with camp beds. Dominating the tents was a large pavilion used as a dining room and recreation space. *The Times* 26 April 1915, described it as: 'a summer holiday camp for young men at a guinea a week'.

Sir William Byrne and Mr Sebag-Montefiore, Chairman and Secretary of the Destitute Aliens Committee, visited the Isle of Man in September 1914, to enquire about accommodating internees on the island, and almost immediately Cunningham's Camp was requisitioned. Lt Colonel Henry William Madoc (1870-1937) Chief Constable of the Isle of Man, was additionally appointed Commandant, a post he occupied for the whole war. Captain (later Major) F.C.C. Bland was his deputy and Dr Robert Marshall was the Medical Officer. The Isle of Man Volunteers provided the first guards.

The camp opened on 22 September 1914 when the first 200 internees arrived. By 24 October, after a party of 200 had arrived from Frith Hill, there were then 2,600 at the camp, its official capacity, but a temporary increase to 3,300 was approved. Men of the National Reserve supplemented the guard.

On 19 November a riot broke out in the dining hall after the mid-day meal. The guard was turned out with loaded rifles and bayonets fixed. They fired a volley over the heads of the prisoners, but that did not quell the disturbance, so they fired again, into the crowd. Five prisoners were killed and 19 were wounded, one of whom died a week later. The US Embassy sent an official, Mr Chandler Hale, to report on the matter. Meanwhile, an inquest was held at which the guards' action was justified. The riot was blamed on the overcrowding, and while poor food had been cited, the Medical Officer said in his evidence that the complaint, of worms in the potatoes, had been remedied some weeks previously. (HO45/10946/266042 and *The Times* 28 Nov 1914)

As a result of the riot Kurt Vausch was charged, and found guilty, at a Court Martial, on 15 December, with incitement which led to the outbreak of violence. Chandler Hale's report for the US Embassy was delivered to the Foreign Office at the end of December and published. He concluded that the food was excellent, that the prisoners were in the wrong and could only blame themselves. The ring-leaders had come from the East End of London and had preached dis-content and insubordination among their fellow internees. He commented on over-crowding and said that the authorities hoped to move about 1,000 to the camp at Peel. (*The Times* 30 Dec 1914 and Cd 7817)

At another hearing, also on 15 December, Otto Lutz and two others were charged with writing letters in invisible ink and with writing under the stamp, both forbidden. Indeed prisoners were not supposed to have stamps at all. Mail which needed stamps should have been handed in with the necessary coin and the censor's office affixed the stamps.

Mr Jackson, of the US Embassy, visited on 9 February 1915 and reported 2,400 present. This confirms the move of prisoners to Knockaloe. Most lived in barracks, 120 men to a hut, but others were still in tents, sleeping one to seven men. Some preferred tents as it gave them more privacy. 'Captains', elected by the internees, had either separate rooms or tents to themselves. In some huts, cubicles for a few men had been built, and their occupants paid a moderate sum for their use. Tradesmen were occupied and Mr Jackson wrote, *more was done here to provide occupation than in any other camp I visited*. The canteen was judged to be adequate, washing, bathing and sanitary arrangements were good. Electric light, a swimming pool and a large hall for recreation, music and dancing were all provided.

As the exercise space was limited, route marches (walks) were arranged. Cunningham's, the owners, provided cooks, including women, under contract, which did not seem to give general satisfaction. Regulations, made by Captains of Companies, and the 'Daily Dietary' were appended to the report. (HO45/10760/269116)

Pre-war postcard of Cunningham's Camp, sent by an internee, Captain Konrad Hass of the Z F Line, in January 1915 to Nürnberg.. The arched roof in the background was the recreation and dining building.

The tented section was the Privilege Camp where the better-off employed servants. Herr F Heickl #673 sent this card, undated, to Frau Else Heickl in Magdeburg

Envelope with a printed cachet for the Alien's Camp at Douglas.
Surely there was more than one alien interned!
A cover to London, posted 13 June 1917, has the correct 'Aliens' Camp'.

In April 1915 the *Liverpool Daily Post* carried a plea from the Jewish authorities to allow all religious Jews then interned, to be allowed to move to Douglas, as that was the only camp where kosher food was provided. This might be a clue to the lack of general satisfaction, regarding food, expressed to Mr Jackson, as non-Jewish people may have been involved in its preparation. In the same month *The Times* referred to the *Camp Echo* but although no other reference to a camp newspaper at Douglas has been seen in official papers in London, two other titles are known and copies are held in the Manx National Heritage Library.

There were a number of escapes from Douglas, but many newspaper reports did not differentiate between Douglas and Knockaloe. Throughout the war many were able to get out of their camp but none succeeded in leaving the island. There were 98 convictions for attempted escape. One of the more active and enterprising men was Georg von Strang, who got out of Douglas four times. On one occasion he tried to swim out to a ferry boat, but the ship got under weigh too soon, so he had to swim back to the shore where a local Constable awaited him.

At another US Embassy visit in June 1915 the report was very positive and described the place as a happy camp, where prisoners took pride in making the place attractive. A new turf playing field had come into use since exercise marches had been given up in May. This is in common with other camps where PoWs, seen out on marches, had lead to ill-feeling after the sinking of SS *Lusitania*. Other facilities mentioned were a gymnasium, tennis courts and shower baths. A Coffee Restaurant had been created in one building, managed by the prisoners, and its price list was given in the report. The library was stated to contain 4,000 books.

At a subsequent inspection, on 1 May 1916, the report (in Cd.8324) mentioned a considerable number of the Jewish faith. That report included details of the layout: the Upper Camp had two compounds; one an ordinary camp, the other a Jewish camp where kosher food was served. The Lower Camp was the privilege camp where 500 lived and they employed 100 servants from the Upper Camp. The privilege camp held 'officer class', or more wealthy internees, who paid extra to improve their diet and accommodation. Ten shillings a week purchased a third-share of a tent; twelve shillings bought a third-share of a hut; twelve and sixpence entitled a man to a half-share of a tent, and for £1 a week they could have sole use of a hut or tent. Both camps had a mixture of hut and tent accommodation. There were 3 patients in the camp infirmary. About 100 internees were employed outside the camps as gardeners and farm labour. Some of these were, very likely, working for Mr Cunningham at Ellerslie Farm, 850 acres, which he purchased in 1915 and from which he later provided the camp with vegetables and dairy produce.

An inspection report of May 1917, mentioned that the Lower Camp internees were allowed the use of tennis courts and parts of an adjacent park, while the Upper Camp had the use of a large grass field for recreation. In November of that year it was reported that 300 men had been transferred to Knockaloe to relieve crowding in the Upper Camp. Apparently these men were selected somewhat indiscriminately so some, who were useful to the camp, and others attending classes, were moved, which caused some disruption.

The 1919 Home Office report (HO45/11025/410118) stated that persistent endeavours were made to organise camp industries, but Douglas was one, of only three, where success could be claimed. Brush making was the industry set up here (and also at Islington, in London). The machinery was installed by contractors, instructors were engaged to teach the inmates, and the products were sold through the contractors to Government departments and the public. Although the enterprise was financially successful, it was criticised by the Brush Makers' Association. The two plants gave continuous employment to about 600 internees, who were paid at ordinary industry rates and were allowed to retain their earnings, less a deduction for their maintenance. On 19 November 1919 the brush making equipment was advertised for sale by tender.

On 4 June 1919, *The Times* reported that the camp had been cleared of internees. The site was handed back to Cunningham's and immediately it reverted to its former use as a holiday camp. In WWII the camp became HMS *St George*, a Royal Naval training school for boys.

Source reference	Inspection Date	German	Austro-Hungarian	Turkish	Bulgarian	other	Total
Cd 7817, p36	30 Dec 14	c 2,000	c 1,300				c 3,300
HO45/10760/269116	9 Feb 15						c 2,400
FO 383/33	19 Jun 15						2,429
HO45/10946/266042	30 Sep 15	1,759	621	12			2,392
FO 383/162	21 Dec 15						2,614
Cd. 8324, p17	1 May 16	1,968	759	14		3	2,744
FO 383/276	5 May 17	1,914	709	10		7	2,640
FO 383/277	26 Nov 17	1,638	529	13	92	108	2,380
FO 383/360	14 July 18	1,621	568			12	2,201
FO 383/432	15 Aug 18	1,612	571	11		11	2,205

Table 7: Douglas: Prisoner population statistics.

The anomalous figures for November 1917 (after the move of 300 to Knockaloe) suggest that some men, then counted as Bulgarian or 'other', had previously been listed as German or Austro-Hungarian. Possibly they included 'friendly aliens' such as Schleswiggers or Polish who subsequently left the camp.

Isle of Man - Internee mail statistics Monthly averages for May, June and July 1916 and 1917							
	Letters, inward		Letters, outward		Registered letters			
	from UK	foreign	to UK	foreign	inward	value	outward	value
1916	32,247	54,433	41,430	83,300	1,666	£4,454	1,292	£1,847
1917	32,228	51,345	26,991	93,896	1,997	£5,450	1,720	£2,013
	Parcels, inward		Registered Parcels	Parcels outward	Luggage inwards	population in May		
	Hostile	other				Douglas	Knockaloe	total
1916	19,236	8,185	333	1,023	717	2,744	20,563	23,307
1917	18,573	12,754	632	958	613	2,640	20,899	23,539

Table 8. Internee mail statistics, drawn from FO 383/359
(Note these figures cover both Douglas and Knockaloe)

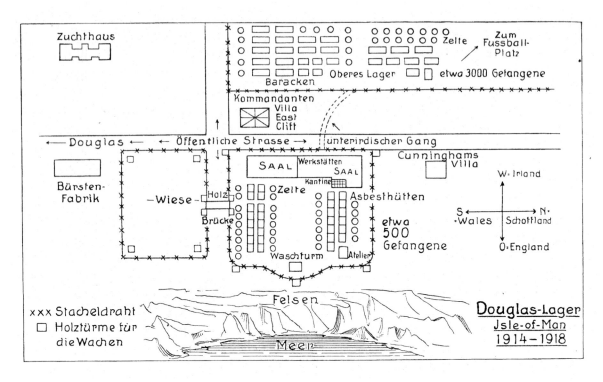

Diagrammatic sketch of the camp at Douglas from F L Dunbar-Kaldreuth's, *Die Männerinsel*

Significant features of this plan are:
About 500 men are shown living in the "Lower Camp" and about 3,000 in the "Upper Camp".

Asbesthütten	= asbestos huts
Atelier	= studio
Baracken	= barrack huts
Bürsten-Fabrik	= Brush factory
Holz-Brücke	= wooden bridge
Holztürme fur die Wachen	= wooden towers for the guard
Kantine	= canteen, ie a shop which sold tobacco, sweets, soap, etc
Oberes Lager	= upper camp
Öffentliche Strasse	= public street, ie Victoria Road
Saal	= hall, assembly room
Stacheldraht	= barbed wire
Unterirdischer Gang	= underground passage
Waschturm	= laundry-tower? Should this be Wachturm = watchtower
Weise	= grass field
Werkstätten Saal	= workshops
Zelte	= tents
Zuchthaus	= prison

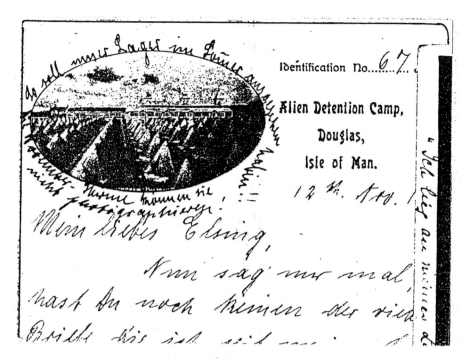

Specially printed notepaper used from Douglas.
The vignette shows rows of bell-tents.

Censor cachet 37 x 24mm

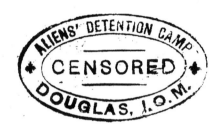

Censor cachet 50 x 28mm

Dyffryn Aled, Llansannan, Denbighshire, N Wales

Officers' Camp   Grid Ref: SH 948 668

This was a country house built in the early 19th century, owned by Lady Dundonald. It lay in the valley of Afon Aled, 1¼m NE of Llansannan. The house name means "Beside the water of Aled". Previously it had been used as a private lunatic asylum (*The Times* 26 April 1915). That paper described the place as inaccessible, gloomy and mildewed-looking. It lacked many modern amenities such as bathrooms, so the officers had to use tin baths. Hubbard (*The Buildings of Wales*, p241) stated the house was demolished in the 1920s.

Macpherson recorded that the camp opened in September 1914 for 90 officers and 30 servants. Among the early detainees was Captain Theodore Schlagintweit, lately the German Consul in Manchester. He was arrested at his home in Whalley Road, Manchester, then appeared before the Manchester Magistrates, who fined him £5 plus costs, and bound him over in the sum of £100, for contravening the Aliens Restriction Act, by travelling outside the 5 mile limit.[7] In answer to a question in the House of Commons, it was stated that Captain Schlagintweit was one of twelve consular officials exchanged in early 1915. (*The Times* 4 March 1915)

Another early detainee was Lt von Tirpitz, son of the German Admiral. He was captured after his ship, the light cruiser SMS *Mainz,* was sunk in the Battle of Heligoland, 28 August 1914.

Chandler Anderson and Chandler Hale, of the American Embassy, visited this and two soldiers' camps and reported to their Ambassador on 14 October 1914. These camps were chosen as 'representing the only types now in use'. Comments were general to all three camps, with no specific criticism. Complaints were, in the most part, restricted to the irritation of capture and confinement, but the exercise area here was not level making sports difficult. (763.72114/62)

When Mr Jackson of the US Embassy visited on 11 February 1915, there were 91 officers, including 25 naval and one Austrian, plus 20 civilian servants and cooks. These civilians had come from Queen's Ferry and were well pleased with their transfer. He reported that the house was good but because it fronted onto a road the windows were barred.[8] One large field was already enclosed and a further field was being fenced. Walks in the woods and surrounds were allowed, escorted by British officers. There were several recreation rooms in the house, and a billiards table has been ordered. Senior officers had single rooms, and there were no more than six in any other room. Captain Schlagintweit was mentioned as being in charge of mess supplies and purchases. The lighting was poor. (HO45/ 10760/ 269116) When the International Red Cross delegates visited they commented that the place was somewhat difficult to access. Otherwise their comments were very similar to those of Mr Jackson and the numbers present were the same.

On 4 April 1915, two officers escaped Ober-Lt Hans Andler (Navy) and Lt Hans Freidrich Rudolf von Sanders Leben (242nd Reserve Infantry Battalion). A £10 reward was offered for their recapture. This escape was one of the earliest, and it certainly caused a major use of newsprint, nationally, as searches for these two were reported.[9] They were re-captured at Llanbedr, 3 miles south of Harlech and about 33 miles from Dyffryn Aled on 11 April. They appeared first before the Festiniog Magistrates and when they faced a Court Martial at Chester (fully reported in *Chester Chronicle* 24 April), Lt Colonel Arthur B Cottell FRCS, late RAMC, (b1855, retired 1901), the Commandant gave evidence. They were awarded 28 days detention.

The *Occurrence Book,* of Blaenau Festiniog Police Station, held in Dolgellau archives, records an interesting account of their arrest:

---

[7] *Hull Daily Mail* 24Aug, p4, *Liverpool Daily Post,* 25Aug, p5f & *Lancaster Guardian* 29Aug, p3f

[8] Possibly the bars were from the previous use of the building as an asylum.

[9] eg *The Times* 6, 7, 9 and 10 April 1915

Sunday 11 April 1915: PC Nathaniel Davies reports apprehending at 3pm this day, near Pensarn railway station, the two German Officers Lts Hans Andler and Rudolf von Sanders Leben, who escaped from the military camp at Llansannan a week ago (4 April). They were brought to Blaenau Festiniog lock-up the same afternoon by Inspector Stephen Owen.

1pm, 12 April - before a full bench of Magistrates they were ordered to be handed over to an escort from Llansannan. Inspector Owen received a wire from the Commandant at Llansannan to hand the prisoners over to an escort of the Denbighshire Constabulary. (J. Jones Morris showed me a telegram from the Home Office ordering the prisoners to be handed over to a military escort.) After consulting with the Chief Constable, on the 'phone, I handed the prisoners over to Superintendent Worlam and Sergeant Evans, of Denbigh, at 4pm.

When the American Embassy visited the camp on 25 June 1915, the report mentioned 69 officers, 43 army and 26 navy, with 29 servants. Major Ritter was the senior army officer and Captain Wallis was the senior naval officer. There was a water shortage due to drought so the latrines were not working. Two playing fields were available, one of 8 acres within the wire, the other a larger field used on parole terms. (FO 383/33)

On 14 August 1915 another escape occurred. This time three officers got out and walked to Llandudno. Lt Hans Werner von Helldorf (army) and Korvettenkapitan Heindrich George von Henning benefited from a plot hatched by Korvettenkapitan Herman Tholens, who had been second-in-command of SMS *Mainz*. When a number of prisoners were exchanged in early 1915 it appears that Tholens sent a message, possibly through Captain Schlagintweit, to the German Naval High Command that a breakout was possible and could a submarine be available to carry them off? Apparently correspondence ensued, in code, which was not rumbled by the censors. Eventually a letter arrived informing Tholens that a lady relative of his would be getting married on a certain date, which confirmed that all arrangements were in place for the night mentioned.

The three got out, reached the planned rendevous and made the agreed signal, but no response was received. They hid up for the day and returned the next night. Again they got no response to their signal. They therefore gave up that idea and decided to split up and make their way to London. Tholens was arrested at Llandudno Junction station and the other two got into a cab, because it was raining, which took them directly to the local barracks, as the driver was suspicious.

The reason the three did not get any response to their signal from the submarine, which was there waiting for them, was because there was a large rock between them and the submarine, blocking the signals they made. Dark nights had been chosen, to give the best chance of avoiding detection, and heavy rain on the second night meant the three could not see the rock which obscured them from their route to freedom. At the subsequent Court Martial at Chester Castle, at the end of the month, they were all sentenced to 84 days at Chelmsford gaol. Tholens became an habitual escaper and will be mentioned at other camps. An account of this escape attempt was carried in *Österreichische Wehrzeitung* of 30 August 1929, upon which this story is based..

In a letter of complaint, written on 13 August, von Heldorf stated that he gave himself up voluntarily to the military authorities at Llandudno. He complained that he was handcuffed on the way back to Dyffryn Aled and about his subsequent sentence of 84 days at Chelmsford. Tholens made similar complaints. (FO 383/65)

In the Spring of 1915 the British Government had adopted a policy of segregating submarine crew PoWs. That policy was abandoned in June 1915 and in September there were discussions at the Admiralty, which no doubt reviewed the escape mentioned above, and fears were expressed that intelligence might get back to Germany through released officers who had mixed with submariners. The Admiralty was especially concerned that details of the Royal Navy's tactics for hunting submarines, and the facts of losses should not get back to Germany. The War Office was consulted and arrangements were made for 40 to 50 additional submarine officers to be moved to Dyffryn Aled, subject to the removal of the military prisoners elsewhere, as the facilities at Dyffryn Aled could not be extended. It was agreed that this camp would become the main camp for submarine officers (ADM1/8446/15). As they were considered the most likely to try to escape, the guard was strengthened and roll-calls were doubled. (Garrett, p131)

A letter from Captain Wallis, the Senior German Naval Officer, was sent by the American Embassy to the Foreign Office, on 5 October 1915. He described the house as neglected and in want of fittings and facilities. The work required took nine months. Windows and doors were ill-fitting, resulting in draughts. The roof leaked. There were smoke problems from fireplaces and chimneys. The fire escapes had been removed and the windows were barred. There was also discontent among the 74 officers at the camp over room-sharing arrangements, which were in the hands of the Commandant, rather than the Senior PoW. A request was made to allow walks outside the camp grounds. He also complained about the removal of the civilian barber and tailor, and their replacement by untrained soldiers. (FO 383/65)

This last point appears to have been remedied, for when the American Embassy made a visit of inspection on 30 March 1916, civilian servants were back in place. The Commandant was then Lt Colonel William Selwood Hewett, late Indian Army (b1851, retired 1906). 81 prisoners were present, 16 army officers, 36 naval officers, with 25 soldier servants, one naval servant and three civilian servants. (FO 383/163)

At a further inspection visit at the end of September 1916 the population was slightly reduced, to 77. The recreation ground, used on parole basis, had been closed because of a recent escape attempt and exercise time had been reduced from 8 hours to 4 hours. Colonel Hewett had offered to reopen the playing field if the PoWs gave their parole, but this they refused. The matter was referred to the War Office and by the date of the report (12 October) the restrictions had been lifted. The un-named officer, who had absconded, was sentenced to imprisonment for nine months, which was commuted to 84 days confinement at the camp. He was allowed exercise in the open air, for two hours each day. Two servants were serving three days confinement for disobeying orders. (763.72114/2126)

Arped Horn, No.261 at Dyffryn Aled, an Austrian officer, wrote a letter of complaint, which was presented to the Foreign Office by the Swedish Legation. He had escaped from Donington Hall and was returned there after recapture, where he was kept in isolation for 41 days with one hour exercise per day. A Court Martial on 29 August sentenced him to 14 days imprisonment, served at Chelmsford. Horn complained of conditions there: no newspapers, no smoking except in the yard, food was rationed yet he had to pay half-a-crown per day, and the cell was wet (FO 383/250). In November 1917 he wrote, from Dyffryn Aled, in good English, to a lady in New York, in which he apologised for not having written for two months. Pending his Court Martial, and while under sentence, he would have been allowed to write only one letter per month.

The Swiss Legation visited on 19 December 1917 when the commandant was Lt Colonel F Winn Sampson (late Militia). The numbers present were 72 army officers and 4 naval officers, 1 Austrian army officer, and 29 German servants. 22 officers had recently been moved to Kegworth, awaiting transfer to the Netherlands and 13 German officers were expected to arrive shortly. The house was described as spacious and comfortable with room for 90 officers. The sports field was in use on parole terms and walks were allowed every second or third day (FO 383/431). From the numbers present it appears that the policy of holding submarine officers at this camp had been abandoned by this date.

In June 1918 Lt W J E Petersen and Engineer Lt H F Burkhardt escaped but they were picked up next day near Wrexham, and in October Franz Laue escaped and was recaptured at Caernarfon, two days later.

The camp was closed on 10 December 1918 and the prisoners were moved to Oswestry and Donington Hall. Subsequently the house was found to be structurally unsound and was demolished. Some have speculated whether amateur tunnellers had weakened the foundations.

International Red Cross postcard (enlarged) showing PoWs playing hockey on what appears to be the open ground which was used on parole terms. The fenced in recreation area below the house, being sloped, was a cause of complaint when the US Embassy inspected the camp in October 1914.

D.A.

This marking is usually found with the circled P.C. handstamp in precisely the shade of red, suggesting that both instruments were held at the camp. Overall length 23mm

```
DETENTION BARRACKS,
  OFFICERS PRISONERS OF WAR.
      "DYFFRYN ALED,"
  LLANSANNAN, ABERGELE,
       NORTH WALES.
```

Overall dimensions 57 x 18mm

```
PRESIDENT
German Officers'
Smoking Canteen.
```

Cachet (enlarged) seen on the flap of a cover to London, posted at Llanfair Talhaiarn 10 August 1917. Length of top line 30mm.

Edinburgh

Four locations in the city have been traced where internees and prisoners of war were held.

Redford Barracks, Colinton Road
Grid Ref: NT 225 692

The barracks, on the south-west of the city, were built between 1909 and 1916. Civilian and military prisoners were held there in the early months of the war, in a tented compound to the south of the main barrack buildings. This camp was not listed by Macpherson.

On 12 August 1914, *Yorkshire Herald* stated that fifty German seamen, from German ships at Leith, were moved under escort to Redford Barracks and two days later *Edinburgh Evening News* expressed disquiet about the Germans at Redford, who had been gathered from all over Scotland, many of them seamen. Over the next two weeks, more were brought in, so there were several hundred there when survivors from SMS *Mainz* arrived at the end of the month. The newcomers included Lt von Tirpitz, son of the Admiral, but he did not stay long.

The Scotsman 3 September, reported that eight German officers, including von Tirpitz, had been taken to Salteford station by char-à-banc, and then to the Caledonian Railway station in Edinburgh, from where they travelled south. No destination was mentioned. A rumour, to the effect that some prisoners had tried to escape from Redford, gained some currency. The authorities stated that the story was baseless but the rumour was published, for example in *Liverpool Daily Post* which reported that von Tirpitz was involved in an attempted escape by 20 at night, but they had been stopped and taken away to Edinburgh Castle.

A postcard from Redford to Edinburgh, written 14 September, said *...we are perhaps 1200 prisoners here ... we can receive no person in weekdays, but Sundays from 2-4.* On 24 September *Yorkshire Herald* reported the arrival at York of 300 Germans, including 70 sailors, from Edinburgh.

On 2 November nearly 500 were removed from Redford. *Edinburgh Evening News* that day, reported that they had gone by train from Georgie station to southern England, but the next day *The Scotsman* announced their arrival at Stobs Camp, near Hawick.

A German report in CAB 37/123/37 alleged bad treatment and conditions at Redford. When Mr Jackson inspected a number of camps early in 1915 he reported, *I was told the temporary camp at Redford, near Edinburgh, had been closed for some time*, but he did mention a temporary receiving depot at Edinburgh, possibly this was at the Castle.

```
COMMANDANT,
REDFORD DETENTION CAMP,
COLINTON.
```

Computer generated cachet. The box is 48 x 23mm and the line lengths (over commas) are 36, 43 and 25mm. Examples seen are struck in red, but a different shade from the circled P.C. which was also applied.

Edinburgh Castle Grid Ref: NT 252 735

The Detention House, Edinburgh Castle, was included in the January 1919 *List of Places of Internment*.

When the alleged break-out from Redford was published in early September 1914, it was said that the prisoners were taken away to Edinburgh Castle. *The Times* 15 April 1915 reported that Germans captured from a Norwegian barque, sailing from South America, had been landed at Kirkwall and moved to Edinburgh Castle.

With the mass arrests in 1915 the authorities must have had a central point at which they could gather those to be interned. With Redford Barracks being cleared, apparently, before the end of 1914, it is likely the Castle was used for a while to hold civilian internees.

Hospitals
The Castle Military Hospital and Craig Lockhart Hospital were both listed as a *Place of Internment* in the 1919 list.

Feltham, Middlesex

Friendly aliens (civil and military)   Grid Ref: TQ 087 725

The Middlesex Industrial Reform School was built in 1869 and early in the 20th century it became part of the Borstal system for juvenile offenders. *The Times* 19 February 1916, reported that the Borstal Institution had been closed the previous day and that it would shortly reopen to house enemy aliens. They would cultivate the 90 acres of pasture land which surround the buildings. Macpherson stated the camp was designed for 1,500 men.

The Commandant was Major Lewis Wentworth Johnson, b1870, late Royal Warwickshire Regt. After retiring from the Army in 1908 he had been appointed Deputy Governor at Portland Prison. He received a temporary commission as Major while Commandant, with effect from 14 February 1916, and on 31 March 1918 he was promoted to Lt Colonel. He was appointed Governor of the Borstal Institution when it resumed its former character after the war.

Mr Boylston Beal of the American Embassy visited the camp on 17 May 1916 and reported that the place had been remodelled, which had done away with the feeling of prison confinement. The report indicated that the first PoWs had arrived there in late March or early April. There were 380 prisoners, of which 201 were soldiers, 4 naval ratings and 175 civilians. The breakdown by nationality was: 319 Germans, 55 Austrians and 6 others. Some ships masters were among the civilian prisoners. 40 to 50 acres of farmland belonged to the camp, where the prisoners worked and grew vegetables. For exercise there was a large indoor gymnasium, an open-air swimming pool and two sports fields. (Cd.8324)

At another inspection visit, on 18 December 1916, (FO 383/276) there were 708 present, comprising 301 military, 10 naval and 397 civilians: 406 were German, 284 Austrian and 18 others. Since the previous visit committees had been properly formed to organise education, industrial activities, carpet weaving, theatrical, sports and other pastimes. The military and civilian sections were separated for dining and sleeping. A British doctor was in charge of the hospital with an RAMC Corporal and 2 German orderlies. There were no in-patients at the time, but 14 out-patients were being treated, all with colds. One death was reported, of liver disease, of a man who had recently arrived at the camp. Six German cooks ran the kitchens, and were issued with the standard rations. It was reported that many prisoners kept rabbits, which supplemented their diet. 70 acres of farmland were then in use for agriculture, horticulture, pigs and cows. Prisoners were also engaged in engineering, concrete block making, shed and hut making, tar spraying, tree felling, tailoring, boot making etc. Three looms had been set up for carpet making. There were no serious complaints. Some Austrians from Galicia, who spoke only Polish or Ruthenian asked to be transferred as they were unable to communicate with others in the camp. There were none in the cells at the time of the visit.

In June 1917, Roumanians were transferred to Feltham, from where it was hoped it would be possible to release them for agricultural work (FO383/247). Lists of men from Alsace and Lorraine, at Feltham in August 1917, can be found in HO45/10760/269510.

Swedish diplomats visited the camp on 11 January 1918 and described the place as being on a treeless plain, 15 miles west of London, and a half-hour walk from the railway station. Their report noted that the men were grouped according to their ten different nationalities, but it only gave numbers of Austro-Hungarians, 118, plus one Armenian and one Arab. 140 men were civilians. Besides the main building, where cubicles for two beds were the usual arrangement on the upper floors, and dormitories for 20 to 30 on the ground floor, there were six huts to provide additional beds. There was some dissatisfaction among the civilians with the catering, because the food was prepared as for the military, and additionally there was some tension because of the mixed nature of the camp. The work was mostly agricultural, both on the camp grounds and for local farmers. All workers, including domestic and kitchen staff, earned wages and received extra rations. The usual sports and recreational facilities were under the guidance of the YMCA. (FO 383/359)

An undated Home Office report, in discussing aliens who claimed to be of friendly races, which included Polish, Czechs, Alsatians, Schleswig Danes, Serbs etc, stated:

Since many of the cases were too doubtful, a separate camp was established at Feltham, in which those of them whom it was thought desirable to intern were collected. This had the double advantage of removing the genuine men from the German camps, where they were unpopular and sometimes ill-treated, and of enabling the authorities to get a better idea of their real sympathies, which, in the German camps, they did not dare to express. Feltham proved a success and it was found possible to liberate a number of the men after they had been sufficiently tested there. Both combatants and civilians were located there. (HO45/11025/410118)

In 1918 the War Office had decided to allow combatant PoWs of Polish race to enlist in the Polish Army in France. Feltham then became a Polish Military centre, at which these men were collected and, after examination, were drafted to France in considerable numbers. However, many who were transferred to Feltham complained about being classified as Polish. (FO 383/433)

The Times 17 March 1919, reported that 300 released Schleswiggers had landed at Copenhagen. While it is not certain they came from Feltham, it does seems the most likely place. On 1 May 1919 there were only 25 interned at Feltham.

13 deaths are known at this camp, nine of which were re-interred at Cannock and four remain in Feltham.

The Feltham Industrial School, before it became a PoW camp

The dining room at Feltham (International Red Cross postcard)

The bakery at Feltham (International Red Cross postcard)

Frith Hill, Frimley, Surrey
later called Blackdown Camp in some sources

Civilians and Other Ranks in 1914
Other Ranks from April 1915, and civilians for a short time
ORs again from July 1916 but a different site
re-opened for ORs in August 1918
May 1919 civilians again

Grid Ref: SU 903 587
and nearby

The first camp was on heathland, two miles east of Frimley, about 360 ft above sea level, between the Blackdown Barracks and the Brompton Sanatorium on the west side of the road which ran along the crest of the rise. Later the camp was extended to the west. The site was poorly drained and most of the accommodation was in tents. The camp was closed in December 1914, but it reopened in April 1915 and subsequently it was closed and reopened a number of times during the war.

The camp was first opened very early in the war, for there were reports in newspapers as far away as Yorkshire on 12 August 1914, that the Royal Engineers were constructing a 40 acre camp at 'Blackdon (*sic*), a few miles from Aldershot'. In mid September the local papers wrote of plans to extend the camp when there were about 2,800 held there in two sections, one for internees, the other for military and naval PoWs. In the early weeks officers are mentioned in some reports, but whether those were accurate is not known.

In early October, the first batch of prisoners to be put to work left Frith Hill for Longmoor Camp, about 19 miles away. About 100 were employed there for about 11 weeks, making a rifle range and re-aligning a railway track to avoid the new range. They left Longmoor before Christmas for one of the ships anchored off Ryde.[10]

On 14 October, Chandler Anderson and Chandler Hale, of the US Embassy, inspected this camp, and two others, which were chosen as 'representing the only types now in use'. All comments were general to the three camps with no specific criticism. Complaints referred merely to the irritation of capture and confinement. Some prisoners claimed Red Cross immunity (763.72114/62). On 23 October Sir Edward Grey, the Foreign Secretary, wrote to the American Ambassador ... *the combatant prisoners are at present, in the main, interned at Frith Hill Camp.*

Throughout September and October new arrivals were recorded in the local newspapers and, from late October, departures. Some 200 civilians went to Douglas in the third week of October and 400 soldiers to Templemore, in Ireland. Further batches went to Douglas over the next few weeks, so that *Camberley News* was able to announce on 28 November that all civilian internees had been moved to the Isle of Man. The PoWs were also moved but there are conflicting reports as to their destination. *The Times* 16 December, stated that all the military and naval PoWs had been moved to the ships, a statement that was also reported by other papers. By contrast, *Dorset County Chronicle* of 17 December, reported the arrival of 500 military PoWs at Dorchester from Frimley.

Frith Hill was reopened in April 1915 when parties of Germans arrived. *Aldershot News* 16 April, stated that it had not been intended to use the camp again, but the decision was reversed and 1,530 had arrived in three batches, on 13, 14 and 15 April, from ships at Southend-on-Sea. The American Embassy soon sent along an inspector, on 29 April, who recorded 1,637 prisoners, mostly from SS *Ivernia* at Southend, but 32 had just arrived from Neuve Chapelle and Hill 60. Accommodation was still in tents, but now they had floors. Twelve Privates, or eight Corporals, or four Sergeants per tent. New latrines and shower blocks had been built with cement floors.

On 17 May 1915 *Yorkshire Post* reported 500 civilians arrived at Frith Hill. *Camberley News* also reported the arrival of civilians after the sinking of SS *Lusitania* (7 May) but that paper stated that the civilians were moved on to other camps. George Kenner, writing his reminiscences in 1929, explained that he was arrested after the sinking of SS *Lusitania*

---

[10] *Hampshire Herald* 3 & 10 October and 26 December 1914

and held at Frith Hill, where ... *the wealthier grouped together to form a 'Paying Section', which was allowed by the English Command ... 120 men in the section, with four in each tent.* He went on to explain that this group set aside their space and marked it with poles, which were regularly knocked over by their poorer neighbours. When 600 were moved to the Isle of Man, Kenner moved into the Paying Section and, after another batch of 600 went to Stobs and more were sent to the Isle of Man, only the Paying Section remained. On 29 September 1915 Kenner was moved to Alexandra Palace.[11] Mail is known from this period. An example was written by Benno Gernhuber, Paying Section, Tent 5 Camp 1, Frith Hill, which confirms Kenner's account. The cover was postmarked London 7 August 1915 after passing through the POWIB.

On 29 July 1915 Paul Heilmann, one of the civilians being moved from Frith Hill to the Isle of Man jumped overboard from TSS *Duke of Clarence* into heavy seas. A body, believed to be his, was found at Southport on 23 August (FO 383/305).

A War Office letter of 30 September 1915, to the Foreign Office, stated that the civilians were removed 'some time ago' [*ie* Whitehall obfuscation for the day before!] and that the place 'would be abandoned as a place of internment within the next few weeks' (FO 383/34). *Leigh Chronicle* 5 November 1915, mentioned the arrival there of a batch of 39 PoWs from Frimley. An indication that the camp was closed was provided in the Spring of 1916 when American Embassy officials visited many camps, but Frith Hill, or Frimley, was not reported upon, suggesting it was not in use during that period.

The first escape from the camp was reported by *The Times* on 31 August 1915. A German airman Ernst August Junght got away, but no report of his recapture has been traced. An Hungarian account mentioned a German who stole an aircraft and flew away and that two weeks later a letter was received from that man, written from Germany. However, that account did not mention a date, the name of the man, nor the place from which he escaped.[12]

---

[11] Harringay Archives, Bruce Castle, Local History Collection 960.1

[12] Benedek B, *et al*: *Hadifogoly Magyarok Története*

A new camp was formed on 17 July 1916, and the American Embassy inspected it in September. The Commandant was Lt Colonel John Hall, Lancashire Fusiliers (retired 1908). It was stated that this was not the same camp as that called Frith Hill in 1914 and 1915. This was a working camp with PoWs brought from Eastcote to build a railway. There were 1,499 PoWs, all German, of which 58 were sailors, 32 were Warrant Officers and 100 were Corporals. Bell tents were the sleeping quarters for both the prisoners, and the guard, with up to ten men per tent. Washing facilities were in a long shed with a cold water supply. About one thousand were engaged on the railway project, one to three miles from the camp. Others were working on drainage of the camp and there were the usual quotas of tailors, cobblers and cooks. The camp had a recreation ground 'about the size of two football fields' (763.72114/2045).

Nottingham Evening Post 26 September 16, reported five men had escaped from railway work at Deepcut; and that three were recaptured at Esher and the other two at Wokingham. This report places the project the PoWs were working on as the 'Bisley Military Railway' which branched off the LSWR main line, at Brookwood station to serve Bisley Camp, Deepcut Barracks and Blackdown Barracks.

In the House of Commons it was reported on 17 October 1916 that Frith Hill was to close shortly. This was only three months after the camp had been reopened, suggesting that the railway work was not large scale, although 1,000 men had been drafted in to carry out the task. Whether they laid or re-laid the track, realigned it or extended it, is not known.

When the American report, of 2 September 1916, reached the German Government, they raised objections to PoWs having to sleep under canvas, referring particularly to Frith Hill where the tents lacked floorboards. Reprisals were threatened. The War Office wrote to the Foreign Office on 3 November, to state that the move to get all PoWs into huts had begun before this threat had been made and that it was expected to be complete by 25 November (FO 383/164).

In August and December 1917 escapes were reported from Cove Heights and Farnborough respectively. It is believed they were both from Cove Heights, a work camp, for that had a postal address of Farnborough. PoW labour was requested by the local councils of the area to clean out the Blackwater River, but no reports of that work being done have been seen.

The camp was re-opened for PoWs in August 1918 and the Swedish Legation inspected it on 3 October 1918. The commandant was Lt Colonel W S Smyth (not traced). It was a tented camp of 2.6 acres with room for 5,000 men. Germans were held in A compound but, as the Swedish delegates did not represent the German interest, their number was not stated. 562 Austro-Hungarian prisoners from the Piave (June 1918) and Sette Communi (May 1916) were in B Compound. 45 of them were employed on camp duties, the remainder went out to work in forestry, road-making, laying drill and exercise grounds, construction, carpentry, agriculture etc. No complaints were made and it was reported to be a well-established camp.(FO 383/360)

When Dorchester Camp was inspected by the Swiss Legation on 29 March 1919, it was stated that 49 Austrian PoWs there were shortly to be moved to Frith Hill, which was then reserved for Austrian combatant PoWs. Similarly, when Brocton was inspected in that same week, 22 Austrians were about to leave for Frith Hill. The movement of civilians from Alexandra Palace to Frith Hill in May 1919 (see below) indicates that there were still two separate compounds, as there had been in 1914-15, and when the Swiss inspection took place in October 1918.

Although Austrian and Hungarian PoWs were mentioned at Frith Hill in reports of October and 1918 and March 1919, no further report of their presence in Britain has been seen. The Hungarian history supported the accounts given in the inspection reports, particularly mentioning Blackdown camp, but gave no date for the PoWs being moved away from there, nor of their repatriation.[13]

In May 1919, when there were rather less than 5,000 civilians left in the internee camps, a committee sat to review applications for exemption from deportation. At that time Frith Hill came back into use for civilians, because Alexandra Palace was taken over by the Government for other purposes; there being insufficient room in other camps relatively close to London and Knockaloe was too far away.

The move of men, back to a tented camp, raised a storm of protest from the internees, their families and friends, and the Swiss and Swedish diplomats. Questions were asked in Parliament about the suitability of the site. It was said in reply that the move was temporary and that a tented camp was satisfactory in summer (*Hansard HC* 2 June 1919, vol.116, col.1713). Nevertheless, observant Jews were moved to Islington and internees who could justly claim to be unfit to live under canvas were moved to Belmont Hospital. As applications for release were approved, the Commandant at Frith Hill was instructed to release no more than 100 per day 'in order not to attract too much attention'. The camp was finally closed on 22 September 1919 when the remaining 150 men were moved to Islington (HO45/11025/410118/3).

The Times 8 May 1920, advertised the sale of huts and materials for 19 May.

---

[13] Benedek B *et al*: *Hadifogoly Magyarok Története*,

Frongoch, Bala, Merionethshire

1915-16 Other Ranks
1916 Irish prisoners
from 1917 ORs again.

Grid Ref: SH 904 393

This camp was 3 miles northwest of Bala, a stone-built whisky distillery, with ancillary buildings, constructed round a courtyard. The distillery had been founded in 1887, by RJ Lloyd Price of Rhiwlas (a large house just north of Bala) and Robert Willis. The capital of the venture was £100,000. They chose Frongoch because of the peaty land and the good water of the Trywaryn valley. However the business had difficulties because of the local Free Church beliefs which did not approve of either the making, or taking, of liquor. Supplies had to be brought in, and the product sent out, under cover of darkness so that the anonymity of the carriers could be preserved. Queen Victoria and the Prince of Wales (later Edward VII) were both presented with barrels of the product so the trade name *Royal Welsh Whisky* was adopted. In 1900 the company went into liquidation and the site was sold for £5,000 in April of that year.

Macpherson gave only the year of opening, 1915, with room for 1,800 men (originally for about 1000, but expanded when the Irishmen arrived) but much more than that number were present during 1919. The earliest indication of moves to Frongoch, found to date, was in *Wilmslow, Alderley & Knutsford Advertiser* of 9 April 1915, which reported transfers from Handforth. Major K C Wright was the first Commandant, who had moved from Leigh.

The US Embassy inspectors visited on 26 June 1915. Their report stated that the camp had opened on 25 March 1915 and that 997 were present, of which four were sailors and one a merchant ship captain. There were six dormitories, the largest for 250 men, the smallest for 21, and four huts, each with 35 men. A 2½ acre playing field was adjacent. One death was reported, of pneumonia after being wounded. Five patients were in the hospital ward, none were serious. Route marches for 200 went out each morning for two hours. Classes were organised in German, English, French, arithmetic and shorthand. Entertainments were provided by a brass band, piano, violins and a 70 voice choir, which gave many concerts. No complaints were made. (FO 383/33)

In November 1915, Sir Louis Mallet (British Ambassador in Constantinople 1913-14) visited Frongoch and reported that 600 parcels were received each week (FO 383/106).

When the US Embassy made their next inspection on 31 March 1916, there were 990 prisoners, all German, seven were naval ratings, the remainder were soldiers. By this date another prisoner had died, from tuberculosis. (Cd 3832)

On 13 April 1916, four escaped (they were not named in the newspapers) and they were recaptured 48 hours later by a Police Constable from Bwlchgwyn (near Wrexham). They were making for Liverpool. All had originally been taken at Neuve Chapelle, in March 1915.[14] On 12 October 1916, the US Ambassador sent a letter from two of these complaining of their treatment after their recapture. Julius Reinhard Kock and Unteroffizier Heinrich Brinkmann wrote from the camp at Jersey. They had got out of Frongoch on 13 April with Gefreiter Wilhelm Arenkens and Hans Schönherr, and were recaptured on 15 April. They were returned to Frongoch on 17th and sentenced to 84 days at Woking. The War Office refuted all allegations of mistreatment. (FO 383/164)

Cambrian News, 2 June 1916, reported that the German PoWs had been moved out, 'to southern England' and that a few soldiers were left to guard the premises. The southern England statement suggests Dorchester. That camp had recently sent a large number of PoWs to France as labourers and an American Embassy visit to Dorchester, on 1 June, commented on the reduced numbers there.

After the Easter Rising, of April 1916, Irish internees were held at Frongoch. OMahony wrote that 2,519 Irishmen were deported from Ireland to British gaols in May and June 1916. Some 650 were released within the first few weeks and the remaining 1,863 were sent to Frongoch. The first of them arrived there on 9

---

[14] *The Times* 15 April 1916 and *Cambrian News* 21 April.

June. Although most of the German PoWs had left, a few remained in the sick quarters, but they were moved elsewhere as soon as the authorities realised the Irishmen and Germans were fraternising.

The new Commandant was Colonel F A Heygate-Lambert, known to the Irishmen as *Buckshot*. Previously he had been at Stratford, where he was considered harsh. The Adjutant was Lt Burns, who OMahony stated, p159, had been involved in an army canteen affair called *The Lipton Scandal* some years earlier.[15] The first censor was an ex-serviceman named Armstrong, a sedate grey-haired individual, and later Lt Bevan, who had been wounded. A photo in Dolgellau Archives (ZS/52/17) of the staff shows and names both Mr Armstrong and Lt Bevan.

A Cabinet paper of 15 May 1916, discussed the Irish Rebels. There were 1,800 prisoners. They could not be tried in England under civil law, nor under Martial Law, as the offences had occurred in Ireland. They could not be tried in Ireland in the civil courts because juries could not be relied upon, and they could not be tried in Ireland under Martial Law owing to strong political objections. Therefore Regulation 14B of DORA was applied, which allowed the detention of persons of hostile origin or associations. (CAB 37/147/36)

Frongoch then comprised two camps: South Camp was the dis-used distillery with adjoining buildings and a recreation field. The buildings formed two squares with courtyards. The main distillery building was divided into dormitories and the other buildings provided the hospital, censor's office, coal depot, gaol (six cells), cookhouse, dining room, and workshops. There were also four wooden huts. Three dormitories held approx 250 each and two held 150 each: but the greatest number of Irishmen held was 936. North Camp, on higher ground across the road, had 35 wooden huts in two rows, each for 32 men (max 1100), but during the Irish internment the highest number reached was 896. This camp had its own cookhouse, plus latrines, wash-houses, drying rooms, etc. The Irishmen laid paths and roadways in this camp because, during their first month there, the underfoot conditions were very wet. Later this 'RE party' went on strike in protest against their 1½d per hour pay-rate. Accordingly they were punished.

The Irishmen appointed their own commandants, adjutant and barrack captains. Their commanders were JJ O'Connell (south) and MW O'Reilly (north), the adjutant was W Brennan-Whitmore [who died 27 December 1977, the last of the Frongoch internees]. In July, thirty of the Irish leaders were removed to Reading gaol because the authorities thought that by moving the leaders out it would be easier to manage the rest. However, new leaders emerged and further removals were made from time to time.

During July 1916, The Sankey Committee reviewed the cases and many were released. To attend these hearings the prisoners were taken to London in batches and held at Wandsworth or Wormwood Scrubs prisons. This author wonders whether the question of taking the prisoners to the Committee, or bringing the Committee to Frongoch was ever asked.

By mid-August only about 600 remained at Frongoch. North Camp was closed at this time and all prisoners were moved to South Camp. However, the prisoners asked to be moved back to North Camp, which was approved on 21 October. South camp was then only used as a punishment station. On 1 September the 'RE Party' were offered quarry work at 5½d per hour, but subject to deductions of their daily train fares and 17s/6d a week (about three-quarters of the potential wage) for board and lodging. That work was refused and likewise agricultural work. OMahony reported one escape, of Devitt, who was recaptured after 4 days only a few miles from Frongoch, but no date was given.

In the House of Commons a complaint about the treatment of Irish detainees was raised, and it was asked whether the US Embassy and Irish Chief Sanitary Officer could inspect the camp. The reply stated that two inspections by the Home Office, in July and August, and by RAMC, also in August, had all reported favourably. Personal visits were allowed, one per month, for 15 minutes, supervised by the censor, on Tuesdays and Thursdays. (*Hansard HC* 17Oct16, vol.86, col.413)

On 25 October 1916, the US Ambassador wrote to his Secretary of State in Washington, that complaints had reached him about conditions at Frongoch where some American citizens were interned. These alleged overcrowding, insufficient food, bad sanitary conditions and harsh treatment. A letter was also written to the Foreign Office and the reply from Lord Grey stated, *inter alia*, that it was probable the Irish prisoners would soon be moved to the North Camp

---

[15] This was possibly 2nd Lt J Burns, a Reservist, late 8th Hussars; Hon.Lt/Adj/QM in 1917 Army List.

[this happened] to make room for German PoWs in the South Camp [but this did not happen]. Lord Grey also mentioned the three inspections, by Home Office and War Office staff, which had found that all was satisfactory. Overcrowding was denied and full statistics of room size and maximum numbers held were given. Food was on the same scale as PoW camps. No specific complaints had been made about harsh treatment, but the Embassy was invited to submit any detailed matter for investigation. It was mentioned that some prisoners had been punished for refusing to carry out fatigue duties (763.72114/2123).

On 14 December 1916, Dr Peters from Bala, the camp medical officer, took his own life. He had been intimidated and overworked by the camp authorities, particularly by *Buckshot* Lambert. Lambert himself, accused the Irishmen of hounding the Doctor to his death with a campaign of lies which, naturally, was immediately denied by the prisoners. It was announced in Parliament, on 21 December 1916, that all the Irishmen were to be released, without conditions.[16] The first 130 were released on 22 December, and the last batch of 28, from Reading, arrived in Dublin on Christmas Day. In all, 628 were returned to Ireland.

So by Christmas 1916 the camp was cleared, but it soon came back into use for German PoWs, but the date has not yet been ascertained. The first evidence found of the return of the PoWs was an escape. *The Occurrence Book* of Blaenau Festiniog Police Station, for Thursday 14 February 1917, recorded:

> PC25 Nathaniel Davies reports that at 10.15pm this day on the Talsarnan and Harlech road he apprehended Wilhelm Jensen, a naval warrant officer, and John Rastenbolz, a Sergeant Major, two German PoWs who escaped from the internment camp at Frongoch, Bala, during the night of 13 February. Both were lodged in the cell at Harlech for the night and handed over to a military escort at 2.15pm, 15 February. (Dolgellau Archives ref. ZH/5/11/4)

In April 1919, 400 PoWs were transferred from Leigh and a further 500 in May.[17] The first transfer was reflected in the increased numbers reported when the Swiss Legation visited on 29 April 1919. There were then 2,815 present, which was well above the normal number due also to 1,500 being sent in from working camps, pending their transfer to France. Their departure was expected daily. There were still 24 working camps controlled from Frongoch, but the numbers were decreasing as lumber camps were being closed. Lt Colonel Richards (probably A C Richards, previously at Jersey) was named as Commandant. At the next Swiss inspection, in June, the numbers were 2,106. The arrival of 500 from Leigh was noted in that report, as well as 300 from working camps at Kerry, Brecon and Dolyhir.

The *Cell Book* of Penrhyndeudraeth Police Station, for 11 October 1919, reported an escape of a PoW, named Defitanske, who absconded from Llanfrothen, 3 miles northeast of Portmadoc. (This is not recorded as a working camp, so possibly he had got away from a farm or itinerant working party). He was brought into the station in the early morning of Saturday, and was handed over to a military escort at 4pm. On 21 October 1919, the same *Cell Book* recorded the arrest of Johann Slochold on a charge of larceny of a hen coop. He was fined 15 shillings and handed over to a military escort at 5pm the next day. (Dolgellau Archives ref. ZH/13/1 8596)

The Times, 24 November 1919, reported that 2,000 had departed. This was the last batch and the camp then closed.

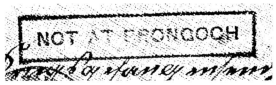

Boxed cachet 53 x 9mm seen on a cover redirected in March 1916 to Dartford War Hospital.

```
MEDICAL OFFICER IN/C,
PRISONERS OF WAR CAMP,
FRONGOCH,
NORTH WALES.
```

Camp Medical Officer's cachet, 52 x 22mm.

---

[16] *Hansard HC,* 21 December 1916 vol.88, col.1763

[17] *Leigh Chronicle* 17 April 1919 and *Leigh Journal* 27 May 1919

Postcard of the old distillery buildings and huts at Frongoch.

German PoWs parade for roll-call at Frongoch

Hackney Wick, London E

Civilian work camp	Grid Ref: TQ 364 851

This camp was not listed by Macpherson as it was a Home Office establishment. It was a disused workhouse, The Hackney Union Casual Ward, in Gainsborough Road, Hackney Wick, which was taken over in 1916. The camp was closely associated with Cornwallis Road, Islington, with which it shared a Commandant. There was no hospital ward - patients were treated at the German Hospital in Dalston (1½ miles away)

A group of highly skilled mechanics, selected from all the civilian internment camps, were brought to Hackney. These men were employed by Vickers Ltd who planned to make sewing machines with a view to driving out German manufactured products which, until the war, had dominated the British market. Vickers provided the machinery and paid the men. The work of this first group of skilled mechanics was to make the machine tools required to manufacture some 360 parts of the sewing machines. Making the machine tools took about a year. Then further men, less skilled, were brought in to assemble the machines. From the Autumn of 1917, the machines were turned out and sold in increasing numbers. (HO45/11025/410118/2)

Little information has been found about this industrial project. The Vickers' company archives are silent on the matter and no mention has been found in *The Times* of setting up the works at Hackney, nor of its production.

The report of the US Embassy representatives, who visited on 10 October 1916, stated that the place had been opened on 1 June 1916 and was guarded by the police. At that time there were 57 Germans and 8 Austrians present, and more were expected when additional workshops and machinery had been installed. There were 100 sleeping cubicles, 22 on the ground floor, 40 on the first and 38 on the second floor. The canteen, dining room, kitchen and offices were also on the ground floor. Outside was a flagged yard, 1½ acres of vegetable garden, a skittle alley and an army-style hut for recreation. Visitors were allowed twice a week for two hours. The work was described as making approximately 1,100 tools, 200 fixtures and 300 gauges for the manufacture of sewing machines. 53 of the men, some previously employed by Vickers, did this work, the other twelve worked in the kitchen, laundry, barber etc. The wages for the skilled men were stated to be 9¾d to 1s per hour, and their weekly earnings ranged from 13s.5d to £3.2s.4d. For maintenance the Government deducted 33% of the wages up to a maximum of 15 shillings. There were complaints about these deductions and about the quantity of the rations. (FO383/164)

Erwin Kerry, the Chief Captain, sent a letter to the Swiss Legation on 29 June 1917, saying that the internees had been served with tax demands for the nine months to 1 July. The Home Office reply, of 28 July, confirmed that internees were liable to income tax just as any other person resident in the country and earning wages. They also confirmed that the work was not connected with operations of war; it was chiefly the manufacture of sewing machines, but also the manufacture of agricultural machinery. (FO383/306)

When the Swedish Legation reported on the camp in December 1917, it was described as a healthy site between Hackney Marshes and Victoria Park. The guard was one police sergeant and three constables. There were then 182 internees present; 116 Germans, 59 Austrians and 7 Hungarians. A further twenty Austrians or Hungarians arrived early in the new year. About 80 men lived in the old building, the others in five huts for 20 men each. The inspector supported a claim for extra rations as the men complained that in view of their work they should receive more than men in non-working camps. The hours of work were stated to be 7am to 8pm with a one hour break at mid-day and ½ hour for tea. Work finished at 5.30pm on Mondays and at noon on Saturdays. (FO 383/359)

At the December 1918 inspection, the workers requested to be allowed home visits on parole once a month. On 18 July 1918, in the House of Commons, it had been announced that the internees might be allowed out on parole for good conduct and industry every 2½ to 3 months. (*Hansard* HC, 10 July 1918, vol.108, col.330)

On 4 June 1919 *The Times* announced that the camp at Hackney Wick had been vacated. After the war the manufacture of sewing machines was continued by Vickers Ltd at a plant in Crayford, Kent. The site at Gainsborough Road was redeveloped as Hackney Baths, but now it appears to have been lost under a motorway.

Pictures of Vickers sewing machines can be found on the internet on www.needlebar.org.

Cachet 48x32mm on a registered cover to London WC2

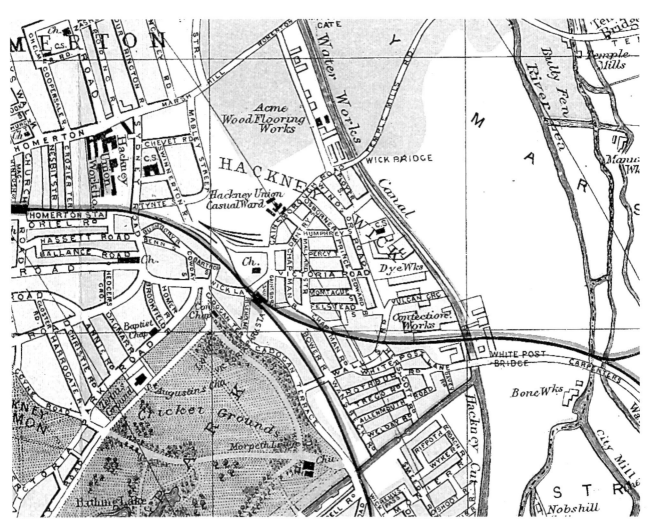

Extract from a 1908 Atlas and Guide to London, by Bacon & Co Ltd, Strand.
The Hackney Union Casual Ward became an internment camp in 1916.

Handforth, Cheshire

Other Ranks & civilians   Grid Ref: SJ 860 828

This camp was a factory building, about ¼ mile south of the railway station, east of the railway viaduct, and on the south bank of the River Dean. It had been built in 1910 by the Bradford Dyers Association to expand their print works, but it remained empty and never saw that business. Early in 1914 The Lancashire Rubber Co purchased the building, intending to use it as a synthetic rubber plant. Again, the projected work never came to the site and it was reported (source not traced) that the German proprietor of that venture was an early inmate.

Upon the outbreak of war, the local Army Command planned to use the buildings as a barracks for 2,000 men of the Manchester Regiment (two battalions), but the War Office had other ideas and they requisitioned the buildings for a PoW Camp. Macpherson wrote that it opened in October 1914 with accommodation for 3,000.

Wilmslow, Alderley & Knutsford Advertiser reported on 9 October 1914, that engineers were converting the buildings for use as a PoW camp, and on 5 November, that the first group of about 500 PoWs had arrived. By 20 November, their numbers had been doubled, to more than the population of the parish of Handforth. *Edinburgh Evening News* of 23 November, included a report by a Press Association special correspondent, that conditions in the camp were good and that there were about 1,000 men in the camp, but that was to be increased by 600 shortly. In the event 573 prisoners, mostly from German East Africa, arrived on 27 November. In December another 650 men were brought from Dorchester when the civilians were moved out of that camp. (*Dorset County Chronicle* 17 Dec 1914)

When Mr Jackson of the US Embassy visited on 12 February 1915, there were some 2,000 present, of which 400 were sailors from SMSs *Blücher* and *Gneisenau*, sunk at the Battles of Dogger Bank, 24 January, and the Falkland Islands, 8 December, respectively. The sailors were in separate compounds under their own Deck-Officers. The civilians were in several compounds, one of which was for the 'better classes'. The building was reported as fairly new, with a good roof. It was roomy, airy and dry, heated by steam pipes and electric light was installed. An exercise ground was available and a football field was being prepared. Washing and bathing facilities were adequate. The kitchen was large and well arranged with German cooks who had worked in London restaurants. The hospital had several wounded patients. Among the inmates there was some discontent over Anglo-Germans having taken Captains' positions, while many Anglo-Germans complained that their arrest and detention, caused financial loss. Some had been gambling, so they had been put to road making as a punishment. No other work was provided at this time. (HO45/10760/269116)

In March 1915 the Commandant was Major Hugh Charles Claude Ducat-Hammersley, late Gurkha Rifles (b1866, retired 1911) who was later in command at Shrewsbury. An April 1915 American report mentioned sailors from SMSs, *Nürnberg* and *Leipzig*, both sunk at the Battle of Falkland Islands, who may well have been already present at Mr Jackson's inspection.

The Times 7 April 1915, carried a report that Herbert Greenwood, of the canteen staff, was charged with receiving letters to be delivered to a PoW, H Herting, at the camp. Greenwood was found guilty and sent to gaol for three months. In that same week some PoWs were transferred from Handforth to Frongoch.

Following the sinking of SS *Lusitania*, on 7 May 1915, large numbers of civilians were rounded up and interned. Many from Liverpool were brought to Handforth (Heusel, p43) but later they were transferred to Knockaloe. Panayi (p64) stated civilians were held at Handforth until early 1916 but, in fact, almost all were moved out earlier (see below).

When the US Embassy conducted their next series of visits, in June, it was noted that sailors previously at Handforth in March, were then at Stobs, and all at Handforth were civilians. On Handforth the report stated: *No camp in Britain has shown greater improvement in the morale and general atmosphere!* Various committees were mentioned, which were well supported by the Commandant. A new hospital, with 60 beds, had 28 patients that day. Crafts, classes, an orchestra and a theatre company were mentioned. Jewish men had separate messing. Daily route marches were permitted for 300 at a time. There were no complaints. (FO 383/33)

By the date of the next recorded inspection, 12 December 1915, the nature of the camp had entirely changed as the civilians had been replaced by combatant PoWs, but two civilians were still there, in the hospital. The Commandant was Lt Colonel A H C Kenney-Herbert (late Northants Regt, previously at Shrewsbury as second-in-command) and his deputy was Major R E Firminger. The senior German, was Feldwebel-Leutnant Hemmers, described in the report as 'the Chief Representative'. 17 patients were in hospital of which three were in isolation. Various occupations were mentioned including crafts, a band, and educational classes. 20 acres of exercise area with a wired perimeter were available. No serious complaints were made. The day of visit was frosty with snow on the ground, nevertheless the buildings were warm and cheerful. The inspector, Mr Buckner, talked to a PoW in the isolation hospital who had leprosy. He was in pain but had no complaints about his treatment. Soon afterward that man was moved to Dartford PoW Hospital (763.72114/1259).

In early May 1916, two prisoners escaped, Offizierstellvertreter Cahn of the Artillery and Fähnrich-zur-See Johl of SMS *Blücher*. They were recaptured at Gorton, and both were sentenced to 6 months in prison which they served at Woking Detention Barracks. They were interviewed there by the US Embassy inspector in August.

When the PoW labour camp at Le Havre was inspected on 6 July 1916, that report stated that the PoWs there had come from Handforth and Frongoch on 26 May. The next inspection of Handforth did report a decrease in numbers there compared with the figures on 1 April 1916 (see table overleaf).

The next American Embassy visit was 17 August 1916 when more details of the infirmary were given in the report. It was staffed by two British doctors with three British and six German attendants. There were 18 in-patients, one in the isolation ward with a mild case of scarlet fever, and 42 out-patients. Three deaths were reported to date; two were civilians, one of chronic bronchitis the other pulmonary phthisis, and one after it became exclusively a military camp, of pleurisy. Bread had previously been purchased outside the camp, but now it was to be baked on the premises. Prisoners' occupations included sewing mailbags, crafts, tailoring and shoemaking. Two work-camps (not named) were operating. Two theatre companies and musical groups were mentioned. There were no serious complaints but some had no work because of continuous shifting of groups of prisoners between camps. Use of the cells for punishment was rare, but there were about 80 cases per month of defaulters, who were punished by being put on cleaning fatigues around the camp (763.72114/1956).

In August 1916, three PoWs escaped. Lt Karl Reitz and Gefreiter Joseph Haneche were recaptured at Bingley, and the third (not named) at Otley, Yorks.[1] The first named was unlikely to have been a Leutnant, but the British press did have difficulties with the German NCO ranks. *The Times* 29 September 1916 reported four sailors, on charges of theft at Wilmslow, were sentenced to 3 months.

Lt Colonel Thursby Henry Ernest Dauncey, late 6th Dragoons (born 1861 retired 1909) was the Commandant when an American inspection took place on 7 December 1916. The report noted that among new committees an Income Tax Assessment Committee had been formed by the PoWs. A lithograph machine had been set up on which a camp newspaper was published. In view of larger numbers of NCOs (113 Feldwebel and 501 others) there has been considerable rearrangements to the sleeping quarters. In the infirmary there were then two additional German attendants. 25 in-patients and 80 out-patients were reported, all with minor ailments. The cooks then numbered 24, all German. No serious complaints were made. One man was in the cells for disobedience. Two work camps were mentioned: Rowley, with 110 men, and Stanhope, 370 men, both quarries in Co Durham (763.72114/2286). In September other work camps under Handforth, at Redesdale, Healeyfield and Stanhope had been inspected and reported on. (When Catterick became a parent camp it took over responsibility for these working camps in northern counties.)

Staffordshire Advertiser 24 March 1917 reported Lt-zur-See Emil Lehmann, a PoW being transferred from the Isle of Man to Kegworth, had escaped in Manchester. He was found at Upper Elkstone, five miles ENE of Leek, on Sunday 18 March. He had been seen in a local chapel and it appeared he had

---

[1] *The Times* 22 Aug and *Stockport Advertiser* 25 Aug and 1 Sept 1916

burnt some bibles. On Thursday (22nd) he was removed to Handforth. Handforth was not an officers' camp, but reports of escapes by officers are mentioned. This may be another misunderstanding, or confusion, of German naval Petty Officer ranks.

Feldwebel Richard Eber and seaman Albert Groensky escaped from Hanforth on 12 or 13 August 1917. Their recapture was reported a few days later, but the following week that was denied. At the end of that month they were still at large, and it was believed they were being sheltered by friends. (*The Times* 14, 17, 25 and 31 August 1917)

In November five sailors got out. Wilhelm Otto, Emil Mandey and Georg Marienfeld were recaptured at Stalybridge while Heindrich Stoldt and Emil Stehr were picked up at Portsmouth a week later.

On 3 June 1918, *The Times* reported the fifth death at the camp, of Carl Liborius, and in August an inquest was held into the death of William Schmidt, shot by a guard, Private John Taylor of the Royal Defence Corps. The verdict was 'Accident'. In September 1918 PoWs from Handforth, who were employed on drainage works at Frodsham, Cheshire, went on strike because some from their team were lent to farmers, for the harvest, and were paid more. The strikers wanted the same higher allowances. This was not conceded, instead they were put onto a bread and water diet.

In February 1919, when the Swiss Legation visited they reported that the influenza of November and December 1918 had resulted in 200 cases, of which eleven died. In all there were 19 deaths at this camp.

In early May 1919, 1,000 men departed, but their destination was not stated. They were replaced, later that month by a similar number moved from Leigh, when that camp was closed down. With the closure of Leigh the four working camps which it had controlled were passed over to Handforth.

The Times reported, on a significant date, 11 November 1919, that the first parties had been sent off and the remainder were expected to depart for Germany over the following few days. The next week the same paper stated that the site was to be used for manufacturing, but the industry was not specified. However, maps of the inter-war period show the buildings as disused and in WWII they became a tank depot.

date	total	civilians	sailors	soldiers	airmen	comment
5 Nov 1914	c500	c500				
31 Dec 1914	c2,200	c2,200				
12 Feb 1915	c2,000	c1,600	c400			later, sailors were moved to Stobs
June 1915	2,100	2,100				later, civilians were moved to IoM
12 Dec 1915	2,236	2*		2,234		* in the hospital
1 Apr 1916	2,713	1†	313	2,399		† as a concession so that he could visit his sick wife in Manchester
17 Aug 1916	2,160		306	1,854		
7 Dec 1916	2,948		274	2,674		
Feb 1919	2,774		30	2,736	8	

Table 9: Numbers present at Handforth on various inspection visits:

P.C. **P.C.**
HANDFORTH W.
HANDFORTH.

Cachets used at Handforth. The reason for the two different P.C. handstamps is not apparent. The length of the word HANDFORTH is 28mm in both cases. The oval office cachet is 46 x 32mm

This cachet was illustrated by Alan Brown, in 1973, but has not been seen used by this author. Dimensions 43 x 21mm

The gardens at Handforth Camp

Christmas 1916 and New Year 1917 card from Handforth Camp

Holyport, near Maidenhead, Berkshire

Officers Camp

Grid Ref: SU 895 781

This was "Philberds", a manor, 2 miles south-east of Maidenhead, with a history going back to the early 13th century. The buildings probably dated from 18th century. The previous house, in the high-Tudor style, was the home of Nell Gwyn in the 1670-80s. The manor was purchased from the Dean and Canons of Windsor by Charles Pascoe Grenfell in 1860. It became a school, founded by Reverend Edward H Price (1823-1898)[2], and when he retired in 1879, he was succeeded as head by his son, also Edward. Around the turn of the century the school took on a military focus. The Headmaster from 1908 was Mr EGA Beckwith MA (1869-1935)[3], who had established The Army School at Stratford-on-Avon. He was appointed head of Imperial Service College, Windsor, upon its founding in 1912, and took with him the pupils of Philberds, merging the two schools. In 1914 the buildings were not in use, and available for requisition by the War Office.

The first Commandant was Major, the Hon. Eustace Henry Dawnay (b1850, Lt Coldstream Guards 1871-83, appointed temporary Major 26 October 1914), the Quartermaster/Adjutant was Captain Armstrong. The guard was provided by Devonshire National Reserve.

The first PoWs, about 40 officers, arrived on 25 November 1914 and were taken to the camp from Maidenhead station by taxis. Two days later, a squad of soldiers arrived to be servants, but they had to march the two miles (*Maidenhead Advertiser, 2 December1914*). The same paper, 15 January 1915, reported the arrival of some survivors of the Battle of the Falklands. By that date, the numbers had reached over 100 officers with about 50 orderlies. At the end of that month a Norwegian visitor gave a favourable report which was published in the local paper and in *The Times* of 29 January 1915.

---

[2] ed Rugby and St John's, BA 1845, MA 1863, ordained 1846: curate, Lutterworth 1845-53; Master of Philberds School 1854-79; vicar, Kimbolton, Hunts, 1880-84; Holy Trinity Eastbourne 1887-88; Willey, Warks., 1888-98. Death notice in *The Times* 26 September 1898.

[3] ed Winchester & Magdalene, BA 1892, MA 1899, died 26 January 1935

On that same day Mr Jackson of the US Embassy inspected the camp. 140 officers were present so the place was overcrowded, but 40 were about to be transferred to Donington Hall. There were 40 soldier servants. The Senior German Officer was Korvetten-Kapitan Hans Pochhammer, of SMS *Gneisenau*, who had a room to himself, but others slept up to 15 in a room. As the building had not been used for some time, the ground floor rooms were still damp and some attic rooms draughty, but repair work was proceeding. The house and immediate grounds were fenced with barbed wire but a football field was not fenced, so guards were posted on the perimeter when it was in use. Some colonial officers were present who complained of their treatment upon arrest and before transfer to Britain. Reservist officers complained they had not been paid. English cooks were employed with German assistants. A swimming tank (*sic*) was mentioned, but it was empty at the time. (FO 383/106)

In March 1915 Gunter Plüschow, who had flown out of Kiao-Chow, a German enclave in China, but was arrested at Gibraltar when trying to return to Germany, arrived on transfer from Dorchester, having established his officer status. On 1 May, in a party of 50, he was moved on to Donington Hall.

Delegates from the International Red Cross visited and in their report, dated March 1915, they noted that among the PoWs were some taken from neutral ships at Gibraltar. They had arrived at Plymouth on 29 December, but their luggage had not been received at the camp. There were 146 present and the potential transfer of men to Donington to relieve overcrowding was mentioned. Religious services were conducted for Protestants every two weeks by a German, Pastor Schulten, but catholic services were more difficult to arrange as there were too few priests available in Britain with sufficient command of the German language.

An attempt to tunnel out, discovered by Captain Armstrong, was reported by *The Times*, 7 April 1915. A new Commandant was also named in the report, Major Bertram Robert Mitford Glossop, 5th Dragoon Guards (b1870), in place of Major Dawnay who had retired due to ill health. The paper stated that there were over 100 German Officers with 40 soldier servants in the camp. Questions were asked in the House of Commons, on 20 April, about the tunnel and the lack of vigilance on the part of the guard.

Two other attempts to tunnel out were reported in newspapers. Air Force Lt Thelen and naval Lt Keilbach were sentenced to nine months detention in Chelmsford Detention Barracks for attempting such an escape in January 1916.[4] Both had previously got away from Donington Hall and both made later escape attempts from other camps. The third tunnel was discovered in March 1916, which resulted in naval Lt Freiherr von Grote also being sentenced to nine months at Chelmsford.[5]

The US Embassy visited again on 27 April 1915, and reported there were 100 at camp compared with 140 in February. The Commandant had been ordered to send 50 to Donington, but none had volunteered, so he decided who should go (Plüschow was one of them). The English cooks, previously employed, had been replaced by Germans. The swimming tank was full of water and in regular use. (FO 383/33)

Huts were erected in the grounds, so that when the American Embassy inspection took place on 5 December 1915 there were 176 at the camp, comprising 124 officers, of which one was an Austrian, 49 German soldier servants and three civilians. There was no comment about the civilians but they were identified in a later report. Interviews were conducted with Captain Pochhammer and a number of other inmates, including the senior NCO. The huts needed attention as cracks had developed. The heating of rooms, hot baths, lighting and religious services were all subject of complaints as being inadequate. The officers asked for wines to be sent from Germany and cigars to be duty free. They also requested regular visits from a German pastor (763.72114/1259).

At the next US Embassy visit, on 24 February 1916, the Commandant was Lt Colonel Sir John Gladstone (1852-1926, late Coldstream Guards). The roll was 33 naval and 90 army officers, plus 47 men and 3 civilians (all German except one Austrian). The report stated there was no real infirmary, any serious cases being sent to Dartford. A local Doctor visited daily and he had a dispensary. Two were sick at time of visit but neither was a bed-case. There were no serious complaints, but heating, slow mail and duty on tobacco were points raised by the prisoners. (763.72114/1337)

There was yet another Commandant, Colonel John Robert Harvey DSO (b1861, Mayor of Norwich 1902-3, late 4th Norfolk Regt at Gallipoli) at the American inspection on 25 May 1916,. The roll call was 89 army officers, 29 naval officers, 47 orderlies and 3 civilians (two cooks and a barber), all German. The house was described as large, with 23 rooms used as bedrooms, for between one and 26 men. There were three huts previously, but this had been increased to 17, although not all were then in use. Up to 25 prisoners at a time were allowed to take country walks under the supervision of a British officer and orderly. (Cd. 8324)

Maidenhead Advertiser 16 November 2001, had an item about these walks which caused annoyance at a public house close to the camp in Holyport Street. 'The Eagle' displayed a sign of the Prussian eagle and when the prisoners passed it, they saluted. Therefore, the landlord changed the name, of his establishment, to 'The Belgian Arms'.

In September 1916 more prisoners arrived, so when the US Embassy inspected on 13 October there were 429 present, all Germans, 297 army and 39 naval officers, 89 soldiers, 2 sailors and 3 civilian servants. The house was full and some officers slept in tents at their own request. A new bath-house had been built and new sewage arrangements were completed. There were five patients in the sick bay, but only two in bed, one was wounded, the other had rheumatism. No deaths had been reported since opening. Walks were allowed for groups of 40 officers, up to two hours, five days a week. They also had compulsory exercise, 90 minutes, twice a week, weather permitting. The recent large increase in numbers was remarked upon by the inspector, and complaints of overcrowding were made, but the space still comfortably exceeded the regulations. The usual complaints about poor heating of rooms were made. The kitchen facilities were in need of some upgrading, in view of the extra numbers present. Some complaints about treatment before arriving at Holyport were submitted to the War Office (763.72114/2127).

---

[4] *The Times* 1 Feb 1916 and *Maidenhead Advertiser* 9 Feb 1916

[5] *Maidenhead Advertiser* 12 March 1916 and *The Times* 15 March 1916

The Times 9 and 11 December 1916, reported the escape of two officers, and their recapture near Old Windsor. One was Lt Otto Thelen, who had just returned from detention at Chelmsford, the other was Lt Anton Cmentek. They had hidden in waste paper. In the following June the sun must have been hot for there were complaints of German officers appearing insufficiently clothed in the field adjoining their huts. 'Suitable orders will be given' was the response to a Parliamentary Question. (*Hansard HoC* 21 June 1917, vol.94, col. 1968)

The Times 27 and 29 August 1917, reported another escape. Two pilots, Joseph Flink and Orbun von Scholtz, escaped, apparently with the intention of stealing an aircraft and flying it to Germany. They were recaptured at Beckenham, Kent. Further escapes were reported; on 26 September when Lt Franz Henrard got away by bicycle, and on 12 November, when Lt Gerhard von Nassau and Lt Helmuth Burkhardt escaped but they were recaptured at Bath on a London to Bristol train.

In May 1918, the Commandant was Colonel Cecil Hodgson Colvin CB DSO (b1858, late Essex Regt) who must have had a surprise in October when he received a parcel containing a German uniform and Iron Cross. Heinz Heinrich Ernst Justus, on being transferred from Holyport to Lofthouse Park, according to his own account, jumped from a train at South Elmshall (between Doncaster and Wakefield). He wrote that he only knew the address of Holyport, so sent the incriminating clothes there.[6] The account of this incident in *Sheffield Daily Telegraph*, 26 October 1918, said Justus escaped from Wakefield, and *The Times* stated that he was dressed as a woman. (Justus's escape when dressed as a woman was earlier and from Colsterdale, *qv*.)

In July 1918 the Swiss Minister requested information on a German statement that 40 German officers were moved from Holyport to a reprisal camp in the London area. A further letter stated 40 were transferred on 22 April and 40 more on 25 April. These appear to be transfers to Lewisham and Stratford, *qv*. The reply, dated 26 July, was that there were no reprisal camps and that the British Government reserved the right to establish PoW camps in any locality (FO 383/441). However, *The Times* 16 March 1918, p6c, had reported that German prisoners would be placed in air-raid zones as reprisal for similar German tactics.

When a reporter of the *Windsor Eton & Slough Express* visited on the day the terms of the armistice were announced, 9 November 1918, he found a subdued spirit among the PoWs. He also mentioned in his report an earlier visit, two years previous, when two prisoners had escaped and were captured at Old Windsor.

In June 1919, the Swiss Legation visited the camp in response to a complaint that two officers had been shot by a sentry, who claimed that he was provoked (FO 383/508). However, no newspaper coverage of the incident has been seen and no names were mentioned in the Foreign Office file.

Three died in the 'flu epidemic of 1918, and were buried at Bray churchyard (possibly a fourth and another burial at Taplow, but the records are not clear). *The Times* 14 November 1918, reported the funeral of Lt Mahn, and next day the burial of Lt Mannhausen and Unteroffizier Matuszak. The following month a local paper reported that the inhabitants of Bray objected to the 'desecration' of their churchyard by the interment of Germans who had died, and that the Parish Church Council was seeking permission to have them removed. (*Windsor, Eton & Slough Express* 14 December 1918)

The camp must have been closed by October 1919 as the War Office advertised the sale of fir poles from the fencing on 15 October. The buildings were demolished shortly afterwards.

Camp censorship cachet. The 3rd initial is believed to be I, for Interpreter.

---

[6] Justus HEH: "An unconducted tour of England" in Durnford H et al: *Tunnelling to Freedom*

Philberds, at Holyport, when used as an officers' camp. (International Red Cross postcard)

Christmas and New Year cards made for PoWs at Holyport in December 1916

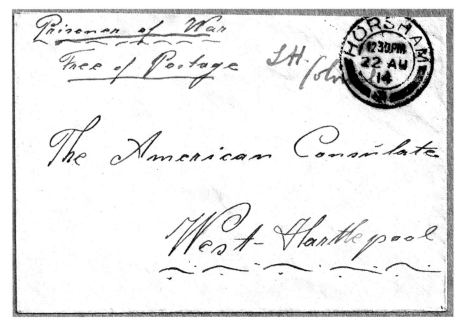

A cover from an internee at Christ's Hospital, Horsham (the only one known to this author, ex the late David Cornelius). The marking *SH Colonel* (in red) to authenticate the item for free postage, was applied by Colonel Hamilton. He has not been identified, but was reported by the local newspaper to be in command at the camp.

Horsham, Sussex

Civilians and military

Grid Ref: TQ 147 286

This was Christ's Hospital School, which had been founded in London, by King Edward VI, in 1552. The 1,200 acre site, near Horsham, was purchased in 1897 and the school moved from its original site, close to St Paul's Cathedral in the City of London, to the new buildings in 1902.

The school was used by the War Office only during the school summer holidays in 1914, and it appears to have been the earliest and shortest lived prison camp in this country during the Great War.

Christ's Hospital School, which had accommodation for about a thousand scholars, was taken over by the Military in the early hours of Thursday, 6 August (only two days after war was declared by the British Government), to hold German PoWs.[7] Batches of sailors arrived from Sheerness, Dover and Harwich. The group from Harwich had been rescued from the mine-layer *Königin Luise*, sunk on 5 August, and had been held temporarily at Shotley Naval Barracks.[8] By the end of the week, the total held was about 150, mostly sailors.

The next edition of the Horsham weekly newspaper reported many more arrivals. Early on Monday morning, 10 August, a special train with 219, said to be mostly waiters, came from Folkestone. At 5.50 pm that day 72 German Reservists arrived from Dover and at 7.44 pm four more reached Horsham station and were conveyed by cabs to Christ's Hospital. On Tuesday eight arrived from Yarmouth, two from Bedford, four from Dover and three others. More came on Wednesday taking the total to about 500. Most were reservists trying to return to Germany but they had been stopped at British ports. Colonel Hamilton (not traced) with a detachment of Royal West Kent Regiment provided the guard. On Thursday 13 August, 200 prisoners were removed to Queen's Ferry by train.

Hull Daily Mail, 8 August, had reported the 219 Germans (mentioned above) being arrested at Folkestone as they tried to board the Flushing boat. That paper stated they were marched to Shorncliffe (a barracks two miles west) and their baggage followed in motors. No doubt they were put on a train the next day for the journey to Horsham.

During the following week more than one large group of prisoners departed for Queen's Ferry. However the local paper stated the destination to be Chester Castle. These transfers of prisoners, coupled with the teaching staff being notified to be ready to start on September 15, or soon after, pointed to the resumption of the school routine being expected very shortly.[9] Reports of damage to school fittings by the prisoners were denied by the headmaster.

Christ's Hospital minutes state the maximum number held was 630.

---

[7] *West Sussex County Times and Standard*, Saturday 8 August 1914.

[8] *Lancaster Observer* 7 August 1914 p8

[9] *West Sussex County Times and Standard*, 22 August 1914, p8.

Islington, London N

Home Office camp for aliens   Grid Ref: TQ 302 867

This was a Poor Law workhouse in Cornwallis Road, built in 1866 by the West London Union. It was transferred, first to the City of London Union, then to the Islington Guardians in 1882, who adapted the buildings to hold up to 611 inmates. In the Spring of 1915 the inmates were moved to other workhouses when the Islington Guardians agreed to a Government request to take over the premises. The local paper, *Islington Daily Gazette* of 24 June 1915, speculated that up to 800 would be accommodated, but in the event it does not seem that figure was ever reached.

This camp was not listed by Macpherson as it was a Home Office responsibility, not a War Office camp. It opened on 26 June 1915 and generally held married internees whose wives were British-born and residents of London. Visits were regular and frequent and, occasionally, internees could leave during the day, on a parole basis, to attend to business or other urgent matters. This last point was confirmed in Parliament. (*Hansard HC,* 28 June 1916, vol.83, col.865)

The Commandant was Sir Frederick Loch Halliday CIE MVO (1864-1937) late Commissioner of the Bengal Police, who had commanded a number of prisons in India. He also took charge of the Hackney Wick camp, when that was set up a year later. He had the assistance of civilian adjutants, the first of whom was Barnard Lailey KC (a County Court Judge from 1916). This official was described as also assisting the internees with legal matters.

The US Embassy's first visit was on 23 August 1915 when there were 720 internees - all German. Dormitories held 6 to 30 beds. The sick bay had six beds. In the two months since opening, four serious cases had been sent to the German Hospital at Dalston. The report (in FO383/34) mentioned a journal being published but no copy has been traced by this author.

The following month, one Dutch and two American journalists visited and were impressed with the place and the tact of the Commandant. It was noted that there was no formal guard but 'half-a-dozen policemen at the entrance'. Of the 720 internees, most worked, but 160 who did not paid 2s.6d per week, which included 6d for laundry. Single rooms were available at an extra charge. Weekly visits were allowed and some prisoners were permitted to attend to their businesses on certain days. Two cells were used solely as display rooms for carvings done by the inmates. They noted that William Allen Jowitt, b 1885, a barrister, managed part of the camp. (*The Times*, 28 September 1915.) Whether Jowitt had replaced Lailey is not clear. Jowitt was elected as an MP in 1922, he was also appointed KC in that year, and served as Attorney-General 1929-32.

At the next US inspection, on 1 March 1916, there were 714 present, of whom 709 were German and five were Austrians. About 500 were working for wages, employed in tailoring, shoemaking, mailbags, carpentry etc. and a further 100 were engaged on various duties within the camp. The guard consisted of one police Sergeant and four Constables. There had been no escapes, nor any need for cells. For exercise the prisoners had 3½ acres of grounds, a skittle alley, gymnasium and a billiard hall with 3 tables. Visits were allowed on an approximately weekly basis. (FO383/162) In July a reporter from *The Times* visited the camp when he recorded 722 inmates. Otherwise he wrote in similar terms to the March report of the US Embassy.

Three interned British citizens, Ferdinand Kehrhan, Graeme Scott and Edward Hodgson, escaped at night on 18 November 1916. Scott and Hodgson were recaptured at a boarding house in Bloomsbury on 23rd, but Kehrhan's re-arrest has not been traced. However, he must have been found, for in the following April he appealed against his sentence.[10] The presence of British citizens in internment seems unusual, but in a Parliamentary statement in December 1916 it was confirmed that there were in fact 39 British subjects held at Islington.[11] *Islington Daily Gazette*, 21 November, stated that Scott, 35, the son of a retired British Army officer, had lived in Germany for some time and, on returning to Britain,

---

[10] *The Times* 21, 24, 28 November 1916 and 13 April 1917, *Hansard HC* 30 Nov 1916, vol.88, col.478

[11] *Hansard HC,* (?) December 1916, vol.88, col.1454

it had been shown that he had been 'associating with the enemy'. Kehrhan, also 35, was British born of German parents, a well-known socialist, who's public speeches gave grounds for his internment. Hodgson, 40, a mining engineer had claimed American nationality, was shown to have been involved with business in Germany and had been found guilty by Magistrates on a charge of abetting a German woman to avoid registering as an alien.

The Swiss Legation visited the camp on 7 March 1917 when yet another barrister was on the staff. This was St John Hutchinson (Middle Temple 1909, Recorder from 1928 and Prosecuting Council for the Post Office 1931-35). The Chief Captain of the internees was Mr Junker, who had a committee of twenty. 651 were present, of whom 644 were Germans. Huts had been erected to provide workshops, bath-houses and recreation rooms. A camp magazine, *Hinter dem Stracheldraht*, a fortnightly publication, was mentioned; up to 150 copies were sold for 2d each. Among the occupations, glass-blowing for the chemical industry, was mentioned. Church services were held every Sunday for Anglicans and Catholics, and on Wednesdays for Methodists. Lutheran services were held monthly. Like other reports, this pointed out that the cells were not used, but it was explained that anyone guilty of an offence such as insubordination was removed to another camp. About 30 had been sent away to date. (FO 383/276)

In July 1917, after the second daylight air-raid on London, in which 54 were killed and 190 injured, there was, apparently, open talk of a reprisal raid by local people upon the camp and its inmates. However the police got wind of the plan and turned out in force with both Regular and Special Constables. Reports of disturbances were published in *The Times* on 9, 10 and 11 July.

A visit by the Swedish Legation on 22 October 1918, found 643 Germans, six Austrians and two Hungarians present. The Austrian and Hungarian prisoners requested one day leave, on parole, every two months to visit their families (FO 383/360). In May 1919, when the Swiss Legation paid another visit, the Commandant was Major R F Godfrey-Faussett (not traced). The report stated that the industries had ceased at the end of January owing to protests of competition from trade unions. (FO383/507)

A Home Office report (HO45/11025/410118/2), discussing industrial work, explained that persistent endeavours were made throughout the war to organise camp industries, but brush making at Islington was recorded as one of only three considered a success. Machinery was installed by contractors, instructors were engaged, the inmates taught and the output sold through the contractors to government departments and the public. The enterprise was financially successful but it was criticised by the Brush Makers' Association. The plant gave continuous employment to some interned aliens, who were paid ordinary rates and were allowed to retain their earnings, less a deduction for maintenance. A similar brush-making industry was set up at Douglas, Isle of Man, *qv*.

A later Home Office report, discussing repatriation, exemption and release, stated that at the end of May 1919, the Alexandra Palace building was taken over, for other Government use, and the internees were transferred to Frith Hill. That raised a storm of protests but one of the few positive measures taken was the transfer of about 100 observant Jews to Islington, where a kosher kitchen was installed. On 22 September 1919, 150 men then remaining at Frith Hill were brought to Islington and on 25 September instructions were given that those remaining at Knockaloe, by then less than 300, were to be moved to Islington. However, their transfer was delayed by the national railway strike. The total number of internees was then less than 500, and steps were taken to close Islington as soon as possible. On 17 November 1919 the last of the internees departed. (HO 45/11025/410118/3)

After the war the site was redeveloped by the GPO as a depot and the Postal Order Office. The south wing of the main building was destroyed in WWII by a land mine, and the whole site was cleared in 1987 and sold for housing development.

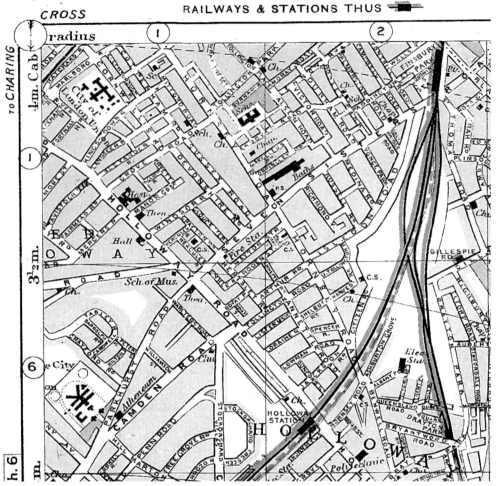

Extract from a 1908 Atlas and Guide to London, by Bacon & Co Ltd, 127 Strand.
Cornwallis Road is at the top left corner. The Workhouse was still named City of London
Union on this map, although it had been transferred to the Islington Guardians by this date.

Camp cachet 1, dimensions 48 x 33mm

Camp cachet 2, dimensions 48 x 32mm.
The first word of the top line is 'THE'.

Censor cachet, length over stop 69mm.

At right: the cachet is 37mm over the comma. The
initials JEW? or SGW? Have not been identified.

Konzert Programm

Sonntag 21. Mai 1916

Lager Kapelle
Kapellmeister O.W. Bayer

1) Marsch: " EINZUG DER GLADIATOREN " .... Fucik
2) Ouvertuere: " DIE DIEBISCHE ELSTER " .... Rossini
3) Gesang: " JA, DU BIST MEIN " .... Marschner
   (Herr Stock)
4) Gavotte: " ROCOCCO " .... Aletter
5) WALZER: " WEIN, WEIB & GESANG " .... Strauss

- - - - - - - - - - - -

6) UNGARISCHE TAENZE Nos: 5 & 6 .... Brahms
7) STAENDCHEN .... Schubert
8) Novelette: " KIRSCHBLUETE " .... Albert
9) Walzer: " DER EWIGE WALZER " .... Fall
10) Fantasie: " TANNHAEUSER " .... Wagner

The Islington Camp had a very active company of musicians, who appear to have given concerts about once a week, under their conductor Herr O.W. Bayer. This programme was for Sunday 21 May 1916.

"ISLINGTON" LAGER-THEATER
SONNABEND 10 NOV 1917
ANFANG 7 UHR
GANZ-NEU
ZUM ERSTEN MALE 1914
IN BERLIN GESPIELT
GEMÜTS-MENSCHEN!
SCHWANK in 3 AUFZÜGEN
von FRITZ FRIEDMANN-FREDERICH

Personen.

Fritz Stangenberg, Rechtsanwalt	P.F. Brietsche.
Lotte, seine Frau	M. Schurig.
J.M. Hartmann	H.E. Hessel.
Sanitätsrat Felsing	F. von Seeler.
Frau Sanitätsrat Felsing	P.S. Fehr.
Lilli, beider Tochter	H. Haeffner.
Hans Buchwaldt, Dr. ing.	O. Müller.
Daisy Blunt	W. Urmetzer.
Mr. Seamon	P. Dammert.
Geheimrat Schmidt	W. Löhner.
Emma	U. Fasching.
Sarah	K. Schatz.

1. & 2. Aufzug: Stangenbergs Wohnzimmer in Berlin.
3. Aufzug: Halle eines Seebad-Hotels.
Zeit: Gegenwart.

Nach dem 1.& 2.Aufzuge je 20 Minuten Pause.

Zwischenaktmusik vom kleinen Orchester unter Leitung des Herrn Kapellmeister O.W. Bayer.
1. a.) Puppchen Polka.
   b.) Das kann ein Herz nur.   } Gilbert.
2. Potpourri: Geschiedene Frau.   Fall.
3. Walzer: Dollar Prinzess.   Fall.
4. Marsch-Lied: So bummeln wir.   Gilbert.

Perrücken & Friseure: Kostüme:
P. Seil, J. Zarembowicz, J. Hahlschnee.   H. Schweitzer.
                                     gedr. i.d. Zeitgs.
                                     Druckerei.

In Vorbereitung.
- - - - - - - -

Ein unbeschriebenes Blatt.   Der Strom.
Lustspiel in 3 Aufzügen von   Schauspiel in 3 Aufzügen von
Ernst von Wolzogen.   Max Halbe.

Islington also had an active theatre where plays and cabaret shows were staged.

Jersey, Channel Islands

Other Ranks 1915-17; NCOs only 1918-19

In August 1914 the War Office ordered a temporary camp to be set up on Jersey. Although two sites were prepared, neither of them was used for PoWs; one was the agricultural show-ground which became first a barracks and then an Army Service Corps Depot. The other was a school building which was converted again, this time to a hospital. In December 1914, the War Office enquired if a site could be found for 1,000 PoWs and a area, previously used for military manoeuvres, was selected at Quennevais, also known as Blanches Banques, in the southwest of the island, not far from the shore of St Ouen's Bay. The principal problem was water supply, but wells and local springs were used successfully.

The camp was opened on 20 March 1915 when approximately 500 prisoners arrived. A further party of 500 arrived on 22 March (*The Star* 23 March 1915) and a third batch of 500 arrived later, in 1916. The guard numbered 130.

There were six Commandants at this camp during the war, each received temporary rank of Lt Colonel, if they did not already hold that rank:
- Lt.Colonel Gregory Sinclair Haines, late Royal Warwickshire Regt., b1853, previously at Newbury and later at Stratford
- Lt.Colonel Ludovic Seymour Gordon-Cumming, late Notts & Derby Regt., b1861
- Major Arthur Carew Richards, late Hampshire Regt., b1865, later at Frongoch.
- Lt Colonel W A Stocker, Channel Island Militia,
- Major E P Allpress, Special List, late Bedford Regt.,
- and Major Owen Christopher Pulley, b1885, 16 Rajputs, Indian Army.

US Embassy inspectors visited the camp at the end April or early May 1915. It was described as a 300 yards square compound. There were 48 dormitory huts plus the usual offices, stores, kitchen, dining hall, baths etc. Most of the 995 prisoners present at that date had come from the ship *Scotian*. 350 were sailors and 645 were soldiers. (FO 383/33)

On 20 April 1916 the US Embassy made another inspection. Lt Colonel Gordon-Cumming was in command, in the absence of Lt Colonel Haines. There were 1,197 prisoners, all German, 883 soldiers and 314 naval ratings. Among the sailors were crewmen from SMSs *Königin Luise, Blücher, Nurnberg, Mainz* and a number of smaller craft. One man was in the cells for an attempted escape. A British doctor with three assistants attended the infirmary where there were five in-patients with minor cases and one in isolation with scabies. One death was reported, from epileptic fits. The kitchen was staffed by 10 assistants and one stoker, under the direction of a Sergeant-Major, previously a master-cook, all were Germans. Prisoners' work included tailoring and boot-making for the Government. Work about the camp had previously been a feature but this was nearly finished. Crafts, theatre, lectures and educational classes occupied nearly half the men. The exercise area, 310x120 yards, was available for football and other games. Route marches of 5-6 miles were arranged twice or three times a week. There were no serious complaints. The camp was described as *almost a model of its kind* (Cd. 8324).

At a third American Embassy visit, on 14 September 1916, the Commandant was Major Richards and there were 1,500 prisoners all German, 1,177 army and 323 naval. Since the arrival of 500 from Dorchester the former dining huts and drying hut had been converted into dormitories. Problems arose from the lack of room for prisoners, since the arrival of men from Dorchester, and this prompted many petty complaints. However, the space per man was well within the regulations, it was simply that when the camp was only two-thirds full the men had more room. There were eight in-patients and 53 out-patients at the infirmary, where the doctor had six British attendants. Two deaths were reported since the previous visit: one of cancer, the other drowned while bathing at the beach. The 15 cooks were all German. Detachments of men walked to a local quarry for materials for roads and pathways at the camp. A new YMCA hut was being erected. Sea bathing, for parties of 400, was permitted six days a week. (763.72114/2166)

Two prisoners at the Jersey camp, Julius Reinhard Koch and Heinrich Brinkmann, wrote to the US Embassy complaining about their treatment after escaping from Frongoch on 13 April 1916, with two others. On 12 October 1916 the US Embassy forwarded this letter to the Foreign Office, and on 16

December the War Office rebutted all allegations. (FO383/164)

Up to 60 prisoners were employed at various times at a local barracks laying a parade ground, widening and making roads, and levelling a recreation ground, all under the supervision of Royal Engineers. However, there was no work for many of the PoWs, so all except 300 were moved to England, in two parties on 13 and 16 February 1917. Those who remained were employed during the potato harvest season, loading the produce onto ships. On 29 August 1917 they were also transferred to England and the camp was closed. It is not clear from the records to which camp these PoWs were transferred.

The camp was re-opened on 12 April 1918, for NCOs who were surplus to requirements for supervisory duties at camps on the mainland, and some reports said they had been something of an irritation to their camp authorities. The NCOs were not obliged to work, but they had to look after their own domestic and sanitary chores. 1,000, mostly soldiers, were moved from Britain.

The Swiss Legation visited on 29 and 30 January 1919, when Lt Colonel Pulley was Commandant. There were 1,098 NCOs present, Feldwebel, Offizierstellvertretter, Fanriche and Unteroffiziers. Each hut had 35 beds. The hospital had 50 beds with eleven patients. There had been five deaths since the camp reopened, three of bronchial pneumonia following influenza (reported in *The Times* of 22 Nov 18), one of dysentery and one of acute gastritis. Small parties of up to six men went out to work on farms (FO 383/505).

There were several escapes from the camp but all were re-captured. Two tunnels were dug; one was discovered before it could be used, the other was used successfully but the six or seven who got out were rounded up next day at St Brelade's Bay. No reports of these escapes were found in *The Times*.

The camp was closed in October 1919. The first group of nearly 900 left on 5 October by the German steamer *Melitta* to sail direct to Germany. The remainder departed the following day (*Guernsey Weekly Press*, 11 October 1919).

Censor cachet 34mm diameter

42 x 30mm

Postcard showing a view of the camp

Kegworth, Derby

Officers' Camp   Grid Ref: SK 505 263

Although named 'Kegworth, Derby', by the War Office (but Kegworth is in Leicestershire) the camp was actually in the parish of Sutton Bonnington, in Nottinghamshire, 1½ miles southeast of Kegworth, but less than half-a-mile from Kegworth railway station. Some references to PoWs at Kingston are found in the local newspapers. Kingston-on-Soar was the original site of the Midland Agricultural College, founded 1895, as the Midland Dairy Institute, indicating some confusion at the papers for the buildings used for the PoW camp were newly built at Sutton Bonnington (a mile south of Kingston) in 1915, for the Agricultural College, but it had not moved to the new site. Hence the buildings were taken over by the War Office in 1916.

The camp opened on 2 October 1916 with accommodation for 800, per Macpherson, but his figure was the eventual size after a number of hutments had been added. The Commandant, Lt Colonel FS Picot, was also in charge at Donington Hall, and his deputy was temporary Major, Kenneth Struan Robertson, Royal Scots. Douglas James Bedford, the local GP at Kegworth, and a temporary Captain RAMC, was the medical officer for both Kegworth and Donington.

Very soon after opening, on 19 October 1916, the US Embassy made an inspection visit. They reported the camp had opened at the beginning of that month with accommodation for 250 officers. 136 officers were present, five of whom were naval officers. One was Captain von Müller of SMS *Emden* who had just arrived from Malta (he was removed from Malta as he had been bullying his colleagues). The Senior German Officer was Major Nau, of the Prussian 76th Infantry. 50 orderlies then slept in the main buildings, in two large rooms, but a barrack hut was to be erected for their dormitory. The British doctor, with three RAMC orderlies on his staff, had only one patient, with a wound to his right shoulder, but he was not confined to bed. The kitchen staff included two British cooks, two German cooks and six German assistants. The ration allowance for Officers was 2s/7d per day. The lecture theatre was described as capable of seating 80 on fixed benches with desks rising in tiers. (The raked floor of this room was later to play a significant role in the story of this camp.) A grass field, 250 yards square, and two indoor recreation rooms were also mentioned. There were no complaints (763.72114/2148).

At the monthly meeting of Nottinghamshire County Council, at the end of October 1916, it was noted that the Midland Agricultural and Dairy College had been taken over by the government and that 100 German officers and 50 servants were quartered there. One speaker observed that the prisoners in the building were, no doubt, more comfortable than their guards who were under canvas.[12]

When the Swiss Legation visited on 22 March 1917, there were 320 officers, 12 of them naval, plus 75 servants, and all of them German. Nine wooden huts, one of them a recreation room, had been erected. In the college building 55 small rooms had 1 to 3 beds, and there were 14 larger dormitories. Servants' dormitories were in the huts. The infirmary had 15 beds attended by three RAMC orderlies and three Germans. On that day there was one bed case and 25 out-patients. One death was reported; a case of fatal appendicitis of a man who had, at first, refused treatment. One had been sent to an asylum. For recreation, the report mentioned two lawn tennis courts, football and hockey games, a gymnasium and gardens. Outside walks were permitted for forty at a time, for one to two hours, daily (FO 383/276).

Lt Konstantin Maglic, *the Dandy Hun*, who has been mentioned before for his escape from Alexandra Palace, had his sentence commuted in December 1916. Then, as his officer status had been established, he was moved to Kegworth, where he fell ill. On 23 March 1917 the US Embassy presented a telegram from Vienna proposing the exchange of Captain Charles Wilson (not traced) for Lt Maglic and Lt van Georgevitz. The War Office did not agree to this and pleas, by two brother officers for Maglic, were sent in. On 9 August Capt Wilson was released to Berne and on 28 August the Spanish Ambassador at Vienna was informed that in view of the release of Capt Wilson, Lt Maglic would

---

[12] *Nottingham Evening Post* 31 Oct and a similar report in *Nottingham Daily Guardian* 1 Nov 1916

be released without conditions. Two days later it was stated that Maglic would leave for Holland by the next available Great Eastern Railway Coy boat, but Maglic wrote that it was 10 November before he crossed to The Hook of Holland by SS *Marylebone*.[13] It seems likely the delay was due more to his illness rather than officialdom.

The largest breakout of German prisoners, from a camp in Britain, occurred at Kegworth. On 24 September 1917, twenty-two escaped by a tunnel, but ten were recaptured the same day and six more within 48 hours.[14] The soil removed from the excavation was dumped under the raked floor of the lecture theatre. Captain von Müller (ex SMS *Emden*) and Lt Otto Thelen (who appears to have got away from every place he was held, and was described by *The Times* as 'the chief instigator') were among those who escaped, but all were recaptured according to *Loughborough Monitor*. However *The Times* recorded only 21 being caught; Mallmann being the exception. The names per *The Times* 26 September - some of them mis-spelt, some without forenames:

Berschmann, Kurt	Loewe, Wilhelm
Boenicke, Ferdinand	Lutz, Gustav
Boerner	Maier, Karl
Burchagen, Walter [a]	Mallmann, Joseph
Feeberger, Carl	Müller von
Gemest, Herman	Prondzynski, Stephan von
Hodzmann, Hans	Routenberg, Hans
Koch, Carl	Schorling
Kraus	Schwarz
Landoverg, Eric	Thelen, Otto
Lehmann, Emil	Thomsen

a) name given as Burghmann in the edition of 29 Sept and Burghagen in *Police Gazette* 28 Sept.
b) named Seeberger in *Police Gazette* 28 Sept.
c) named Stolymann in the 29 Sept edition and Stolzmann in *Police Gazette* 28 Sept.

Sutton Bonington - a patchwork, pp33-36 gives an account of the escape and describes how well supplied with provisions the fugitives were. The Chief Constable called for the civilian-run canteen to be examined from a security point of view. Weiland & Kern *In Feindeshand* (1931) p.445, related that the spoil was dumped under the stage of a theatre as well as below the raked floor of the lecture room. None of those who escaped through the tunnel got very far from Kegworth before they were arrested.

In September and October 1918 there were two other escape incidents, each involving two prisoners. In the earlier attempt Julius Stachelbauer, 26, and Paul Bastoen, 20, got out on 5 September. They planned to steal an aircraft but were caught a few days later at Kneeton (on the River Trent, half-way between Nottingham and Newark, and 18 miles from camp). On 9 October Ernst Johannes Steinhardt, 25, and Eduard Hauser, 23, escaped. Their recapture was reported on 14 October but the location was not stated.

Early in February 1919 there were 549 officers and 149 orderlies, with Major Meier the senior German officer (FO 383/506) and on 17 February the camp was closed when everyone moved to Oswestry. Colonel Picot also moved to Oswestry at that time, and became Commandant there.

Weiland & Kern, p434, stated that the influenza epidemic of the autumn of 1918 resulted in 470 of the 650 PoWs at Kegworth falling ill and Macpherson, p153, reported that 34 deaths, out of a total of 35 at this camp, were due to influenza. This is a much higher proportion of deaths, when compared with other camps and the early closure of this site may have been a response to the high infection and mortality rates.

Although the War Office moved out in February 1919, the College did not regain the use of its buildings until October of that year. Moreover, in 1923, two local newspapers reported that the War Office still owed £5,000 rent to the college in respect of the period of occupation as a PoW Camp. (*Derbyshire Advertiser* 3 Aug and *Leicester Advertiser* 4 Aug 1923)

Today the buildings form part of a campus of the University of Nottingham.

No camp cachet or censor mark has been recorded, to date, for Kegworth.

---

[13] FO 383/250, also Maglic *The Dandy Hun*

[14] *The Times* 26, 28 & 29 Sept 1917, also *Loughborough Monitor and News*, 27 Sept and 4 Oct 1917.

Knockaloe, Peel, Isle of Man

Home Office camps for Aliens

Grid Ref: SC 240 820

This was, by a long way, the largest camp in the British Isles. The Isle of Man authorities had a major part in running it on behalf of the British Government, where the Home Office was the responsible department, but the War Office appointed the Commandants and provided the military guards. Its eventual size can be judged from some statistics of material used: 50 million feet of timber, 1 million bricks and over 700 miles (Lands End to the Shetland Isles) of barbed wire. The camp circumference was approximately three miles. One extension from the railway line from Peel to St Johns was constructed to serve the camp and another, down to the quay at Peel Harbour, was laid to assist in moving stores to the camp.

The Destitute Aliens Committee (of the Home Office) visited the Isle of Man, for the second time, on 24 October 1914, seeking additional accommodation for internees. The site chosen was at Knockaloe Moar, 2½ miles southeast of Peel, on an area previously used as a military camping ground for Reservists etc. Clay soil of the area proved a problem for drainage. First plans were for a camp for 5,000 men, but the need to accommodate more and more meant that eventually there were plans for five camps and a maximum population of 25,000. In the event, it did not reach that number and only four camps were constructed. The guard and staff numbers totalled approximately 2,000.

The camp opened in November 1914 under its first Commandant Lt Colonel John Maxwell Carpendale (late Indian Army, retired 1909). In February 1916 he was succeeded by Lt Colonel Francis William Panzera CMG, b1851, who had been Commandant at Libury Hall since November 1915. Panzera died on 4 June 1917, while inspecting the camp, and Major Taylor, his deputy, took temporary charge until Lt Colonel Bertram Metcalfe-Smith (b1863, W Yorkshire Regiment, late Assistant Commandant at a camp in England, awarded a CBE in 1919) was appointed on 21 July 1917. Major C H Cholmondeley (not traced) was the first deputy, but for most of the war Major Grahame Taylor (also not traced, but named in a number of documents) served in this capacity. Each of the four camps had a sub-commandant, all of whom received the temporary rank of Major:

I - A B R Kaye (King's Shropshire Light Infantry, Hon.Major retired),
II - H N Fyfe Scott,
III - J Q Dickson DSO (Colonial Secretary, Falkland Islands 1913-14)
IV - A Nodin (late Captain Lancs Volunteers).
The staff at Knockaloe included seven full-time and four part-time British medical officers.

Early in 1915 the guard was commanded by Colonel Henry Best Hans Hamilton (b.1850) who had previously been Commandant at Queen's Ferry. He was a County Court Judge and presided at Military Courts in the Isle of Man. Although in his mid-60s, he later commanded a Battalion of Territorials in England and became a Town Major in France. Hamilton was succeeded in June 1915 by Lt Colonel William Arthur Ince Anderton, Royal Defence Corps, (b.1855, late Grenadier Guards). As Knockaloe expanded a headquarters staff was formed in Douglas, for all camp guards on the island, under Brigadier Edward Algernon D'Arcy Thomas CMG (b.1858, late Worcester Regiment) who was appointed Area Commandant on 24 February 1917. The maximum guard numbers reached 2,500 (for the whole island).

Mr Jackson of the US Embassy inspected the camp on 9 February 1915. (The previous visit had been by Mr Chandler Hale, on 24 November, following the riot at Douglas.) 2,000 internees were then in two separate compounds and three additional compounds were under construction. The camp was described as being in a hollow, on clay soil, so cinders were used to make the early roads, but they quickly disappeared into the soil. Therefore, plank roads were built. There was little space within the enclosures for exercise and no work was available, except camp duties. Marches, under guard, in the locality were allowed, but in winter most inmates preferred to stay in their huts, reading, playing cards etc. Each hut accommodated 100 men, who slept in bunks, three high against a central partition and two high against the outside walls. Tables and benches occupied the spaces in between. Huts were heated by stoves and electric light was installed. Showers were in a separate building.

The cooks were German, and the food generally good. Hospital accommodation was reported to be ample and no deaths had been recorded to date. Inmates were allowed to order food by post from London, but on the day of the visit there was considerable discontent as all sausages had been cut open. This was because a newspaper had been discovered, hidden in a sausage. The canteen would provide the sausages in future and, as certain English newspapers were then permitted, the temptation to smuggle papers would be diminished. Cigars had also been cut open for the same purpose. Various addenda were included with the report: a Sanitation notice, 'Information for the Guidance of the Commandant', 'Regulations Respecting Stores', 'Prisoners' Banking Facilities' (prisoners were allowed to keep only 5s/-), 'Rules for Prisoners' (no limit was stated on the number of letters a man could send), 'Daily Dietary' and 'Canteen Prices'. (HO45/100760/269116)

In March there were 2,587 at Knockaloe and a similar number at Douglas. Space for a further 2,500 was to be provided at Knockaloe at a cost of £28,000 (*Hansard HC*, 9 March 1915, vol.70, col.1263.)

When the ships, moored in the Solent and Thames estuary, were cleared between February and June 1915, many of the civilian internees were moved to Knockaloe. Visiting arrangements, at both Isle of Man camps, were three ½ hour visits per quarter for non-resident visitors, and one ½ hour visit every two weeks for Isle of Man residents. (*The Times* 23 March 1918) Due to these restrictions, and travel difficulties facing families from the mainland wishing to visit, a number of men, who had lived in the London area, were transferred to Alexandra Palace, during 1915.

In May 1915, following the sinking of SS *Lusitania*, the camp was doubled in size again, from 5,000 to 10,000, which required alterations to the water supply and drainage systems. The plan had been to build the new camps and then intern the aliens, but the government gave way to popular feeling after the sinking of the *Lusitania*. Hence facilities were not complete when men arrived. There was no furniture, nor wash-houses or latrines to start with, and such problems were repeated as the camp was successively extended to 15,000 and finally to 23,000 prisoners.

Cohen-Portheim's account,[1] he was at Knockaloe from the end of May 1915, confirmed these points. He described his compound as a dozen or more long, low wooden huts, each of which housed about 40 men. Five compounds formed a camp and there were five camps (*sic*). He mentioned a Captain for each hut and a Chief Captain for the compound. He supposed they had been elected, but evidently he did not partake in the election. *One was allowed to write twice a week, on one page of glazed paper, and it was forbidden to mention either the war or conditions in the camp. Of course all letters had to pass a censor.* Upon arriving at Knockaloe he applied to move to Lofthouse Park, one of two 'gentlemen's camps' (the other was at Douglas) and was successful, so he was moved, in a group of 60, after two months, but he did not give a precise date.

On 19 and 20 June 1915, the US Embassy made another inspection, when 8,470 were present. 2,000 had arrived the previous week and a further 1,000 were expected each week. The inspectors reported that when completed there would be five compounds, each for 5,000 men, in barrack huts for 180-200 each. 510 men were still in tents but they were to be moved into wooden huts. Dining halls were not then erected, so the men ate in their huts, but when the inspectors returned to London in July and prepared their reports, Home Office officials stated that the dining halls were being erected. Wooden roads had been laid. 22 acres of playing fields had been added, and 2,000 were sent there each day for exercise. Classes had begun and about 1,000 attended them. An exhibition of crafts had been arranged. 3 deaths were reported. There were complaints from men who had been at the camp some time but newer arrivals seemed content (763.72114/689).

The postmark "The Camp, Knockaloe, Peel", a double-ring datestamp, appears in the *Steel Impressions* book dated 23 July 1915, but this sub-Post Office was not listed in contemporary Post Office Guides. Massy, in *Isle of Man Postmarks*, showed this office operating during WWI only, and did not give a sub-postmaster's name. The postmark is known used until 1919.

---

[1] Cohen-Portheim P: *Time Stood Still, my internment in England 1914-1918*

Christmas greetings cards for 1915 and 1917 sent by internees to their friends in Germany.
Both cards were marked as passed by the censor in the camp.

Censorship was under the control of Mr A Knox and Mr WM Holmes and the Camp Bank was under the direction of the Chief Purser, Mr A Harris. (Sargeaunt, p71)

In August 1915 a report by an internee at Knockaloe described the camp and conditions, comparing them favourably with his previous camps at Newbury and Douglas (FO 383/34). In September when the US Embassy made another visit the report noticed the reduced crowding and stated that Camps I, II and III were practically complete and filled, while Camp IV was half occupied but a further 2,000 men were expected the following week.(HO45/10946/266042)

At the end of the year there were complaints about the weather-proofing of the huts, that the stoves in the huts were inadequate, about the mud under foot, and the lack of clothing. 28 had died by 31 December 1915.

Early in 1916, a tunnel, 89 yards long, was discovered under the floor of the theatre in compound 1 of Camp II. W Druschke #1913, was charged and sentenced to 14 days hard labour and B diet. E Muller #3843, R Wilcher #1258 and W Peterson #1508 were also implicated in the tunnel venture, but their sentences, if any, were not mentioned in the file.[2] In February, Colonel F W Panzera, previously at Libury Hall, was appointed Commandant.

The gaol on the Isle of Man was small and, incidentally, was just across Victoria Road from the Douglas camp (*qv*), therefore some convicted internee offenders served their sentences at Liverpool (*The Times* 3 March 1916).

On 16 April 1916, August Uccusic #21,507, and two others were shot and wounded in Camp IV. A prisoner had been chased by others so he took refuge with the sentry. The guard tried to disperse a crowd who gathered, without success, so he eventually

---

[2] HO 45/10946/266042. A full report was given in *Isle of Man Times*, 20 January 1916

opened fire hitting three men. The following month Uccusic claimed compensation, but the file did not state whether he was successful in his claim (HO45/10946/266042).

When the US Embassy next visited, at the end of April 1916, there were 192 patients in the hospitals and there had been 42 deaths up to the date of the report. Burials were at St Patrick's Church, close by the camp. About 72% of the internees had work. 30 acres or so were under cultivation for vegetables. Two men were in the cells. Two news-sheets, produced at the camp, *Knockaloe Lager Zeitung* and *Knockaloe Lager Echo* were mentioned (Cd.8324). Specially printed wrappers are known for these news-sheets when sent out by post.

By October 1916 the population of 22,435 internees included 2,500 men over 45 years old (*Hansard HC* 24 October 1916, vol.86, col.979). The previous week a tunnel had been discovered and the Captain of the compound was arrested. Thereupon the other Captains resigned in protest. A meeting to select new Captains was called but it was dominated by one speaker, so the authorities removed him to another camp. A riot followed and the Captains were assaulted and beaten. A Beirich, W Wunderle and O Kohler were charged with mutiny and assault (*The Times* 19 October 1916). *A report of 'stone throwing and rough hooliganism' in Camps III and IV was carried in Isle of Man Weekly Times of 28 October,* which may have been connected to the same incident.

On 22 February 1917, the War Office issued an amended scale of rations for PoWs (ACI 323) which came into effect on 2 March. This was brought in because the food situation had become critical and the general public was also rationed. Unrestricted submarine warfare, declared by Germany, had reduced grain imports. The lower scale of rations prompted the internees' welfare committees to write to the US Embassy protesting the insufficiency of their diet. Mr Page, the Ambassador, wrote to his Secretary of State asking for the calorie value of the new scale to be investigated. By the date of this letter, 16 March 1917, USA had severed diplomatic relations with Germany and Mr Page stated that the Swiss Legation was then dealing with the interests of interned Germans. The Swiss calculated the calorie value as 2,100, while they considered that 2,300-2,600 calories should be received by the men. It was learned that a fresh ACI would be issued to bring the calorie intake up to 2,500. (763.72114/2524)

In a follow up letter of 30 March, Mr Page sent a copy of a letter from Captain Schwyzer, of the Swiss Legation, who had calculated the calorie values as 2,213 for the normal diet and 2,684 for the enhanced diet for labourers. These figures compared unfavourably with 2,427 and 3,000 given by the British Government. Moreover, Captain Schwyzer stated that his calculation was based on top quality food, which he doubted the PoWs received. He considered the new scale insufficient for grown men, even if they did no work. A new scale of rations was published by the Isle of Man Government which differed from the ACI only in small details. Dr Taylor (of the University of Pennsylvania) wrote, on 20 April, that neither list was entirely accurate. He calculated the new scale as 2,315 calories while a non-working PoW required 2,400 (763.72114/2550). For comparison, it should be noted that the official PoW ration in Germany during the period June to October 1916 was 1,750 to 2,050 calories per day.

The variety of trades practised by the large numbers of internees meant that many useful articles were produced in the workshops as well as souvenirs and knick-knacks. Furniture was made to special orders and, after the end of war, pre-fabricated housing and flat-pack furnishings were made for homeless families in the devastated areas of northern France and Belgium. The handicraft industries were under the supervision of James Baily, a Quaker.[3]

Gangs of men were employed from time to time on the camp sewage system, while others went out for quarrying, road building, land clearance and drainage. Work camps for agricultural gangs were set up at Regaby (2 miles NW of Ramsey) and Ballaugh (6 miles W of Ramsey). In 1916 a gang of 200 worked on canalising the Sulby River to reclaim land. This site was 4 miles W of Ramsey, and they were conveyed there daily by train. In September 1916 it was reported that a further 100 men were to be sent to this work.

After the USA had declared war on Germany, on 6 April 1917, Switzerland and Sweden became the protecting powers and their Legations made visits to the camps. Dr A L Vischer, a Swiss, visited in May and noted that youths had been separated from the men and put into their own compound. He also wrote to the Home Office explaining depression among the

---

[3] Baily L: *Craftsman and Quaker, the story of James T Baily 1876-1957*

prisoners and recommended that those under 20 years should be segregated under a Pastor, or similar official, who could supervise them, their education and occupations (FO 383/276). When the Swedish officials inspected the camps on this Isle of Man, they reported that in view of the isolation, difficulties of communications and strict supervision, a more liberal attitude could be adopted. For example, movement between the compounds without a pass and an escort, and permitting walks in the surrounding country. (HO45/10946/266042)

In November 1917 the Swiss inspector noted that about 500 youths, all under 21, had been moved to compound 8 in Camp IV. Mr Rehbehn, the Captain of that compound, had previously been an estate manager for Baron von Bredow, in Pomerania, and after that he was in the Cameroons. However, he did not stay long for in April it was stated that Mr Bac, a much younger man, had taken over, and in August 1918 the leader was named as Mr Balzer, an elderly man, stated to be well fitted to be leader of this compound (FO 383/277 and /432). This special regime did not last, for the Home Office wrote to the Foreign Office, on 8 November 1918, proposing to break up the group and distribute the juveniles into the main part of the camp.

In February 1918 Sir James Cantlie, a leading surgeon and Council Member of the British Red Cross inspected the camp and reported in some detail, *inter alia*, on the parcel post arrangements, which he found quite satisfactory, particularly how broken and unaddressed items were dealt with. (HO45/10947/266042)

During the night of Sunday 26 May 1918, 500 internees arrived at Douglas by steamer, and were taken by train to Knockaloe. *Isle of Man Examiner,* 1 June, stated that a rumour of their pending arrival from Dublin had prompted speculation that they would be Irish Nationalists, but in fact they were internees from Oldcastle, as that camp was closed.

Another movement of internees was referred to in June 1918 in a *Note Verbale* from Berlin about 48 Germans, previously in Brixton Prison, then in compound 4 of Camp III. The British reply was that those prisoners had been moved at their own request and that all in that compound had criminal antecedents, or their characters were such that it was in the interests of other prisoners to keep them separate (FO 383/440).

On 8 and 10 October 1918 the civilians at Lofthouse Park were also transferred to Knockaloe, and compound 4 in Camp IV then became a privilege camp. After this move Lofthouse Park became a PoW officers' camp.

There were many escapes from Knockaloe but no internee ever got away from the island. In newspapers many reports refer simply to events in the Island. As there were many times the numbers at Knockaloe, compared with Douglas, it is assumed, in the lists, that such items refer to Knockaloe unless there is evidence to the contrary.

When agreements were made to repatriate older prisoners, this gave the opportunity for men to lie about their age, or for others to assist in falsifying the records, for some consideration. Internees, Karch, Lassen and Gey, who had worked in the camp office, were charged with altering records to make men appear to be over 45, so qualifying for repatriation. (*The Times* 14 September 1918)

Statistics for Knockaloe Camp, to the end of 1917:					
	Admitted to camp	transferred or released	deaths	lunatics	Total strength at last day
up to end 1915	23,477	2,169	50	18	20,308
1916	4,578	4,188	47	47	21,698
1917	2,780	6,017	76	27	18,461
Totals	30,835	12,374	153	92	

Table 10: Statistics from FO383/432. Unfortunately the cross-casts do not tally with the right-hand column. However an indication of numbers is given by these figures.

At the end of hostilities it was reported that there were 26,000 internees on the Isle of Man and that the mortality rate, of three per thousand, was less than that of the general population. By January 1919 the internees were being moved to camps in England for release, or repatriation, at the rate of about 1,000 per week.

Statistics for the two camps on the Isle of Man from January 1916 to 21 March 1919 were given in HO45/10947/266042:
Average daily population 20,981
Average weekly expenditure £10,759
   (equals 10s/3d per man per week)

The population in 1919 reduced as follows:
January 1919	16,234
February	11,666
March	4,722
27 May 1919	1,376

By September 1919 there were less than 300 at Knockaloe, so on 25 September instructions were given to transfer those remaining men to Islington, but the actual move was delayed by a railway strike. James Baily, who had been in charge of the craft industries at the camp since they were first set on a formal basis, wrote:

> *One morning in October 1919, I stood at the camp gate and watched the last 175 march out under escort ...... en route to freedom.*

An International Red Cross postcard, based on a sketch by an internee, B. Heinecke.

The wooden buildings of the camp, depicted in this artist's impression, were dismantled and many were re-used in parishes around the island, as British Legion huts. In 1920 the railway extension to Peel Quay was removed and in 1924 the site of the camp was sold and it became an experimental farm.

An official envelope, printed with a camp cachet, posted at Peel 29 August 1915, addressed to one of the three German Banks in London which were placed under official supervision in August 1914.

Similar envelopes, 120 x 95 mm have also been recorded.

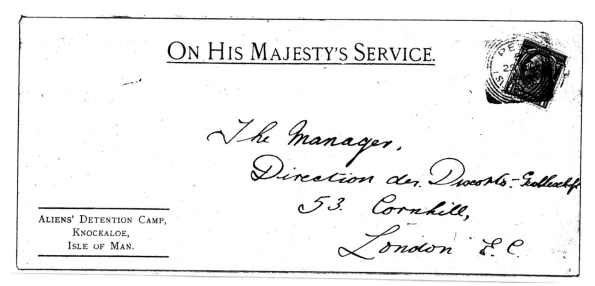

Printed letterhead for internees' use at Knockaloe.
This letter, dated 27 Září (September) 1915 was addressed to Mr Jan Ćupík at Mnichovo-Hradiště, 75 km north-east of Prague.

Three versions of the smaller 'censored' cachet: all three 47 x 29mm
A. With crosses paté   B. Without crosses   C. With simple crosses and lower central line missing

The larger 'censored' cachet, 53 x 31mm

Camp cachet 41 x 27mm

Camp Post Office

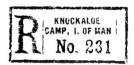

Registration label

Date stamp
(Proofed 23 July 1915)

In addition to these a Camp Bank cachet is recorded. A double circle, 40/31mm with a date across the centre and '............ BANK / KNOCKALOE PEEL I.O.M.' around the rim. This was on a registered letter from London 7 August 1918 to Camp 3 (London & Brighton Auctions, May 1984)

1916 Christmas card designed by FW Kehrhann, who is mentioned in the section on Islington Camp.

Two news-wrappers from Knockaloe, showing the names of the two newspapers which were produced there in two different camps.

This cachet, on the flap of a cover to Munich, without any postal markings, translates as:
    Editorial Office,
    Knockaloe Camp Newspaper
    formerly "Stobsiade",
confirming the point, made in the Stobs chapter (*qv*), that the civilians began a newspaper at that camp and after they were moved to the Isle of Man, in July 1916, they started it up again.

Lancaster, Lancashire

Civilians   Grid Ref: SD 484 633

For many years until the first decade of the 20th century the wagon works at Caton Road, Lancaster (¾ mile northeast of the town-centre), had been a major employer of labour, building tramcars and railway rolling stock. The works closed in 1908 (per Potter) and the site was still vacant in August 1914.

For a short while that month the works became a temporary barracks for the 5th Battalion, The King's Own (Royal Lancaster Regiment), but soon the buildings were being prepared for an influx of 2,000 internees.[4] Macpherson gave the accommodation figure as 4,000, which seems an over estimate. However, for some reason he linked Lancaster with Templemore and 4,000 is the likely total for the two camps combined. Panayi (p64) described this as 'an old wagon works, which had been empty for 17 years'. That is not accurate, for if the business closed in 1908, the buildings had been empty for only 6 years.

Colonel Hugh Cecil Cholmondeley CB, late Rifle Brigade (1852-1941), was the first Commandant, but in September he was posted to Shrewsbury. Major William deBathe Hatton, late Seaforth Highlanders was his deputy and Dr Faulkner the medical officer. Captain Fairclough, Royal Warwickshire Regt and Lts Graves and Ackerly were also named in *Lancaster Observer* of 21 August 1914. A company of Royal Welsh Fusiliers provided the guard.

The first batch of prisoners arrived by train from Liverpool on 24 August, escorted by men of the Cheshire Regiment. Later that day another batch arrived from Hull and by the end of the week the total had reached about 380.[5] Throughout September more were arrested around the country. Many from the Manchester area were sent to Lancaster and others arrived from The Potteries, Tyneside and Carlisle, so that in October there were about 2,000 held at the camp. Meanwhile, the guard was relieved by National Reservists and some of the 'better class' prisoners were transferred to Douglas during October.

Lancaster Gazette, 21 November, reported that prisoners had attempted either an escape or a raid on the stores. They broke through the roof and caused damage amounting to £30. At the same time the paper reproduced a report of good treatment and conditions by an internee, which denied allegations to the contrary from Germany.

The Times 3 December, carried a report of a riot, in which one was seriously hurt, but no mention of such an incident has been found in local newspapers. However, it was referred to in Shrewsbury and Portsmouth papers where it was stated that the Commandant, Colonel Ainslea, (not traced) did not confirm the story. The incident was also mentioned briefly in a German report, dated 20 January 1915 (in CAB 37/123/37).

A more detailed item in *Yorkshire Evening Press,* 4 December, reported a serious conflict between PoWs at Lancaster. The armed guard went in with bayonets fixed and one prisoner was wounded. However, the Commandant, named as Colonel Ainstre (not traced) declared 'not a word of truth in it'. He explained that, in consequence of the release of a few men from Alsace, the Germans in the camp began booing, so the guard turned out, but there was no conflict. About 2,000 at the camp had been very tractable since the events at Douglas.

Mr Jackson inspected the camp, for the US Embassy, on 12 February 1915. He reported about 1,800 men and 200 boys being present. Many of the youths had been taken from fishing vessels or from bands of itinerant musicians. He understood that boys under 17 were being concentrated at Lancaster with a view to their repatriation. There were considerable numbers of Hungarian and Polish men and several over 55. The buildings were described as an old wagon works, disused for some years. The floors were bad, but they were being concreted as funds become available. The Commandant (not named) was commended for his attitude. A boxing ring had been set up and gymnastic apparatus ordered. Schooling was arranged for the boys and voluntary instruction for others. In some parts the beds had been tented to protect them from a leaking roof. The better classes of men occupied a separate building. While the heating was satisfactory,

---

[4] *Lancaster Observer* 21 August 1914, p5

[5] *Lancaster Guardian* 29 August 1914, 5f

the lighting was poor. Washing facilities were fair but there were few baths. Each mess had a small kitchen, which seemed to be a satisfactory arrangement. The canteen facility was adequate. The hospital, well arranged, was full of ex-Africa patients, one with black-water-fever and several malaria cases. Two deaths were reported. Venereal cases were in a separate enclosure. (HO45/10760/269116)

A House of Commons delegation visited and their report, quoted in *The Times* 26 April 1915, described 'an old machine works' and stated: *... at Lancaster the members were impressed with the complete confidence which the prisoners seemed to have in the authorities' sense of justice and fair play.* However, other impressions of the camp were not so flattering. The American report, mentioned above, and Thomas, p46, wrote critically of the camp, *...for several weeks conditions in this camp at Lancaster were, to say the least, deplorable.*'

When the next US Embassy visit took place, on 16 June 1915, conditions had improved. There were 2,097 held, and this still included about 200 boys under 17, whose sleeping quarters were again noted as being separate from the men. Repairs had been made to the roof and floors were being concreted. A technical school had been started, staffed by prisoners. Route marches with their own band had been allowed, but were suspended in May because of public hostility [probably a reaction to the sinking of SS *Lusitania*]. Recreation space was limited but an additional playing field was being acquired (FO383/33).

The date of evacuation of the prisoners and the whereabouts of their new abode has not been traced, but the most likely destination would be Knockaloe. Mail from internees at Lancaster has been seen up to mid-August 1915. After they were moved out the place was used for the manufacture of torpedoes until the end of the war (Potter). The site was sold to a Carlisle firm, Morton Sundour Fabrics, in December 1922.

The Times, 5 April 1919, reported the funeral at Lancaster of three PoWs who died of pneumonia. Lancaster Castle was a work camp under Leigh, and the victims must have been there.

Note: The Commandant, mentioned in various newspapers under different names was probably Lt Colonel John Henry Ansley, (b 1863, retired 1913) late Loyal North Lancashire Regt, listed as Commandant of a PoW Camp in the March 1915 edition of *The Monthly Army List*. Later he was Commandant at Pattishall in 1916, and then at Leigh from late 1917.

```
O.H.M.S.
PRISONERS OF WAR
POSTAGE FREE.
```

This cachet, 69x27mm, is found on some early mail from Lancaster, (and also from Queen's Ferry).

Leigh, Lancashire

Other Ranks   Grid Ref: SJ 653 997

This was a mill building in Pennington, on the south side of Leigh. Construction had begun in January 1914 for Lilford Weaving Co Ltd, but it had not been completed at the outbreak of war. The War Office intention of using the buildings for a PoW camp was announced in the *Leigh Chronicle* of 30 October 1914, but it was not until the end of January 1915 that the first prisoners arrived, although 200 Reservists had arrived to serve as the guard just before the New Year.

Leigh Chronicle 18 December 1914, named the first Commandant as Captain Kenneth Crause Wright, late Bedford Regiment (b.1867, retired 1907) but he was moved to Frongoch, just as the first PoWs arrived. He was succeeded by a Captain Lindsay (not traced), and he in turn by Major George Goulbourn Tarry, late Leicestershire Regt (b.1859, retired 1900) who arrived on 7 April 1915 from Templemore, where he had been Commandant, but he did not stay long for in June he went back to Ireland as DAQMG.

The official opening date, given by Macpherson was 28 January 1915, and he wrote the capacity of the camp was 1,785 men. However, within a month that number was exceeded. The first PoWs arrived in five batches, each of approximately 360 men, between 29 January and 19 February 1915. In all 1,855 were transferred from Templemore, Co Tipperary. Most were soldiers, but there were some sailors. Local papers in Leigh said that Templemore Barracks had been condemned but that was not correct.

In April 1915, forty PoWs were sent to Donington Hall to act as orderlies for officer prisoners. Also in that month Friedrich Schwenke, a soldier, escaped but was recaptured at London Road station, Manchester, and returned to the camp. At the end of the month he faced a Court Martial. He had deliberately ruined his uniform and had been supplied with overalls, similar to those worn by artisans, and a jacket, giving him the opportunity to escape simply by walking out, with the contractors' workers, with a 'toolbox' on his shoulder.[6]

On 30 May 1915, Friedrich Schmidt, was shot and killed while attempting to escape. The verdict at a coroner's inquest was 'justifiable homicide'. Schmidt was buried at the local cemetery (*The Times* 1 and 2 June 1915). The following week there was another attempt to escape when an un-named prisoner hid in a swill-tub, but he was discovered near to suffocation. He received a sentence of 28 days for his foolish efforts.

Sixty 'ambulance men' left for Germany on 26 June 1915, to be exchanged for British personnel. This was part of a larger exchange of disabled PoWs and medical orderlies (*Leigh Chronicle* 2 July 1915). Two days later the US Embassy visited the camp and reported 1,688 soldiers and 39 sailors present. The smallest of six dormitories held 80 Feldwebel and NCOs, while the largest contained 519 men. All had low wooden beds with a palliasse and three blankets. Fifteen patients were in the hospital. A hut had been provided by the YMCA, for recreation and concerts. Bands of string and brass instruments and a choir of twenty voices were noted, as well as the organisation of classes and craft occupations. No complaints were aired. The Commandant, not named, had only recently been appointed (763.72114/689). The new Commandant was Colonel Henry John Blagrove CB, late 13 Hussars (b.1854, retired 1901) who was in charge until 1917.

The discovery of an escape tunnel led to a Court Martial in July. Three (unnamed) were sentenced to three months with hard labour at Woking Detention Barracks. The discovery was made during a thorough search of the camp as a result of the fatal attempted escape, by Schmidt, at the end of May.[7]

The camp was visited again by US Embassy staff on 21 February 1916. In the report the commandant was named as Col. Blagrove, and the Quartermaster/Adjutant as Lt Ashby. There were 1,770 prisoners, all German, of which 38 were sailors, the remainder

---

[6] *The Times* 12 April 1915, *Liverpool Daily Post* 28 April and *Leigh Chronicle* 16 and 30 April. (*The Times* report stated that Schwenke was recaptured at Salford Docks)

[7] *The Times* 14 July 1915, p5d and *Leigh Chronicle* 16 July

soldiers. Various committees were mentioned and craft work was a particular interest. There were complaints about the lack of fresh vegetables, but the inspectors recognised these were scarce in winter. Two fields, each of 2 to 3 acres, were available for exercise, one cinder, the other grass. Drill, three times a week, kept the men fit. A tank for swimming was available in summer. Poor heating had previously been an issue but a new boiler had been installed, so this was no longer a cause of complaint. Parcel opening arrangements were criticised and complaints were made by those, who claimed to be ambulance men, that they should be released. Five were in the cells, including one man who had struck the Provost Sergeant twice, and received 14 days for each attack. A list of the complaints was not in the file but the Commandant's replies were there (763.72114/1364).

Another US Embassy visit was made on 8 September 1916, when there were 1,357 prisoners. The reduction in numbers was because 475 had been sent out to working camps. 200 and 110 were at forestry camps at Crickhowell, Breconshire, and Sproxton Moor, Yorkshire, respectively, and 165 at quarry work at Rowrah in Cumberland. A further 26 went daily, to work at the pit-head of a local coal mine. A British doctor was in charge of the hospital with a Ward-Master/Dispenser, five RAMC and two German orderlies. There were 17 in-patients and 27 out-patients on the day of the visit. One man was in isolation with pulmonary tuberculosis. He had been transferred from Frongoch in late 1915 and had gained 18 lbs (8kg) in weight. He was referred to the medical referees for transfer to Switzerland. Two deaths of enteric fever, two of tuberculosis and one of heart failure, were reported since opening. A British dentist visited one day a week and one of the prisoners, a dentist, was available daily. The 10% rebate from canteen takings, amounting to about £600 per month, was spent for the benefit of the prisoners. A new hut had been provided for the carving school. Besides this and other craft occupations, men were employed in sack-making, harness-cleaning, cotton-picking and building trades. A third recreation ground (grass) had been added since the previous report. There were no complaints. Four were in the cells for breaches of camp orders. The average number of parcels from Germany was one, per man, per week. Mostly these contained foodstuffs. Cash drawings were limited to £1 in any month. Weekly church services were arranged for Catholics and Protestants and a German pastor visited every fortnight (763.72114/2039).

Local newspapers of late 1916 & early 1917 reported the move of PoWs to Abergavenny, in South Wales, and to the nearby colliery at Atherton. Also mentioned about 200 going to work at Partington Steel Works at Irlam, (6 miles away) but this latter site was not mentioned in any of the reports seen of official visits.

On 6 December 1916 there were 1,474 prisoners, all German, 33 sailors, the others all soldiers. With the onset of winter an extra blanket has been issued to each man. 200 had returned from forestry work at Crickhowell, a few weeks previously, due to inadequate quarters during inclement weather. It was anticipated that they would return there in about 10 days [presumably huts were being built in place of tented accommodation]. There were 23 in-patients at the infirmary, 10 recently arrived with slight wounds or illness, and 55 out-patients, of whom 40 were recent arrivals from France with slight wounds. One death was reported, since the previous visit, of enteric fever. The occupations of 425 men at Leigh were listed: among these 300 were engaged in cotton-picking, 43 sewing sacks, 24 tailors and 14 bootmakers. Dependant working camps were listed, giving the numbers of prisoners at each:

Harperly, Co Durham,	199,	forestry
Eastgate, Co Durham,	196,	forestry
Sproxton Moor, Yorkshire	110,	forestry;
Rowrah, Cumberland,	180,	quarry
Atherton Collieries, Lancs,	26.	

No serious complaints were made. Five were in the cells for insubordination or refusing to work. The American inspectors wrote: *the general tone of this camp was excellent.* (763.72114/2284)

In the autumn of 1917 three escapes were noted in the local paper. None got very far, the most-distant recapture was near Preston. (*Leigh Chronicle* 19 & 26 October, 2 & 16 November 1917.)

At the end of November 1917, Colonel Blagrove was succeeded as Commandant by Colonel J H Ansley. He had previously been Commandant at Pattishall and may have been at Lancaster at the end of 1914.

In January 1918 four sailors escaped. They managed to travel much further than previous absconders from this camp. Two got to Grimsby and the other pair reached Gloucestershire before they were apprehended.[8]

---

[8] *The Times* 21 January 1918, p3d and 28, p3f and *Leigh Chronicle* 25 January 1918

400 prisoners were transferred to Frongoch in April 1919. A further 500 went there in May and 800 were moved to Handforth. About fifty then remained at Leigh to clear up, and they departed on 30 May 1919, when the camp was closed.[9] With the closing of Leigh the work-camps under its control were passed to Handforth (FO 383/508). There had been 13 deaths at the camp: one was shot in trying to escape in May 1915, six died during 1915-16, and six more during the influenza of late 1918.

For this account of Leigh Camp this author is grateful to acknowledge the work of Leslie Smith. His book *The German Prisoner of War Camp at Leigh 1914-1919*, published in 1986, quoted extensively from the local newspapers. National newspapers did not always agree on the details of an individual story, but this author assumes the local reporters and editors were better able to check the facts than Fleet Street men.

No camp or censor cachet has been recorded for Leigh. That a censor mark has not been recorded to date can be explained by the fact that the inmates were combatant PoWs from the rank and file, so were much less likely to have correspondence with people living in Britain. Almost 100% of their mail would be to countries outside Britain and therefore subject to censorship at the PW Department in London.

---

[9] *Leigh Journal* 27 May 1919 and 3 June & *Leigh Chronicle* 17 April and 6 June 1919

Lewisham, London SE

Officers' camp   Grid Ref: TQ 385 757

Five reprisal camps were opened in the Spring of 1918 to hold German officers in areas liable to Zeppelin or aircraft bombing. *The Times* 16 March 1918, p6c stated this action was taken in retaliation for the Germans moving prisoners to areas near the battle lines. However, the British Government denied that this, and the four similar sites, were reprisal camps, in a letter to the Swiss Minister, dated 26 July 1918. That was in reply to his request for information. (FO 383/440) Nevertheless, Farquharson, p384, did list them as 'Reprisal Camps (Officers)'.

Macpherson gave the opening date as 23 April 1918 and described the accommodation, for forty officers and ten servants as a "Mansion House". Lewisham Library has identified this as 2 Belmont Grove, a substantial 1850s house on the Blackheath-Lewisham borders (personal communication, March 2005). The enquiry from and the reply to the Swiss Legation in July 1918, mentioned above, established that the officers at this camp came from Holyport, near Maidenhead, in April.

The Times of 4 July 1918, p3f, reported the escape, on 2 July, of Lt Walter Tarnou, German Air Force, and his recapture at Farnborough. There are two towns with this name and it is easy to assume it was the one in Kent, only 8 miles to the southeast. However *Kentish Mercury*, 5 July 1918, reported that Tarnou was apprehended by the Hampshire Constabulary, so it must have been the other Farnborough, near Aldershot, over 30 miles away. Was he looking for an aircraft to make good his escape, or were his navigation skills a bit rusty?

A Home Office document listed Lewisham as closed on 10 December 1918. It has not been ascertained to where these prisoners were then moved. Back to Holyport is a possibility but inspection visits, which usually give numbers present, have not been traced for that camp at the critical time. On the basis, that those at Margate were moved to Oswestry in January, that is another possible destination for those from Belmont Grove. Sandhill Park, from where officers were transferred to other reprisal camps in April, was unlikely to be their new camp as, according to a Swiss inspection report, that was already back in use for officers in August 1918.

Belmont Grove is a turning off Belmont Hill, which runs across the middle of the map.
Reproduced from 1916 OS map (Crown Copyright)

Libury Hall, Ware, Hertfordshire

A Home Office camp   Grid Ref TL 345 235

In 1899 Libury Hall, 6 miles north of Ware, and 3 miles west of Puckeridge, with 300 acres of land, was purchased by Baron Sir (John) Henry William Schröder (1825-1910), head of the family banking house. His father, Johann Heinrich Schröder (1784-1833), was a Hamburg merchant who had moved to England and the sons became naturalised in 1864.

Sir Henry founded a German Farm Colony at Libury Hall, which opened on 29 September 1900, to provide temporary work, shelter, board and lodging, to German speaking unemployed and destitute men. The farm was designed to be self sufficient, which it was in all respects, 'except for certain cuts of meat'. An adjacent 25 acre farm was purchased later. In 1914 the three trustees of the estate were Baron Bruno Schröder, Baron William Henry Schröder (both nephews of Sir Henry, who had died without issue) and Mr C A Bingel. Up to the outbreak of war, over 7,200 men had passed through the colony, most spent only a few weeks there, but some older men had become long term residents. The manager from 1900 until 1920 was Willi Müller.

On 11 September 1914 the Destitute Aliens Committee wrote to the Home Office recommending the German Farm Colony, at Libury Hall, be utilised for the accommodation of up to 300 destitute Germans and Austrians. Practically all the candidates were married men whose families were being supported by charitable institutions. They proposed an English superintendent and that a police guard be provided. The Home Office replied on 27 November that the Secretary of State agreed, retrospectively to 20 August 1914. The approval allowed for up to 250 at the colony, which was to be a place of internment for old and physically incapable Germans and Austrians who, owing to long residence in UK, had lost all connections with their native countries. The Colony was to be under the overall command of a military officer and an armed police guard was provided from 9 September, for which the Home Office undertook to defray the expenses.

Early in September, local people complained that inmates were permitted to go where they pleased, within a five-mile radius, and that the Aliens Restriction Orders allowed this. The Chief Constable of Hertfordshire wrote to the Home Office regarding these complaints. Whether the armed police guard was a result of the public misgivings, or some other policy, is not clear.

On 2 December 1914 the Destitute Aliens Committee stated there were then 42 elderly inmates and 24 employees at Libury Hall. The Army Council, which had opposed the establishment of the place as an internment camp, was requested to reconsider their position, which they did in the New Year, and Colonel William James Smyth Fergusson CMG (b.1864, late King's Dragoon Guards, retired 1910) was nominated as Commandant.

The Times 2 February 1915, reported that at Hertfordshire Quarter Sessions it was alleged the colony was 'too near the coast'! A glance at a map reveals it was 34 miles to the River Thames at Purfleet, about the same to the Blackwater Estuary, at Maldon, and rather more to Colchester. A long walk for the elderly or infirm!

In April 1915 there was a proposal to replace the police with a military guard, and Eastern Command agreed to supply men from the Supernumerary Territorial Force. The police guard handed over on 14 April when men of 3rd Battalion, Hertfordshire Regiment arrived, but then the War Office had second thoughts and objected. The soldiers were withdrawn after one week and armed police resumed guard duties. The guards lived in three cottages which were part of the estate.

In June a plan to expand the 'camp' to 500 selected men was opposed by the War Office. On 30 July 1915 the Chief Constable wrote to the Home Office and enclosed a list of the 29 men at Libury Hall of military age, ie under 55. These were 28 Germans, mostly aged between 44 and 53, but one of 41 and one 31, and one Austrian who was 38 years old. The Chief Constable stated he intended to have them arrested on 4 August, but instructions by letter from the Home Office stayed his hand.

In September 1915, a parliamentary answer revealed that there were only 89 Germans, average age 59, and four Austrians, average age 55, at Libury Hall. Most of them were suffering from serious infirmities. Mr Muller, the manager, was mentioned in the statement as being confined to the camp (*Hansard HC* 28 September 1915, vol.74, col.712).

Further public disquiet was revealed in the Autumn of 1915 when allegations that arms and ammunition were stored at Libury Hall. The police made a search, but no trace of arms or ammunition was found. However, security needed to be tightened, as the inmates could easily leave, for the wire fencing was inadequate and the guard, of one Sergeant and eight Special Constables, was considered insufficient to prevent a break-out.

The Chief Constable reported to his Police Committee, on 8 October 1915, that the Home Office had broken their promise that only elderly and infirm would be held there, as there were men of military age, and the Home Office had given instructions that they were not to be arrested for internment. He recommended closure of the colony, or failing that, only aged and infirm be allowed there, and that a military guard be provided. In addition the Home Office had failed to keep their promise to pay the expenses for the police guard, £530 for the period from September 1914 up to 15 April 1915, although some expenses had been reimbursed. The cheque for these expenses was eventually received on 5 January 1917.

When Home Office officials inspected the place, on 10 October 1915, there were 99 inmates of whom 33 were under 50 years old. Two patients were in the infirmary. The guard comprised one Sergeant and two Special Constables. A new Commandant was appointed on 25 November 1915, Lt Colonel Francis William Panzera CMG, (1851-1917), late Resident Commissioner Bechuanaland, but he did not stay long for in February 1916 he was transferred to Knockaloe.

In March 1916 the Unionist Business Committee (of MPs) criticised the arrangements at Libury Hall. A full list in inmates was attached to their statement. There were 74 over military age or physically unfit, and 21 of military age. Captain Merry, the new Commandant (not traced) was confidentially informed by the Home Office of a possible visit by these hostile MPs. They did visit and their report, of 6 April, was very bland, although they commented adversely on the size of the guard; only four were on duty at any one time. The Home Office reaction was *they had to find something to criticise*. This visit was followed by another, by Sir John David Rees KCIE MP, Director of the Prisoners of War Information Bureau.

On 29 May 1916, Mr Boyston Beal, of the US Embassy inspected. 188 were living there, of whom 178 were German and 10 Austrian, and the accommodation was sufficient for 244. 38 residents, including nine staff members, had been there from pre-war days. Some had wives and children with them. Besides the main buildings there were eight cottages (three were occupied by the guard, per an earlier report, and presumably the families lived in the others). The infirmary had 50 beds, under the care of an English doctor and a German nurse. There were three in-patients and twelve out-patients that day. Seven deaths were reported, mostly from old age. There was no military guard, and the police were not mentioned. (FO 383/163)

At the end of 1916 Captain Merry listed 235 inmates, of which 28 had opted for repatriation, but 32 had been adjudged by the Committee to qualify for repatriation. This was at the time when internees' cases had been examined by a panel in connection with an agreement with the German Government for the mutual repatriation of invalids.

Two visits by the Swiss Legation have been traced. The first, on 9 May 1917, was a few days after Captain Merry had died and a Police Sergeant was acting Commandant. There were 197 inmates and twelve staff, comprising 203 Germans and six Austrians. The hospital has 20 cases that day. The many occupations of the internees were mentioned in a very positive report. On the second visit, in September 1917, Lt Butcher in command, overseeing 222 Germans and ten Austrians. A skittle alley was being built which, it was stated, would be greatly appreciated. There were 23 patients in the hospital ward. (FO 383/276 and FO 383/277)

This was the last internee camp remaining, after Frith Hill had been closed in September, Knockaloe in October, and Islington on 17 November 1919. On 23 December 1919, Captain A P J Armstrong, upon termination of his appointment as Commandant, submitted a list of 83 inmates remaining at Libury Hall, including eight women and four children. Home Office papers recognised that almost all the men were old or infirm, and many of them, exempted from repatriation, preferred to stay where they were. They were not fit to look after themselves and if sent out would, for the most part, have drifted into the workhouse. They were less expensive where they were, until some new arrangements could be made. During the period of internment 32 had died and were buried in the churchyard of Little Munden.

At some point after the war, date not discovered, the Trustees found it impossible to continue the colony, and it was handed over to the Society of Friends for Foreigners in Distress. Today Libury Hall is a home for elderly people.

This account has, to a large extent, drawn upon two Home Office files in The National Archives at Kew: HO 45/11006/264762 and HO 45/11025/410118, and files of the Police Committee Reports and Minutes held at the Hertfordshire Records Office.

Commandant's cachet, used as a censorship mark, 32mm diameter

Lofthouse Park, Wakefield, Yorkshire West Riding

Civilians, until October 1918, then Officers

Grid Ref: SE 334 253

Lofthouse Park, 3 miles north of Wakefield, on east side of the A61 road to Leeds, was developed in 1907-08 as an amusement park, said to be the first of its kind in Britain, on 60 acres around the Hall, which had been built in 1801 by the Dealtry family. The main pavilion, along the lines of a similar structure at Great Yarmouth, (largely of timber construction) provided a stage and auditorium, grill room, cloakrooms and administration offices. There was an orchestra alcove from where music could be provided for dancing, in the auditorium or outside, according to the weather. A conservatory, of iron and glass construction, was added where refreshments were available. The venture was initially successful but, after only a few years, the novelty wore off and the place was closed at the end of 1913. To the east of the site an airfield was laid out, where Blackburn Aircraft were first built and flown.

The Howden and Derwent dams had been built in the Peak District between 1902 and 1912 by the Derwent Valley Water Board. The War Office was a major buyer of the temporary buildings from the labour camp at Birchinlee, which had housed the workforce for these dams, and those timber and corrugated iron buildings were moved to Lofthouse Park as the initial accommodation for the internees. Macpherson recorded that it opened in October 1914 as an officers' camp with accommodation for 874 officers and 250 servants, but that is incorrect for it began as a civilian internment camp and was larger. It only became a PoW officers' camp in the autumn of 1918.

The Times 24 October 1914, reported about 1,000 German prisoners were being lodged at Lofthouse Park, and on the same day *Liverpool Daily Post* stated that about 150 were sent there from Manchester. It was all they could take. However, either *The Times* figures were an exaggeration or many must have been released or transferred for, on 13 February 1915, when Mr Jackson of the American Embassy visited the camp, there were only 225 on the roll. He reported that more huts were being built to expand the capacity, that the kitchens were good, and staffed by Germans. Inmates, who preferred pork, complained that beef was served every day. Most of those held at the camp had lived in Britain for some time so visits were allowed by their wives, many of whom were British by birth. Three patients were in the hospital. This was the briefest of the reports of the February 1915 visits. (HO45/10760/269116)

Two escaped on 28 May 1915; Frederich Weiner, age 35, (who had been brought from Edinburgh on 29 April) and Alfred Klapproth, 30, (who had been moved from Donington Hall on 24 April, lately an officer of the Hamburg-America line). The *Police Gazette* on 1 June, carried a notice of their escape together with a portrait of Weiner, and that was repeated on 18 June. At the end of the month a report of their arrival in Copenhagen was published (*The Times* 2 and 29 June 1915). They were the first of five that managed to get out of Britain during the war.

On 14 June 1915 the US Embassy made a second visit. The report described the camp as three compounds, each of which had a library: The South compound held 486 internees in 15 huts, with a gymnasium, a hospital with 50 beds, and a dining hall. The Winter Garden, part of the original buildings, was used by tailors as a workshop. The North compound had 503 men in 23 huts, one hut was the Post Office, another a canteen. All internees in that compound paid extra for better food. A recreation hut was being built, meanwhile a YMCA tent had been provided. The West compound was a new extension of the camp with 221 men in 15 corrugated iron huts. 26 of these men paid extra, but the remainder, who had come from Dorchester, could not afford the extras. Two huts were provided for recreation (763.72114/689). Lofthouse Park was a 'privilege camp', where internees who could afford it, paid for better food and less crowded sleeping accommodation. Later in the war they were even allowed to erect small huts for their exclusive use. The Swedish Legation reported, in August 1918, that the huts cost between £20 and £30 each. (FO383/360)

Cohen-Portheim wrote that he moved from Knockaloe in mid-1915. He described Lofthouse Park as a large estate with fine old trees surrounding the house, a simple Georgian mansion, which was the abode of the

Commandant. He described the three sub-camps each holding about 500 men: South Camp, where the hall stood, *pleasantly irregular and untidy*; North Camp, regularly planned, *wooden huts in serried rows and a corrugated iron hall*, on flat ground; West Camp, on sloping ground, the latest and smallest, with corrugated iron huts, *a treeless, grassless, sandy waste*. The canteen had a much better variety of goods than he had seen available in the Isle of Man.

He defined Lofthouse as a 'Gentlemen's Camp' where men could pay ten shillings a week towards a better diet. They were also allowed to draw up to £3 a week from the camp bank, whereas £1 had been the limit in Knockaloe. The inmates built paths, planted shrubs etc, and built a tennis court. Huts were divided into rooms, and furnishings were acquired or made. He commented that, in 1917, men who could afford to purchase and erect small private huts were permitted to do so in South Camp. Food rationing came into force when the Germans declared 'unrestricted submarine warfare' and as a result, parcels from friends in England were forbidden and parcels from Germany or Austria were scarce as rationing applied there also.

In May 1916 a serious breach of security occurred and a Minister was questioned in Parliament. An internee by the name of Hitner had apparently obtained, by post, samples of pocket lamps, and then ordered and received 2 dozen of them. (*Hansard HC* 15May16, vol.82, col.1112)

The US Embassy visited again on 8 June 1916, when the commandant was Major E T Lloyd (late Agra Volunteers), vice Lt Col F S Low, away sick. There were 1,447 internees, of whom 1,322 were Germans, 122 Austrians and three Turks. No serious criticisms of the camp arrangements were made, but as two camps were higher than the third, water shortages were noted if the gardens and tennis courts were being watered in the lower compounds. *We found the camp in a very much better condition than it was at the time of our previous visit on 16 March*. It appears from the report that one problem had been the under-foot conditions, but in June everything was dry, and promises were made that cinders and slag would be provided to improve pathways etc. (Cd.8324)

From October 1915, lectures by internees were held. At first *ad hoc*, but in 1917 more formal arrangements were made, with Freiburg University in Germany, so that courses could be accredited. However, in the event the University declined to accept the course-work after the war. Early in 1918, exchanges of some internees were arranged, and these included the Principal and about half the lecturers, unfortunately disrupting the timetables. The 'Camp College' officially closed in March 1918, although some courses continued until May. Wakefield Library holds a copy of the balance sheet and accounts of the 'Camp College' dated 15 May 1918. Unofficial courses began again in September 1918 and there were plans to recommence full courses in January 1919, but by then all the civilians had been moved to the Isle of Man.[10]

In February 1918, when the Swiss Legation inspected the camp, Lt Colonel G S Haines was commandant (previously at Newbury, Stratford and Jersey). 1,430 were present, of whom 180 had been noted for repatriation on grounds of their age, and eight patients had recently been repatriated from the hospital. (FO 383/432)

In June 1918, the German Government alleged bad conditions at Lofthouse, in particular that the camp was divided into compounds by wire fences! The reply was given that it was proposed to close the camp and move the internees to the Isle of Man (FO383/419). However that move did not take place until after another inspection by the Swiss Legation on 12 and 13 September 1918, when Lt Colonel Archibald H T Rouse (late Indian Army) was in charge. The population was then:

	North	South	West	Total
German	312	327	278	917
Austrian	26	41	35	102
Turkish	-	4	2	6
Totals	338	372	315	1,025

A patent letter-sheet, written on 2 October 1918, paid 1½d, addressed to Bradford, included the message: *We have just received information that our camp will be transferred to Knockaloe on Tuesday next*. On 10 and 12 October all the civilian prisoners were transferred to Camp IV at Knockaloe, where a privilege section was established. A *Note Verbale* from Berlin, dated 16 December, was delivered which complained about the removal of the internees to Knockaloe at 3am on 14 October. The German Government alleged that when the first order to move was published on 12 October, no limitation on the

---

[10] Ibs Dr.H: *Herman J Held 1890-1963* (trans Sharp) extract held in Wakefield Library

amount of baggage was stated but, when they came to move, a limit was imposed on the heavy baggage which meant that books and personal furniture had

Some of the small private huts in the South Compound

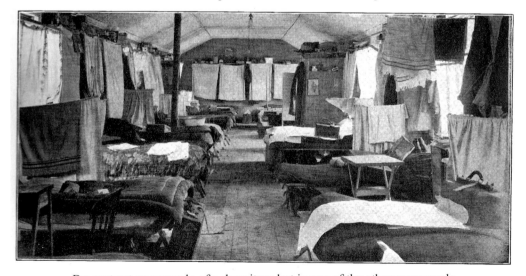

By contrast an example of a dormitory hut in one of the other compounds

had to be left behind, along with provisions and vegetables growing in the gardens. Dogs were not allowed to travel, although there were dogs already at Knockaloe. Upon arrival at the Isle of Man most hand baggage was confiscated and had not been returned. (FO383/505. The discrepancies in the dates cannot be explained.)

The following week, on 19 October 1918, Lofthouse Park became an officers PoW camp and within a week, the first escape was reported. Not actually from Lofthouse, but by a prisoner being moved to the camp. Heinz Heinrich Ernst Justus, who had made attempts to escape from other camps, jumped from a train at South Elmshall, 6½ miles southeast of Wakefield, on the line from Doncaster. He was being brought from

Holyport in a party of fifty. He got rid of his uniform by posting it, together with his Iron Cross, in a parcel to the Commandant at Holyport. He walked back to Doncaster and travelled to London by train. There he caught an infection, probably influenza, but later went on to Cardiff, hoping to get on board a neutral ship in dock. He surrendered to the Police when he became too ill to stay on the run. He was returned to Lofthouse Park and recovered with good medical treatment. He was then sentenced to 56 days at Chelmsford and received back his uniform from Holyport. Justus wrote of his various escapes in "An Unconducted Tour of England" [11]

There were 400 officers and 120 orderlies in the North Camp and 452 officers with 132 orderlies in West Camp when the Swiss Legation visited on 22 February 1919. Graf von Budingan was the senior officer in North Camp, while Major Schulze was senior in West Camp. It was reported that the gates between the two camps were left open. No mention was made of South Camp not being in use, but that was where internees had been permitted to erect their own private huts.

During 1919 *The Times* reported five escape attempts involving seven officers. In June 1919, after the German High Seas Fleet was scuttled at Scapa Flow, some of the naval officers were sent to Lofthouse Park, while the others went to Oswestry. Those at Lofthouse wrote a long letter of complaint, on 2 July, about their treatment at the sinkings and subsequently on board British Battleships (FO 383/508). Most of the PoWs were repatriated in October and November 1919, but the crews from Scapa Flow were not released. Officers at Lofthouse, and those from Oswestry, were moved to Donington Hall in November.

The Times 13 November 1919, p9f, reported that an escape tunnel had been frustrated, and that twenty naval officers, ex Scapa Flow, were involved in the scheme. Their 'navigator' must have miscalculated the distance, for a guard noticed a surface collapse just outside the wire. It seems likely that this report was of an incident of a week or so before, because the last letter written at Lofthouse Park, North Camp, by a German naval officer, was dated 4 November and numbered #15, while his first from Donington Hall, #16, was written on 8 November.

The Times 8 May 1920, advertised the sale of huts and materials on 25, 26 and 27 May. In 1921 there was an attempt by businessmen to revive the amusement park but the place was burnt out in April 1922. In the 1930s it became part of a brickworks and later an engineering depot of the local council.

Other Sources:
Walling J: "Held - Prisoner at Lofthouse Camp" in *Mitteilungsblatt 50* (Anglo-German Family History Society) Dec 1999
Wood PI: "Lofthouse Park", in *Aspects of Wakefield*, ed Taylor K (1998)
— "The Zivilinternierunglarger at Lofthouse Park" in *Aspects of Wakefield 3*, ed Taylor K (nd)

Camp Bank cachet
37 x 23mm

This Camp Bank cachet has been recorded on the back of an OHMS envelope, posted 25 March 1918, to London. The smallest of the Camp cachets (see below) has been recorded on receipts given to internees for money received by remittances and credited to the internee's account.

---

[11] First published in *Escapers All,* The Bodley Head Ltd, London 1932, republished 2004 in *Tunnelling to Freedom.*
The Times 26 October 1918, has an inaccurate story, for the escape described there was an earlier bid for freedom by Justus from Colsterdale

Christmas 1915 greetings sent from Lofthouse Park to a lady in St Gallen, Switzerland.

Postcard written at La Paz, Bolivia, 24 January 1917, to an internee at Lofthouse Park.
The censor removed the added adhesive postage stamp, in case there was a message
written beneath it, and marked the space with the common encircled P.C.

Frame: 46 x 16mm

28 x 15mm

35 x 26mm

27mm diameter

Outer rims strengthened

33mm diam. 33mm diam.
Small star Large star

Lofthouse Park appears to have the largest number of different censor cachets. As there were three compounds, this writer has surveyed a number of covers to see if any of these cachets could be associated with a particular compound, but the result was negative.

Carter and Brown recorded two camp cachets, which this writer has not seen used on mail or other documents, but a smaller cachet has been seen used on receipts for remittances to internees:

70 x 40mm 50 x 29mm 36 x 23mm

Margate, Kent

Officer Reprisal Camp   Grid Ref: TR 356 709

Five camps were opened in the Spring of 1918 to hold German Officer PoWs in towns liable to Zeppelin or aircraft bombing. *The Times* 16 March 1918, p6c, stated that this was in retaliation for the Germans moving British prisoners near to the battle lines, but in July the British Government denied this and the other four were reprisal camps. This denial, dated, 26 July 1918, was made in a reply to a request for information by the Swiss Minister (FO 383/440). Nevertheless, Farquharson, p384, did list them as 'Reprisal Camps (Officers)'.

Macpherson wrote that the camp opened on 20 March 1918 and he described the building as a "house", but in fact it was Margate College buildings, about 200 yards from the harbour. Wilde, in his history of the college wrote:

> It certainly took the enemy a long time to dislodge Margate College [commenting on bombing raids] and it would seem this was achieved only by providing so many prisoners of war that the school buildings had to be requisitioned for the purpose of housing them. The boys were moved away from Margate in 1917 to new premises at Hale [between Farnham and Aldershot] and captured Germans were installed in the old school. A relic of the visitation remained in the building right up until it was bombed in 1940. Some Teutonic artist had carved into the wall of Dormitory IV the words *Gott Strafe England*.[12]

The prisoners came from Sandhill Park Officers' Camp, near Taunton, and the senior German officer was Captain Fischer. (FO 383/432)

Mr Joynson-Hicks [Unionist, Brentford] asked, in the House of Commons, how many German prisoners there were at Margate College, how many German servants waited on them, how much the cork carpet had cost, and how many pianos had been sent in for their use.[13] Mr Macpherson, the Under Secretary at the War Office, replied on 7 May (after enquiries), that 80 German officers and 25 other ranks had been interned at Margate. Similar numbers had been sent to Southend and Ramsgate. They had been in their new homes about a month. No expense had been incurred on account of carpets or floor coverings, as none had been provided. There was no dug-out in the garden and prisoners were not allowed to walk on the promenade. Officers had made local arrangements to hire a piano. All the officers had come from Sandhill Park and that camp had been closed temporarily. In their letters, prisoners were allowed to mention their move, but not the buildings in which they were housed. There were other batches of German officers in English places considered subject to air bombardments.

On 10 January 1919 *The Thanet Times*, p3, reported that the German prisoners at Margate College had been evacuated on Monday morning 6 January. Officers and servants, totalling 104, had entrained at Margate West station shortly after 9am and their special carriages were attached to the 10.13 up train, en route for Oswestry.

---

[12] Wilde, Laurie A: *A Short History of Margate College 1873-1940*, no date, no ISBN, no pub., p28

[13] *Hansard HC* 11 April 1918, vol.104, col.1667, and *Isle of Thanet Gazette* 20 April 1918.

Newbury, Berkshire

Civilians and PoWs   Grid Ref SU 484 667

Newbury racecourse had opened in September 1905. The War Office took compulsory possession early in the war, which put an immediate stop to horse racing at this venue. The prisoners lived in the horse boxes - a similar situation to Ruhleben - and also in tents. This writer believes that the Germans used Ruhleben racecourse from November 1914, as a direct response for the British using Newbury from the previous September.

Newbury Weekly News, Thursday 3 September 1914, ran an account of the arrival of the South Midland Mounted Brigade, the previous Sunday and Monday (August 30-31). While these Yeomanry troops were encamped on the centre area of the racecourse, arrangements were being pushed forward, at the stables, for a detention camp for German PoWs.

The next edition of this weekly paper reported the arrival of the first three Germans on Friday 4 September, followed by 150 on Saturday and more each day, so by Wednesday the total was about 600. Most were civilians and reservists arrested in this country, but there were six PoWs, one of them an officer. The racecourse had 145 horse boxes, each taking seven men, so there was room for about 1,000, but barbed wire enclosures were being erected where tents or huts would be used to expand the camp.

The Commandant was Lt Colonel Gregory Sinclair Haines (b1858, retired 1913) who had previously commanded military Detention Barracks and, later in the war, was in charge at other camps. His office was in the Weighing Room, his deputy was Major R E Firminger and the Adjutant was Lt H H Bacon. The Guard, under the command of Captain Harding, were named by the paper as 'Lancashires', but they were soon relieved by National Reservists.

Western Morning News, of 15 September, reported that about 100 men, taken from German vessels, recently brought into Falmouth, had left by train for Newbury, while the local Newbury paper reported on 17 September that there were then 1,300 prisoners including Uhlans, sailors, stokers, spies and suspects. By the 24th, the prisoners numbered 1,400, and were in two sections. Nearly 1,000 were in the stables, still guarded by the 'Lancashires', while a compound established on the northern side of the course, with tents, held mostly aliens liable for military service, and was guarded by 'Berkshires'. The 'Lancashires' departed at the end of that month, for Plymouth.

On 10 October, 386 civilian internees were removed to the Isle of Man. Their journey by train took them to Fleetwood and then by TSS *Duke of Cornwall*. They landed at Douglas and then marched two miles to the camp. New arrivals at Newbury included first class passengers taken from a German ship and 60 soldiers in uniform. A further 400 civilians were sent off to Douglas on 14 October and that cleared the 'lower camp'. The paper stated that Newbury was then to be used solely for the reception of PoWs (*Newbury Weekly News* 15 October 1914). However, that idea was soon reversed.

While more German combatant PoWs arrived almost daily during the second half of October, the Government's move to arrest all German and Austrians, of military age, resulted in civilians also being brought to Newbury. By early November, about 3,000 were held there.

The first death reported at the camp was of an Austrian, Jacob Hock who's funeral took place at Greenham on 23 October.

Newbury Weekly News 19 November, reported that the Yeomanry, camped on the racecourse, had departed. They had gone to Norfolk. The reporter also understood that the detainees in tents were to be moved to ships off the south coast. On 3 December the paper stated that the canvas compounds had been cleared and men were then being moved from the stables to the ships. The next edition stated the camp was to be closed forthwith. A War Office letter, 20 December 1914, to the Foreign Office (in FO 383/34), confirmed closure of the camp.

When the US Embassy inspected the ships in February 1915, it was reported that civilians from Newbury, then on SS *Canada*, were pleased with their transfer (but see below), and Mr Jackson commented that he was informed that Newbury had been closed 'for some time'.

Yorkshire Evening Press, 1 December, p3, reported an item in the *Norddeutsche Allgemeine Zeitung* which expressed dissatisfaction with an American report on Newbury (not seen by this writer). The York paper went on to say that it did not follow, from the report, that the German complaints were unfounded, as it did not report on the Commandant and his relations with the PoWs, nor deal with inadequate arrangements of the camp and the resulting abuses. The German views of the conditions at Newbury were reported to the Cabinet (CAB 37/123/37). Among the points made in the German press were: men were housed in stables, eight to a stall; straw was not changed for two months; no opportunity given to air the blankets; and the food was bad. However, *The Times* correspondent, on 30 October, had painted a rosy picture.

The Times 8 February 1915, carried an article, by an Austrian, previously at Newbury, which countered German reports of atrocities there. The man, then on parole, wrote that he was at Newbury from 25 October until 13 December. He described the stables and two tented compounds, with 4,000 prisoners there. He also mentioned the hierarchical arrangements of 'seniors' and 'captains', elected by the inmates, for the internal administration. He wrote complimentary remarks about the running of the camp. He declared that the food was good and sanitary arrangements were adequate. He concluded with a remark, heard on the decks of SS *Canada*; *If we only could go back to good old Newbury*.

A B Thomas wrote, pp46-47:
> The prisoners were housed (as at Ruhleben) in horse boxes, in each of which from six to eight men lay side by side on straw. Here too there was neither heat nor light, the prisoners being locked up at sunset until next morning ... deep mud prevailed throughout the camp ... after some months the camp was closed ... as soon as the camp in the Isle of Man was finished.

This was not quite accurate, for although some civilians were moved to Douglas during October, Newbury continued in use and more civilians and military prisoners arrived. The camp was eventually cleared to the ships in December. Panayi was also mistaken when he wrote, p63, that although the War Office was conscious of the poor conditions, and intended to close the camp before the onset of colder weather, it remained open until the beginning of 1915. Official papers show that In fact it was closed in mid-December 1914.

Horse racing resumed in March 1915. The War Office ceased its occupation on 6 April 1916 and the Ministry of Munitions took over certain areas, but they did not interfere with racing up to August 1916. After that meeting the Ministry took over the whole racecourse for tanks, and they did not release the area until early in 1919. (Osgood F: *The Story of Newbury Racecourse*)

Camp cachet

44 x 30mm

Carter and Brown both illustrated a similar handstamp with COMMANDANT'S HOUSE around the top and dated 14 SEP 1914. This writer has not seen such a handstamp and wonders whether a poor strike of the instrument shown here had been mis-read.

The Commandant's office was in the Weighing Room of the racecourse.

Oldcastle, Co Meath, Ireland

Civilians

Irish Grid Ref: 2555 2805

This was the Oldcastle Workhouse, built in the 1840s, demolished in the 1950s. Oldcastle is 71 miles northwest of Dublin and in 1914 it was described as a small market town with a population of less than 700. This figure was almost doubled by the internees and their guards.

Major Robert Johnston VC, (1872-1950) late Royal Inniskilling Fusiliers, won his VC at Elandslaagte, during the Boer War, was Commandant. He had joined the Irish Prison Service in 1911 and was appointed to Oldcastle with the temporary rank of Major on 10 November 1914. From 1915 he was Governor of Maryborough Prison (per *Who's Who* entries), but he was still at Oldcastle in July 1917.

Mr Jackson's report to the US Embassy of his visits to camps in February 1915 stated that he did not go to Oldcastle ... *because of the time such a visit would require.* Meanwhile a statement in Parliament reported 304 enemy aliens were interned in Ireland (*Hansard HC*, vol.69, col.260, 8 February 1915).

The American Embassy did visit in June 1915. The report described 26 dormitories, in two blocks of stone-built buildings, housing 435 Germans and 99 Austrians. The hospital ward, in a detached building, had no patients. There were four recreation yards and two playing fields, each about 2 acres. Route marches, lasting 2-3 hours, for about 100 men at a time, were allowed. Some of the internees were captains or officers of merchant ships, who had individual rooms or shared two or three to a room. Two theatres and organised classes were mentioned, but no manual crafts were organised, other than tailors and bootmakers who had set up workshops. (FO383/33)

During 1915 and early 1916 a few escapes were reported, but none got far before they were arrested. In August 1915 two ship's officers, Carl Marlang and Alfons Grien, were believed to have got away disguised as women, but when apprehended one of them was dressed as a clergyman. A week later it was reported that Charles Fox had been charged with aiding two PoWs to escape. (*The Times*, 13, 14 and 21 August 1915)

When Mr Lowry of the American Embassy visited on 10 June 1916, there were 579 prisoners, all civilian except one naval officer. Of these 468 were German, 110 Austrian and one 'other nationality'. They were divided approximately equally between those who were living in Ireland before the war and merchant seamen taken off ships in Irish ports. Ships' captains and officers had separate rooms and a separate mess. The men had dormitories, the largest sleeping 30. Again there were no patients in the hospital and no deaths were reported. Major Johnson was named as Commandant. (Cd.8324)

The Times 22 September 1916, reported an escape. One, named Bockmeyer, was shot in the attempt. His colleague, Kreuz, got away but was recaptured. Another escape, by Ehlers, and his recapture was reported by the same paper in August 1917.

A paper in FO383/284 dated January 1917, stated that Dr Theodore Lenders #741, was to be held at Oldcastle for at least two months. He had come from India, via South Africa, and sailed from Cape Town on 26 December 1916, on SS *Briton*. His eventual return to Germany was delayed further by the suspension of sailings by the Dutch ships.

The Swiss Legation inspectors visited the camp on 26 July 1917. Major Johnston was still in command. As this was their first visit, the situation was described quite fully. 494 civilians held, of which 398 were German, 95 Austrians or Hungarians and one other. Dormitories had from 4 to 23 beds. The hospital ward had 31 beds, but only five patients on the day. There had been no case for the isolation ward up to that time. Serious cases were sent to the King George Hospital in Dublin. Up to the end of 1916 two had died at the camp and four had been removed to the Mullingar Asylum, but there had been no deaths nor cases of lunacy during 1917. (FO383/277)

In May 1918 all the internees were moved from Oldcastle. *Isle of Man Examiner*, Saturday 1 June 1918, reported the arrival of 500 aliens by steamer from Dublin on Sunday night (26 May) and their transfer to Knockaloe by train. Rumour of their impending arrival from Dublin had prompted speculation among the Manx population that they would be Irish Nationalists. Such speculation is understandable, for on 17 and 18 May a number of leading Irish Republicans had been arrested in Ireland and removed to prisons in England, under suspicion of a treasonable plot.

Hansard HC, 3 June 1918, vol.106, col.1250, recorded a statement that, for reasons of economy, it had been decided to close down Oldcastle, and transfer the internees to the Isle of Man.

The London Gazette, Supplement Friday 2 October 1914, listed 115 enemy vessels detained in British ports. Among those, only four were listed at Irish ports, all German ships:

ship	tonnage	detained at
Excelsior	1407	Berehaven
Odessa	3046	Berehaven
Senator Dantziger	164	Tralee
Terpsichore	2025	Limerick

These four vessels seem unlikely to provide the numbers alluded to in Mr Lowry's comments about half the 579 internees being taken off German ships at Irish ports when he inspected in mid 1916. Some additional seamen may have been added to the numbers during 1915, having been landed from vessels of other nationality. Another possibility is seamen being transferred from ports in Great Britain.

Camp cachet 49 x 30mm   Camp cachet 44 x 21mm   Censor cachet 36mm diam.
All three of these markings have been seen on a number of examples of mail to internees

Olympia, London W

Clearing station for civilians Grid Ref: TQ 243 790

An undated Home Office Report, written at the end of the war, stated 'internment of enemy subjects commenced at the beginning of the war with some 200 suspects who were interned at once at Olympia and at Frimley'. (HO45/11025/410118/2)

The Times 14 August 1914, reported that the number of German prisoners at Olympia showed a marked diminution, in spite of constant fresh arrivals. The well-to-do, arrested the previous week, had explained themselves and had been released. *A miscellaneous collection of German suspects remained*, many of them were sailors taken from ships detained in British ports. The report continued with a description of the conditions in the large hall, where the men were confined, which in August was quite hot because of the steel and glass construction of the building. *The prisoners are enjoying every comfort and recreation compatible with their position.* Their food was provided by *a well-known firm of contractors*.

By 25 August, *The Times* was able to state that there were less than 100 held at Olympia.

The Home Office Report, mentioned above, referred to circulars being sent to the police in September and October 1914 which led to 20,000 being interned. Olympia was listed as one of the places used. As examples: *The Times*, of 18 October, reported that twenty waiters at the Vienna Café, in New Oxford Street, were arrested and sent to Olympia. The following Saturday, the same paper stated that nearly 1,000 were arrested in London on Thursday, and slightly fewer on Friday. 500 had been moved to Frith Hill from London, also on the Friday.

Liverpool Daily Post, 24 October, mentioned serious overcrowding at Olympia. Therefore aliens were being detained in Police Stations pending men being moved out from Olympia, allowing others to enter for processing. The Home Office Report recognised that accommodation for the increasing numbers being interned was a problem, and in November steps were taken unilaterally by the War Office to release about 100 men from Olympia.

The buildings were apparently needed by the Government for other purposes, but exactly what purpose has not been discovered. Soon the internees were moved away to other camps or released, for when Mr Jackson began a tour of inspection of camps, on 28 January 1915, he was told that Olympia had been closed for some time (HO45/10760/ 269116). Envelopes from Olympia post-marked up to 25 November 1914 have been recorded by this author.

A German report on the camps described Olympia as "dismal". (CAB 37/123/37)

At the end of March 1915 the last of the Belgian refugees at Alexandra Palace, some 300-400, were moved to Olympia (*Hornsey Journal* 3 April 1915). This might be the alternative use alluded to above, but it is known that Earl's Court buildings were used over a long period to accommodate Belgian refugees.

Camp cachet 36 x 23mm.
Most mail was struck with this mark and then passed through the POWIB receiving their cachet also.

Oswestry, Shropshire

Officers, Other Ranks and Hospitals

Grid Ref: SJ 310 315

Park Hall, 1½ miles northeast of Oswestry, was a large, fine, Elizabethan timbered mansion dating from the late 16th century, with later additions. Mrs Wynne Corrie had purchased the estate in 1871, but she died in 1913 as a result of the lift, which she had had installed in the house, crashing to the ground while she was in it. An obituary appeared in *The Times* of 23 June 1913.

The south aspect of Park Hall, Oswestry
(from an old print)

In 1914 the Army took over the estate. The Hall became the Officers Mess. At Christmas time 1918, the mansion was badly damaged by fire. After the war the Camp Hospital was rebuilt and it re-opened in 1921 as an orthopaedic hospital. The camp itself was closed after WWI, but the area was taken over again by the War Office in WWII. Park Hall Camp and Park Hall West Camp postmarks are recorded from 1915 to 1919.

Macpherson recorded that the Other Ranks' camp opened in April 1918, with huts for 10,000 men, and the Officers' camp in September 1918 for 1,800 officers with 450 servants. The hospital also opened in September. The January 1919 POWIB list showed five locations for PoWs at Oswestry: Officers Camp, Eastern Camp, Western Camp, P/W Hospital, and Park Hall Hospital. Ruge (p127) gave details of what he saw: Camps E1 and E2 were tented camps for several thousand NCOs and men. E3, E4 and E5 camps each held about 500 officers in barrack huts.

On 3 July 1918 the local paper *Border Counties Advertiser* (abbreviated to *BCA* hereafter) recorded the death of a German PoW, Alfred Burkind, at Park Hall PoW Hospital, of a wound sustained in action. The 20 November edition of the same paper reported a fire in the generating station at Park Hall. Temporary lights were fitted up, but they were said to be poor substitutes.

The Swiss Legation inspected the officers' camp, on 1 December 1918 when the Commandant was Lt Colonel F G Waddington (Sherwood Foresters). The first 46 officers had arrived on 18 September and on the day of the visit there were 575 officers present with 146 orderlies. Hauptmann Fritz Baldamus, 46th Infantry, was senior German officer and Dr Konrad Teicher, 19th Bayern Infantry, was the senior German medical officer. The accommodation was 28 huts, each for 20 or 21 officers, three ablution sheds with latrines, a bathhouse with 20 showers and three dining huts each sitting 90. Conditions under-foot were not good, so duckboards and ashes were supplied. Also in this report Colonel Turner RAMC (not definitely traced, but probably William Aldren Turner) was mentioned as Commandant of the Oswestry Hospital. (FO383/506)

The Times 28 December 1918, carried an account of the fire, which destroyed a large part of the Hall and the next edition of the *BCA*, 1 January 1919, p6, stated that after the fire, some PoWs assisted in moving the furniture and fittings, which had been rescued from the mansion during the fire, into the remaining section.

In 1919 *The Times* reported three escapes: Vincent in January, Lt Screinuller in March and Waldhausen in April. Meanwhile on 17 February 1919, Kegworth officers' camp was closed and those prisoners were moved to Oswestry. Lt Colonel Picot also moved from Kegworth to become Commandant at Oswestry.

BCA 12 March 1919, reported that the War Office was considering converting the army camp into a permanent base for both infantry and artillery. However, the correspondent observed, the scheme could hardly proceed until the 12,000 PoWs, then present, had gone home. The next week the paper stated that the Demobilisation Centre, at Park Hall, had been closed, but in fact it continued, at least for a while. In the 9 April edition an account was given of 'advance parties', totalling 350 officers and men of the 42 Division arriving, and that fifty PoWs were detailed to assist with unloading the trains. In fact these were not advance parties, they were the Divisional cadre, returning from France after most of the men had been demobilised.

When the Swiss Legation visited Beachley on 31 March 19, their report indicated that camp would soon close and the PoWs would be transferred to Little Fern Hill. Similarly, when Shrewsbury was reported on, on 24 April, it was stated that the camp was to close in May and the prisoners would be shifted to Oswestry. (Both reports in FO383/507)

The Swiss Legation visited Oswestry on 26 and 27 April 1919, when they reported that the camps had grown considerably since their previous visits. The description was:
- West Camp: four compounds, about 5,300 present, capacity 5,600.
- East Camp: compounds, 1 and 2, about 2,700 present.
- Officers' Camp: 'known as East Camp' compounds 3, 4 and 5, over 2,000 present.
- Hospital: 1,600 beds
- Two large canvas camps, known as Little Fern Hill and Henlle, close to Gobowen railway station, not then occupied, but were intended to receive transfers from Shrewsbury, Beachley and other, smaller centres.

Lt Colonel Picot was in overall command and Commandant of the officers' camp. Lt Colonel Bertie Cunynghame Dwyer-Hampton DSO, Leicestershire Regt, (b.1872) commanded the soldiers' camps. Their main camp had been a British army training facility. The compounds were open during the day. No electricity was available following the fire in the generating station, so oil lamps were used (see *BCA* 20 Nov 18 above). The hospital was under the charge of Major William Parker RAMC. At the previous visit in December, all 1,600 beds were occupied, but at this inspection there were only 340 patients, including 40 officers, of whom ten were Austrians. In the officers' camp conditions had not been satisfactory, as it was equipped at very short notice, but this report noted that it had been much improved under Colonel Picot. (FO383/507)

German sailors, from scuttled fleet at Scapa Flow, arrived by train at Gobowen on Tuesday 24 June 1919. Admiral von Reuter, the commander of the fleet, went to Park Hall Camp, while the seamen and officers went to Henlle (*BCA* 25 June 1919). Henlle is 3 miles northeast of Oswestry and about 2 miles from Gobowen station by road. Ruge (later an Admiral in the German Navy), p126, confirmed they de-trained at Gobowen and marched for half-an-hour to reach their camp. He was one of four sub-Lieutenants among some fifty officers to go to Compound E5.

A week later three German officers were escorted into Oswestry, by car, to exchange a quantity of German paper money, but the Bank Manager refused to take it. Word of their visit got around the town, and on their return journey they were assaulted by a woman, who struck out, and a youth, who threw a cabbage (*BCA* 2 July 1919). Admiral von Reuter was soon moved to Donington Hall with his Flag Lieutenant. This provoked questions in the House of Commons, complaining that the Admiral had been met by car on arrival at Oswestry, and was escorted by the Commandant when taken by car to Donington on 3 July (*Hansard HC* 7 July 1919, vol.117, col.1394).

A German PoW, Willi Oster, was shot dead during disturbances at camp E1 on 12 July. Officers in the adjoining compound were reported to have been throwing parcels over the fence to the men. The sentry shot at random, to drive away PoWs who were throwing stones at him. Oster was hit when on the roof of a building retrieving a parcel. A verdict of misadventure was returned at the Coroner's Court (*BCA* 16 July 1919). Ruge wrote that an officer threw bread over the narrow gap between the compounds, which was forbidden. In protest against the shooting the PoWs 'went on strike', ie they refused to attend parades, so the guard was called out with fixed bayonets to drive the prisoners out of their huts. This incident was reported in a letter published in *Hamburger Nachrichten*, and subsequently picked up by the British press. (eg *BCA* 13 August 1919, p5)

It was believed by the camp staff that the PoWs plotted to burn down their huts. Therefore the German officers were summoned to a meeting with the Commandant, who told them that, if anything should happen along such lines, no replacement accommodation would be provided (*BCA* 23 July 1919). This conflicts with Ruge's impression that the seamen were in tented camps, and he made no suggestion of such a plot among his fellow officers.

Henlle Camp was closed on Sunday 26 October 1919, and Fernhill Camp was scheduled to close in the following week. The German PoWs were reported to be going away in batches of a few hundred (*BCA* 29 October 1919). Fernhill is about ½ mile west of Henlle and about one mile north-east of Park Hall. *The Times* 17 November 1919, stated that the German seamen had been moved to Park Hall Oswestry (presumably the main camp) after they had dismantled the camps at Henlle and Fernhill.

At this point local and national newspapers appear to overlook the continued presence of 1,640 German sailors. The local paper, on 26 November 1919, reported, *Now that all the German PoWs have been sent home, the guards have been dispersed and their magazine 'On Guard' is suspended until the next war.* Two days later *The Times* also ignored the seamen from the German fleet, when it reported that 20,000 PoWs had been repatriated from Oswestry and that the property was to be sold the next month. If Macpherson's figures of camp capacities, 10,000 men and 1,800 officers, were correct, there was either a mistype, or an exaggeration by the reporter. Alternatively, it is possible that Oswestry had latterly been used as a transit camp.

However, the next day *The Times* did mention the sailors remaining in camp after the general repatriation. The officers had been moved to Donington Hall and the sailors were put to work to clear up the old camps. They became discontented and refused to obey orders, so the guard turned out with fixed bayonets and work resumed. The local paper (*BCA*) on 3 December, carried a similar story, but it stated that the camp authorities had responded by withholding rations, and that the PoWs had made an appeal to the British public (but it is not clear how that appeal was made). This report of the hunger punishment reached the German press but *The Times*, of 9 December, carried a denial of the matter.

Towards the end of November two unnamed prisoners escaped, and a report of both being re-captured locally was carried in the local paper of 3 December 1919. Another escape, by Paul Simon who was recaptured at Harwich, was reported by *The Times* of 15 December.

Right at the end of their time at Oswestry one the sailors, Stoker Johann Beck, committed suicide by taking morphia on 24 January 1920. At the inquest it was stated in evidence that *while at Henlle Camp he often took morphia to induce sleep* (*BCA* 28 January 1920). We must assume he had access to the hospital dispensary in order to obtain the drug.

The 1,639 sailors were moved by train, on 29 January 1920, from Oswestry to Hull where they joined their officers, who had travelled from Donington. At Hull they embarked on two German steamers for their return to Wilhelmshaven for repatriation. (*The Times* 30 January 1920, p9e)

An advertisement in the *BCA* of 4 February 1920, for the sale of effects from Park Hall Camp, including huts, posts, duck-boarding, timber, barbed-wire etc., indicated that a chapter of local history was drawing to an end.

The final act was reported in both national and local papers in April; the departure of the last PoW from Oswestry. He was not named, but it was stated that he was a U-boat commander, who left for Scotland under escort. No further details were published, so it is not clear why he was so late in being released. It seems most likely he had been ill in hospital when the others were released at the end of January.

109 PoWs died at Oswestry and, as from other camp sites, their remains were removed to Cannock in the 1960s.

Only one cachet has been recorded to date, and that was by Brown, not seen by the current author, but others should exist.

Camp cachet 51 x 29mm

Eastcote, near Towcester, Northamptonshire, later named Pattishall.

Civilians until July 1916
Other Ranks from Spring 1916

Grid Ref SP 678 542

This camp was originally called Eastcote, but from late 1916 or early 1917 the name Pattishall was used. Eastcote is a settlement to the east of, but within, the parish of Pattishall, close to the A5 road, seven miles southwest of Northampton.

At the outbreak of the war, Eastcote House, with 60 acres, was being purchased, from a Mr Gresham, by the National Sailors' and Firemen's Union of Great Britain and Ireland with the intention of using it as a retirement home for their members. The Union begged the Government to allow the premises to be used for the internment of German merchant seamen, members of their Union, who had been put ashore by British ship owners. The Government agreed, and up to 1,000 were held there, watched by the local constabulary, and under the overall control of the Home Office. The house could not accommodate such numbers so at first tents and a marquee were used, which were later replaced by wooden huts erected in the grounds.

The camp was initially run by Joseph Havelock Wilson (1859-1929), General President of the National Union of Seamen. He lived in the house, until the War Office took over. He had helped found the Union in 1887, was an MP from 1892. For his obituary, see *The Times* 17 April 1929.

Northampton Mercury 25 September 1914, reported that fifty men at the camp, guarded by the police and Boy Scouts, were making preparations for others, expected within a few weeks, when there would be up to 1,000 men there. Towcester Rural District Council was concerned about water supply and sewerage. A week later the same paper mentioned that the dining hall and assembly room was a large marquee, and that the sleeping quarters were bell tents. On that same day, *Northampton Herald* stated that two German doctors, then interned elsewhere in the country, would be transferred to Eastcote to serve in the hospital being fitted out in two cottages.

At the end of October Alfred Stockhurst escaped from the camp and was arrested at Fosters Booth (a mile west of the camp, a cross-roads on the A5). When he appeared before the Magistrates at Towcester, on a charge of escaping, he told them that he wanted to join the British Army. Two weeks later about 20 German internees were removed from Eastcote. They were held briefly at Northampton Prison, then taken by train to Frith Hill. (*Northampton Mercury,* 30 October and 13 November 1914.) On 5 January 1915, *Northampton Daily Echo* reproduced the text of a letter dated 17 November 1914, which had been published in the German press, praising good treatment at Eastcote.

Mr Jackson's report, of 27 February 1915 for the American Ambassador, stated *inter alia*, that he did not visit Eastcote, but a Home Office paper a week before mentioned 240 men interned at the camp. A Foreign Office file included reports of a number of inspections in May 1915 but again Eastcote was not visited. Meanwhile, a letter of 5 March from the National Sailors' and Firemens' Union stated the cost per man was 11s.7d per week, that 700 were present, but there was room for a thousand. (FO 383/33 and HO 45/10946/266042)

Good relations with the Union were shattered in the aftermath of the sinking of SS *Lusitania* on 7 May 1915. The German seamen celebrated the event, which went down very badly with the British Trade Unionists. Soon after there was a visit by Members of Parliament, and a report appeared in *The Times* on 15 May 1915. 779 were held there at that date under a "commander" who appeared to be responsible neither to the Home Office nor the War Office. Nine constables guarded the place. An un-named escaper was mentioned. He was recaptured after three months when working on a British collier supplying the Royal Navy.

On 20 May, Havelock Wilson offered the house and land to accommodate up to 5,000 or even 6,000. The War Office agreed, on 1 June, to extend the camp to 5,000 at their expense and later wrote to the Home Office explaining that the War Office would take over the camp under DORA. The question of compensation to the Union would be referred to the Defence of the Realm Losses Commission (HO45

/10946/266042). Considerable expansion of the camp was planned, with a complete water supply, drainage and sewerage system being installed. A hospital and other facilities were to be built. The accommodation was enlarged to hold up to 2,000, as a first stage.

In August 1915 three un-named prisoners broke out and when arrested they were taken away to 'a military camp near Crewe' (the nearest PoW camps to Crewe were Leigh and Handforth. Leigh was entirely a PoW camp, while Handforth held only civilians at that time, so seems more likely). The following month the escape, and recapture at Northampton, of Wilhelm Wetzel and Herman Yarus were reported. (*Northampton Mercury* 13 August and *The Times* 14 September 1915.)

In December 1915 all the prisoners were moved, to Alexandra Palace, while the Eastcote camp was being rebuilt and enlarged (FO383/162). The date of the return trip has not been discovered but a visit by the US Embassy on 2 February 1916 shows the internees were not away for long. The report of that visit named the Commandant as Lt Colonel J H Annesley.[1] 660 civilians were present, of which 60 were Austrian. There were 4 compounds, each with 5 dormitory huts (200 beds each), but only one compound was in use at that time. The compounds covered 4 acres and there was a field of 9 acres. Part of one hut was the infirmary, with sixteen beds, and it had 15 in-patients that day. A new hospital was being built, and when completed the camp would come into full use.

At the next visit, 11 April 1916, there were 1,559 prisoners; 705 German soldiers in one compound, and 749 Germans and 105 of other nationalities in the civilian compound. The report mentioned that buildings for workshops and a theatre/hall were almost complete, but the hospital although built had not then been fitted out. 19 in-patients were in the temporary ward. *The prisoners in this camp do not seem inclined to do much work.* (Cd. 8324).

The civilians were moved out in July 1916, but no specific report of their move has been found to date. This then became a camp for combatant prisoners only, still called Eastcote. In September there were 1,447 Germans and one Austrian PoW, of which 33 were sailors. Some were away working in forestry camps, 131 at Woburn, Bedfordshire, and 167 at Panshanger, Hertfordshire. The hospital had two wards, each of 38 beds, and an isolation ward of 8, staffed by two doctors, one Sergeant and four men, all of the RAMC, with two German attendants. 37 in-patients and 38 out-patients, non serious, were noted that day. There had been two deaths – one of heart disease (a civilian) and one of meningitis. Route marches, for 300 men, were permitted four days a week and physical drill for one hour daily. The prisoners had created a pond on a stream which flowed through the recreation ground. The theatre/concert-hall was then complete and in use. Fahnrich von Schweinichen (see Woking Gaol) was one of the delegation reporting to Mr Brantingham the US inspector. No serious complaints were made, but Red Cross men, as usual, wanted to be exchanged, more hot water was needed, and better lighting was requested as the evenings were getting shorter. No one was in the cells. (763.72114/2074)

On 11 and 12 May 1917, the camp was visited by Dyke Acland MP and Colonel Charles Anstruther (late Life Guards). In their report the camp was referred to as Pattishall; this is the first occasion traced for the change of name. They found *2 or 3 men in the cells* who had been before a Court Martial that morning. They had escaped and were caught in Suffolk (not traced). The report, in FO383/276, was dated 16 August 1917, so it is not surprising that the authors could not remember how many men were in the cells three months earlier!

The Swiss Legation inspected the camp on 16 May 1917 and their report also called it Pattishall. The Commandant, since April, was Lt Colonel O'Donnell Colley Grattan DSO, late Liverpool Regt, b.1855. 2,043 were present; 1,994 soldiers and 49 sailors, all German. Three were in the cells. The report mentioned two large huts in each compound for dining and recreation. The infirmary, with 36 beds and a 10-bed isolation ward, had 33 in-patients with old wounds, splinters, or amputations not yet healed. One death was reported since January and six cases had been removed to an asylum since the camp opened. Twelve work camps were listed where 1,600 men were employed. The inspector called for the amputees, 42 with one leg, 27 with one arm, one man with only one leg and one arm, with others from Handforth, and those with shattered jaws who could not eat properly, to be brought together in one place where they could be better looked after by German Red Cross men. (FO383/276)

---

[1] Wrong spelling. He was John Henry Ansley, late N Lancs Regt. He was correctly named in the April 1916 report. In Nov 1917 he was Commandant at Leigh.

In September 1917, seven prisoners escaped; their surnames were given as: Ball, Gitzen, Harte, Kerst, Muller, Schultz and Schulte. The whole group were recaptured at Denton, 6 miles southeast of Northampton and 10 miles from the camp. (*The Times* 1 and 3 September 1917)

When the Swiss Legation visited on 23 October 1917 there were 3,493 present, of which 42 were sailors. Previously there had been complaints about inadequate diet but the nutrition was judged satisfactory at this time, following the addition of 4oz vegetables and 4oz potatoes daily. There were 42 patients in the hospital, mostly surgical cases following wounds. 4 deaths since 1 June 1917 were reported. (FO 383/277)

In April 1919, when the Swiss Legation visited (the last inspection of this camp traced), there were 4,509 present. Horseflesh was stated to be on the menu. There were 12 patients in the hospital. Pattishall was then a parent camp for 161 working camps, employing 14,537 men. 1,500 of those at Pattishall were awaiting transfer to France as labourers. (FO383/507)

The Times 11 August 1919, reported the escape and recapture of Schulby, but he was named Heinrich Schultz in *Northampton Mercury* of 15 August. Was this the same Schultz, one of seven who got out in September 1917? He was charged with burglary of a house at Castlethorpe (10 miles SE of the camp), near to where he has apprehended, and committed to the Quarter Sessions (*Northampton Mercury* 29 August 1919). No subsequent report has been seen, but he may have been released before his case came up.

A letter written from Pattishall by Herman Schroder, a soldier, on 8 September 1919, to his parents near Soltau, mentioned that PoWs were no longer being sent to France as labourers, as the cost to the British Government was too great. He also wrote that the sick and disabled had nearly all been released at that date and that three letters a week were now allowed, on Monday, Wednesday and Saturday. Whilst no mention of this relaxation of the number of letters has been seen in official records, the letters of Lt Edmund Beutter, at Holyport, do bear out this statement. He wrote ten letters (sequentially numbered 421-430) to his parents between 12 September and 5 October.

Northampton Mercury 28 November 1919, reported a case of theft of blankets and unserviceable clothing. In evidence, Mr Darnell, appearing for the defence, said *inter alia* 'there are no Germans at the camp now'.

During the camp's five years of use 31 inmates died, 24 of them in 1918 and 1919, mostly due to the influenza epidemic. A full list of the burials was published in *Pattishall - a parish patchwork*.

No camp or censor cachets have been recorded for Eastcote or Pattishall, but an interpreter's initials handstamp E.L.S. (boxed) has been seen on a letter addressed Trieste.

In February and March 1920 the sale of huts and building materials was advertised. *Northampton Independent* 14 August 1953, reported: 'The dining hall from Eastcote was re-used in 1925 as the garage of Abington Motors Ltd, in Wellingborough Road, Northampton. Previously it had been a Palais de Dance.'

Letterhead used by Alfred Bremer, No. 1390, on 6 November 1914, for his letter to Germany.

An International Red Cross postcard, naming the camp Pattishall, formerly Eastcote, showing the water-wheel, which drove the merry-go-round.

A group photo, sent undated by Joseph Müller, No.5376 and Julius Bölle, No. 3123, from Pattishall, undated, to Germany in an envelope.

Queen's Ferry, Flintshire

Civilian camp, but some soldiers are recorded

Grid Ref: SJ 324 683

Note that the 1914 *Bartholomew's Gazetteer* showed this town as two words 'Queen's Ferry', to distinguish it from Queensferry, North and South, by the Forth Bridge, in Scotland. The Post Office also adopted this spelling.

The camp was a disused engineering works of Williams & Robinson, at Chemistry Lane, between Queen's Ferry and Sandycroft, on the south shore of the River Dee, and about 5 miles west of the centre of Chester. Previously the plant had produced water-tube-boilers for the Navy but that production had been moved to Rugby. The site was requisitioned by the War Office soon after the outbreak of war.

The first report found of the movement of prisoners to Queen's Ferry was in *West Sussex County Times* of 13 August 1914, which said 200 prisoners were removed from Christ's Hospital School to Chester Castle (Queen's Ferry?) by train, and corroborated by *The Chester Chronicle* of 15 August which reported that 500 had arrived at Queen's Ferry on Tuesday evening (11th) by three special trains. An escort of Lancashire Fusiliers marched them to the camp where Colonel Thomas Alured Wynne-Edwards, late 4 Royal Welsh Fusiliers (b.1855) was Commandant. The guard was initially provided by the Cheshire Regt, under Captain William Arthur Vere Churton (b.1876, a solicitor, who at the end of the war was a Lt Colonel, with a DSO, and three MiDs).

The next week *The Chester Chronicle* said four hotel waiters from that city were arrested and conveyed under military escort to Queen's Ferry. It also stated that there were 600-700 prisoners at Christ's Hospital, Horsham, and that *numbers of them were being sent to the concentration camp at Chester*. There were then about 1,000 at Queen's Ferry. The same newspaper, on 5 September, reported that 200 Royal Welsh Fusiliers had replaced the guard of the Cheshire Regiment, and that there were then about 1,500 internees.

Liverpool Daily Post, 22 September, recorded that 200 Germans gathered from Queen's Ferry, and other camps in England, were moved to the Isle of Man (they went to Douglas) from Liverpool in SS *Tynwald*.

However, this did not do much to relieve pressure at this camp for *The Chester Chronicle*, on 26 September, reported over 2,000 present and that despite the accommodation being taxed to the utmost, a further 200 had arrived on 24th. The camp was also named as 'Sandycroft'.

On 14 October, Chandler Anderson and Chandler Hale, officials of the US Embassy, inspected the camp and reported to their Ambassador. This and two other camps were chosen as *representing the only types now in use*. Their comments were general to the three camps with no specific criticism. Complaints referred merely to the irritation of capture and confinement. Some claims of Red Cross immunity were lodged with the inspectors. The report was published by *The Scotsman* on 13 November.

A reporter from *Birmingham Daily Post* visited the camp and gave his impressions in the edition of 26 November 1914. 2,200 were interned, including soldiers, officers and men of the German merchant marine, clerks, hotel staff and others. The reporter seems to have been impressed by the organisation and regulations. One prisoner had died of heart failure, and two had been transferred to a hospital outside the camp.

A letter from some detainees at Queen's Ferry, dated 1 January 1915, complained that they were destitute and requested their salaries from the German Colonial Office. 243 of them had been deported from West Africa, including 49 from the Cameroons, one from Togoland, three military officials from Cameroons and two Post Office employees.[2] Kavanagh, pp46-47, stated that the effects of Germans captured or interned from the Cameroons and other German dependencies were stored in the basement of the British Museum.

---

[2] FO 383/32.
Later a letter from the US Embassy 18 August 1915, to an internee at Lofthouse Park, explained that the German Foreign Office had stated that their Colonial Troops were not entitled to receive pay from Colonial funds during their imprisonment, so no advance could be made.

When Mr Jackson, of the US Embassy, visited on 10 February 1915, there were 2,200 civilians and a small number of soldiers held. He commented, *The general atmosphere of this camp was the most depressing of all those I visited*. Little had been done to improve the original poor conditions. The buildings, an old machine shop, were divided into two compounds. The glass rooves had many leaks. The floors were stone or cement. No separate accommodation for better class men was available, but some had built 'tents' around their beds to protect against leaks and draughts. The prisoners seemed listless and not inclined to improve matters. There were no work opportunities. Washing facilities were limited and the latrines insufficient. New kitchens were being built, the existing one was dirty and inadequate. Two deaths in the camp were reported, and one outside after surgery. The sick quarters were full and there were complaints about having to wait for treatment. Many cases of venereal and other contagious diseases were noted. There was no library and the exercise ground was small. *Much money would be needed to put this camp into good condition*. Complaints were made about sausages and cigars, received by mail, being cut open to look for contraband (see also the report on Knockaloe which was visited the day before), and that only one hot meal was served each day. Beer had been allowed, but one of the 'Captains' got drunk, so the privilege was withdrawn. Some older sea-captains were present, and other older men were detained as possible spies. Some from Africa had similar complaints to those on board ships off Ryde (*qv*).[3]

When the delegates from the International Red Cross visited the camp early in 1915, they recorded about 2,000 prisoners, in twelve rooms, holding 100 to 200 men each, and heated by radiators. The diet was standard but there were complaints that the food was insufficient and that margarine had been substituted for butter. However, purchases could be made at the canteen. As with Holyport camp, the men from West Africa complained of the loss of their baggage and money. Religious facilities were provided, in part by an internee, a German pastor who had sailed for Africa just as war broke out. A catholic priest visited from time to time and pastor Scholten had made two visits. They noted the difficulties of running a camp with such a diverse collection of men, from many different areas and walks of life, which would need firm management.

The Chester Chronicle 3 April 1915, speculated that the German prisoners would be removed from the old works at Queen's Ferry and the buildings, which had been purchased by the Government, would be utilised for other purposes in connection with the war. Two weeks later the paper published a rumour that a 'well-known Midland firm of manufacturers' had acquired the premises. Colour was added to the rumour as many detainees had left recently and the paper supposed they had gone to the Isle of Man.

The Times of 25 April 1915 reported on an unofficial inspection by MPs. It was stated that the prisoners had a band which played in fine weather as they walked about the compound. If that is all they had to say, it was clearly a very superficial investigation. No report on this visit has been seen in *The Chester Chronicle*.

In May 1915 the compounds were cleared and the prisoners were transferred to Alexandra Palace, but six of their number did not make that journey, as they had developed mental problems and had been removed to the North Wales Asylum at Denbigh. The American Embassy report, of 21 May 1915, on Alexandra Palace, confirmed that the first to arrive there, on 7 May, had come from Queen's Ferry, which had been abandoned. (See also *Flintshire County Herald*, 21 May 1915.)

The names of three who died during the eight months of the camp's existence, and buried at Howarden Old Cemetery were:
 Captain Friedrich Segelken, 16 November 1914
 Julius Pekukes (age 52), 6 March 1915
 Hugo Haedler (age 23), 8 April 1915.
Mr Jackson also mentioned three deaths but his report, dated 27 February 1915 predates two of these funerals.

---

[3] HO 45/10760/269116. In contrast a Swiss official, Col. Schindler, who visited on 20 December 1914, described conditions as 'rather comfortable' (FO 383/107)

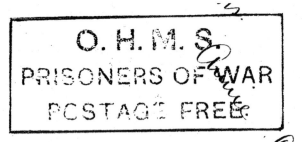

Postage Free cachet 68 x 27mm,
seen used on inland mail during September 1914.
(A similar marking was used at Lancaster)

Camp censor cachet
39mm diameter

Back of a cover, flap gone, showing handstamped marking:
Place of Internment, / Prisoners of War, / Queen's Ferry,

Postcard written 19 December 1914 at Baja, in Hungary, to Mathias Kleinert at Queen's Ferry. Censored in Vienna. An additional postage stamp (to make up the foreign rate) was removed by the censor in London. Marked *released* when delivered to the camp.

Isle of Raasay, Inverness-shire

A working camp, under Stobs.　　　　　　　　　　　　　　　　　　　Grid Ref: NG 555 356

Although this was a labour camp, so outside the general run of this study, its unique function and because its history has been well researched, by others, makes it worthwhile including as a chapter.

A deposit of iron ore prompted William Baird & Co, of Coatbridge, to purchase the island of Raasay in 1911, and work began on the infrastructure required to mine, treat and ship the ore. By the outbreak of war the pier was built, kilns erected, railway laid etc but, owing to the local men joining the forces, mining operations could not begin.

In 1916, with the threat to British shipping from the submarine campaign, local ores were looked to, in order to reduce the need for imports. The Ministry of Munitions proposed that the work force required for mining should be provided by PoWs. In January 1916, Baird's offered to supply a Motherwell steel works with 50,000 tons of pig-iron, beginning at 3,000 tons per month in May 1916, providing they could secure PoW labour. It took some months to persuade the government that PoW workers would be in order (the Foreign Office was particularly against the idea) but eventually the proposal was accepted, on the basis that the Baird Company would run the mine on behalf of the Ministry of Munitions, while the War Office would provide the 200 PoW labourers required.[4]

The first PoWs reached Raasay by early June 1916, and their numbers had increased to 100 by July, at which point the Scottish Command enquired when the further 100 would be required. Draper & Draper believe that the first batch of 18 prisoners were sailors from SMS *Blücher*, but they were soon withdrawn for fear they would escape by boat. The maximum number of PoWs on the island was about 260 but some have suggested higher figures. The Baird Company records indicate 250 Germans and 60 British workers in April 1917. Macpherson, p153, recorded 253 prisoners at the camp, of which 94 were miners, while the others worked at the pit mouth, at the pier-head, and on camp duties.

Draper and Draper showed an interesting photograph of PoWs posing on a Bucyrus steam drag-line during the course of its erection, while a Scottish soldier carrying a rifle, with bayonet fixed, stands guard. They also showed a splendid picture of the PoWs band, complete in lederhosen.

The Company had built housing, intended for their workers, and part of that was fenced off as living quarters for the PoWs. 32 two-roomed cottages in the PoW compound, indicate that eight or nine men lived in each unit, assuming one or two cottages would be used for messing, sitting rooms etc. The guard, staff, infirmary, etc occupied cottages in the adjacent section. The guard was commanded by Captain K G MacLeod, Gordon Highlanders, a noted athlete, who had been wounded in action. The Quartermaster was QM Sergeant Skea of The Royal Scots, who had survived the Gretna rail crash in 1915.

One prisoner, Paul Sosinka, died in an accident in December 1916, another, Georg Kagerer died (cause unknown) in May 1917. Twelve others died in the influenza epidemic of early 1919.

An outbreak of scurvy occurred in June 1917, affecting 82 men, which was attributed to poor diet, due to overcooking their food. This was cured by changing the method of cooking. It appears that calorie counts were almost the only concern of the medical authorities - vitamins, minerals, fibre, etc., were not mentioned in any of the reports on the diet,[5] although it was vitamins that were destroyed by the overlong cooking.

There were a number of escapes but none managed to get away from the island. When arrested or surrendered the escapees were sent to Woking Detention Barracks to serve their sentence and they were not replaced.

---

[4] Draper & Draper, *The Raasay Iron Mine*

[5] Macpherson WG et al: *History of the Great War ..... Medical Services, Hygiene of the War*, vol.II. This was not the only case of scurvy among PoWs. In FO383/431, a Swiss Note, dated 16 January 1918, referred to scurvy in No. 92 PoW Company in France.

In 1917 and early 1918 there was industrial unrest. Trade Unionists complained that the PoWs, by being paid less, were taking jobs from British workers. They also complained that the local population was being denied use of land by the prisoners' sports ground. Questions were asked in Parliament. Many of the allegations were quite false, but eventually the British employees on the site did receive a substantial increase in wages.

Production from the mine was nearly 30,000 tons of ore in the second half of 1916, nearly 66,000 tons in 1917, rising to 88,000 tons in 1918.

As a result of the Armistice, the Government sought to terminate their contract with the Baird Company as quickly as possible, and took steps to achieve this by 21 December. Three months notice of termination was required and the agreement was ended on 30 April 1919. A Home Office document found in ADM1/8506/265 stated that the camp closed on 21 March 1919. There is no indication as to where the PoWs were transferred, but it was probably back to Stobs

This author is pleased to acknowledge the research of Lawrence and Pamela Draper, who published a prize-winning study *The Raasay Iron Mine, where enemies became friends.*

Ramsgate, Kent

Officer Reprisal Camp   Grid Ref: TR 381 653

This was one of five reprisal camps opened in the Spring 1918 to hold German officers in areas liable to Zeppelin or aircraft bombing. *The Times* 16 March 1918, stated this action was taken in retaliation for the Germans moving prisoners to areas near the battle lines. However, on 26 July the British Government denied that this, and the four others, were reprisal camps, when they replied to the Swiss Minister who had requested information (FO383/440). Nevertheless, Farquharson, §384, did list them as: 'Reprisal Camps (Officers)'.

Macpherson gave the opening date of this camp as 2 April 1918, with accommodation for 120 officers and 35 servants in a "house". However, the building was in fact Chatham House School, in Chatham Street, Ramsgate. The pupils had been evacuated to Gloucester in 1916, so it would appear that the buildings were vacant in the Spring of 1918 when the War Office decided to move in. The prisoners were brought from Sandhill Park, near Taunton.

The Times, 20 January 1919, p5c, reported that an Austrian officer Friedrich (no other name) was taken off a Norwegian ship *Dicto*, at Deal, as a stowaway, along with two Russians. The report stated that he was being sent to Ramsgate as an escaped PoW. The incident was also reported in *Thanet Times* of 24 January 1919, p3.

A typewritten Home Office document dated April 1919 (in ADM 1/8506/265 120667), gave the date of closure as 19.2.1918. This was probably a typographical mistake, either 2 for 12, or 1918 for 1919. On the basis of the report of a PoW officer being sent to Ramsgate in January 1919, mentioned above, it appears that 19 February 1919 is the more likely date of closing. So far, it has not been possible to discover any report of the departure of the PoWs from Ramsgate, nor of their arrival at, nor the whereabouts of, their new abode. However it is known that officers from Margate were sent to Oswestry when moved from that camp.

Redmires, Sheffield, Yorkshire West Riding.

Officers' Camp   Grid Ref: SK 275 860.

This camp was on Lodge Moor, overlooking the Rivelin Valley, 5 miles west of Sheffield and about half-a-mile east of the Redmires reservoirs of Sheffield Corporation Waterworks. The camp area is 1,000 feet above sea level. A correspondent has informed this writer that a horse racing course was planned before WWI, but he was unsure whether any racing was actually held there. However, the name Racecourse Farm is found to the south of the camp site. In the 19th century it was within a gunnery exercise area for the Sheffield Artillery Volunteers.

The camp was shown in some detail on the 1920 provisional edition 6" OS map, and traces of the foundations of buildings can still be seen today, southwest of the Sportsman Inn, in pine woods which now cover the site. Part of the site, and adjacent land to the west, was used during WWII for another PoW camp. Whether the traces of occupation date from WWI or WWII is not clear.

The first wartime occupants of the camp were the 12th Battalion, The York and Lancaster Regiment, which was raised by the Mayor and City of Sheffield on 5 September 1914, and they moved to Cannock Chase in May 1915 (James p100). They were followed by 16th Battalion, The Sherwood Foresters (the Chatsworth Rifles), who were at Redmires from June until September 1915, when they moved to Winchester in the 117 Brigade (James p87). Other units are recorded in Sheffield, but whether at Redmires is not known.

Macpherson wrote that the camp had room for 650 officer PoWs with 156 servants (with provision for guards and staff, the total would approximate the numbers for a British infantry battalion). The camp opened on 8 October 1918. This date was confirmed in a report of an inspection by the Swiss Legation on 22 January 1919. The Commandant was Lt Colonel Ernest Cooke, b.1856, late Scottish Rifles. At that visit there were 501 German and four Austrian officers, with 156 orderlies, present. Eight patients were in the hospital ward. Daily walks for 2 hours were permitted for 100, escorted by a British officer. (FO383/505)

Sheffield Daily Telegraph 19 October 1918, reported that Emile Franke, a PoW from Redmires, was admitted to Firvale Hospital suffering from gunshot wounds. He and two others, who had been engaged in preparing the camp for PoWs, had got out at night to steal potatoes and turnips. The two not wounded were remanded for one week and were named by the paper, in the following week's edition, as Karl Braun and Richard Kummeth, when charged with stealing potatoes from Soughley Inn Farm. The charges were withdrawn at the Police Court and the prisoners were handed over to the Military authorities.

The Times, 7 February 1919, p5d, carried a small item that Lt Plessing had escaped from Redmires and was recaptured at York.

No camp cachet has been recorded for Redmires.

No mention in newspapers of evacuating the camp has been found, but in March 1920 the huts and other buildings were sold by auction.

Ripon, Yorkshire North Riding

Officers & Other Ranks   Grid Ref: circa SE 294 724

Ripon was a major garrison town for much of the war. North and South Camps are known and maps in Ripon Library shows how extensive they were, but the actual location of the PoW compounds is not known, the Grid reference given above is the centre of the known barrack area.

The Book of Ripon, p107, records that in the first month of the war navvies arrived to build camps, which soon spread over three sides of Ripon from Littlethorpe over Red Bank to Studley Roger and Coltherholme, ie clockwise from southeast to northwest. Early in 1915 parts of the camp were ready, and the first soldiers to arrive were 15 West Yorkshire, the Leeds Pals, who had been at Colsterdale (*qv*). It was said that in 1917 there were 70,000 soldiers at the camps, many of them Scottish third line battalions. At the end of the war South Camp, Ripon, was a major reception centre for British PoWs released from imprisonment or internment. The first to arrive, on 17 November, were the Royal Naval Division men from Groningen.

Macpherson wrote that the PoW camps were opened in October 1918 (but *The Times* reported an earlier escape) with hutted accommodation for 720 officers with 216 servants, and an ORs camp for 1,200 men. No camp cachet has been recorded so far, but a distinctive censor mark is known. No.3 Camp was for the officers, while No.8 North Camp was for the Other Ranks but, as stated above, it is not known where they were, precisely.

The Times 18 March 1918, p5b, reported the escape of six officers from Ripon; Frank Kaars, Augustus Hiller, Rudolf Schneider, Lorenz Hellselder, Helmuth Reinavorss & Fritz Spraub. This is a puzzle for according to Macpherson the camp had not opened at this date. Colsterdale was not far away and it could be from there that the escape was made. No mention has been found in *The Times* of their recapture.

On 13 January 1919, p5d, *The Times* mentioned that two crewmen from Zeppelin *L33*, who had got away from Ripon, were recaptured at Hull, and that a U-boat officer, named Boedt, had escaped.

On 25 February 1919 the Swiss Legation visited the officers' camp where they recorded 675 officers, with 219 orderlies, living in concrete huts. The Senior German Officer was Major Claus of 86th Reserve Regiment. The Commandant was Lt Colonel H Sturgis (not traced). It was noted that there had been no influenza at the camp. (FO383/506)

It was reported by *The Times*, 4 June 1919, that the camp had been vacated, but whether this was the soldiers' camp, or the officers' camp, or both, is not clear. This is quite early for the closure of a major PoW camp and too early for repatriation. If the report was correct, the PoWs must have been moved to other camps, but no report of arrivals from Ripon have been traced. The letter-sheet shown below, from a soldier, is dated after *The Times* report of clearing the camp.

Part of a letter-sheet sent from No.8 Camp North, Ripon, on 29 July 1919 to Birmingham, thanking the addressee for a cheque for £4.10s.0d.
Note: the unique P.C.RIPON. handstamp, 25mm diameter, tying gummed slips, and that the postage stamps were added after censorship. Ripon Camp postmarks are known from 1915 to 1919.

Sandhill Park, Taunton, Somerset

Officers' Camp   Grid Ref: ST 156 299

Sandhill Park is 5½ miles northwest of Taunton and 1 mile west of Bishops Lydeard. It had been the nominal home of Sir Wroth Periam Christopher Lethbridge, 5th Baronet, (1863-1950). He had served in the Grenadier Guards and retired in 1903, but rejoined his regiment in 1914 as a Captain and was appointed Deputy Assistant Censor to BEF in 1914. Later he served in a Divisional Base Depot, also in Egypt, and as a member of the Military Mission to USA in 1918.

The Lethbridge family had acquired the estate in the mid 18th century and the 4th Baronet had become deeply involved with iron mining on the Brendon Hills, and the early steel industry in South Wales. These ventures nearly bankrupted him in mid 19th century. Hence the estate was let for much of the later part of the 19th and early 20th centuries, but it was unoccupied in the years immediately before WWI (per *Kelly's Directories*).

On 29 June 1915, two companies of Army Service Corps soldiers, about 600 men, arrived at Bishops Lydeard under the command of Lt S G Spoor. They were Mechanical Transport units officially numbered 344 and 345 Companies ASC MT. Within three weeks, the Bell Inn, in the village, had to be placed out of bounds to soldiers from Sandhill Park. They departed in September (*Somerset County Gazette* 3 and 24 July, and 18 Sept 1915) and the next occupants were 130 men and several hundred horses, which suggests the place had become a Re-mount Depot. Their arrival and departure dates have not been discovered.

Macpherson gave the opening date as a PoW camp as 26 March 1917, for 400 officers, but the local newspapers indicate an earlier date. *Wellington Weekly News*, 20 December 1916, reported that 'a batch of German prisoners, under guard, were brought to Bishops Lydeard where preparations had been in progress for accommodating PoWs at Sandhill Park'. The article went on to speculate whether the PoWs were officers or men, and called for all prisoners to be put to work on farms etc.

The following month, Mr G G Stevens claimed compensation of £150 for 17 weeks occupation of a house by the War Office, which had been requisitioned as a reception unit for German prisoners. (The location of the house was not stated and has not been traced.)

Despite this new use of the premises, the estate was put up for sale early in 1917. On 10 February 1917 the *Somerset County Gazette* reported that Lot 1, the mansion and 19 acres, occupied by the War Office and housing PoWs, had been offered at £6,000, but was unsold. The auctioneer remarked that he was not surprised there were no bids. Twelve of 20 other lots found buyers.

When the Swiss Legation inspected the camp at Dorchester, in March 1917, their report included a list of the dependant work camps and among them was Sandhill Park. However, no clue as to the numbers of men, nor the nature of their work has been found. Indeed, when the Swiss visited Sandhill Park on 25 May there was no mention of a work camp, only officers. At that inspection Lt Colonel Harrison Midwood, (b.1857, late Highland Light Infantry, retired 1907) was Commandant, Dr Edward Frossard, the local GP, was medical officer, and Lt E C M Hart was censor. There were 138 army officers, eight naval officers and 56 orderlies, in all 202, of whom one was Austrian. 31 rooms were used as dormitories with two to ten beds per room. Lighting was by oil lamps and heating by coal fires. The water supply was inadequate for full bathing facilities. There was no fire escape from the upper floors, but one had been ordered. To ease overcrowding a number of huts were being erected. Part of the 2-acre exercise area, outside the wired perimeter, was used on parole terms. Route marches for up to 40 were permitted, also on parole terms. There had been several cases of influenza and bronchitis, but no deaths were reported. Complaints concerned over-crowding, poor bath facilities, the want of a larger sports field, high prices in the canteen and the need of religious services. (FO383/277)

In May and June, the local papers carried items about the German officers at Sandhill Park, their rations, exercise walks outside the grounds, and car journeys to Taunton to visit the dentist. There was local demand for the PoWs to be confined to the grounds at Sandhill

Park and for their diet to be less luxurious. At a public meeting at Bishops Lydeard, to discuss food economy, speeches were made against the prisoners being able to buy extra food at their canteen. There were also letters to the editor on the same lines (*Somerset County Gazette* 26 May and 2 June 1917). All these allegations were denied.

On Saturday 25 August 1917, Lt Block and 2Lt Hertzog escaped. They were arrested at Toller Down, near Evershot, in Dorset, the following Tuesday, and returned to Sandhill.[1] In October three men of 255 Protection Company, Royal Defence Corps, (the camp Guard) were charged with stealing three chickens and a turkey. No doubt they hoped to fatten up one of them for Christmas.

Somerset County Gazette, 19 January 1918, reported the death of a Prussian Guardsman, Wilhelm Hellmich, aged 26, who had been employed as a butcher at the camp. It appears he had a throat cancer, which was successfully operated on, but he choked when using a throat-wash. A verdict of misadventure was returned at the inquest. He was buried in the parish churchyard. This was also reported in two other local newspapers but was not mentioned in the Bishops Lydeard parish magazine.

Early in 1918 there were more articles about the 'fine food' supplied to the PoWs compared with the foodstuffs available to the local population. Allegations about luxury foods going to Sandhill Park were denied by Dr Frossard.

In March 1918 the prisoners were moved from Sandhill Park to newly established Officer Reprisal Camps at Margate, Ramsgate and Southend-on-Sea, towns vulnerable to Zeppelin and aircraft bombing raids. This prompted the local MP, LtColonel D F Boles, who lived in Bishops Lydeard, to press for PoW men to be sent to the camp as agricultural labourers (*Somerset County Gazette* 4 May 1918). While no specific report of soldier PoWs being sent to Sandhill Park has been found, they clearly did come and they lived in tents.

The meeting of the Somerset County Council War Agricultural Committee, on 20 August 1918, received a letter from the Food Production Department stating that it had been decided to reopen Sandhill Park for German Officer Prisoners. The Committee instructed their Executive Officer to see that accommodation at the Prisoner Ploughman Depot at Sandhill was not given up until suitable alternative premises were found. This Depot housed 55 prisoners who lived under canvas. The Committee had a real problem in finding alternative accommodation for these soldiers, for every time they nominated a property, the owner objected, successfully. The War Office sent instructions, that all canvas camps had to be struck by 31 October, but still the Committee had no place to re-house these PoWs. Eventually they decided to use the Taunton Workhouse and the men were moved there on 21 November. This did not please farmers living in the Bishops Lydeard area, who complained of the inconvenience of having to go the 5 or 6 miles into Taunton to collect a team of labourers. (Minute Books of the War Agricultural Committee in Somerset County Records)

The officers' camp was reopened on 29 August, according to a report of a visit by the Swiss Legation on 24 November 1918. At that inspection there were 304 officers and 81 orderlies present, nearly double the previous head count. Some of the officers and all the orderlies slept in huts on the south side of the house. Other huts, on the north side, accommodated the staff and guards. The report (in FO 383/505) made no mention of any soldiers, other than the orderlies, so it is possible the 'Prisoner Ploughmen' were in a separate area of the park, but it is not clear.

To add confusion, a report on a work camp at Marshmoor Sidings, South Mimms, Herts, on 18 March 1919, stated that of 210 prisoners there, most had come from Sandhill Park. A statement that does not easily reconcile with the 55 mentioned in the Minutes of the Somerset War Agricultural Committee. However, the *List of Places of Internment* prepared by the POWIB in January 1919 included both an officers' camp and a work camp (under Dorchester) at Sandhill Park.

At some stage it was proposed that Sandhill Park should be the camp for Austrian and Hungarian officers. Most of these officers were captured on the Italian Front near Asiago in June 1918 and in the last battle in that area, Vittorio-Veneto, 24 October to 4 November 1918. However, it was the Spring of 1919 before about 300 new prisoners arrived. None were German, but three Roumanians, from Transylvania, were in the party. They did not stay long for the Roumanian Embassy requested their release, and they joined the reconstituted army in their country.

---

[1] *Somerset County Gazette* 1 September 1917, also reported in *The Times* 27, 29 and 30 August.

A postcard of Sandhill Park. The message reads:
23/1/18 ... what do you think of this little hut for the poor Huns ...?

The Commandant was again Lt Colonel Midwood, the Adjutant was now Captain EA Brandon (late Quartermaster, Cheshire Regiment) and the Medical Officer was still Dr Frossard. The guard numbered 150 NCOs and men.

The Swedish Legation visited the camp in May 1919 when there were 237 officers and 74 soldier servants, all Austrians and Hungarians. About 200 of the officers had come from camps in Italy, the others had been transferred from camps in England, principally from Donington Hall. There was insufficient room in the house for all the officers so some slept in huts. One hut served as a sick-bay. The dining room was not big enough for all, so meals were taken in two sittings. There was no canteen at the camp but purchases could be made in Taunton, through an NCO on the staff of the Commandant.

The report stated the place was healthy, for the influenza epidemic did not reach this camp. In the sick bay there were some minor hurts gained during a game of football. The doctor visited every morning at 9.00. Brigadier-Colonel Samesch, the senior officer, and his ADC spoke for their colleagues, who were all were satisfied with arrangements, and were grateful to the Commandant and staff for courteous treatment and their efforts to make the PoWs comfortable. The only complaints concerned their time before reaching Sandhill Park, including the allegation that some were taken prisoner 24 hours after the armistice was signed. The inspector concluded his report that his impressions of the camp were: *most favourable ... well situated ... healthy and well administered.* (FO383/478) [2]

A letter written by an Hungarian Officer, Lt Paál, at Sandhill on 27 October 1919, commented that others had been repatriated but he and 110 Hungarian colleagues were still waiting. The Supreme Council in Paris had consented to the repatriation of Austrian and Hungarian PoWs in October, but the occupation of Budapest by Roumanian forces, from 4 August until 14 November 1919, may have been the cause of the delay. The Hungarians' eventual route home was via France to Cologne, where they were handed over to Hungarian representatives, and then on by train. No reports of the departure of the officers from Sandhill Park has been traced.

---

[2] See also *Hadifogoly Magyarok Története*, p351. This account has been drawn upon for the story of this camp during 1919.

Somerset County Gazette, 1 November 1919, carried a report of the departure of sixty PoWs on Tuesday 28 October. They were taken to Dorchester by train, along with others from the west country, prior to repatriation. They were the PoW labourers from the Taunton Workhouse. The newspaper commented favourably on the conduct of these PoWs, and praised the work they did in agriculture and at the County Horse Depot at Castle Green. Similar remarks were made about another group of prisoners who had joined the same train at Tiverton Junction station.

After WWI Sandhill Park was converted into a hospital and home for mentally handicapped children. There were 200 patients in 1927. In 1940 the property was again taken over by the War Office, the patients were moved out, and it became the 41st Military Hospital. Later, under the Americans, it was a neurological hospital with 1,000 beds. The Military moved out in 1944 and after short term use of the hutted wards as emergency housing, the buildings reverted to hospital use, and it became a leading psychiatric institution.

In February 1928 the *Daily Mail* published a letter from an ex-Hungarian officer, Andrew Dush of Novakanjiza, who spent 10 months at Sandhill in 1919. He wrote that he was taken prisoner on the Piave (in Italy) by Scots soldiers. He commented favourably on the treatment he had received. He asked about Sandhill Park, and whether any picture postcards of the place were available.

1917 Christmas card from Sandhill Park

Scapa Flow, Orkney Isles

German naval ships

Grid Ref: ND 350 990 and an extensive area to the south.

On 21 November 1918, the German Navy surrendered at the Firth of Forth. The following day, arrangements were made for them to be sent to Scapa Flow (Newbolt vol.V, pp381-2). 73 German ships were anchored there, with reduced crews totalling about 4,400 men which, incongruously, included a band. Surplus crew members were repatriated from Scapa Flow, beginning on 3 December. Those who remained were forbidden ashore and not allowed radio receivers. Inter-vessel communication was only by flag signals. For food, mail and newspapers the crews relied upon a weekly German naval ship from Wilhelmshaven, but fresh water was provided by a local water barge.

The internment crews as laid down by the British Admiralty were:

5	Battle-cruisers	x 200 =	1,000
11	Battleships	x 175	1,925
8	Light Cruisers	x 60	480
49	Destroyers	x 20	980
	Total		4,385

Admiral von Reuter stated that there was no censorship of mail at the beginning. This conforms to the relaxation of censorship of naval mails by the Admiralty two weeks after the armistice. Mail was distributed at Scapa Flow by a British motor launch which tossed the mail aboard the German ships as no contact was permitted between German and British sailors. However, contact and trade did develop in other ways. English newspapers were supplied by the British, but Ruge wrote that they were several days old when received. Communication was provided by drifters or small trawlers. Such vessels came alongside once in the morning and once in the afternoon to collect official and private mail and, perhaps, also to deliver some.

A different account was given by Brown & Meehan, p130, who wrote that mail from Germany had to go through the British censors in London. This concurs with Farquharson's account, p.378, which recorded 77,800 letters outgoing in November and December 1918, and at p.211, where he stated the censors surmised from letters, the plans of the German crews to sink their ships. This intelligence was passed to the Admiralty, but they do not seem to have heeded the warning.

von Reuter (p56) believed censorship began at the end of December, in London, but was transferred to the Orkneys in January to reduce delays. That arrangement did not last long and London took over all the work again (p66). Censorship was very strict from 8 May 1919 when the peace conditions were made known to Germany (p89).

Ruge wrote, p82, that the mail came pretty regularly to Scapa Flow but it reached them very irregularly. It was brought from Germany, at intervals of one to two weeks, by the cruisers *Regensburg* or *Konigsberg*, or the torpedo boats *B97* and *B98*. These ships took the mail to Germany which the British had censored. At one point, the crews received written assurance that their letters would be sent on uncensored, but they were censored after all. That caused annoyance and, in addition, the examination of letters took so long that the mail only went by the next vessel. Incidentally torpedo boat *B98* was seized by the British (*The Times* 8 July 1919) but the reason is not known.

In May 1919, Admiral von Reuter requested transport be provided so that he could reduce the crews to the bare minimum, partly to get rid of trouble makers. 2,200 departed in transports on 17 June, leaving about 2,000 still on board the ships.

On 21 June 1919, Admiral Freemantle, commanding the 'Watchdog Squadron' on HMS *Revenge*, took his ships out into the North Sea for gunnery and torpedo practice. At 11.20am a coded flag signal was hoisted, on Admiral von Reuter's flagship *Emden*, meaning, 'prepare to scuttle', and shortly afterwards the final order was given. By 1pm the German ships were foundering and Admiral Freemantle was rushing back towards Scapa. Meanwhile, some elements of the Royal Navy lost their heads and began shooting at the German sailors in their sinking ships and in lifeboats. According to *The Times* 23 June, six Germans died, ten were wounded and a number were missing, but von Reuter gave the numbers as ten killed and 16 wounded, while Ruge listed nine killed and named them, and 21 wounded. The Germans were taken on board the British battleships HMS *Resolution* and HMS *Royal Oak* which sailed next day to Nigg, on the Cromarty Firth, from where, after an overnight stay, they were transferred by train to PoW camps at Oswestry and Lofthouse Park.

Farquharson stated, at p.386, *the correspondence of ... the disembarked officers and crews from Scapa Flow, was censored locally*. From the evidence of letters from an officer on one of the German torpedo boats, his letters written on board, were either not opened by the censor, or were closed with the 'coat-of-arms' label (Mark type 17). Farquharson stated that style of label was used to seal letters that had not been read.

This is supported by the fact that the gum on the envelopes is intact, showing the letters had been received at the censorship open, and the label was used to close them 'as a courtesy', to use Farquharson's term. Once this officer was at Lofthouse Park he mostly used the PoW stationery, and his letter-sheets received merely the encircled P.C. marking, until censorship was withdrawn in September 1919.

Sources for this brief account:
Brown M & Meehan P: *Scapa Flow*
Farquharson. Lt Col A S L: *Report on Postal Censorship during the Great War (1914-1919)*
Ruge F, (trans. Masters): *Scapa Flow 1919*
von Reuter, V-Adm L, (trans. Mudie): *Scapa Flow, the account of the greatest scuttling of all time*.

Ships used as places of detention

Kenneth Killeen wrote, in 1993, about the ships moored off Southend-on-Sea, in Portsmouth Harbour and off Ryde, Isle of Wight. Further research has discovered that other vessels, besides the ten identified by him, were used to hold PoWs and Internees. The following list adds four ships, but it is known to be incomplete as some reports in newspapers in 1914 referred to un-named ships being used.

Andania	Solent, off Ryde
Ascania	Gosport, later Solent
Borodino	Hull
Calypso	Hull
Canada	Solent
Ivernia	Southend-on-Sea
Lake Manitoba	Gosport, later Solent
Phryne	Rouen (a French ship, see PoW Companies in France)
Royal Edward	Southend-on-Sea
Saxonia	Southend-on-Sea
Scotian	Gosport, later Solent
Tunisian	Solent
Urania	Plymouth (a German ship)
Uranium	Solent, later Southend-on-Sea

In the early days of the war when German ships were detained in British ports the crews and passengers were usually held on board for a day or two while arrangements were made for the men to be moved to a camp. The Plymouth newspaper *Western Morning News* been searched for such early reports. Some examples:

6 August: *Belgia*, 8,132 tons, taken as a prize off Barry, South Wales, was being held at Newport, Monmouthshire, with 73 German reservists on board.

7 August: *Kronprincessin Cecilie* 8,684 tons, and *Prinz Adalbert* 6,030 tons had a total of 481 Germans on board at Falmouth. Armed guards were put on board the ships overnight. The next day, it was stated that 'several hundred German reservists' were on their way by train from Falmouth to Dorchester, but they were not the passengers on these two ships.

14 August: it was reported that the 481 passengers with 360 officers and crew of these two passenger ships had been landed and were then held in workhouses at Falmouth, Redruth, St Colomb and Truro, and at a barracks in Penzance.

14 August: It was noted that, as Britain was then at war with Austria, the experience of detaining German passengers might be repeated as there were several Austrian ships in port.

12 September: five Germans of the crew of the British barque *Heathfield* were arrested upon the ship's arrival in Plymouth. Five crew and one passenger, all German were taken from the Union Castle steamer *Llanstephen Castle*. All eleven were transferred to the German four-masted barque *Urania*, 3,265 tons, lying as a prize in Plymouth Sound.

25 September: 13 Germans were taken into custody from ships in Plymouth Sound. Whether these were the men on *Urania*, or from other ships, is not clear. The same report mentioned four German soldiers who had recovered from wounds being moved from the Fortress Hospital at Devonport to a compound at Bull Point (Saltash).

The Supplement to *The London Gazette* of Friday 2 October 1914, listed vessels detained in British ports. The following German ships, held at ports in Devon and Cornwall, were listed:

Bolivar	267 tons	held at Plymouth
Caracas	503 tons	Falmouth
Else	223 tons	Falmouth
Erica	141 tons	Fowey
Fritz	2191 tons	Falmouth
Goldbek	2630 tons	Falmouth
Helgoland	247 tons	Falmouth
Johanna	223 tons	Falmouth
Olona	1943 tons	Plymouth
Orlanda	2185 tons	Falmouth
Ossa	1941 tons	Falmouth
Ottokar	957 tons	Plymouth
Ponape	2318 tons	Falmouth
Roland	1377 tons	Plymouth
Schlesien	5536 tons	Plymouth
Urania	3265 tons	Plymouth
Wilhelm	187 tons	Fowey

(No Austrian ships were listed at west-country ports)

Ships at Hull

SS *Borodino*

Wilson Line, 1,870 tons, completed in 1914 for the Baltic trade, with refrigerated cargo space and passenger accommodation. Requisitioned in December 1914 as Merchant Fleet Auxiliary No.6, a stores ship stationed at Scapa Flow and operated by the Junior Army & Navy Stores Ltd.[1] Returned to her owners in February 1919. Requestioned again in 1939 and sunk as a block-ship at Zeebrugge on 27 May 1940, during the retreat to Dunkirk.

SS *Calypso*

Wilson Line, 2,876 tons, built 1904 for the Scandinavian immigrant trade, fitted for 45 first-, 46 second-class and 200 steerage passengers. A further 570 could be carried in temporary accommodation. Three refrigerated cargo holds. Taken up be the Admiralty in November 1914, renamed HMS *Calyx,* fitted with eight 4.7" and two 3lb guns at Hull and employed with 10th Cruiser Squadron from December 1914. Found unsuitable for this service as she could not remain on patrol for twelve days (insufficient coal storage) and withdrawn in March 1915. Returned to her owners in June 1915. Torpedoed by *U53* in the Skagerak on 10 July 1916 while en route from London to Christiania with general cargo. Master and 29 crew were all lost.

In response to the proclamation of 5 August 1914, that all Germans should register with the Police, about 170 reported at Hull up to Friday evening. About half of them were examined and released but the remainder, which included some sailors, liable to service in the German Navy, were detained and moved to SS *Borodino* in Hull Docks. The Court was also removed to the ship so that the Magistrates could continue to hear cases.

On 12 August it was reported in the local newspaper that a party of Germans, the crew of a ship, were taken from Parliament Street Police Station in a motor charabanc, *probably to the Borodino where other Germans were detained.*[2] By 20 August there were over 300 Germans and Austrians under detention at Hull. Until the day before they had been held on SS *Borodino*, but they were transferred to SS *Calypso* in the Albert Dock. (*Hull Daily Mail*, 8, 12 and 20 August 1914)

It has not been possible to trace when these detainees were disembarked from SS *Calypso* and moved to a regular camp. Their closest destination would have been York, but no reports of arrivals there, from Hull, have been found, nor of departures from Hull. However, *Lancaster Observer* of 28 August, recorded the arrival there of a batch of PoWs from Hull. It is highly likely that this was, or included, the men from the *Borodino* and *Calypso*.

No mail has been seen from men detained on either of these ships.

---

[1] For an account of this phase of the ship's history see Allen WJ: *SS "Borodino" M.F.A. No.6*.

[2] *London Gazette* 2 October 1914, listed six German (but no Austrian ships) detained at Hull: *Levensau* 2,153 tons, *Lucida* 1,476 tons, *Nyland* 1,533 tons, *Ursus* 2,190 tons and two un-named small craft.

Leigh Channel Squadron, off Southend-on-Sea

Grid Ref: TQ 880 830

On 17 November 1914, the Surrey Division of the National Reserve arrived at Southend-on-Sea to join the ships as armed guards. The previous week the *Saxonia* took up her mooring, followed by the *Hibernia* (sic), ie the *Ivernia*, and the *Royal Edward*, all lying east of the pier. The first contingent of internees, 500 Germans, escorted by men of the Royal Sussex Regt, arrived by train, 20 minutes late, on Wednesday 18 November, and were marched to the pier.[1] Subsequent arrivals were 300 on Friday, 'a batch from the north of England' on Saturday, and 250 more from Olympia on Sunday. All these appear to have been civilians.

An early attempt to communicate with the outside world was reported in the local paper of 18 December. A letter in a vinegar bottle, thrown from one of the PoW ships, was picked up from the beach, near to the gas works.

The first move of internees from the ships to the Isle of Man was a group of 500 on 1 March 1915, but ten days later some 1,200 civilians arrived at Southend in two trains.[2]

In April there were complaints in the local and national press about litter and rubbish being thrown overboard from the ships, and about the waste of food. In the House of Commons it was stated on 22 April 1915 that the *Saxonia, Royal Edward* and *Uranium* were the only ships still in use and that the first two named were to be released by the end of that month. However, in May it was admitted that all three were still in use and that orders had been issued to eliminate the overcrowding on *Uranium*, which had 922 detainees plus 154 staff and guard on board.[3]

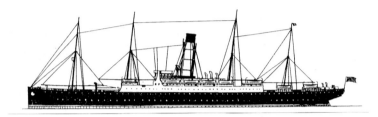

RMS *Ivernia*

Cunard Line, built 1900 by Swan Hunter on the Tyne, 14,067 tons. 164 first-, 200 second- and 1,600 third-class passengers. Requisitioned as a transport in September 1914. Served as a temporary hospital ship in the Mediterranean in mid-1915. Torpedoed by *UB47* off Cape Matapan, southern Greece, 1 January 1917, with 2,800 troops on board. 87 soldiers and 36 crew members lost.

In the first week of December about 1,000 PoWs arrived at Southend-on-Sea. They were chiefly infantrymen, with a few Prussian Guards and some sailors rescued from SMS *Mainz*. On Wednesday evening [9 December] one of these prisoners 'went mad' and had to be removed. He had tried to escape through a porthole and jump overboard. He was taken away to Colchester.[4] These reports stated that the combatant PoWs were put on board *Royal Edward*, but is not correct for the *Ivernia* was the 'military ship' of this squadron.

Mr Jackson, of the American Embassy inspected this ship on 30 January 1915, when there were 1,700 soldiers and sailors on board. Some had been badly wounded but were then convalescent. Two German military surgeons, with 16 sanitary orderlies were on board. The spirits of the PoWs were better than the civilians on other ships. Daily exercises on deck, under their NCOs, were commented upon. On the morning of the visit there had been a funeral, on shore, of an NCO, Johan Meiser, of the 13th Hussars, who had died of food poisoning, after eating a sausage sent from Germany through the post, which had clearly gone bad. Twenty comrades in uniform had attended the funeral (HO45/10760/269116). Reports of the death and funeral, with pictures of the cortege, were carried in the local newspapers.

Delegates of the International Red Cross visited this ship when the count of prisoners was 1,376. They observed that the soldiers

---

[1] *Southend Standard* 19 Nov. 1914, *Southend & Westcliff Graphic* 20 Nov., and *Essex County Chronicle* 20 November 1914.

[2] *The Times* 2 March 1915 and *Southend & Westcliff Gazette* 19 March 1915.

[3] *Hansard HC* vol.71, 22 April 1915, col.386, and 5 May, col.1088

[4] *Southend Standard* 10 December and *Essex County Chronicle* 11 December 1914.

slept in the third-class accommodation on sprung mattresses, while the NCOs used the second-class cabins.

The delegates saw an advantage for the prisoners in that during the winter they would be warmer than in a tented camp, but on the other hand the restricted opportunities for exercise and games was a disadvantage. They recommended that with improving weather conditions the PoWs should be moved to camps on land.

In April, 600 men from *Hibernia* (sic), so presumably PoWs from *Ivernia*, were transferred to York, according to a local newspaper report.[5] However there was no PoW camp at York by this date. Their real destination was most likely Frith Hill, for when the US Embassy inspected that camp on 29 April, the report stated that most of the 1,637 men present had recently arrived from the *Ivernia*. This indicates a probable date of release from prison duties, but the file in The National Archives does not give a date. That file instead, refers to correspondence between the Cunard Company and the Director of Transports at the Admiralty concerning this ship and *Saxonia* (see below).

NOT ON BOARD R.M.S. *Ivernia*

NOT ON H.M.T. "IVERNIA"

Both these cachets were recorded by Brown but only the upper one, 50mm overall, by Killeen. The lower one 64mm overall.

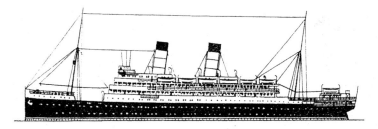

SS *Royal Edward*
Built 1907 as *Cairo* by Fairfield's of Glasgow, 11,117 tons. Purchased 1909 by Canadian Northern Steamships Ltd. Taken up as transport in Autumn of 1914. Torpedoed in the Aegean Sea, 14 August 1915, by *UB14* while employed as a troopship. 132 lost, including the Master

When Mr Jackson of the US Embassy visited this ship on 30 January 1915, he commented that this was *obviously the show ship* with 1,400 on board. The interned were separated into three classes depending partly on social standing, but to a greater extent upon their ability to pay for extras; two shillings a day for first-class mess, and half-a-crown to five shillings a week for first-class cabins (depending upon the number sharing). All payments had to be made in advance. Other prisoners occupied the steerage accommodation, sleeping in tiers of three. Men transferred from camps on land were generally satisfied with conditions on board, but there were some complaints from 'better class' men that they should not have been interned at all. Mail, letters and parcels, arrived with fair regularity. Three German consular officials Wilhelm Julius (Aberdeen) Herr Buchholzke (West Hartlepool) and Herr Köhler (Glasgow) were on board. All prisoners had to be on deck for stipulated hours, but the only opportunity for exercise was to walk round the deck. Two deaths were reported, one from heart failure. Appended were *Rules for Correspondence with Prisoners of War, Rations* (full and light diet) and *Specimen scale of First-class Messing* dated 23 January 1915.[6]

In February, on a happy but bizarre note, four internees were allowed ashore to be married. After the ceremony and a meal, with their guards, the husbands returned to the ship.[7]

Escape, by the traditional tunnel, was not a practical proposition, but one internee did get away for a short time. He dived overboard and swam to a Dutch ship *Elve*, some 500 yards away. When he got there he was promptly fished out of the water and returned to his rightful place on board *Royal Edward*, where no doubt he spent some time in 'the brig'.[8]

The first Zeppelin raid occurred, at 2.45am on 10 May 1915. *LZ38* (Hauptmann Linnarz) appeared over SS *Royal Edward*, and

---

[5] *Southend & Westcliff Gazette*, 16 April 1915

[6] HO 45/10760/269116

[7] *The Times* 26 February and *Southend & Westcliff Gazette* 5 March 1915.

[8] *Southend & Westcliff Gazette* 23 April 1915

dropped a bomb close to the ship. The airship then passed over Southend, from east to west, and dropped four high-explosive and many incendiary bombs.[9] An undated report by the International Committee of The Red Cross stated: *Les prisonniers ont éte un peu émus de ce qu'un jour des avions allemands ont jeté une bombe qui est tombée dans l'eau à une cinquantaine de mètres du navire.* (Trans: The prisoners were somewhat perturbed when one day German airmen dropped a bomb which fell into the water about 50 metres from the ship.)

On 21 May 1915 the *Gazette* reported that more German civilians had arrived at Southend for *Royal Edward*. This seems rather late in the day because official records show the ship was soon cleared of internees. The ship left Southend on 4 June 1915, when she sailed to Avonmouth for cleaning up, and was discharged from Prison Service on 6 June. (MT 23.429)

Censor marking 39x24mm

Censor marking (size not certain)

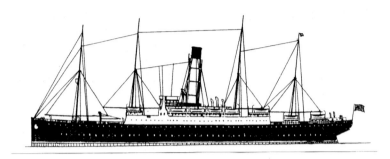

RMS *Saxonia*

Cunard Line. Built 1900 by John Brown on the Clyde, 14,281 tons. 164 first-class, 200 second-class and 1,600 third-class passengers. Requisitioned as a transport in September 1914. Returned to North Atlantic service in May 1915. Broken up in the Netherlands in 1925.

Mr Jackson's report, to the US Ambassador, of his visit on 30 January 1915 (HO45/10760/269116) stated there were 1,800 on board, all treated equally except 'the workers' who were allowed to occupy cabins. It appeared to the inspector that *the rougher element* had been collected on this ship, but there were some of the *better class*. A Court Martial had been held on the day of the visit, of several men for a bid to escape. Visits to the ship by 'undesirable females' had been attempted, causing some trouble. The cooks on board were German. The canteen facilities were not as good on this ship as elsewhere. There were some restrictions on smoking and no alcohol was permitted. The British physician had been taken ill, so he had gone ashore, and consequently the difficulty in getting a doctor, in case of emergency, was highlighted. One death on board was reported. Some prisoners from Frith Hill said treatment there was good, no rough handling, and the food was better on shore.

The Cunard Company wrote, on 5 May 1915, to the Director of Transports at the Admiralty, re RMSs *Ivernia* and *Saxonia* being requisitioned when Cunard had contracted them to the French Government. The response has not been seen, but other records indicate that this ship returned to the Liverpool to New York service on 1 May 1915. So it is not clear what actually happened. (MT 23.411)

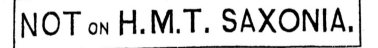

Instructional marking, 110 x 14mm

---

[9] Jones HA: *War in the Air*, vol.3, pp97-8

SS *Uranium*

As noted in the section below on the Solent Squadron, SS *Uranium* was moved from Ryde to the Leigh Channel, off Southend-on-Sea, during May 1915. No reports of the ship have been seen in the Southend local newspapers during the time it was in the Thames estuary, nor of the reason for the move. However, an item of mail is known from this new location dated 25 May 1915, and an inward letter addressed to SS *Lake Manitoba* at Ryde, re-addressed from there 21 May 1915 to SS *Uranium* at Southend, has been shown to this author.

It is not known at present when this ship was cleared of internees, nor to where they were removed.

Fareham Creek, Portsmouth Harbour, later off Ryde, Isle of Wight

Grid Ref: SU 600 045

In the report of his visit to the ships in January, the American Consul at Southampton, Mr Swalm, noted that Major M Graham Taylor (later second-in-command at Knockaloe?) was the military commander of this group of ships and Lt Colonel James A.H. Lindsay, RA, (graded an Assistant Provost Marshall) was in overall command of the PoWs on board ships at both Portsmouth and Ryde.

Mr Churchill, responding on 11 February 1915 to a question in the House of Commons by Admiral Lord Charles Beresford (MP for Portsmouth) replied: *Owing to large numbers [of prisoners] and shortage of time, ships are in Portsmouth Harbour, but this is not satisfactory. Steps are being taken to find alternative accommodation.*

A week later a further statement was made: *Orders have been issued which will result in the removal from Portsmouth Harbour of the vessels by 22 inst.* (*Hansard HC* 11 February 1915, vol.69, col.747 and 18 February, vol.69, col.1293)

Soon after Mr Churchill's statement in The Commons *Ascania* was moved to the Ryde anchorage and she was followed by the other two ships of this group, after the three vessels of the Ryde Group had discharged their prisoners and sailed away. *Ascania* became the headquarters of the squadron.

RMS *Ascania*
Cunard Line. Built 1911 by Swan Hunter on the Tyne. 9,111 tons.
200 first- and 1,500 third-class passengers.
Wrecked off Newfoundland on 13 June 1918, no lives lost.

On 1 February 1915, Mr Jackson of the US Embassy, visited the ships at Gosport. The *Ascania* and *Lake Manitoba* were moored together with connecting gangways. As they were anchored within a 'proscribed area' (Portsmouth Harbour) visits were not generally permitted. There were 1,003 civilians on board and the ship had been in use since 1 December. Better class prisoners had the use of cabins while others occupied the steerage accommodation. All had the same food. There was no compulsory exercise but men took part in rowing and could promenade on deck until 7pm. After that hour all prisoners were locked in, below decks. A British military doctor was on board. No deaths were reported (HO45/01760/269116).

Although Mr Jackson reported that the ship had been in use since 1 December a postcard written a week earlier, by an internee, and postmarked 27 November is known. The message stated that the writer had arrived on board from Newbury the previous Saturday, *ie* 21 November 1914.

The ship was released from Prisoner Service on 4 May 1915, before cleaning up and proceeding to Bermuda (MT 23.429). In June 1915 she served as a temporary hospital ship in the Mediterranean.

In a letter of 27 May 1915, the US Embassy informed the Foreign Office that they did not visit Bevois Mount, Southampton, due to contagious disease. Spotted fever, a form of meningitis, had appeared among prisoners on *Ascania*. Prisoners from this ship were distributed among various camps but no further cases were reported, and it is assumed that men at Bevois Mount were infected, or suspected, cases.

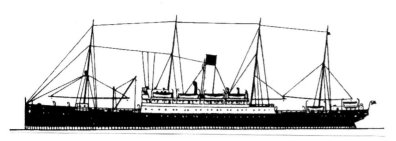

SS *Lake Manitoba*
Canadian Pacific Railway. Built 1901 by Swan Hunter on the Tyne. 9,674 tons. 122 first-, 130 second- and 500 third-class passengers. Gutted by fire at Montreal on 26 August 1918. Hulk sold and refitted as *Iver Heath*. Sold and resold twice more. Broken up in 1924.

As mentioned above, the report of the visit on 1 February 1915, by Mr Jackson, recorded this ship and *Ascania* were moored together with connecting gangways. There were 927 civilians on board. The better class of prisoners had use of the cabins, while others were in steerage accommodation. Lights were allowed until 9.00 or 9.30pm. Prisoners were not locked in below decks at night, as the water closets were on the upper deck.

The ship was cleared of internees by 16 April 1915, when the ship proceeded to Southampton for a refit (MT 23.429). The US Embassy report on *Uranium*, off Ryde on 8 May 1915, noted that most of the internees on board that ship had previously been held on *Lake Manitoba*.

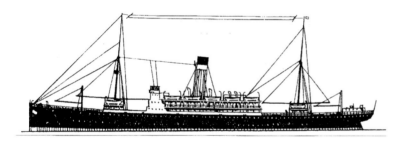

SS *Scotian*
Allen Line. Built 1898 by Harland & Wolff, Belfast, as *Statendam* for Holland-America Line, 10,322 tons. 200 first-, 175 second- and 1000 steerage class passengers. Acquired and renamed by Allan Line 1911. Taken over by Canadian Pacific in 1917. Broken up at Genoa 1927.

Hampshire Telegraph 29 January 1915, reported that Lt Athelstane Nobbs MD RAMC had published in *The British Medical Journal* an article on the treatment and diet of the German PoWs. He was described as being 'in charge' of this ship.

Albert Swalm, the US Consul at Southampton, visited at the end of January and noted that Dr Nobbs had segregated some tubercular cases. The Consul also saw mail arrive from Germany and commented favourably on the distribution system. The Censor, Mr Harrison, had condemned some letters, but a full record was kept.

Mr Jackson's report of his visit on 1 February 1915 recorded that this was the 'military ship' of the group. 936 soldiers, 319 sailors and 3 civilians (total 1,258) were on board, but there was berths for up to 1,400.

The senior NCO was a Deck-Officer Machinist from SMS *Mainz* (sunk at Heligoland Bight 28 August 1914). Also on board were members of the crew of the German ship *Ophelia*, captured in the North Sea on 18 October, purporting to be a hospital ship searching for survivors of a recent naval action in which four German destroyers had been sunk. She was suspected of being a scout and orders discovered on board added to that suspicion.[1]

The report stated that all the men on *Scotian* slept in cabins, NCOs in the first-class. It was stated that there was no steerage on this ship (but details from fleet lists indicate other-wise). The cooks were British, part of the civilian crew of the Allan Line. Exercise included gymnastics on deck and on 30 December a boat race was rowed between a crew from SMS *Mainz* and men from *Ascania*; the professionals had won. A 'Fest-Spiel' programme was appended to Mr Jackson's report. (HO45/10760/269116)

The ship left Portsmouth for Barry, South Wales, on 23 March 1915 (MT 23.429). The US Embassy report on Jersey Camp, in May 1915, stated that of the 995 men in that camp, most were from *Scotian*.

---

[1] *Ophelia* was condemned by the Prize Court on 21 May 1915.

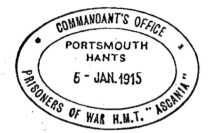

J. A. H.
CENSOR.

This censor mark is known used on mail from *Ascania* and later at Dyffryn Aled.

Cachets used on the ships in Fareham Creek in Portsmouth Harbour.

NOT ON BOARD "ASCANIA"

PASSED CENSOR

This censor mark is believed to have been used on *Ascania*

C. G. H.
CENSOR.

This censor's personal mark is recorded used on *Lake Manitoba* and later on board the *Uranium*.

Cachets used by the ships when off Ryde, Isle of Wight.
No cachets have been recorded used on board *Scotian* when at the Ryde anchorage.

Solent Squadron, off Ryde Isle of Wight

Grid Ref: SZ 580 940

It was originally planned, in October 1914, that this group of ships would be moored in Milford Haven, in south-west Wales (MT 391, file T 20931/1915). The date and reason for the change to Ryde have not been discovered. The ships came on station in the Solent in mid-December 1914. When the US Consul from Southampton inspected, the following month, he mentioned Captain Hancock (possibly G.S. Hancock, temporary Captain 15 November 1914) as the military commander of this squadron and Doctor Peters (probably Edwin Arthur Peters, MD, FRCS, temporary Captain RAMC, 21 December 1914) as the medical officer.

The three ships of this group were all released in February 1915 and their 'passengers' were transferred to camps on land, but their specific destinations are not known. With the release of these three, their moorings were taken up by the three vessels which had been anchored in Fareham Creek of Portsmouth Harbour.

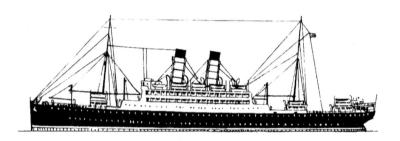

RMS *Andania*
Cunard Line. Built in 1913 by Scotts of Greenock, 13,405 tons. 520 second- and 1540 third-class passengers. Torpedoed by *U46* off Northern Ireland, 27 January 1918. 7 lost.

The Portsmouth newspaper *Evening News*, 1 January 1915, reported a case of theft being brought before the Court. The case was dismissed for lack of evidence to convict. Lt Harrison, this ship's interpreter and censor, was thanked by the Bench.

Mr Jackson of the US Embassy visited on 2 February 1915, and reported that this was the 'military ship' of this group. 579 Germans were on board, mostly soldiers, but some were civilians from Africa, including two pastors, some sanitary officials and some men over 55. These were advised to present their cases for repatriation to the Commandant.

The colonials had only recently arrived, having been taken off SS *Laurentic* at Liverpool, and they were soon to be transferred elsewhere. Some soldiers had come from Handforth and others were convalescent after treatment at Netley Hospital. All the prisoners were in cabins and divided into messes under their NCOs, who compelled their groups to a certain amount of drill. The scale of rations for this group of ships was reproduced in the report (HO45/10760/26916).

The ship was cleared of prisoners on 23 February 1915, and then she proceeded to Barry in South Wales (MT 23.429). The destination of the prisoners is not known at present.

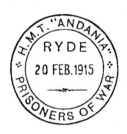

This cachet has not been recorded used on mail. A specimen strike is known, said to have been presented to a well known collector by the son of Captain Hancock the military commander of the squadron.

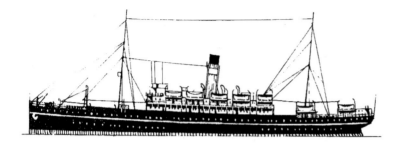

SS *Canada*

Dominion Line. Built 1896, by Harland & Wolff, Belfast, 8,800 tons gross. 200 first-, 200 second- and 800 third-class passengers. Requisitioned as a troop-ship 1914–1918. Sold to breakers in 1926.

This was the Headquarters ship of this group, until she departed, when *Ascania* took over HQ duties.

When the US Consul at Southampton, Mr Swalm, visited this ship in the last week of January 1915, he reported 914 on board. He mentioned an acute case of appendicitis: that man was landed and an operation was performed at 2am. One case of pneumonia (recovered), one of Bright's Disease (kidneys), and other lesser conditions were mentioned as showing a good health record for the ship and commending the medical officer, Doctor Peters. The sick bay had 24 beds. One mental case had been removed to an asylum.

The prisoners had separated themselves into first, second and third-class accommodation 'by a process satisfactory to themselves'. Their internal organisation was described. The canteen did not sell beer or liquor. Internees were limited to £2 expenditure per week. The food was judged excellent and was the same standard as served to the guards. An excessive bread ration, 24oz daily, was criticized, as the surplus was being fed to seagulls by the internees. (763.72114/321)

The following week, when Mr Jackson of the US Embassy inspected, he found 1,026 civilians, including several sea-captains and one man aged over 55, on board. Many had come from Newbury when that was closed, or from Dorchester when that was made a military only camp. Those from Newbury were happy, but men from Dorchester were not. Some, from Africa, complained of lack of consideration for their situation. There were no German cooks as the British galley crews were taken over with the ships, and they were not prepared to work with non-union labour. Consequently, there were many complaints about the food. Mr Jackson considered the conditions less than ideal, but the ships had been taken as a temporary expedient, when wet weather made camps like Newbury and Frith Hill impossible. The report stated that the ships were to be given up as soon as replacement facilities on shore became available. No deaths were reported. (HO45/10760/269116)

No certain date is known for landing the internees, but the ship left Ryde on 9 March 1915, for Barry and Avonmouth (MT 23.429). On 17 March she sailed from Avonmouth to Alexandria, Egypt, with 17 British General Hospital, then served in the Mediterranean as a hospital ship.

Both these cachets are believed to have been used on SS *Canada*. The date of the lower one suggests *Canada* had handed over Headquarters duties to *Ascania*, but the letter was clearly written on SS *Canada*.

This censor cachet, used on *Canada* is also recorded used at Shrewsbury.

SS *Tunisian*

Allan Line. Built 1900 by Alexander Stephen & Sons, Govan. 10,576 tons. 240 first- 220 second- and 1,000 third-class passengers. Taken over by Canadian Pacific in 1917 and renamed *Marburn* in 1922. Broken up in Italy in 1928.

Mr Jackson's report of his visit on 2 February 1915, recorded 795 civilians on board. As with SS *Canada* there were British cooks on board and therefore no Germans were working in the galleys. Conditions generally on this ship were depressing. Two deaths were reported, one from heart disease and one from black-water fever. The sick-bay was full of patients with malaria and other tropical complaints. The ship was paid off at Ryde on 17 February 1915 and left Southampton on 24 February 1915, for Barry (MT 23.429).

SS *Uranium*

Uranium SS Co. Built in 1891 by William Denny & Co, Dumbarton, as *Avoca* for British India. Chartered to other lines and renamed twice. 1908 acquired by New York and Continental Line but that company was wound up the same year and ship sold to North West Transport Line and renamed *Uranium*. 1910 sold to new owners Uranium SS Co. 1916 sold to Cunard and renamed *Felitra*. Torpedoed 5 May 1917 by *UC48* off Waterford, Ireland, 45 lost.

The US Embassy visited this ship on 8 May 1915 when she lay off the Isle of Wight. There were 743 on board, including 300 merchant seamen from the Cameroons. Most had been transferred from *Lake Manitoba*. Prior to the inspection there had been up to 1,000 on board, but although some 250 had been landed to make more room, it was still considered overcrowded (FO383/33). When the Southampton transit camp at Shirley Rink was inspected two days after the visit to this ship there were more prisoners at the Rink than usual. The extra numbers there could well have been the men put ashore from this ship, but that point is not confirmed in the report.

Subsequently *Uranium* was moved to the Leigh Channel, off Southend-on-Sea, but the date of the move is not certain and no reason for it is known. No press reports of the ship at the new location have been seen. However mail to and from this ship at Southend is known.

Ship cachets

C. G. H.
CENSOR.

This censor cachet is recorded used on *Lake Manitoba* and on *Uranium*. Later it is known used at Stratford camp.

Shrewsbury, Shropshire

Civilians initially, later ORs

Grid Ref SJ 500 122

Macpherson did not give an opening date, but he listed the accommodation as 'buildings and railway works' for up to 500 men. The 1919 POWIB List gave the address as Abbey Wood, but Shrewsbury Records Centre thinks the address should have been Abbey Works. It was part of the Midland Railway Carriage and Wagon Works, to the south-east of the town, east of the Shrewsbury to Hereford railway lines, south of the Abbey and near the site of the Abbot's fish ponds. Today the site is a supermarket and car park. Thomas (p47) considered the camp *not suitable for the prolonged internment of men, owing to the situation and narrow limits.*

The earliest mentions of the camp were found in *Liverpool Daily Post* of 2 November 1914 and *Shrewsbury Chronicle* of 6 November: Ernst Koanig walked out of the camp and went to Liverpool to visit his family, as he had not heard from them for a few days. He handed himself into the police, was charged and sentenced to 3 months in gaol for absconding.

In December, the War Office vetoed a concert, planned to be given by the German military PoWs at Shrewsbury. A letter about this, published in the *Shrewsbury Chronicle* 18 December, was written by the Commandant, Colonel Hugh Cecil Cholmondeley CB (1852-1941), late Rifle Brigade. He was first appointed to Lancaster but moved to Shrewsbury in September 1914, which is a clue to the opening date. The following week the paper reported that he had received various donations in lieu of the cancelled concert. Major A H C Kenney-Herbert, late Northants Regiment, was second-in-command. The camp held between 500 and 600 PoWs at that time.

Mr Jackson's February 1915 report to the American Embassy stated, *inter alia*, that he did not go to the camp at Shrewsbury *because he was informed officially that this was to be, and probably was by then, closed.* Although the intention to close the camp was, no doubt, genuine at the time, in fact the place remained open until mid 1919.

The Times 14 June 1915, reported the escape of two men, Bernhardt J Zimpel & Otto R Kirchner, and their recapture at Welshpool.

The report made, after the US Embassy inspection on 30 June 1915 stated that the camp was *not up to standard, ... the authorities several times have contemplated abandoning it.* There were 501 prisoners present, comprising 467 soldiers, 26 sailors and eight civilians. The civilians had been the officers' servants at Dyffryn Aled. Leaking roofs were reported. There were no proper floors, but the soil was hard so there was no dust. Beds were raised off the ground. The recreation area was about 100 yds square. Nine men were in the hospital ward, some recovering from wounds. Their conditions were good and they were cared for by a female nurse. The PoWs had not organised any classes nor occupations, as at other camps, nevertheless the prisoners did not seem discontented or unhappy. (FO383/33)

In November 1915, when Sir Louis Mallet (lately the British Ambassador to Turkey) visited the camp he recorded that although the intention had been to close the camp, that decision had been reversed, so repairs and improvements were being made. 469 prisoners were present. (FO383/106)

A further visit was made by the US Embassy on 18 March 1916. The Commandant was then Major H.C.C. Ducat-Hammersley, who had previously commanded Handforth camp. 464 were present, all German; 411 soldiers, 46 sailors and 7 civilians. Concrete floors had been laid and the washing and latrine facilities had been markedly improved. Prisoners were engaged in tailoring, carpentry and making small articles for sale through a welfare committee. Route marches were arranged four days a week. There were no serious complaints and everything inspected was judged neat, clean, well lit and ventilated. (Cd.3824)

At the next inspection visit on 9 September 1916, there were 500 prisoners, all German, of which 61 were sailors. Two tents had been added to the accommodation previously described, for seven recent arrivals. The sick-bay had one doctor and three assistants looking after 15 in-patients, six of whom had battlefield wounds. Three deaths were reported; one of enteric fever contracted pre-internment, another died-of-wounds and the third of tuberculosis. A

British dentist attended when required. Outside the camp 50 men were employed at each of two local quarries and a 100 more were expected to supplement them shortly. A further 50 were to start at a third quarry during that month. They travelled to work daily by train. A hut for instruction and education had been erected where languages and music were taught. As the days were getting shorter, a request was made for electric light to be provided in this school hut. There were no complaints but NCOs were becoming overcrowded, due to recent arrivals, and asked to have a larger dormitory, or for some to moved elsewhere. One man was in the cells for attempting to pass a letter outside the camp. (763.72114/2040)

The Times 15 January 1917, p3, reported the escape and recapture of Ernst Boldt and Herman Bunte, and on 19 February 1918 the *Police Gazette* listed the escape on 12 February of Otto Krueger, 24, Arthur Leo Fassien, 27 and Max Willi Laessig, 27. Kreuger was recaptured at Rotherham, but no report of the arrest of the other two has been traced. An account of three PoWs climbing out through a disused chimney shaft in 1918, has been seen in *20th Century Shrewsbury*, which could well be the same incident.

Shrewsbury Chronicle 10 May 1918, reported that Walter Henry Booton was charged with receiving a letter, for his daughter, from a German PoW in Monkmoor Road, Shrewsbury. Booton was sentenced to one month in prison. *20th Century Shrewsbury*, p21, stated that the PoWs were employed at Monkmoor Aerodrome. It is likely that the German who gave the letter to Booton was one of a working party at the aerodrome. Monkmoor is about one mile northeast of the PoW camp and bounded on three sides by a loop of the River Severn.

Border Counties Advertiser (an Oswestry newspaper) had a number of reports through the spring and summer of 1918 concerning the agricultural work of PoW labour parties. Although these reports were in an Oswestry newspaper that camp did not have any dependent labour camps. Until May 1919, Shrewsbury controlled all the labour camps in the three border counties of Shropshire, Hereford and Monmouth.

In April 1918, the County Agricultural Committee received good reports of work done at Bromfield and Wem (both in Shropshire), and they agreed to request 200 more PoWs. It was hoped to house them in small camps of 15-20, or in groups up to three on single farms, if the farmer could house them. However, in July, one farmer complained that he was denied a PoW labourer for lack of guards. In August the Committee arranged PoW work under two plans. One provided for migratory gangs of ten men, with two guards, the other allowed groups of PoWs to be despatched daily, by train from Shrewsbury, to convenient stations. Farmers were told to apply at once so that arrangements could be made and numbers would be available for the harvest.

The Times 19 June 1918, reported the escape, and recapture at Tipton, Staffordshire, of Bruno Sens and Ernst J L Clausnidzer. On 17 July 1918 the Oswestry paper reported the death of a German PoW, Otto Wenzel, who was killed in a rock fall while working at Dolgoch Quarry.

On 24 April 1919 the Swiss Legation visited the camp. The Commandant was Major Richard George Tyndal Bright CMG, Rifle Brigade, b.1872. There were 348 prisoners at the camp and a further 1,262 on the strength of dependent work camps. The report stated that on 2 May the camp would commence closure when the resident prisoners, together with 64 from outside parties, would move to Oswestry. The control of work camps then under Shrewsbury would also be transferred to Oswestry. (FO383/507)

In November 1919 and February 1920 *The Times* advertised the sale of huts and building materials from the site.

This censor cachet has been seen on an undated card to Germany. 'Shrewsbury' is 46mm long. (The P.C. mark is also known used on SS *Canada*)

In this censor cachet 'Shrewsbury' is 31mm long

PoWs in the garden of Shrewsbury Camp. The Abbey is in the background.
(International Red Cross postcard)

A group of PoWs, probably a work-party, at Shrewsbury
(International Red Cross postcard)

Skipton, Yorkshire West Riding

Officers' camp   Grid Ref: SD 984 525

Rowley, in *The Book of Skipton*, stated the Bradford Corporation built a camp to the north-east of Skipton town-centre 'in the Hollow' between the girls' school and Raikes Road. This camp was first the home of the 1st Bradford Pals, the 16th Battalion, The West Yorkshire Regiment, between January and May 1915, followed by the 17th Battalion for a short period (James *British Regiments*). Other troops occupied the camp in 1916 and 1917. Macpherson gave the opening date as a PoW camp as 1 January 1918 with huts for 552 officers and 160 servants.

There are photographs in Skipton library, and in books, which show a tented army camp. The area shown is open and nearly level, which means it could not be the Raikes Wood camp. It seems more likely that this tented camp was about a mile out of town to the west of the Grassington Road, between the present by-pass and 'The Craven Heifer'. It could have been a pre-WWI Territorial Camp or, if early in WWI, a temporary site while the Raikes Wood camp was being constructed.

A German account *Kriegsgefangenen in Skipton* by Sachsse and Cossmann, was published in 1920. From sketches in that book, the parish church could be seen from the PoW camp and the description of woods, on either side, place the camp in the (present) Raikeswood Drive and Botheby Wood area. A number of other features described in the book show that the camp can confidently be placed on the 1907 six-inch OS map, south of Raikes Wood and north of the woods above the Grammar School. The present recreation area, to the north-west of Raikes Wood, appears to have been the PoWs' sports ground. This was not marked as a recreation ground on the 1907 map, because it was not donated to the town for such purposes until 1908. Later maps do show it as a recreation ground. A personal contact in Skipton recalled that as a boy he used to play on that field, which was always known to him and his young pals as 'The Camp Rec', but he had never known how it got its name.

At Colsterdale there had been complaints about the exposed nature of the site and that, as much as the number of officer PoWs, may have prompted the construction of a new camp. It was on 12 January 1918 that the local inhabitants witnessed the first party, of 50 to 60, to arrive in Skipton (*Craven Herald* 18 January 1918). From the description, and the date, they may have been ordinary soldiers, arriving to prepare the site, or as servants to the officers. The first Officer PoWs came from Colsterdale a few days later, while the soldier servants came from Brocton. These first arrivals were described as having mixed and worn uniforms which were supplied to the PoWs, both officers and men when their own uniforms wore out. (Sachsse and Cossmann pp28-29 and 285)

On 1 February 1918 the *Craven Herald* reported a fire in a hut used by the officers of the guard and on 22 February a complaint was aired in the paper about the greater amount of food available to the PoWs, compared with civilians in Britain.

Officials from the Swiss Legation inspected the camp on 13 February 1918. The camp was commanded by Lt Colonel William Chevers Hunter (b.1870, late Oxford & Bucks LI, retired 1908). 150 officers had arrived in three parties, on 17, 19 and 21 January, but since then numbers had increased to 230 officers and 124 servants. The accommodation, 24 huts each with 24 beds, and four dining huts would allow about 500 officers. Two patients were in the hospital ward and an isolation ward was being completed. The recreation ground was open from 10.30am until 1.00pm and 2.00pm until 6.00pm. Walks were permitted three days a week. (FO383/432)

Four German officers escaped from Skipton on Sunday morning 30 June 1918. They were named as: Hans Wallbaum, 24, Hans Kraus, 22, Louis Bauneisher, 26 and Hans Laskus. Wallbaum and Laskus were recaptured the same day at Clitheroe, and the other two were retaken on Monday, but the locations was not stated. (*The Times* 2 July 1918 and *Craven Herald* 5 July 1918.)

Another inspection was made by the Swiss Legation on 24 February 1919, when the Commandant was Colonel Robert William Hawthorn Ronaldson CB, (b.1864, late Highland Light Infantry). 530 officers and 124 orderlies were present. The joint Senior German Officers were Major von Kleist and Major von Bültzingsloewen. 279 officers and 28 orderlies (nearly half of the camp population) reported sick on the day of the inspection. 15 officers and 15 soldiers were in hospital at Keighley. Five had died. It was stated that beef and mutton had replaced the 'ill-famed horseflesh' to help improve the possible resistance to infection. (FO383/506)

The 600 PoWs received notice to quit on Saturday 25 October 1919, and spent the weekend packing. They departed on Monday, 27th by rail, travelling via Keighley and Leeds, to Hull, where they embarked for Germany on *Die Lisboa*. (*Craven Herald* 31 October 1919)

When they departed, the PoWs left behind 47 of their colleagues who had died while at Skipton. The influenza epidemic hit this camp quite severely, and the local hospital in Skipton could not, or would not, accept the prisoners as patients. Those in need of hospital treatment were taken to Keighley and the 47 who died were buried at East Morton cemetery. Their names, ranks and places of residence were listed by Sachsse & Cossmann.

The Times 14 February and 8 May 1920, carried advertisements for the sale of huts and building materials. At the sales, Bradford Corporation was the major buyer of huts, but some of them remained in Skipton; three were acquired by the Grammar School, one became a garage, another the office of a timber merchant and a sixth became the village hall at Embsay.

No camp or censorship markings have been recorded by this author.

The local newspaper mentioned a housing scheme in connection with the Raikeswood Camp, but there was no indication at that date, 22 August 1919, as to when the PoWs would leave. The following month it was announced that the site was unsuitable for a housing scheme. Nevertheless, the camp site is now a modern estate of private houses.

A cartoon from Sachsse & Cossmann, possibly conveying something of the characters of the Commandant and his Adjutant.

Slough, Buckinghamshire

also referred to as Cippenham and as Salthill in some sources.

ORs Working Camp   Grid Ref: SU 960 807

Although working camps have not been covered systematically elsewhere in this study, this one was so large and in view of the controversy surrounding it, it should be mentioned.

In June 1917 the War Office perceived a need for a central stores and repair depot for mechanical transport, and the Lands Department was put on notice that a site was needed. In August Longhedge (Battersea) was approved and in September a Mechanical Transport Board was set up to deal with the whole project. However, in October, Slough was suggested as a suitable site, and a sub-committee was appointed to examine this fresh proposal. After ten meetings of the Mechanical Transport Board, a letter was despatched to the Treasury on 12 February 1918, seeking sanction for the expenditure. Approval was received on 23 April 1918.

However, in May 1918, objections to the scheme were lodged by both the Director General of Lands and the Food Production Department, on the grounds that the land proposed was prime agricultural property. An alternative site at Baldock, in Hertfordshire, was considered but rejected for the same reason, that it was arable land under cultivation. The War Office claimed to have examined and rejected eleven other sites in favour of Slough. On 23 May 1918 General Smuts called a meeting of all concerned and, being a good soldier, he decided in favour of the War Office. An area of 700 acres (more than a square mile) was taken over and building work commenced on 11 June.

Meanwhile, in the Spring of 1918 the War Office had been faced with a difficult situation in terms of the repair of vehicles in France. The German Offensive had pushed the front line towards the Channel, thus restricting the area in which back-up operations, such as repairs etc, could be undertaken. Large numbers of damaged vehicles were sent across to Britain and many small yards were used for repairs. Kempton Park Racecourse was used to store the damaged vehicles awaiting repair.

Some 200 Royal Engineers were brought to the site at Slough to build the repair facilities and two camps, one for 1,000 civilian workers, the other for 2,500 PoWs, were erected. On 4 July 1918 it was stated that the supply of PoW labour was insufficient, and it was agreed to press for more. But in September this problem still existed and it was suggested that the Army Council should send a demand to France for PoWs to be sent over, specially, to do this work. 300 Austrians and Bulgarians were brought in during September 1918, but they were withdrawn when 1,000 Germans arrived on 4 November and a further 500 came at the end of that month. In evidence to the committee of enquiry it was stated that the supply of PoW labour had come in small batches and, as soon as sufficient were available, the British civilian workers had gone on strike against the employment of the prisoners.

Visits were made in September 1918, by the Ministry of National Service, to investigate the efficiency with which labour was being used, and to make recommendations whether to employ 2,250 PoWs to expedite the work. In a highly critical report, dated 2 October 1918, the Ministry of National Service, recommended that no further labour be supplied, pending a re-appraisal of the whole scheme. However, pressure, by the War Office on the War Priority Committee, resulted in the labour being provided; 1,000 PoWs arrived on 4 November, as mentioned above.

The PoW camp was also subject to serious critical comment. After the PoWs were moved out [date not certain but from a letter in *The Times* it was probably February or early March 1919] the Army took over their camp to accommodate soldiers, but they only used part of it. During the late 1920s and early 1930s, it became hostel accommodation for workers who hand come, mainly, from the South Wales valleys, resulting in the camp getting the nick-name 'New South Wales'.

Little progress was made from June 1918 until Sir Robert McAlpine & Sons were awarded a contract. It was officially approved in principle on 20 November, informally arranged in December 1918 (when the work started), but contract documents were not actually signed until 16 January 1919. No other firm was considered, nor invited to tender. Moreover, the contract was on a 'cost plus' basis, which ensured the contractor did not loose on the deal, and the taxpayer picked up 'the tab'. Besides the buildings, all on an enormous scale, sidings were to be laid into the area from the Great Western Railway main line.

In May 1919, in response to a Joint Select Committee's questions, the Assistant Financial Secretary to the War Office replied that the original cost was estimated at £990,000 in October 1917. However, he was unable to give detailed responses to some questions as the file was then 'missing'. (How convenient for the Civil Servant!). The eventual cost was about £2 million, not including the purchase of the land.

By early 1920 there were large numbers of rusting vehicles on the large waterlogged site, and the Government was pleased to receive an offer of £7million from entrepreneurs to take the whole lot off their hands in April 1920. This deal also included substantial number of vehicles and quantities of spare parts still in British depots in France and elsewhere. The Government claimed to have realised £4½ million from the sale of vehicles which had been repaired and reconditioned at Slough, over the previous nine months.

The new business, registered as Slough Trading Co Ltd, was headed by Sir Percival Perry and Noel Mobbs. In 1926 the company changed its name to Slough Estates Ltd and has been a great success over the years.

The main sources of information for this brief account have been the 262 page *Report from the Joint Select Committee on Government Works at Cippenham*, House of Commons papers, 3 July 1919, (131) v.5, *The Times* and the files of the *Windsor, Eton and Slough Express* and the *Slough, Eton and Windsor Observer* in Slough Public Library.

No camp or censorship cachets have been recorded by this author.

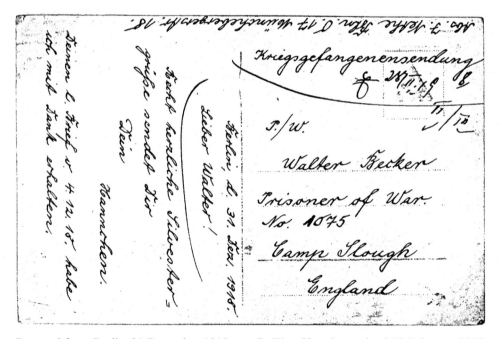

Postcard from Berlin, 31 December 1918, to a PoW at Slough, received 28 February 1919.
This and another card from the same correspondence, dated 5 January 1919,
and received 10 March, do not appear to have been censored.

Southampton, Hampshire

Bevois Mount
Officers transit camp   Grid Ref: SU 423 135

This old manor was purchased by Charles Mordaunt, 3rd Earl of Peterborough (1658-1735) in 1725. He was a successful soldier and a veteran of the War of the Spanish Succession. He added to the house and had the grounds landscaped. A number of literary and musical figures visited the property in his lifetime and during the widowhood of his second wife, Anastasia Robinson, a professional singer (d.1755). The estate then passed through a number of hands over the next 160 years. Some added to the buildings, others had parts demolished. By the 1870s much of the estate had been sold off for housing and some local roads are named after the Earl. The house became a ladies' school, and later a hostel for women students. It was on the north side of Lodge Road, between Cambridge Road and Cedar Road, just over one mile north of the town centre.

The house, and grounds of 1¼ acres, were used as a reception and distribution depot for officer PoWs arriving from France, and for those awaiting transfer to Switzerland. It opened early in September 1914, with accommodation for 85 officers.

Mr Jackson, of the US Embassy, visited on 3 February 1915, when there were 11 army, 9 naval and 17 merchant-ship officers present, with 8 military servants and 20 civilians. Some officers, notably those from SMS *Blücher*, were transferred to Donington Hall before the report was written at the end of that month. The Senior German Officer was Korvetten-Kapitan Ross of SMS *Blücher*. The merchant ship officers were largely from Woermann line vessels. Among the civilians were Baron Plessen (son of a former Prussian Minister at Stuttgart) and Prince Rohan (an Austrian). The grounds of the house, where the prisoners could walk, were enclosed with barbed wire, but the area was small and it was overlooked by the public. Facilities inside the house were barely adequate, but as it was only used as a transit camp that was not considered a problem. No room contained more than nine beds. German cooks were employed. The use of wine and tobacco was freely permitted, and visitors, including women, were allowed. The Commandant was Lt Colonel John Tyrwhitt-Walker (b.1854, late Dorset Regiment, retired 1903). The camp rules were annexed to the report together with 'Instructions relative to prisoners receiving visitors, parcels, letters etc' and the 'German Officers' Mess tariff'. (HO45/10760/269116)

Another US Embassy visit was planned for May 1915 but it did not take place because of contagious disease. Spotted fever (a kind of meningitis) had appeared among prisoners on RMS *Ascania* and PoWs were distributed from the ship to various camps. No further cases were reported. It is presumed that the cases at Bevois Mount were either infected or suspected cases.

When the Embassy did inspect the camp again, on 2 June 1916, the Commandant was Major Ralph James Wilbraham (b.1858, late Duke of Cornwall's Light Infantry, retired 1906). 15 army and one naval officer were present, with six soldier servants. As there were only a few prisoners there were no more than four to a room. No in-patients were in the hospital ward, but all prisoners had been wounded, or ill, so attended as out-patients. (Cd 8324)

A Home Office document of April 1919 listed the camp as closed on 12 February 1919. After the war the house was demolished and replaced by business premises.

"Bevois Mount", the officers' transit camp (International Red Cross postcard)

German soldiers and sailors at Shirley Skating Rink transit camp. Note the man nearest the camera, right centre, has a patch on the back of his civilian style jacket which identified him as a PoW. (International Red Cross postcard)

Shirley Skating Rink,
ORs transit camp

Grid Ref SU 403 134

This was a roller-skating rink on Shirley Road at the junction of Janson Road, about one mile northwest of the present Southampton Central railway station. It had been built only a few years previously, and it was demolished after the war. The building was used as a reception and distribution depot for PoWs arriving from France and for those awaiting transfer to Switzerland. Hence, there were no Committees, nor work for the prisoners. It was opened on 6 September 1914 for 1,000 men.

The first inspection was on 3 February 1915 by Mr Jackson of the US Embassy, when there were 81 German soldiers, 21 naval and 69 merchant seamen held. In addition, there were eight civilian suspects who were kept separate from the others. The men slept on the floor on palliasses. The exercise area outdoors was small, and had only recently been made serviceable by the use of cinders. The sanitary arrangements were poor but improvements were planned. There were no baths, but they were also planned. The prisoners had celebrated the Kaiser's birthday on 27 January. (HO45/10760/269116)

When the US Embassy made their next visit, on 10 May 1915 there were 455 held, including 78 Austrians. All were civilians, except four soldiers who had been servants at Bevois Mount. A new exercise area had been provided in a meadow 200 yards from the camp. Half the men stayed in the camp during the morning, while the other half went to the field, and they swapped over for the afternoons. The four soldiers slept separately from the civilians, in a gallery above the main floor (FO 383/33). No comment was made on the large number of civilians at the camp but, based on the date of inspection, it is quite likely they had been put ashore from one or more of the prison ships. *SS Uranium* was reported to have landed some 250 to reduce over-crowding.

The US Consul at Southampton, Mr Swalm, reported on various matters on 25 November 1915. He wrote that there were nearly 400 present, and all had good overcoats and boots, either German or British. Other clothing was provided as necessary (see postcard illustrated above). Most men had palliasses and four blankets, but those without palliasses were given six blankets. The food was adequate and of good quality. Baths, laundry and lavatory facilities were all inspected and considered good. The Adjutant was named as Major Burrows (possibly Norman Burrows, late South Wales Borderers, retired 1906). The US Embassy visited the same day, and the report dated 2 December, noted some improvements since May. 375 of the military prisoners present, had come from Frith Hill. (763.72114/1054)

240 were present when the US Embassy next visited, on 2 June 1916. Of these 26 were naval, one a civilian, and the others military. The reception and distribution nature of the camp was reiterated. The Commandant was Major RJ Wilbraham, who was also in charge of the officers' camp at Bevois Mount (Cd 8324).

An oblong cachet, 50x30mm, has been seen with a double rim and rounded corners:

COMMANDANT
PRISONERS OF WAR RECEPTION DEPOT
(date)
S O U T H A M P T O N

The lengths of the lines of text were 18, 45 and 42mm. The date was unclear and the strike feint.

The Royal Victoria Military Hospital, Netley, Hampshire

Grid Ref SU 464 076

This hospital had been built in 1857, on the east shore of Southampton Water, with its own pier where hospital ships could dock, so that sick and wounded troops could be landed and easily brought directly into the hospital.

When King George and Queen Mary visited wounded British soldiers at Netley, *The Times* 16 September 1914, noted that a party of wounded German PoWs had just arrived at the hospital.

Southend-on-Sea, Essex

Officers' Reprisal Camp   Grid Ref: TQ 877 864

Five reprisal camps were opened in the Spring 1918 to hold German officers in areas liable to Zeppelin or aircraft bombing. *The Times* 16 March 1918, stated this action was taken in retaliation for the Germans moving prisoners to areas near the battle lines. However, on 26 July the British Government, in a letter to the Swiss Minister, denied that this, and the four others, were reprisal camps (FO 383/440). Nevertheless, Farquharson, in his *Report on Postal Censorship*, p384, did list them as 'Reprisal Camps (Officers)'.

Macpherson gave the opening dates as 2 March 1918 with accommodation for 40 officers and 10 servants in a "house". A Home Office list gave a closing date of 11 December 1918.

The location is not certain but a personal communication quoted a local lady's reminiscences, that the prisoners lived in a large house in Victoria Avenue, which later became the Commercial School, and was situated close to the modern Civic Centre. The lady's account of seeing the German Officers in their grey uniforms with distinctive high collars, some wearing Iron Crosses, concurs with a point made above, about Margate. A Parliamentary reply on 7 May 1918, specifically stated that the German officers were not allowed on the promenade at Margate, but it implied that they were permitted elsewhere about the town. They were probably allowed out, in groups for exercise with escorts, hence the lady at Southend was able to observe the prisoners there. It seems very unlikely that PoW officers would be allowed individual or group freedom to explore the town, even on parole terms.

No mention of this camp has been found in contemporary local newspapers.

Stobs, Hawick, Roxburghshire

Civilians & Other Ranks

Grid Ref: NT 500 095

Stobs Castle, 4 miles south of Hawick, was the home of the Eliott family from 1583. The castle and 3,600 acres were purchased by the War Office, in 1902, and a military camp area was established in 1903. The Castle became the headquarters building for the camp. A siding was provided off the North British Railway line at Acreknowe, about one mile to north, and later it was extended into the camp area. *Post Office Circulars* reported a Camp Post Office opened for a short period in the summer of 1914 and again in the spring of 1915.

Macpherson stated that the PoW camp opened on 22 August 1914, with accommodation that eventually reached 5,960 in huts. *Hawick Express* 14 October 1914, stated that German prisoners were to be held at Stobs, 200 huts were planned, each to accommodate 30 PoWs. The huts were to have concrete bases, corrugated iron roofs and would be asbestos lined. The first prisoners arrived by train from Redford Camp, Edinburgh, in early November 1914 and a picture of them was published in the local paper. *The Scotsman*, 3 November 1914, also reported the first German prisoners to be interned at Stobs Camp had arrived there the previous afternoon. The *Edinburgh Evening News* put their number at 'nearly 500' and reported that they had been taken by a special train, accompanied by a strong military escort.

Mr Jackson reported in February 1915 on camps for the American Embassy. He stated, *inter alia,* that he did not go to the camp at Stobs because of the time such a visit would have required, that there were only 300 prisoners there, and none were soldiers.

In April 1915, 780 Germans were expected and the guard was to be reinforced. In the following month 36 German Navy sailors arrived (*Hawick News* 16 April and 7 May 1915). The latter party probably included crewmen of two Torpedo Boats, A2 and A6, of the 'Flanders Flotilla', sunk off the Dutch coast on 1 May. Later 150 civilians arrived from Liverpool and a further 150 came from Manchester after the 'Lusitania riots' in that city (*Hawick News* 21 May 1915). Orders were issued under DORA to prohibit the public from approaching nearer than ¼ mile of the camp, to deter sight-seers.

The American Embassy visited, on 15 June 1915, when 2,377 were present: 1,098 civilians, 783 soldiers and 496 sailors. The report mentioned an intention to hold up to 12,000. Four compounds had been completed and fifth was in preparation. Huts were arranged for 60 men each, but the average occupancy was only 33 (see comment above about the plans in the previous October). Most of the sailors had previously been held at Handforth in March. (FO383/33)

The Times 22 September 1915, reported the suicide by hanging of Karl Klein, a German sailor from SMS *Blucher*.

The next month four escaped; Gustav Geblin, Alfred Joksch, 26, a Bosuns Mate, Emil Stehr, 26, a ship's officer and Karl Villbrandt, 22. Geblin was retaken at Granton the same day and Joksch at Leith two days later, but the recapture of Stehr and Villbrandt, ex SMS *Blücher*, has not been traced. Another escape by Carl Michalski, also ex SMS *Blücher*, who was recaptured at Newcastleton, was reported in *The Times* 6 and 8 January 1916.

The next American inspection traced was on 4 February 1916 when the Commandant was Lt Colonel Henry James Bowman, (b.1860, late Notts & Derby Regiment, retired 1904). He had 4,616 prisoners under his responsibility, comprising 1,829 soldiers, 504 sailors and 2,283 civilians. Three of the soldiers were from Alsace and, of the civilians, 181 were Austrians, three were Turkish and one was Bulgarian; all the others were German. A marked increase, since the June 1915 visit, was noted in the numbers of educational classes, and those attending them. The subjects included German orthography and grammar, arithmetic, geography and history in the elementary section, while for more advanced students mathematics, physics, navigation, business studies, law, foreign languages, history and classes in agriculture, gardening, and forestry, were available. Dr Markel (see p.6) had assisted in the provision of books and materials. The hospital had beds for 150,

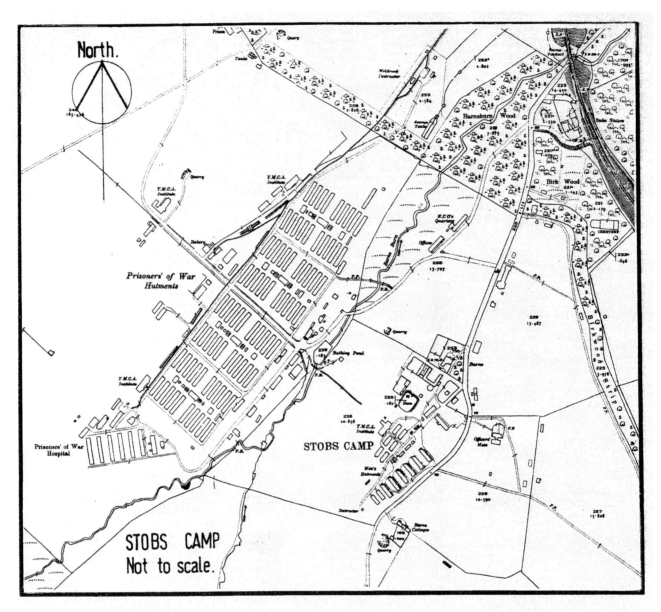

Stobs PoW Camp in its later stage. The railway siding has been laid along the north-west boundary. The plan shows 80 huts in four compounds and the hospital, at the south-west, is separate from the rest of the camp. The guard and staff occupied the huts and buildings to the south-east. The cemetery plot is shown close to where the railway main line reaches the east edge of the map.

and there were 66 in-patients at the visit. On average, the daily attendance of out-patients was 35. The hospital staff included a dentist prisoner and 27 other German personnel. There were two in the cells. Craft work was mentioned and exhibitions of work had been held and sales arranged. This was some of the best handicraft work the inspector has seen in PoW camps. The PoWs asked for walks, under escort, as the recreation areas were too muddy. The Commandant approved the desire, but he had insufficient troops for all the duties to permit walks. Various other requests were put forward. Good relations between staff and PoWs were mentioned. (763.72114/1336)

Boylston Beale of the US Embassy visited on 13 April 1916, when there were 4,592 prisoners: 1,821 soldiers, 502 sailors and 2,269 civilians. Of the civilians, 178 were Austrians, two were Turkish, all others and the soldiers and sailors were Germans. Compounds A and B were civilian, holding 1,102 and 1,098; C and D mixed naval and military 1,081 and 1,209 respectively. In addition 28 hospital staff and 65 patients were in the sick quarters and nine were in prison, of which six were awaiting sentences on charges of pilfering the contents of parcels to fellow PoWs. Three soldiers from Alsace were in one of the civilian compounds. There had been twelve deaths in the camp during 18 months of operation. 500

prisoners were employed in road building. (Cd.8324)

The camp newspaper was mentioned, in Mr Beale's report, as *Neu Stobsische Zeitung*, however wrappers are known printed *Neue Stobser Zeitung*, but a copy of the paper seen, the last published edition, January-February 1919, shows that the title was then *Stobsiade*. Murray and Horne both mention the camp newspaper under this latter title. Coltman and Horne both reported that the civilian internees had started the newspaper venture. When the civilians were moved to Knockaloe, in July 1916, the military PoWs who came in their place, found a stock of back-numbers. They therefore decided to continue the publication, but that cannot account for the 'New' in the title as reported by Mr Beale, three months before the civilians departed.

25 issues of *Stobsiade* were published, every three weeks from October 1916 until the last in 1919. The typesetting was done by the prisoners and, after approval by the censor, it was printed in Hawick. One issue, number 23, was not passed by the censor, but there is no information as to why it was suppressed. The earlier 'civilian' issues of the paper are said to be extremely scarce.

Hansard HC 26 July 1916, vol.84, c1702, reported a question about PoWs making boxes, photo frames and other small articles. The reply stated that this was permitted and that the PoWs were allowed to benefit from sales income, after deducting the costs of the state [materials, tools?]

The first issue of *Stobsiade*, 16 October 1916, produced by the military PoWs.

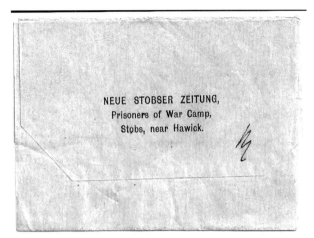

Wrapper for the camp newspaper, undated, sent to a cigarette manufacturer in Baden-Baden.

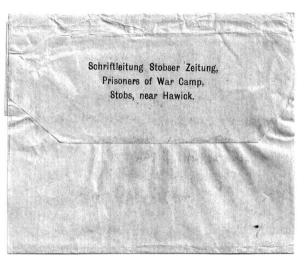

Another wrapper, this for the editorial staff, sent undated, to a Committee in Berlin which provided gift parcels to PoW graduates.

Horne commented on the school established by the PoWs. A hut was set aside for instruction and about 70 students could use the facility at a time, but a total of 3,500 pupils passed through the school, which was staffed by 67 teachers, themselves prisoners. The subjects included commercial studies, motor engineering, architecture, interior design and languages (a shorter list than that mentioned by the American inspector in February 1916).

A number of escapes were made in 1917, the most daring of which was reported in *The Times* of 25 August 1917. Six got away: Wilhelm Jensen and Max Ammerlich (Zeppelin crew), Walter Dusselmann, Emil Schultz, Paul Butz and Bernhard Haak. They reached the coast near Cresswell, Northumberland, and stole a boat, intending to sail to freedom. However, they were picked up by the Royal Navy well out to sea, some seven miles off-shore, which produced a legal problem. As they had managed to sail out of the three-mile territorial limit, had they escaped British jurisdiction? It was held that, as they had not been able to re-join their units, it was in order for them to be taken back into captivity (Belfield p17 and *Hawick Express* 21 September 1917). Some other accounts indicate these PoWs were nearly half-way across the North Sea when found by the Royal Navy.

After the USA joined the war, the inspection of camps was carried out by Swiss and Swedish officials. However, it is surprising that no reports of visits to Stobs, by either Legation, have been traced.

A large number of work camps, dependent on Stobs, were established in Scotland. Many of these camps were engaged in timber cutting but a significant exception was where the PoWs were engaged in laying a pipeline from Loch Eildemor for an aluminium plant at Kinlochleven. When that camp was visited in September 1916 three prisoners, who had come from Cameroons, complained of the cold and that the work was too hard, so they asked to be sent back to Stobs. Another unusual work camp was Raasay, which is described elsewhere in this study.

No reports have been traced, of the clearing of the camp of PoWs. Generally that took place in the Autumn of 1919. The last issue of *Stobsiade*, early in 1919, might suggest an earlier clearance, but letters from the PoW hospital, recorded up to September 1919, indicate otherwise.

35 soldiers, 4 sailors and 6 civilians were buried in a special graveyard, near to the railway station.

The camp came back into regular use during World War II as a training area, but in the 1950s its use declined and it was abandoned. Huts and fittings were auctioned on 15 December 1959, but one hut remains. It is used by a farmer to store feedstuffs for his animals.

Censor's cachets.
The larger type, 33mm diameter, is known in two versions, with six-point and eight-point stars.
The smaller type, 29mm diameter, is known as illustrated, with and without lettering in the rim.

A camp newspaper cachet 56 x 18mm

Commandant's cachet 46 x24mm.

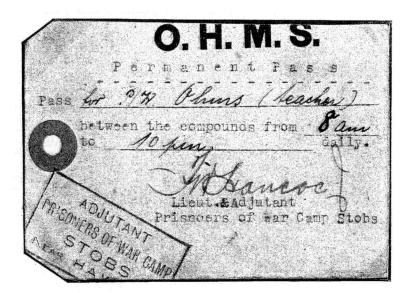

Pass issued to PoW 7801, Willi Ohms, a school-teacher in civilian life, permitting him to move between the compounds.
Note the Adjutant's cachet, also 46 x 24mm. F.W. Hancock was appointed temporary Lieutenant on 12 October 1915, and promoted to temporary Captain on 3 August 1917.

Stratford, London E

Civilians   Grid Ref: TQ 384 840

Richard Noschke, an internee, and Mr Jackson, the US Envoy, both identified this as Ritchie's works, a disused jute factory. It was on the west side of Carpenters Road, immediately to the south of the railway bridge carrying the main line out from Liverpool Street. A 1950s A-to-Z atlas showed this area as a recreation ground.

Boro of West Ham, East Ham & Stratford Express 28 November 1914, reported that a camp was being prepared, in Carpenters Road. For nearly three weeks, contractors had employed over 100 men to get the building ready for the 'foreign guests'. The building was to be heated and well provided with slipper and spray baths. There were to be commodious kitchens and store rooms. A similarly worded report was printed in the *Essex County Chronicle* of 4 December.

Panayi (p64) gave incorrect dates for this camp, but rightly stated that the inmates condemned the accommodation as poor and the administration as intolerant. Thomas (p47) wrote that it was *not suitable for prolonged internment of men, owing to the situation and narrow limits*, a comment he also made of Shrewsbury.

The first batch of German prisoners arrived on Tuesday 15 December,[1] and on 2 January, *Stratford Express* reported that there were then about 100 at the camp, but it could take up to 2,000, which seems an exaggeration. There was also a report of a Christmas service held by a Lutheran Minister and that the prisoners had a Christmas tree and gifts from German ladies. The Commandant was named as Colonel De Burke. (There was no officer of that name in the 1914 Army List, but see footnote overleaf).

Mr Jackson of the US Embassy visited on 28 January 1915. He reported that the camp opened 'about 20 December', and that about 400 were present. Steam heating was installed and electric light was fitted, but used sparingly in the mornings, and switched off at 9.15pm to save expense. Internal governance of the men was in the hands of a 'Senate' who enjoyed their own messing, dormitory and other privileges. The rest slept in one large hall on wooden beds with palliasses. The floor was cement and dry. Internees also ate in this hall, but in a different part, and that space could be used for exercise in bad weather. In good weather the men had to be outside but there was no compulsory drill. There was no opportunity for any occupation except the camp chores and local improvements like making paths or shoe repairs etc. Visits were allowed, including female members of families. Occasional parole had been permitted. The prisoners had organised their own Post Office. The kitchen was under charge of a chef, previously at the Trocadero. A canteen was available but no alcohol was allowed. Two cases had been sent to an outside hospital (probably the German Hospital in Dalston). No deaths were reported. Cases of venereal disease were isolated as far as possible, using separate baths and WCs. A circulating library had been organised by the inmates, and they had a piano. A concert had been organised for the Kaiser's birthday, the previous day (27 January). The cells were empty, but 24 hours bread and water was the maximum punishment given. Camp Rules, in German, and the concert programme were annexed to the report. (HO45/10760/269116)

Stratford Express 6 March 1915, reported that about 400 prisoners were marched out to the railway station, among them 'several Turkish officers'. They were being transferred to the Isle of Man. Both the *East Ham Echo* and the *Stratford Express* of 15 May 1915, carried reports of riots and looting in the wake of the sinking of SS *Lusitania*, which lead to further arrests of German nationals.

Noschke was held there from 23 July 1915 and wrote of his experiences. There were 400 men there before he arrived, and the new total was about 750. The guard was 128 strong. Noschke complained of a leaking roof, poor food and inadequate drains. The recreation area, 50x80 yards, was not big enough for 750 men. A YMCA tent was erected, but it would only take 200 men. A converted stable was used as the hospital. The Commandant 'Marquis de Burr' was *very proud* and he kept the five cells well occupied

---

[1] *West Ham & South-East Essex Mail* 18 December 1914 and also in the *Stratford Express*.

with men on a bread and water diet. At end October 1915, 500 men were removed to the Isle of Man, but later some of them returned to Stratford awaiting repatriation. In early spring 1916, 'de Burr' left and was replaced by Heygate-Lambert, who seemed even worse. He was very strict on internees' letters and denied Noschke the opportunity to lodge an appeal for release. In July 1916 Heygate-Lambert was posted to Frongoch, where the Irish Republicans were held. His replacement was Col Haines, previously at Newbury, *a perfect gentleman in every way*, and conditions began to improve, but soon he was moved on, and succeeded by Col Lushcombe, and the bad old ways were quickly re-established.[2]

Cohen-Portheim was one of many arrested in the aftermath of the sinking of SS *Lusitania* (7 May 1915) and when he was told he was going to Stratford, he imagined he was being taken to Stratford-on-Avon, but quickly had that delightful prospect shattered. By the end of the month he had been moved to Knockaloe.

At the next American inspection, on 22 May 1915, there were 740 prisoners, compared with 400 at the previous visit. Most were from Cameroons and South West Africa. The 20 bed hospital had two cases that day. (FO383/33)

In June 1,000 men left Stratford, in two batches, and were marched to the station (*South Essex Mail* 25 June 1915) which must have emptied the camp. However in September 1,000 aliens were arrested in London, and of those 400 were sent to Stratford, and the others went to Alexandra Palace. (*The Times* 28 September 1915)

US Embassy inspected again on 14 February 1916 when the Commandant was Heygate-Lambert. Three military PoWs were there, temporarily, with 266 German civilians, 62 Austrians, 8 Turkish, and two others. The report stated that the camp was being used as a short term holding place, either for those just interned, or brought there for repatriation, hence life

---

[2] The Commandants mentioned here were: possibly, Colonel Ulick George Campbell de Burgh CB (1855-1922), late staff, retired 1908 (the closest name to 'de Burr' or 'de Burke' found in Army Lists)
Colonel Frederick Arthur Heygate-Lambert, late County of London Yeomanry, b.1857
Lt Colonel Gregory Sinclair Haines, late Commandant of Detention Barracks, b.1858, retired 1913
Major GA Luscombe (promoted to temporary Lt Colonel in June 1917).

was not so well organised as in other camps (but Noschke's experience was of a much longer stay). One large room had 700 men and an outbuilding held 50. All was neat and clean, well warmed, in well-ventilated rooms and well-lit. The hospital was separate and had 15 patients, one an Armenian was serious, but the others were not serious cases. In response to German *Notes Verbale* of 15 and 26 January about the condition of the building, the inspectors wrote that it was old and in constant need of maintenance, but there was only one leak in the roof after recent rain. Food was plentiful and of good quality. Medical care was satisfactory, serious cases being sent to the German Hospital at Dalston. There were fewer present than on the previous visits and conditions generally improved. (FO383/162)

On 20 May 1916 the numbers present were reduced again, for Colonel Heygate-Lambert had only 174 prisoners in the camp, of whom 141 were Germans, 30 Austrians and three Turkish. Most of these men were internees awaiting repatriation, but a few were there at their own choice to be close to their families. (Cd. 8324 and FO 383/163)

The Times 30 December 1916, reported the escape of Emile Schmidt (alias Revosa), age 25, a ship steward. No report of his recapture has been seen.

In February 1917, Richard Noschke applied for, and obtained, a transfer to Alexandra Palace.

Stratford Express 16 May17, reported that Isaac Judah Hannar, Austrian 37, had been charged with maliciously wounding a German inmate Frederich Rauchstadt. When the case was heard Hannar was discharged as the other man, a bully, caused the fracas while Hannar was shaving and the razor was not used intentionally. (It is a little surprising that an open razor was available to an internee, but safety razors were not common at the time.)

On 23 May 1917 the War Office wrote to the GOC Eastern Command, Lt General Sir James Wolfe Murray, informing him that it was proposed to close Stratford but retain the facility for repatriation purposes when that was resumed. Major Luscombe, the Commandant was posted to Alexandra Palace as Commandant, vice Lt Colonel Frowd Walker, who had died. All the prisoners and staff moved to Alexandra Palace (FO383/276).

However, when the Dutch steamers resumed the repatriation sailings in October 1917 (they had been suspended since the previous February) the route was no longer from the Thames, but from Boston, Lincolnshire (HO45/11025/410118). So it seems unlikely that Stratford ever came back into use.

A single oval cachet for Stratford has been seen in a Home Office file, 50 x 30mm, with wording:
PRISONER OF WAR CAMP
* (date) *
STRATFORD

Two International Red Cross postcards of the camp at Carpenters Road, Stratford

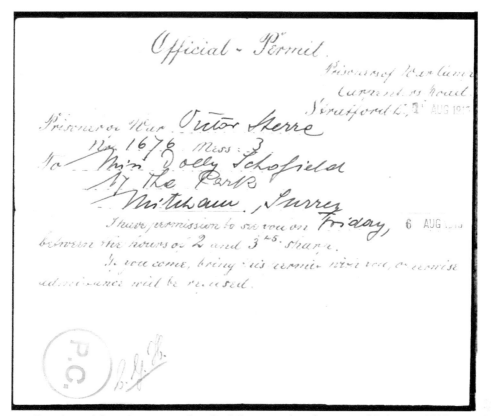
Permit to visit an internee at Stratford Camp on the afternoon of 6 August 1915.

New Year greetings card from Stratford

Stratford-by-Bow, London E

Officers' Reprisal Camp   Grid Ref: TQ 394 847

This was one of five camps opened in the spring of 1918 to hold German officers in areas liable to Zeppelin or aircraft bombing, in response to the Germans moving prisoners to areas near the battle lines. Although *The Times* 16 March 1918 had described them as such, the British Government denied they were reprisal camps, when they replied, on 28 July 1918, to a request for information from the Swiss Minister. Nevertheless, Farquharson, p384, did describe them as Reprisal Camps and listed this one as 'Stratford B' ('Stratford A' being the camp at Carpenters Road).

Macpherson gave opening dates and the size of the accommodation for the other four reprisal camps, but not this one. However, it was the only camp, of this group, with a street address in a Home Office list, dated October 1918. The address was 11 & 13 Water Lane, E15. These were two large houses on the west side of the street opposite The Green, and close to the Artillery Barracks.

It appears from the enquiry from, and the reply to, the Swiss Legation, mentioned above, that the officers came from Holyport, near Maidenhead, in April 1918. (FO 383/440)

The Times 11 June 1918, p3c, reported the escape of three officers, and the recapture of two, at Walsham, was reported two days later. However, the *Stratford Express* 15 June, account of the incident, gave the recapture of three at Walton-on-the-Naze on Wednesday 12 June. The three who got away were Edmund Klaiss, a U-boat commander, Hugo Karl Thielmann and Johann Diedrich Braue. However, a Sergeant and another officer, who also got out, were caught at Ilford quite quickly. The five had tunnelled from the kitchen out to the garden and escaped on Saturday 8 June. Questions were asked in the House of Commons about the tunnel, said to be 40 feet long, how long had it taken to dig, and questioning the level of supervision. A Court of Enquiry was promised. (*Hansard HC* 17 June 1918, vol.107, col.37)

This camp was closed on 11 December 1918. Whist no report of the destination of these prisoners has been seen, it is likely they went to Oswestry, to where it is known that officers from other reprisal camps were transferred.

Templemore, Co Tipperary, Ireland

Other Ranks

Irish Grid Ref 2110 1715

This camp was Richmond Barracks, Templemore, 79 miles southwest of Dublin. Macpherson bracketed this camp with Lancaster, but his reason for this is not understood.

Building of this barracks began in 1800 and was completed by 1810. It was the third largest barracks in Ireland with accommodation for 54 officers and 1,500 men, plus married quarters etc. There were two parade squares, formed by the buildings, and in view of the numbers quoted it would imply 2 battalions of infantry at peace-time strength. The April 1914 Army List did not show any military units located at Templemore.

Soon after the outbreak of war, the two squares were made into 4 compounds with barbed wire fences, guard platforms and searchlights. Shelters were built in the open yards for the prisoners.

OMathuna wrote that civilians living in Ireland were arrested and taken to Templemore on 5 September but they must have been removed to Oldcastle during the next month or so. The first PoWs at Templemore were a batch of 300 (per OMathuna, but he did not give a date).

The first report in *The Times* of prisoners being sent to Templemore was on 23 September 1914, when it was stated that 400 PoWs, transferred from Great Britain, were taken to 'a military barracks in the centre of Ireland'. A further report, of 400 soldier prisoners being moved from Frith Hill 'to Tipperary' was carried in *The Times* of 24 October and no doubt other batches were also sent. A German report on camps (in CAB 37/123/37) mentioned that the PoWs at Templemore had come from Newbury.

During February 1915 the whole population of Templemore camp, 1,855 PoWs, were moved to Leigh, in Lancashire, in five batches. A local paper at Leigh (26 February) reported that 'the barracks at Templemore are now entirely free of German prisoners'. Another Leigh paper, reporting the arrival of the first party of prisoners, stated that the barracks at Templemore had been condemned but, from the subsequent history of the barracks, that appears to be inaccurate. Mr Jackson, in his report to the US Ambassador of February 1915, stated that he did not go to Templemore because, he was informed officially, that it was to be, and probably was by then, closed.

Walsh speculated about the reason for moving the PoWs out in early 1915. He suggested the British Government feared an Irish Nationalist rising, during which the PoWs would be released. This theory is quite plausible, and was supported by OMathuna, but the internees at Oldcastle were not transferred to Britain. The latter though, being mostly civilians and merchant seamen, would have been considered a much lower risk.

In March 1915, the Royal Munster Fusiliers arrived and Richmond Barracks became a regular training facility. James, in *British Regiments* recorded a number of battalions at Templemore up to the end of 1917. After the war a battalion of the Northampton Regiment was stationed there, until they marched out on 13 February 1922, when the Provisional Irish Government took over the premises.

During the Civil War the facility was used by the IRA who renamed the place McCan Barracks. Later the Irish Army used the barracks until 1929, and again during the 1939-45 war. Subsequently it became a Training Centre for the Gardai (the Irish Police Service).

York

Civil and Military, mixed camps.

Three sites have been located in this City from local newspaper reports:

    York Castle   Grid Ref: SE 605 514
    The Exhibition Buildings   SE 600 523
    Leeman Road   SE 590 523.

Because of movements of prisoners between the three camps it seems better to consolidate the short history into a single narrative:

York Castle was first used on 8 August, a very early date. It is possible that initially the old debtors' prison was used. That building was demolished in the 1930s and stood where there is now a car park. However, the curators at York Castle Museum have no knowledge, or record, of PoWs or internees being held in any part of their buildings. At the end of August 1914, newspapers reported that the square before the Castle buildings was occupied by a tented camp. Later barrack huts were planned, but it seems unlikely that they were ever built.

The wooden Exhibition Buildings, behind the City Art Gallery in St Leonards Place, had been closed as unsafe since early 1909, but they were not demolished until the 1940s. Parts of the buildings were used by the military from early August 1914, as billets, but internees were held there from about 11 September. City Council records show that the Art Gallery was closed from 15 September until 22 October. However, on 27 October internees were put there again, temporarily. The date of final evacuation of these men has not yet been determined, but they had been moved out by 19 November.

Leeman Road was the disused works of the York Engineering Company, to the south of Leeman Road and Carleton Street, about 700 yards northwest of the railway station. The first 'guests' arrived about 25 September 1914. Again the date and circumstances of clearing this camp are not known, but it appears from the absence of information in local papers in 1915, and from a War Office file (see below), that the prisoners were moved elsewhere early in 1915.

A local paper, *Yorkshire Herald*, 9 August 1914, reported that a party of 50 had arrived at the station on Saturday 8 August, and were marched to York Castle where they were placed in the 'Detention Barracks'. Later it was learned that most of these men were from Harrogate, so it is likely they were hotel staff. There were also reports of arrests elsewhere. Men from Selby were brought to York. Those arrested at Pontefract were detained at the Barracks in that town, while others arrested in Bingley were held in the local Police Station. From Shipley men were taken to Bradford, but for those detained in Leeds there was no indication of what happened to them, but mail to Leeds is known, sent from Leeman Road camp. The following day the same paper published a picture captioned; *Released Germans crossing Lendal Bridge on their way to York Station* with a short statement, that some of the men arrested and brought to York Castle on Saturday and Sunday had been released.

On 11 August the same paper reported that a party of 20 were moved from East Retford to York Castle. It was stated that the previous Saturday (8th), 16 men employed by an Anglo-German syndicate to sink a mine at Harworth (2½ miles southwest of Bawtry) had been arrested as they were of military age and were taken to East Retford.

Yorkshire Gazette, 15 August, reported that batches of Germans had been brought to York Castle during the past week. No antipathy had been shown to them. Another York paper had said, on the Wednesday (12th), that there were about forty held at the Castle, but that figure seems too low.

More short reports of arrivals were carried in York papers and at the end of August, *Yorkshire Herald* mentioned 130 prisoners at the Castle, living in tents. The following week the paper expected a further 250 to arrive, but also that a new camp was planned which would take up to 1,500 men. When more Germans and Austrians did arrive the existing accommodation was insufficient so 100 were moved to the Exhibition Buildings, where palliasses were provided. Yet more were expected, 300 to 400 were mentioned, for which arrangements were being made pending the completion of the new camp in Leeman Road, on land previously occupied by York Engineering Company. (*Yorkshire Herald* 12 September 1914)

On 24 September, the same paper (and *Yorkshire Gazette* 26 September) reported that 300 Germans, from Redford Barracks, Edinburgh, including 70 sailors, had arrived by train and that they went to Leeman Road. Two days later, those who had been in the Exhibition Buildings, were moved to Leeman Road. Nearly 100 were transferred, under armed escort, marching via St Leonards, Museum Street and Lendal Bridge. Prior to the move of this York party, others had arrived at the new camp from Burton, Newcastle, and Sunderland.

At the end of September, the Castle was cleared of detainees. 280 were marched across the city, to Leeman Road, escorted by 51 men of Royal Scots Greys. This took the total at Leeman Road to over 1,000. In October there were reports of daily visits by large crowds to watch the PoWs taking exercise. The number in the camp was stated to be 1,180, with men from all walks of life. There was comment on the extraordinary amount of baggage the prisoners had brought, which was stored in one of the bigger sheds of the camp. There was no apparent lack of money among the detainees, who had a shop in the camp selling tobacco and cigarettes. An extension of the camp was reported as 'planned for a further 500' (*Yorkshire Gazette* 3 October 1914).

Yorkshire Herald, 5 October, also mentioned the numbers held at the camp and commented on the crowds who gathered to watch exercise periods. The report went on to say that the internees would shortly be removed to Wakefield.

Lofthouse Park Camp, at Wakefield, was opened in October 1914, but although reports that month mentioned 1,000 there, the numbers were much less when the US Embassy inspected the camp in February. The ships at Southend-on-Sea and Portsmouth are other possible destinations for men from York, but they did not begin to take internees until the second half of November.

However, many more civilians were brought to York from all over the north of England. All went to Leeman Road, except one party which, by mistake, were marched off to the Castle. The accommodation at Leeman Road was stretched to the limit. The paper said that any more arrivals would have to go elsewhere. Hoardings were to be erected *to arrest public curiosity* and prevent sight-seeing.

Because of the overcrowding 150 civilians were moved to the Exhibition Buildings, as a stop-gap, and it was said they would be moved on to York Castle after a few days. (*Yorkshire Herald* 24, 26 and 27 October 1914)

At the end of the month internees were still living in the Exhibition Buildings and a report (*Yorkshire Herald* 30 October) that tents in Castle Square were to be replaced by huts, suggests there were more internees held there. By the middle of November, with the Exhibition Buildings still in the hands of the War Office, the Post Office was faced with a dilemma. For some years they had used that building as a temporary sorting office for the Christmas post, so alternative space had to be found (*Yorkshire Gazette* 14 November). In the event the Guildhall was used for the mail.

The internees must have been moved out of the Exhibition Buildings, for Lady Plumer was able to have a tea party there, for 1,000 wives of soldiers and sailors, on 19 November (*Yorkshire Herald* 20 November). In the Spring of 1915, the Exhibition Building was mentioned as the venue of a Soldiers' Recreation Club, and later that year it was used as offices by the Army Pay Corps.

Papers in the German Federal Archives state that Leeman Road was closed in 1915 due to unsanitary conditions. It has not been possible to verify this statement from contemporary newspapers, nor from the minutes of the City Council, a body which one would expect to have been concerned with drainage and sanitary matters in their area.

The PoW list No.22, dated 13 February 1915, (WO900/45) sent by the Prisoner of War Information Bureau, to Germany, did not include York as a place of detention, which seems to indicate that it may have been closed by that date.

Prisoners of War Camp,
YORK.

Camp cachet, overall length of top line 53mm.

Other places of detention

In the early days of the war a number of reports were made of aliens being held in various towns, in all sorts of buildings, as temporary places of detention, before the men were either released, on being able to give a good account of themselves, or were moved to one of the early tented camps.

Among these reports were:

Western Morning News 14 August 1914 reported that the workhouses in Falmouth, Redruth, St Colomb and Truro, all in Cornwall, were being used to hold passengers and crew landed from two German liners held at Falmouth. At Falmouth the Guardians raised questions about the expenses of feeding and maintaining the aliens and a resolution was passed protesting against the landing of aliens at their port without the government making adequate provision for their supervision, accommodation, maintenance or clothing. This resolution was sent to the Local Government Board in London.

On 21 August that paper stated that 110 destitute aliens had been in Truro workhouse. Eight of then had sufficient money for the fare to London and had been permitted to travel the previous Monday. Seven or eight more were Jewish and the Clerk of the Guardians was in touch with the Jewish Society in London regarding them. It was also stated that the Truro Guardians had sent a bill for their expenses to the Local Government Board. At Penzance the local barracks was used to hold some of the men landed from the ships at Falmouth.

In Swansea, 85 prisoners were held under guard at Lutland Street School, pending formation of a permanent camp. (*Western Morning News* 11 August 1914)

At Gosport, 120 Germans were landed, on 10 August, from an un-named German steamer anchored off Yarmouth, and marched to Fort Elson (*Western Morning News* 11 August 1914 and "The First Prisoners" in *Yesterday No.4,* August 1988).

At Exeter, 46 Germans from Plymouth and elsewhere were lodged at St Sidwell's School, under guard. A further batch was expected. Two days later it was reported that many at St Sidwell's had been released on parole. (*Western Morning News* 12 and 14 August 1914)

Throughout the second half of August and during September more reports were carried in the west-of-England papers of Germans and Austrians being taken off ships at Falmouth and Plymouth. By then, the camps at Dorchester and Newbury were in use, and trains were soon arranged for the men to be moved, under guard, to those camps.

No doubt similar reports of Germans and Austrian citizens being arrested and detained at other ports can be found in other areas of the country. A supplement to *The London Gazette* of 2 October 1914 listed 116 ships of German or Austrian registration detained in ports of the United Kingdom from Kirkwall and Wick to Falmouth and Fowey and from Yarmouth and King's Lynn to Tralee and Berehaven.

From a postcard addressed to the Captain of a German ship seized at Blyth it appears there was some sort of holding place at Newcastle-upon-Tyne. The card, from USA, was addressed to him at 'Concentrate Camp, Newcastle' and it passed through the office of the Chief Constable on 28 November 1914. It is quite likely that a local Police Station was used as a temporary holding place, but equally it could have been a ship in dock, as a Hull.

Postcard from New York 15 November 1914, addressed to the Captain of the German ship *Gamma* (which had been seized at Blyth) at "Concentrate Camp, Newcastle". Marked with the Chief Constable's Office cachet 28 November 1914.

Prisons

A number of prisons have been identified as holding PoWs or internees from time to time, but only a few of them have stories which have been gleaned from newspapers and the public record.

Brixton Grid Ref: TQ 305 742

Brixton Prison, in south London, 3½ miles south of Trafalgar Square, was built in 1819. During the Victorian era it served at different times as a female prison and a military prison. In 1898 the gaol was returned to the Prison Commissioners and it was then used as a trial and remand prison for the whole of London.

Early in the war about 100 aliens were held in Brixton under the Defence of the Realm Act (DORA). The intention appears to have been to begin expulsion proceedings against these men but for some reason that did not happen. In late 1915, some were moved to Reading, but enemy nationals with criminal convictions remained at Brixton until 1918.

Lt Matthias Peterson, who had been detained at Gibraltar and then transferred to UK, attempted an escape from Southampton on 23 March 1915. He faced Court Martial at Southampton, on 8 April, and was sentenced to 3 years imprisonment on 12 April. The term was commuted to 4 months which he served at Brixton until 7 August 1915.

Ober-Lt Hans Andler of the German Navy wrote, from Brixton on 7 May 1915, to complain to the American Embassy that his Court Martial on 23 April for an escape from Dyffryn Aled, was irregular in terms of Article 8 of Chapter 11 of the Annex to the Hague Convention. The War Office responded to this point by stating that Section 22 of The Army Act covered the offence of escape (FO 383/65).

On 13 June 1918 the Swiss Minister forwarded a *Note Verbale* from Berlin about 48 Germans previously in Brixton, then at Knockaloe, Camp III, compound 4. The Foreign Office response was that they had been transferred from Brixton at their own request. It was stated that 'all in that compound had criminal antecedents or were of character such that it was in the best interest of other prisoners to keep them separate' (FO383/440).

Chelmsford   Grid Ref: TL 717 071

Chelmsford Prison was built in 1828, half a mile east of the town centre. It was badly damaged by fire in 1978.

This appears to have been the usual place of detention for officers sentenced to prison terms for escapes after mid 1915, for two officers who escaped in April 1915 served their sentences at Brixton (see above). Chelmsford then served as a military prison during the war, but a complaint by an Austrian officer in 1917, indicated that civilian convicts were also held there. It is presumed that military prisoners were held in a separate wing, apart from civilian convicts.

On 11 November 1915 a German *Note Verbale* protested about conditions at Chelmsford. In response the War Office wrote to the Foreign Office to say the American embassy was welcome to inspect the place. On 29 November Mr Lowry visited and reported satisfactory conditions. Three German officers under sentence, who he met there, Thelen, Keilback and Tholens made no complaints. (FO 383/65)

A *Note Verbale* from Berlin dated 2 July 1917 concerned Lt Otto Thelen and Lt Lehmann who had escaped from Chelmsford on 26 May, and were recaptured two days later and returned to Chelmsford. The War Office informed the Foreign Office on 2 August that no proceedings had been taken against the two officers. Both had been released from their previous sentences, Thelen on 25 June and Lehmann on 29 July. Both were then at Kegworth (FO383/285) and both got out of that camp in September 1917 among the 22 officers who escaped by tunnel.

In October 1917 the Swedish Legation presented a letter from Arped Horn, an Austrian officer then at Dyffryn Aled, which he wanted to send to the Austro-Hungarian Government. He complained about his treatment at Chelmsford, and of being kept in solitary confinement for 41 days after recapture and, that after being sentenced to 14 days imprisonment, he was held at Chelmsford. He considered the place inappropriate for his status as an officer, citing the size of the cell, its condition, the ban on smoking, except in the courtyard for one hour morning and evening, food restrictions, a ban on newspapers and that he was held among English convicts. (FO383/250)

Reading   Grid Ref: SU 720 735

Reading Prison was built in 1844. It was unused from 1919-39, and in 1940 it became first a Borstal, then a Detention Barracks for the Canadian troops. It was a prison again in 1946. Parts of the buildings were demolished in 1972.

As mentioned above, early in the war about one hundred aliens were held in Brixton Prison and others were held in gaols around the country, all were detained under DORA pending the enforcement of Expulsion Orders. However, conditions in convict prisons were not good, so the Home Office, in consultation with the Prison Commission, decided to transfer the detainees to Reading Prison which would be designated a place of internment for aliens awaiting deportation or expulsion, with a special regime. The convict population was moved out of Reading in November 1915 and internees from Brixton, Birmingham, Leeds, Liverpool, Wakefield, Stafford and Manchester prisons, arrived at Reading during December 1915 and January 1916.

On 4 July 1916 the British Government, responding to a *Note Verbale* from Berlin, dated 17 May, stated that Reading Gaol was not a camp for PoWs. It contained many persons who were not aliens who were guilty of grave acts of espionage and their identities could not be disclosed. The US Embassy was welcome to inspect the conditions under which German civilians were detained there.

The inspection took place on 8 July 1916 and the report described Reading as a former gaol, but cleared of convicts in latter part of 1915. Three wings, each of 3 floors, were in use. The cells were 8 x 14ft, with a wooden bed, table and chair. Additional furniture was permitted and many cells were comfortably furnished with an iron bedstead, carpet, easy chair, mirror, table and table cloth etc, which were hired for 2s.6d per week. Almost every man had a sprung bed, costing them 9d per week. A small building in the yard served as a canteen and club room. Light wines and beer could be purchased, but these had to be served with meals in the dining room. Exercise periods were for one wing at a time. Cells were locked from 9pm until 7am, otherwise detainees could move about their own wing at leisure, but not to other wings. Two letters per month, both in and out, were permitted. There were no complaints and all seemed on excellent terms with the Governor. No details of the numbers or nationalities were stated in the report. (FO383/193)

On 3 November 1917 four escaped, Carl Hemlar (Austrian) Carlos Kuhne Escosuras (Spanish) Curt Muller, alias Charles Neller (a German) and Louis Class (also German). Class surrendered in London, at Cannon Row Police Station, while Escosuras was believed to have sought sanctuary in the Spanish Embassy. It was supposed that the men had made a key to allow them access to the exercise yard and then they scaled the 18ft wall. (*Berkshire Chronicle*: 9 November 1917) *The Times* 5 November, p5c, gave three of the names as Jenlar, Burt Muller and Louis Cress. Escosuras was described as a German spy using a Spanish name, and an alias Diaz.

Many of the men held at Reading became discontented and demanded an improvement in their conditions. Therefore, in November 1917, the Home Office moved them to Knockaloe, where they were held in Compound 4 of Camp III (FO383/272 & 436)

In response to another *Note Verbale*, in June 1918, it was stated that the move to the Isle of Man was at their own request, and that *all in that compound had either criminal antecedents or characters such that it was in the interest of other prisoners at Knockaloe to keep them separate* (FO 383/440).

In a Swiss report of an inspection of Knockaloe in August 1918, (report dated 11 September) it was observed that prisoners transferred from Reading were simply segregated, and that no special restrictions were applied. (HO45/10947/266042)

Letter of 18 September 1917, from Richard Koch, who had been interned for two years, to the Netherlands, explaining that in future he would correspond with his parents through the Thomas Cook service.
There is a feint War Office oval cachet on the face of the cover.
The postmark appears to be 17 December and addressee's note is dated 27/12/17.

Stafford Detention Barracks
Grid Ref: SJ 923 238

A group of 59 NCO PoWs were charged with stealing from the Quartermasters' Stores at Catterick in March 1918. All were found guilty and sentenced to six months with hard labour by a military court. The sentences were commuted to 84 days military confinement and were served at Stafford Detention Barracks. (FO 383/440, 13 June 1918)

Woking Detention Barracks
Grid Ref: SU 946 590

This was the usual place of detention for rank and file and NCO prisoners committed to prison or detention.

The US Embassy visited on 7 August 1916, to interview Fahnrich von Schweinichen, Lt Kahn of the Bavarian Artillery and Lt Johe of SMS *Blucher*, at the request of German *Notes Verbale*. Von Schweinichen had been released on 24 June, having received five months remission of sentence and was returned to Dorchester. Papers in FO 383/190 state he had attempted to escape from Stobs (no date given). In September 1916 he was at Pattishall and was interviewed by the US Embassy inspector, Mr Brantingham.

The other two prisoners referred to were in fact Offizierstellvertreter Cahn and Fahnrich-zur-See Johl; neither were commissioned officers. Their names were different from those given in the German communique, but that was, very likely, due to wrong spellings in the British reports of their escape. Both men had been sentenced to six months for attempting to escape from Handforth and had arrived at Woking on 7 May.

Two Berlin *Notes Verbale* of 18 June 1917 enquired about Clemens Rücker and Johann Biercher. The Foreign Office replied that the former had been sentenced to one year imprisonment at Woking because he had persistently refused to work and openly defied authority. The latter had also persistently refused to work at Winchester, and had been sentenced to 9 months on 9 March 1917. (FO383/306)

Farquharson, at p384, listed Camps and Hospitals in his *Report on Postal Censorship*. In addition to those prisons described above, he included Bodmin, Cromwell Gardens and Hereford, but no press comment has been seen, nor any papers in Foreign Office files, concerning these places. Chatham and Devonport Detention Barracks were also listed by Farquharson, and reference to them will be found in chapter 2 of this study. Whether these two latter locations were used after the policy of segregation of submarine crews was ended, is not known.

PoW Labour Companies in France

Although some may consider this falls outside the title of this study, it seems appropriate to include this topic, particularly as the two major camps at Le Havre and Rouen were treated by the War Office as camps within the UK. Initially the prisoners were transferred from camps in Britain in the spring of 1916, but later many prisoners captured on the western front were held in France, for employment in labour gangs, rather than being sent over to Britain.

The proposal to employ PoWs with the British Army in France was first made early in 1916. Initially the C-in-C, General Sir Douglas Haig, declined the offer as he feared escapes, that a great number of guards would be required, the expenses, and he expected a poor performance from such labour. However, Kitchener persuaded Haig to accept 1,000 PoWs on an experimental basis, but rather more than that number were transferred from Britain to France. 750 went to Rouen on 5 April 1916, and 700 to Le Havre on 26 April. Initially they worked in the ports unloading ships, but they did not handle munitions, and a further 500 followed to Le Havre in early May. With the demands on manpower for the Battle of the Somme, which began 1 July 1916, PoW labour was employed more extensively, in quarries and forests, on road works and in the Lines of Communication. A statement in the House of Commons on 10 July 1916 confirmed that 2,700 prisoners had been moved to France, but they remained under the same conditions as when they were in UK, and had not been handed over to the French.

In response to the British moves to employ PoWs in France, the German government announced, on 10 May 1916, that two thousand British PoWs would be put into labour companies in occupied areas of Poland and France. (Cd..8260 and *Hansard* 10 July 1916, vol.84, col.6.)

The American Embassy inspected the camps at Le Havre on 6 July 16, where the Commandant was Lt Colonel K C Wright (previously at Leigh and Frongoch). One 'camp' was a French registered ship, SS *Phryne*, where 20 NCOs and 452 Privates slept in bunks, in 3 tiers, arranged around the sides of four upper holds. Hatchways above were always open, but a roof has been built over them, several feet above the deck to provide ventilation. An Offizierstellvertreter had a cabin on deck and the NCOs had the use of a saloon as a recreation room. Nine prisoners were under confinement on board. Newspapers were being withheld, because three had tried to escape, but that restriction was to be removed shortly. No serious complaints were made.

Nearby, in a barracks of wooden huts, on Quai de la Gironde, 735 prisoners were accommodated, and in a further, partly completed, barracks near the Quai there were 200. Total at Le Havre 1,407. Most of these PoWs were reported to have come from Handforth and Frongoch on 26 May, but some had been recently captured. In the barracks, the bunks were in tiers of four. Previously these barracks had been used by German PoWs of the French, but they were to be vacated for a new camp to contain 1500, at that date already partly built. Washing and bathing arrangements, were at the time adequate, but in the new camp they were said to be excellent. Every two weeks the prisoners went to a sanitary station to be 'thoroughly cleaned'. There was only a Sick Bay, which an English doctor visited each day. Hospital cases were sent to the British military hospital in Le Havre. No epidemics or deaths were reported.

The PoWs were engaged in unloading cargo from ships and loading barges and railway wagons. They worked for the French Government and for contractors, and were supervised by French NCOs, but under British guards. They worked irregular hours but the average was 8 hours per day, 6 days per week. The average number employed each day was 950. Other prisoners were engaged in erecting the new camp. The report commented that in the new camp there would be little exercise space and suggested it should be increased. (763.72114/1797)

The US Embassy inspected Le Havre again on 7 December 1916, when there were 1,479 soldiers and 88 NCOs present, living in four large barrack huts, each for 390 men. There was no heating in the huts in view of the great fire risk. The huts lacked floors, which had been ordered, and the Commandant promised to urge no further delay in laying them. 1,100 were employed on labour parties and the remainder on camp duties, including 15 cooks. The sick were treated at the British hospital nearby. To date there had been three deaths, including one suicide.

There was a complaint that the work of shifting 200 lb (89kg) sacks was too hard, but the Commandant's reply was that the work was being done for the French Government and he therefore had no say in the matter. The prisoners also complained that they had only one rest day in three weeks (a more rigorous regime than at the previous visit), which was insufficient, and Colonel Wright promised to see what he could do on that point. (FO383/284)

Clearly, the regime of PoWs in British custody working for the French Government was not satisfactory and on 18 February 1917 the War Office wrote to the POW Department of the Foreign Office seeking the release of these men back to full British control. The British Army needed the labour for its railways and Lines of Communications. The French responded by releasing the 3,000 prisoners to the British authorities, in batches of 500, from the end of April; each batch made up of equal numbers from Le Havre and Rouen. (FO383/284)

In July 1918 the Swiss Legation sent in a *Note Verbale* from Berlin, dated 14 June concerning eleven German NCOs in prison at Rouen. They had refused to turn out for supervision work on 28 December 1917, claiming it was their rest day, but the work schedules had been altered, on account of Christmas. (FO383/442)

By early 1918 PoWs were, for preference, being held in France, rather than transferred to Britain. They were processed through the holding cages and sorted into trades. The occupations had been expanded to include road-making, quarrying, forestry, railway construction, salvage, laundry, construction and repair in RE and ASC workshops, ordnance work and unskilled labouring. PoW Companies were not employed within 30km of the front line, but previously they had been as near as 8km until the German Government objected and threatened reprisals. PoW labour could not be used on any work in connection with defence, nor which had a direct connection with military operations, nor handle munitions. However by November 1918 it was permitted to employ the PoWs in handling derelict rifles and used shell cases in old battlefield areas outside the 30 km limits.

At the beginning of October 1916 there were 12,300 prisoners serving in 29 PoW Companies and the Adjutant General at GHQ, BEF, Lt General Sir George Fowke, estimated a need for fifty Companies. By early 1917 the numbers had increased to 20,445, employed in 47 Companies and in November 1918 there were 343 PoW Companies with a total strength of 1,032 officers and 180,000 other ranks (prisoners and escorts).

The January 1919 POWIB *List of Places of Internment* listed Companies 1 to 372, but 28 of those were noted as having been closed. Brown (*in FPHS Newsletter* #122, p11) recorded an undated cachet of No.400 PoW Coy. and that of No.505 Coy. on an official cover of November 1919 is shown below. These higher numbers suggest a further enlargement of the labour force attached to the Clearing-Up Army in France and Flanders. It is likely the system did not reallocate the number when a Company was disbanded.

Initially the Companies comprised 425 prisoners: 400 labourers with 10 NCOs for supervision, plus 6 interpreters, 2 tailors, 2 shoemakers, 4 cooks and 1 medical orderly. Later an additional 20 labourers and 11 NCOs were added, bringing the nominal strength to 456. Labourers, orderlies, tailors and shoemakers were all paid 4d a day, while the interpreters and NCOs received 6d per day. Initially cooks, sanitary men and others employed on camp routines were not paid so those jobs were rotated on a daily basis. Later the cooks were employed on a long term basis, and they were then paid out of canteen profits.

The Company staff comprised the Commander, a Company Sergeant-Major, a Quartermaster, one Sergeant, four Corporals and a clerk. The escort/guard varied between 46 and 90 enlisted men, 12 to 19 NCOs and one officer. The strength of the guard depended on the nature of the employment and the degree of scattering of individual working parties.

Canteens were set up in every camp which were supplied from the Expeditionary Forces Canteen. These canteens had to be managed by the prisoners and the profits from their sales of sweets, chocolates, tobacco, toiletries etc. were divided, presumably after paying the cooks. 50% went towards losses, wear and tear, or damage which could not be attributed to a specific individual, and the other 50% was used by Commandants to purchase items of benefit to the Company as a whole, such as musical instruments, games equipment, gramophones.

In 1918 metal token coinage was introduced in PoW Camps in France, in a similar move to that in camps in Britain. Tokens of 1 franc, 50 centimes and 10 centimes, were issued in exchange for any French or British money in the possession of PoWs. They could spend these tokens only in the canteens within their camps. Camp staff were instructed to be aware of the possibility of counterfeiting but, as any losses due to the circulation of spurious coins would reduce the benefits accruing to the prisoners, it was not seen as a problem. On leaving one camp for another, or for hospital, or on transfer to UK, a PoW had to hand in his tokens and he was credited with the equivalent value in his account with the paymaster.

Peter Burrows, in his 1987 book *'I am Well'* illustrated postcards issued by the British Army for the use of PoWs. These included cards with space for the sender's address part-printed as:

    Absender:
    No.____ PRISONER OF WAR CO.,
    BRITISH TROOPS IN FRANCE.

A special printing of the PoW letter-sheet (the patent design) was also made, with a part-printed sender's address:

No. ..... NAME ....
No. ..... PRISONERS OF WAR COMPANY IN
                                      FRANCE
Care of G.P.O., LONDON
ENGLAND

However, it should be noted that some of these specially printed letter-sheet were used by PoWs in Egypt, in 1919.

Besides official records, this account of the PoW labour force has drawn upon two articles by Peter T Scott, cited in the bibliography, to whom grateful acknowledgement is given.

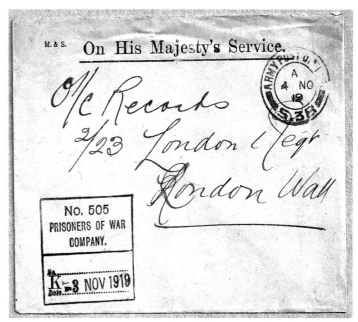

The cachet, 35mm square, on this official cover is the highest PoW Company number recorded. Brown also reported a similar divided box cachet 30 x 35mm, with the same wording, and another 28 x 21mm inscribed:

          PRISONERS OF WAR
                SECTION
         G.H.Q. 3RD ECHELON.

The date and the address of this cover, suggest that it was possibly sent on winding up the Company after the prisoners had been repatriated to Germany.

Censor mark (37mm diameter) used in France on outward PoW mail, but not invariably. Numbers up to 18 have been recorded. Most mail was going to Germany and much of that was also censored in the PW Branch in London.

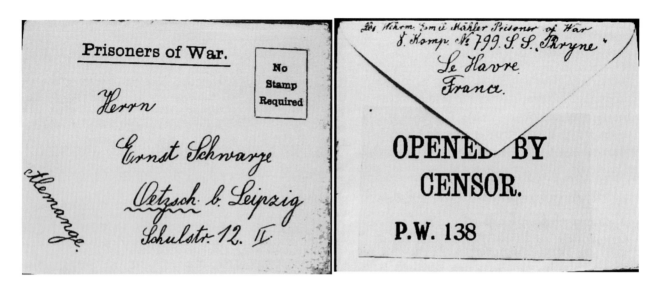

Cover from a prisoner on SS *Phryne* at Le Havre

Pre-printed cover from Germany to a PoW Unteroffizier in France, sent from Frankfurt am Main 4 August 1919.

Camp List, Introduction

The list which follows has been compiled from five different lists found in The National Archive. Parent camps were not always shown on some lists, and the nature of some camps was not given. As the lists were dated in 1918 and 1919, camps that had already closed (eg Beech Abbey, Queen's Ferry, Templemore, York etc) are not included.
The following abbreviations have been used:

Type (ie the nature of the camp)
- a = Agricultural camp
- ad = Agricultural depot
- c = Civilian camp
- cw = Civilian work camp
- f = Female camp
- h = Hospital
- o = Officers' camp
- p = Prison
- t = Transit camp
- w = Work camp
- w.c = indicates a change of status, work camp then civilian camp (or v-v)

Insufficient data has been found to categorise work camps by the nature of their work, but forestry, quarries, mining, drainage projects, road, railway, and workshop employments are recorded.

Although parent camps were not always stated, it appears that with few exceptions each parent camp had a well defined 'parish', so assumptions can be made. Where a name appears in capital letters that is a parent camp. Some major camps did not have subsidiary working camps.

Most locations can be pinpointed from the postal address, but care is needed as in some cases the postal address was the office of the local commander, not the place where the prisoners lived. The agricultural and work camps in the counties of Monmouth, Hereford and Shropshire are good examples as most of them have the same address which must have been an office in Leominster.

The county column gives the location of the camp, irrespective of the postal address. The contemporary county boundaries have been used for this rather than later changes in local government areas. Beachley is an example for the camp was in Gloucestershire, but the postal address was Chepstow in Monmouthshire.

For ease of sorting on the computer the next column shows the country
- e = England
- i = Ireland, Isle of Man and Jersey
- s = Scotland
- w = Wales and Monmouthshire

The right hand five columns show the dates of the various lists seen and a tick '/' in the column shows that the camp was listed in the document of that date. A date in the column is the date of closing the camp as per the list (which does not always agree with other information seen).

CAMP NAME	TYPE	PARENT CAMP	POSTAL ADDRESS	COUNTY		Jan.18	May.18	Oct.18	Jan.19	Apr.19
Abbess Roding	a	Pattishall	The Old Rectory, Abbess Roding, Ongar, Essex	Essex	e				/	
Abbey Dore	a	Shrewsbury	42 West Street, Leominster, Herefordshire	Hereford	e			/	/	
Aber Llowyn House	a	Frongoch	Aber Llowyn House, Llanfarian, Aberystwyth, Cardigan	Cardigan	w			/	/	/
Abergavenny	a	Shrewsbury	The Garage, Monmouth Road, Abergavenny, Mon	Monm	w				/	/
Aberglasney	a	Frongoch	Aberglasney, Golden Grove, Carmarthen, S Wales	Carm	w				/	
Addington Park Hospital	h		Addington Park War Hospital, Croydon, Surrey	Surrey	e			/	/	
Addlestone	w	Feltham	Wey Manor Golf Cub House, Addlestone, Surrey	Surrey	e			/	/	
Aldborough	a	Pattishall	Aldbrorough, Norwich, Norfolk	Norfolk	e			/	/	
Aldershot Isolation Hospital	h		Isolation Hospital, Aldershot, Hants	Hants	e			/	/	
Alexandra Palace	c	ALEXANDRA P	Alexandra Palace, Wood Green, London N22	London	e	/		/	/	12.10.18
Alton	w	Dorchester	Alton, Hants	Hants	e			/	/	
Ambergate	w	Brocton	Crich Matlock, Ambergate, Derby	Derby	e		/	/	/	
Ampthill	w	Pattishall	Bird-in-Hand, Ampthill, Beds	Beds	e		/	/	/	
Angmering	w	?	Angmering, Worthing, Sussex	Sussex	e		/	/	/	
Appleton	w	?	Appleton, Stretton, Warrington, Lancs	Cheshire	e			/	/	04.12.18
Ardler	w	?	Keillor, Ardler, Meigle, Perthshire	Forfar	s			/	/	
Arrington	w	Pattishall	Kardwick Arms, Arrington, Royston, Herts	Cambs	e		/	/	/	
Ashbourne	ad	Brocton	Ashbourne, Derbyshire	Derby	e			/	/	
Ashby-de-la-Zouch	a	Brocton	Queens Head Hotel, Ashby-de-la-Zouch, Leics	Leics	e			/	/	
Ashwell	w	Pattishall	Ashwell, Baldock, Herts	Herts	e			/	/	
Atherstone	w	Dorchester	Atherstone, Warwickshire	Warks	e			/	/	
Auchterarder	ad	Stobs	Auchterarder, Perth, Scotland	Perth	s		/	/	/	18.02.19
Avington Park	c		Mornhill, Winchester	Hants	e			15.09.18	/	
Axbridge	a	Dorchester	The Workhouse, Axbridge, Somerset	Somerset	e			/	/	
Aylesbury	f		State Inebriates Reformatory, Bierton Road, Aylesbury	Bucks	e			/	/	
Badsey Manor	w	Dorchester	Badsey Manor, Badsey, (Evesham) Worcs	Worcs	e			/	/	
Baldersby Park	a	Catterick	Home Farm, Baldersby Park, (Ripon) Yorks NR	Yorks NR	e			/	/	
Baldock (aka Bygrave)	w	Pattishall	Malting House, Baldock, Herts	Herts	e	/		/	/	
Balgowan	a	Stobs	Balgowan, near Perth, Scotland	Perth	s	/		/	/	
Banbury	w	Dorchester	Banbury, Oxfordshire	Oxon	e	/		/	/	
Barnstone (aka Langar)	a	Brocton	Langar Hall, Barnstone, Nottingham	Notts	e			/	/	
Barry	w.c.	?	Barry, Cardiff	Glam	w	/w	/c	19.06.18	/	
Beachley			Beachley, Chepstow, Monmouthshire	Glos	e		/w	/	/	
Beaminster	a	Dorchester	Beaminster, Dorset	Dorset	e		/	/	/	
Beauly	w	Stobs	Beauly, Lentran, Inverness-shire, Scotland	Inverness	s		/	/	/	
Beckenham	w	Feltham	Beckenham, Kent	Kent	e				/	
Bedford Military Hospital	h		Bedford Military Hospital, Bedford	Beds	e				/	
Bedley Hall	w	?	Bedley Hall, Redditch, Worcestershire	Worcs	e				/	/
Belmont House	a	Pattishall	Belmont House, Chigwell, Essex	Essex	e				/	
Belmont PoW Hospital	h		PoW Hospital, Belmont, Surrey	Surrey	e				/	
Berkhampstead	a	Pattishall	Berkhampstead, Herts	Herts	e				/	
Berkswell	w	Dorchester	Berkswell, Hampton-in-Arden, Warwick	Warks	e		/	/	/	

Name	Type	Parent	Location	County	Status			Date
Bethnall Green Military Hosp	h	Pattishall	Military Hospital, Cambridge Road, Bethnal Green, E2	London	e	/		
Billericay	w	Pattishall	Billericay Union, Billericay, Essex	Essex	e	/		
Billingford	w	Pattishall	Billingford Maltings, near Diss, Norfolk	Norfolk	e	/		
Binegar	a	Dorchester	Binegar, Gurney Slade, Somerset	Somerset	e	/		
Birmingham Hospital	h		1st Southern General Hospital, Edgbaston, Birmingham	Warks	e	/		
Bishops Stortford	w	Pattishall	Oak Hall, Bishop's Stortford, Herts	Herts	e	/		
Blairfield (aka Chichester)	w	?	Blairfield, Chichester	Sussex	e	/		
Blaisdon	ad	Dorchester	Blaisdon, Longhope, Gloucestershire	Glos	e	/		05.02.19
Blandford (prev a parent camp)	w	Dorchester	Blandford, Dorset	Dorset	e	/		
Bletchley	a	Pattishall	Walting Street, Bletchley, Bucks	Bucks	e	/		
Blunham	w	Pattishall	Blunham, Sandy, Bedford	Beds	e	/		
Boddam	w	Stobs	Boddam, near Peterhead, Aberdeenshire, Scotland	Aberdeen	s	/		
Bolsover Castle	a	Catterick	Bolsover Castle, Chesterfield, Derbyshire	Derby	e	/		
Boroughbridge	a	Catterick	Boroughbridge, Yorks WR	Yorks WR	e	/		
Boston Dock	cw	Brocton	Boston Docks, Lincs	Lincs	e	/		
Bovington	w	Dorchester	Bovington, (Wareham), Dorset	Dorset	e	/		
Bowithwick	w	?	Bowithwick, Altarnum, Launceston	Cornwall	e	/		
Bracebridge	ad	Brocton	Bracebridge, Lincoln	Lincs	e	/		
Brackley	w	Pattishall	Brackley, Northants	Northants	e	/		
Bradford Abbas	a	Dorchester	Bradford Abbas, near Yeovil, Somerset	Dorset	e	/		
Braemore	w	Stobs	Braemore, Garve, Ross-shire, Scotland	Ross	s	/		
Brailes	a	Dorchester	Springfield House, Brailes, Banbury, Warwickshire	Warks	e	/		
Bramley	a	Pattishall	Bramley, near Basingstoke, Hants	Hants	e	/w	/w	
Brampton	a	Pattishall	Brampton Park, Huntingdon	Hunts	e	/		
Braughing	w	Pattishall	Braughing, Ware, Hertfordshire	Herts	e	/		
Brecon	ad	Frongoch	County Prison, Brecon, Wales	Brecon	w	/		
Bretby Hall (aka Swadlincote)	a	Brocton	The Stables, Bretby Hall, Burton-on-Trent, Staffs	Derby	e	/		
Brighton General Hospital	h		2nd Eastern General Hospital, Brighton	Sussex	e	/		
Brightwell	a	Dorchester	Brightwell, (Wallingford), Berks	Berks	e	/		
Brixworth	w	Pattishall	The Grange, Brixworth, Northampton	Northants	e	/		
Broad Marston	w	Dorchester	The Priory, Broad Marston, Mickleton, Glos	Glos	e	/		
Brockenhurst	w	Dorchester	Brockenhurst, Hants	Hants	e	/		
Brocton Camp		BROCTON	P/W Camp, Brocton, Staffs	Staffs	e	/		
Brocton PoW Hospital	h		PoW Hospital, Brocton, Cannock Chase, Staffs	Staffs	e	/		
Bromfield	a	Shrewsbury	42 West Street, Leominster, Herefordshire	Salop	e	/		
Bromyard	a	Shrewsbury	42 West Street, Leominster, Herefordshire	Hereford	e	/		
Broom	w	Pattishall	Broom Hall Stables, nr Biggleswade, Bedfordshire	Beds	e	/		
Buckminster	w	?	Buckminster, Grantham, Lincs	Leics	e	/		
Bucknall	a	Brocton	Tupholme Hall, Bucknall, Lincoln	Lincs	e	/		15.09.18
Bulford	cw	Dorchester	Bulford, Wiltshire	Wilts	e	/		
Buntingford	w	Pattishall	Hare Street, Buntingford, Herts	Herts	e	/		
Burbage (see Stanley Moor)								
Bures	w	?	Bridge House, Bures, Suffolk	Suffolk	e	/		

Name	Type	Parent	Description	County	E/W	Date
Burnham Beeches	w	?	Sunnycroft, Burnham Beeches, Maidenhead, Berks	Bucks	e	/
Burnham Market	w	Pattishall	Burnham Market, Norfolk	Norfolk	e	/
Burnham Norton	w		Maltings, Burnham Norton, Norfolk	Norfolk	e	/
Burton Hall	a	Brocton	Burton Hall, Burton, Lincoln	Lincs	e	/
Burton-on-Trent	w	Brocton	Burton-on-Trent, Staffs	Staffs	e	/
Buxton (aka Peak Dale)	a	Brocton	Peak Dale Quarries, Doveholes, Buxton	Derby	e	/
Bygrave - see Baldock						
Caersws	a	Frongoch	The Workhouse, Caersws, Montgomeryshire	Mont	w	/
Camberley	w	?	Camberley, Surrey	Surrey	e	/
Cambridge	w	Pattishall	Newmarket Road, Cambridge	Cambs	e	/
Cambridge Hospital, Aldershot	h		Cambridge Hospital, Aldershot, Hants	Hants	e	/
Cambridge Military Hospital	h		Cambridge Military Hospital, Cambridge	Cambs	e	/
Canterbury	w	?	Hanover Place, Canterbury, Kent	Kent	e	15.11.18
Caolas-na-Con	w	Stobs	Caolas-na-Con, near Kinlochleven, Argyllshire	Argyll	s	/
Cardiff 3rd Western Gen Hosp	h		3rd Western General Hospital, Cardiff, S Wales	Glam	w	/
Carlton-on-Trent	a	Brocton	Carlton-on-Trent, Newark, Notts	Notts	e	/
Carmarthen	ad	Frongoch	Carmarthen, S Wales	Carm	w	/
Castle Bromwich	w	Dorchester	Castle Bromwich, near Birmingham	Warks	e	/
Catterick (opened as "w" to Brocton)		CATTERICK	Catterick, Yorks	Yorks NR	e	/
Catterick Military Hospital	h		Military Hospital, Catterick, Yorks	Yorks NR	e	/
Cawood	w	Catterick	Fosters Flour Mills, Cawood, Selby, Yorks WR	Yorks WR	e	15.02.19
Caxton	w	Pattishall	Caxton, Cambridge	Cambs	e	/
Caythorpe	a	Brocton	Caythorpe, (near Grantham), Lincs	Lincs	e	/
Chapel Oak	a	Dorchester	Chapel Oak, Iron Cross, Salford Priors, Warwickshire	Warks	e	/
Chapel-en-le-Frith	a	Brocton	Bank Hall, Chapel-en-le-Frith, Derbyshire.	Derby	e	/
Charlbury	w	?	Charlbury, Oxfordshire	Oxon	e	/
Charlton Kings	w	?	Charlton House, Charlton Kings, Cheltenham	Glos	e	/
Chatham Naval Barracks	o		Chatham	Kent	e	/
Cheam	w	Feltham	Cheam House, Cheam, Surrey	Surrey	e	/
Chelmsford	w	Pattishall	Chelmsford, Essex	Essex	e	/
Chelmsford Detention Barracks	p		Detention Barracks, Chelmsford, Essex	Essex	e	/
Chelsea Hospital	h		2nd London Gen Hosp, St Mark's College, Chelsea, SW3	London	e	/
Cheltenham	w	Dorchester	Cheltenham, Gloucestershire	Glos	e	/
Cheriton Bishop	w	Dorchester	Cheriton Bishop, Exeter, Devon	Devon	e	/
Chesterton	w	Pattishall	Chesterton, Cambridge	Cambs	e	/
Chevington	w	Pattishall	Chevington, Bury St Edmunds, Suffolk	Suffolk	e	/
Chigwell	w	?	Belmont House, Chigwell, Essex	Essex	e	/
Chigwell (aka Foxburrow)	w	Pattishall	Foxburrow Farm, Chigwell Row, Essex	Essex	e	/
Chippenham	a	Dorchester	Avon House, Chippenham, Wiltshire	Wilts	e	/
Chipping Norton	w	Dorchester	Hillside House, Chipping Norton, Oxfordshire	Oxon	e	/
Chipping Ongar	ad	Pattishall	Bowes House, Chipping Ongar, Essex	Essex	e	/
Chisledon	w	Dorchester	Chisledon, Swindon, Wiltshire	Wilts	e	01.01.19
Chisledon Military Hospital	h		Military Hospital, Chisledon (near Swindon), Wiltshire	Wilts	e	/

Name			Location	County								
Cholsey	ad	Dorchester	Cholsey, Berks	Berks	e						/	
Churchdown	w	Dorchester	Chosen House, Churchdown, Gloucester	Glos	e					/	/	
Churt	w	Dorchester	Churt, Farnham, Surrey	Surrey	e			/			/	
Ciliau Aeron	a	Frongoch	Ciliau Aeron, (near Aberayon) Cardiganshire, Wales	Cardigan	w			/			/	
Cirencester	w	Dorchester	The Old Vicarage, Thomas Street, Cirencester, Glos	Glos	e					/	/	
City of London Military Hospital	h	Pattishall	42 Clifden Road, Homerton, E5	London	e						/	
Claydon	a	?	Claydon, (near Ipswich) Suffolk	Suffolk	e			/			/	
Claypole	w	?	Manor Farm, Claypole, Newark, Notts	Lincs	e						/	
Clee Hill Dhu	w	Shrewsbury	Clee Hill Dhu, Shropshire	Salop	e					/	/	
Clent	a	Dorchester	Clent, Stourbridge, Worcestershire	Worcs	e						/	
Cleobury Mortimer	a	Shrewsbury	Cleobury Mortimer, Shropshire	Salop	e						/	
Coal Aston	w?	?	Coal Aston, Sheffield	Derby	e	20.05.18		/			/	
Codford	cw	Dorchester	Codford St Mary, (near Warminster), Wiltshire	Wilts	e			/			/	
Coggeshall	w	?	Coggeshall, Essex	Essex	e						/	
Colchester Hospital	h	?	Military Hospital, Colchester, Essex	Essex	e			/			/	
College Town	w	Dorchester	College Town, Camberley, Surrey	Berks	e						/	
Colsterdale	o		Colsterdale, near Masham, Yorkshire NR	Yorks NR	e						/	
Combe Down	w	?	Combe Down, Bath, Somerset	Somerset	e			/			/	
Compton	ad	Dorchester	Roden House, Compton, Newbury, Berkshire	Berks	e						/	
Coningsby	a	Brocton	Coningsby, Lincolnshire	Lincs	e			/			/	
Connaught Hospital	h		Connaught Hospital, Aldershot, Hampshire	Hants	e						/	
Conveth Mains	w	Stobs	Conveth Mains, Laurencekirk, Kinkardineshire	Kinkard	s						/	
Copt Hewick Hall (aka Ripon)	a	Catterick	Copt Hewick Hall, near Ripon, Yorkshire	Yorks NR	e			/			/	
Corby	cw	Pattishall	Corby, near Kettering, Northamptonshire	Northants	e		/ c					
Corfton Hall (nr Ludlow)	a	Shrewsbury	42 West Street, Leominster, Herefordshire	Salop	e		/ w					
Cove	w	Dorchester	Cove, Farnborough, Hampshire	Hants	e			/				
Cranleigh	w	Pattishall	High Park, Cranleigh, Surrey	Surrey	e						/	
Crawford	w	Stobs	Crawford, Lanarkshire, Scotland	Lanark	s						/	
Crichel	w	Dorchester	(Long) Crichel, Blandford, Dorset	Dorset	e			/			/	
Crickhowell	w	Frongoch	Crickhowell, Brecknockshire, Wales	Brecon	w			/			/	
Crondall	w	Dorchester	Churchill House, Crondall, Farnham, Hants	Hants	e						/	
Crowthorne War Hospital	h		Crowthorne War Hospital, Crowthorne, Berkshire	Berks	e			/				
Croxton Park	ad	Brocton	Croxton Park, Melton Mowbray, Leicestershire	Leics	e						/	
Cuddington	w	Handforth	Cuddington, (near Northwich), Cheshire	Cheshire	e			/			/	
Cumnor	a	Dorchester	Cumnor, Oxfordshire	Oxon	e						/	
Dalmellington	w	?	Dalmellington, Ayrshire	Ayr	s			/			/	21.08.18
Dartford War Hospital	h		Dartford PoW Hospital, Dartford, Kent.	Kent	e						/	
Dawyck	w	Stobs	Dawyck, Stobo, Peebles, Scotland	Peebles	s							
Deal Royal Marine Infirmary	h		Royal Marine Infirmary, Deal, Kent	Kent	e							
Deddington	a	Dorchester	Stoneleigh, Deddington, Oxfordshire	Oxon	e						/	
Denby (aka Kilburn Hall?)	w	Brocton	Denby, near Derby	Derby	e							
Denham Lodge (aka Uxbridge)	ad	Feltham	Denham Lodge, Uxbridge, Middlesex	Middx	e						/	
Devizes	ad	Dorchester	Fairview, London Road, Devizes, Wiltshire	Wilts	e			/			/	

Name	Type	Camp	Location	County	Side	Date
Devonport Hospital	h		Military Hospital, Devonport, Devon	Devon	e	/
Digby	a	Brocton	Digby, (near Sleaford), Lincolnshire	Lincs	e	/
Dolgwilyn	w	?	Dolgwilyn, Hebron, Carmarthenshire	Carm	w	/
Dolyhir (Old Radnor)	w	Shrewsbury	Dolyhir, Kington, Herefordshire	Radnor	w	/
Donington Hall	o		Donington Hall, Castle Donington, Derby	Leics	e	/
Dorchester		DORCHESTER	Dorchester, Dorset	Dorset	e	/
Dorking	w	Feltham	Deepdene, Dorking, Surrey	Surrey	e	/
Dorking	w	?	The Fort, Ranmore Common, Dorking, Surrey	Surrey	e	/
Douglas		DOUGLAS	Douglas, Isle of Man	IOM	i	/
Dover Military Hospital	h		The Military Hospital, Dover, Kent	Kent	e	/
Downham Hall	w	Pattishall	Downham Hall, Brandon, Suffolk	Suffolk	e	/
Drim Wood	w	Frongoch	Drim Wood, Narberth, Pembrokeshire, S Wales	Pembs	w	29.01.19
Droitwich (aka Doverdale)	w	Dorchester	Doverdale, Droitwich, Worcestershire	Worcs	e	/
Drumburgh	w	Stobs	Drumburgh, Methven, Perthshire, Scotland	Perth	s	/
Dulverton	ad	Dorchester	Barlecombe House, Dulverton, Somerset	Somerset	e	/
Dunmow	w	Pattishall	Dunmow, Essex	Essex	e	/
Dyffryn Aled	o		Dyffryn Aled, Llansannan, Abergele, N Wales	Denbigh	w	10.12.18
Dykebar War Hospital	h		Dykebar War Hospital, Paisley, Renfrewshire, Scotland	Renfrew	s	/
Eardiston	w	Dorchester	Eardiston, Tenbury Wells, Worcestershire	Worcs	e	/
Eartham (aka Slindon)	w	Pattishall	Eartham, Slindon, near Chichester, Sussex	Sussex	e	/
Easingwold	a	Catterick	The Workhouse, Easingwold, Yorkshire NR	Yorks NR	e	/
Eassie	w	?	Eassie, Glamis, Forfarshire	Forfar	s	28.02.19
East Dereham	w	Pattishall	East Dereham, Norfolk	Norfolk	e	/
East Grinstead	w	Pattishall	218 London Road, East Grinstead, Sussex	Sussex	e	/
East Harlsey	w	?	East Harlsey, Northallerton, Yorkshire NR	Yorks NR	e	/
East Leake	a	Brocton	Hetchley Plaster Pit, East Leake, Loughborough, Leics	Notts	e	/
East Leeds War Hospital	h		Harehills Road, Leeds	Yorks WR	e	/
East Preston	w	Pattishall	East Preston, Angmering, (Worthing) Sussex	Sussex	e	/
Eastcote	a	Feltham	Eastcote, Pinner, Middlesex	Middx	e	/
Eastcote (later called Pattishall)		PATTISHALL	Pattishall, Towcester, Northamptonshire	Northants	e	/
Eastgate	w	Catterick	Rosehill Farm, Eastgate, (near Stanhope), Co Durham	Durham	e	/
Easton-on-the-Hill	w	Pattishall	Easton-on-the-Hill, Stamford, Lincolnshire	Northants	e	11.02.19
Edinburgh	p		The Detention House, Edinburgh Castle, Edinburgh	Midloth	s	/
Edinburgh Castle Hospital	h		Castle Military Hospital, Edinburgh, Scotland	Midloth	s	/
Eggesford	ad	Dorchester	Eggesford House, Eggesford, Devon	Devon	e	/
Ellesmere	a	Shrewsbury	42 West Street, Leominster, Herefordshire	Salop	e	/
Elton	w	Pattishall	Elton, Peterborough, Northants	Hunts	e	/
Ely	w	?	Ely	Cambs	e	/
Enfield	w	Feltham	Clayhill Lodge, Enfield, Middlesex	Middx	e	/
Enstone	w	?	Enstone, Oxfordshire	Oxon	e	/
Epping	w	Pattishall	Coopersale House, Epping, Essex	Essex	e	/
Esher	w	?	Mill Meadow, Esher, Surrey	Surrey	e	04.11.18
Estuary Road	w	Pattishall	Estuary Road, King's Lynn, Norfolk	Norfolk	e	/

Name	Code	Camp	Location	County	Type	Date											
Ettingshall (aka Bilston)	w	Brocton	Bilston, Staffordshire	Staffs	e		/	/					/				
Etwall	a	Brocton	The Ash, Etwall, Derby	Derby	e		/	/					/				
Evesham	w	Dorchester	Evesham, Worcestershire	Worcs	e		/	/					/				
Eye	w	Pattishall	Eye, Suffolk	Suffolk	e		/	/					/				
Falmouth Military Hospital	h		Falmoth Military Hospital, Falmouth, Cornwall	Cornwall	e		/	/					/				
Fargo Rolleston Military Hospital	h		Fargo Rolleston Military Hospital, Salisbury, Wiltshire	Wilts	e		/	/					/				
Faringdon	a	Dorchester	Pidnell House, Faringdon, Berkshire	Berks	e		/	/					/				
Feltham		FELTHAM	Feltham, Middlsex	Middx	e		/	/					/				
Fladbury (aka Craycombe House)	w	Dorchester	Craycombe House, Fladbury, Pershore, Worcestershire	Worcs	e		/	/					/				
Flowerdown	w	Dorchester	Flowerdown, Winchester, Hampshire	Hants	e	14.09.18	/	/	00.09.18				/				
Folkingham	a	Brocton	Folkingham, (near Grantham), Lincolnshire	Lincs	e		/	/		/			/				
Forgandenny	a	Stobs	Forgandenny, Perth, Scotland	Perth	s		/	/					/				
Forteviot	a	Stobs	Forteviot, Perth, Scotland	Perth	s		/	/					/				
Fovant	w	Dorchester	Fovant, Salisbury, Wiltshire	Wilts	e	19.01.19	/	/					/				
Foxhill	w	?	Foxhill, Round Bridge Farm, Woking, Surrey	Surrey	e		/	/		/			/				
Frampton-on-Severn	w	Dorchester	Frampton-on-Severn, Stonehouse, Gloucestershire	Glos	e		/	/					/				
Frith Hill		FRITH HILL	Headquarters, Blackdown, Surrey	Surrey	e	02.11.18	/	/					/				
Frodsham	w	?	Frodsham, Warrington, Lancs	Cheshire	e		/	/					/				
Frome	w	Dorchester	The Tannery, Keyford, Frome, Somerset	Somerset	e		/	/					/				
Frongoch		FRONGOCH	Frongoch, Bala, Merionethshire, Wales	Merion	w		/	/					/				
Fulham Military Hospital	h		St Dunstan's Road, Hammersmith, London W6	London	e		/	/					/				
Gamlingay	w	Pattishall	Gamlingay, Sandy, Bedfordshire	Cambs	e		/	/					/				
Gargrave	w	?	Gargrave, Leeds, Yorkshire WR	Yorks WR	e		/	/					/				
Garn Dolbenmaen	w	?	Brynkhir Hall, Garn Dolbenmaen, Carnarvonshire	Carn	w		/	/					/				
Gayton	w	?	The Workhouse, Gayton, King's Lynn, Norfolk	Norfolk	e		/	/		/			/				
German Hospital	h		German Hospital, (Graham Road), Dalston, London E8	London	e		/	/					/				
Gillingham	ad	Dorchester	Gillingham, Dorset	Dorset	e		/	/					/				
Gisburn	a	Catterick	No.19 PW Agricultural Group, Gisburn, Yorkshire WR	Yorks WR	e		/	/					/				
Glasgow	h		3rd Scotish General Hospital, Glasgow	Lanark	s		/	/		/			/				
Glasgow	h		4th Scotish General Hospital, Glasgow	Lanark	s		/	/					/				
Glastonbury	w	?	Glastonbury, Somerset	Somerset	e		/	/					/				
Glatton	w	Pattishall	Glatton, Peterborough, Northants	Hunts	e		/	/					/				
Glemsford	w	?	Glemsford, Long Melford, Suffolk	Suffolk	e		/	/		/			/				
Glendevon	w	Stobs	Glendevon, Dollar, Clackmannanshire, Scotland	Clack	s		/	/					/				
Glentham	a	Brocton	Glentham, Market Rasen, Lincolnshire	Lincs	e		/	/					/				
Gore Farm (aka Dartford)	w	Pattishall	Gore Farm, Dartford, Kent	Kent	e		/	/					/				
Grantham	w	Brocton	Belton Park, Grantham, Lincolnshire	Lincs	e	20.02.19	/	/					/				
Grassington	cw		Grassington, Yorks WR	Yorks WR	e		/	/					/				
Grays	w	Pattishall	The Wouldham Cement Co, Grays, Essex	Essex	e		/	/					/				
Great Baddow	w	Pattishall	Great Baddow, Essex	Essex	e		/	/									
Great Coggeshall	a	Pattishall	Great Coggeshall, Essex	Essex	e		/	/					/				
Great Hale	a	Brocton	Great Hale, Heckington, (near Sleaford) Lincolnshire	Lincs	e		/	/									
Great Hampton	w	Dorchester	Great Hampton House, Evesham, Worcestershire	Worcs	e		/	/					/				

Place			Location	County						Date
Great Offley	w	Pattishall	Great Offley, Hitchin, Herts	Herts	e	/			/	
Great Ouseburn	a	Catterick	The Workhouse, Great Ouseburn, York	Yorks WR	e	/			/	
Great Parndon	w	?	North Brook Farm, Great Parndon, Harlow, Essex	Essex	e	/			/	
Great Witley	w	Dorchester	Hillhampton, Great Witley, Worcester	Worcs	e	/			/	
Green Lane Farm (aka Doncaster)	a	Catterick	Green Lane Farm, near Doncaster, Yorkshire WR	Yorks WR	e	/			/	16.10.18
Gringley-on-the-Hill	a	Brocton	Gringley-on-the-Hill, Gainsborough, Lincs	Notts	e	/			/	
Guilsborough	w	Pattishall	Guilsborough, Northampton	Northants	e	/			/	
Hackney Wick	c	?	Gainsborough Road (now Eastway), Hackney Wick, E9	London	e	/			/	
Haddenham	w	?	Haddenham, Ely, Cambridgeshire	Cambs	e	/			/	
Hailsham	w	Pattishall	Roseneath, George Street, Hailsham, Sussex	Sussex	e	/			/	
Hairmyres	w	Stobs	Hairmyres, East Kilbride, Glasgow	Lanark	s	/	20.07.18		/	
Halam	a	Brocton	Halam, Southwell, Nottinghamshire	Notts	e	/			/	
Hale Farm	w	?	Hale Farm, Wendover, Buckinghamshire	Bucks	e	/			/	
Halesworth	w	Pattishall	Halesworth, Suffolk	Suffolk	e	/			/	
Hallatrow	a	Dorchester	Hallatrow, (near Radstock), Somerset	Somerset	e	/			/	
Halling (aka Snodland)	w	Pattishall	Lee's Cement Works, Halling, Snodland, Kent	Kent	e	/			/	
Halstead	w	Pattishall	The Workhouse, Halstead, Essex	Essex	e	/			/	
Halton Park	w	Pattishall	Halton Park, Wendover, Buckinghamshire	Bucks	e	/			/	
Hammersmith Military Hospital	h	?	Ducane Road, Shepherd's Bush, London W12	London	e	/			/	
Handforth		HANDFORTH	Rubber Works, Handforth, Cheshire	Cheshire	e	/			/	
Harewood	a	Catterick	Harewood Arms, Harewood, Leeds, Yorkshire WR	Yorks WR	e	/			/	
Harperley	w	Catterick	Harperley Station, (near Bishop Auckland), Co Durham	Durham	e	/			/	
Hatfield	w	Pattishall	Hatfield, Hertfordshire	Herts	e	/			/	
Hatfield	w	?	Hatfield, Doncaster, Yorkshire WR	Yorks WR	e	/			/	
Hatherleigh	w	Dorchester	Fishleigh House, Hatherleigh, Devon	Devon	e	/			/	
Hatherton	w	Handforth	Hatherton, near Nantwich, Cheshire	Cheshire	e	/			/	
Hatley St George	w	Pattishall	The Rectory, Hatley St George, Gamlingay, Sandy, Beds	Cambs	e	/			/	
Haughley	a	Pattishall	Haughley, Suffolk	Suffolk	e	/			/	
Haverfordwest	w	Frongoch	Shoals Hook Farm Rifle Range, Haverfordwest, Pembrokeshire	Pembs	w	/			/	
Hawkesbury	w	Dorchester	Hawkesbury Upton, (near Chipping Sodbury), Glos	Glos	e	/			/	
Haywards Heath	w	Pattishall	Summerhill, Haywards Heath, Sussex	Sussex	e	/			/	
Heacham (aka Snettisham)	w	Pattishall	Heacham, (near King's Lynn), Norfolk	Norfolk	e	/			/	
Hemel Hempstead	ad	Pattishall	Gemmaes Court, Hemel Hempstead, Hertfordshire	Herts	e	/			/	
Hendon	w	?	Hendon, NW9	London	e	/			/	11.11.18
Hendre	w	?	Hendre, Glyn, Chirk, Denbighshire	Denbigh	w	/			/	
Henfield	w	Pattishall	Henfield, Sussex	Sussex	e	/			/	
Hentland	w	?	Hentland, Harewood End, Hereford	Hereford	e	/			/	
Hermitage	w	Frongoch	The Hermitage, Crickhowell, Brecknockshire, Wales	Brecon	w	/			/	
Hersham	w	?	The Drill Hall, Hersham, Surrey	Surrey	e	/			/	
Heveningham	a	Pattishall	Heveningham, Saxmundham, Suffolk	Suffolk	e	/			/	18.02.19
Hogsthorpe	a	Brocton	Hogsthorpe, Alford, Lincolnshire	Lincs	e	/			/	
Holbeach	a	Brocton	Holbeach, Lincolnshire	Lincs	e	/			/	
Hollowell	w	Pattishall	Hollowell Grange, Creaton, Northampton	Northants	e	/			/	

Name		Camp	Address	County								Date
Holsworthy	w	?	Thuborough House, Holsworthy, Devon	Devon	e	/	/	/	/	/	/	/
Holyport	o		Holyport, near Bray, Maidenhead, Berkshire	Berks	e	/	/	/	/	/	/	/
Honiton	a	Dorchester	Combe Raleigh House, Honiton, Devon	Devon	e	/	/	/	/	/	/	/
Hook Norton	w	?	Hook Norton, Banbury, Oxfordshire	Oxon	e	/	/	/	/	/	/	/
Horsham	w	Pattishall	28 North Street, Horsham, Sussex	Sussex	e	/	/	/	/	/	/	/
Houghton	w	?	Houghton, Huntingdon	Hunts	e	/	/	/	/	/	/	/
Houghton	w	?	Houghton, Kings Lynn, Norfolk	Norfolk	e	/	/	/	/	/	/	13.01.19
Houghton Regis	w	Pattishall	Grove Farm, Houghton Regis, Bedfordshire	Beds	e	/	/	/	/	/	/	/
Houghton-on-the-Hill	a	Brocton	Houghton Lodge Camp, Leicester	Leics	e	/	/	/	/	/	/	/
Hove (aka Brooker Hall)	w	Pattishall	Brooker Hall, Hove, Sussex	Sussex	e	/	/	/	/	/	/	/
Huntingdon	w	Pattishall	Huntingdon, Hunts	Hunts	e	/	/	/	/	/	/	/
Hunton Bridge	w	Pattishall	Hunton Bridge, King's Langley, Hertfordshire	Herts	e	/	/	/	/	/	/	/
Hursley Park	w	Dorchester	Hursley Park, Standon, Hursley, Winchester, Hampshire	Hants	e	/	/	/	/	/	/	/
Hyde Park	w	?	Hyde Park Barracks, St John's Road, Sheffield	Yorks WR	e	/	/	/	/	/	/	09.12.18
Ilchester	w	Dorchester	Ilchester, near Yeovil, Somerset	Somerset	e	/	/	/	/	/	/	/
Ilkeston	a	Brocton	Oakwell Colliery Buildings, Ilkeston, Derbyshire	Derby	e	/	/	/	/	/	/	/
Illeston	a	Brocton	Illeston Grange, Market Harborough, Leicestershire	Leics	e	/	/	/	/	/	/	/
Inverkeithing	w	Stobs	Inverkeithing, Fife	Fife	s	/	/	/	/	/	/	/
Inverlaidnan	w	Stobs	Inverlaidnan, Carr Bridge, Invernessshire, Scotland	Inverness	s	/	/	/	/	/	/	/
Ipswich Military Hospital	h		Military Hospital, Ipswich, Suffolk	Suffolk	e	/	/	/	/	/	/	/
Isleworth	w	Feltham	Warton Road, Isleworth, Middlesex	Middx	e	/	/	/	/	/	/	/
Islington	c		St Mary's Institute, Cornwallis Road, Islington, London N19	London	e	/	/	/	/	/	/	/
Itton	a	Shrewsbury	Cottage Farm, Itton, nr Chepstow, Monmouthshire	Monm	w	/	/	/	/	/	/	/
Itton	w	?	Howick Farm, Itton, nr Chepstow, Monmouthshire	Monm	w	/	/	/	/	/	/	/
Ivybridge	w	Dorchester	Lee Mill, Ivybridge, Devon	Devon	e	/	/	/	/	/	/	/
Iwerne Minster	w	Dorchester	Iwerne Minster, near Blandford, Dorset	Dorset	e	/	/	/	/	/	/	/
Jersey			Jersey, Channel Islands	C I	i	/	/	/	/	/	/	/
Joyce Green	w	?	Joyce Green, Dartford, Kent	Kent	e	/	/	/	/	/	/	/
Justinhaugh	w	Stobs	Newmiln of Craigeassie, Justinhaugh, Forfarshire, Scotland	Forfar	s	/	/	/	/	/	/	/
Kedington	w	Pattishall	Kedington, near Haverhill, Suffolk	Suffolk	e	/	/	/	/	/	/	/
Kegworth	o		Kegworth, Derby	Leics	e	/	/	/	/	/	/	17.02.19
Kelham	ad	Brocton	Kelham Brickfields, Kelham, Newark, Nottinghamshire	Notts	e	/	/	/	/	/	/	/
Kempshott Park	ad	Dorchester	Kempshott House, Kempshott Park, Basingstoke, Hampshire	Hants	e	/	/	/	/	/	/	/
Kenilworth	ad	Dorchester	Little Woodcote, Kenilworth, Warwickshire	Warks	e	/	/	/	/	/	/	/
Kenninghall	w	Pattishall	Uphall, Kenninghall, East Harling, Norfolk	Norfolk	e	/	/	/	/	/	/	/
Kerry	a	Frongoch	Kerry, Newtown, Mongomeryshire	Mont	w	/	/	/	/	/	/	/
Kettleburgh	w	Pattishall	Kettleburgh Rectory, Wickham Market, Suffolk	Suffolk	e	/	/	/	/	/	/	/
Keyston	a	Pattishall	Keyston, Huntingdonshire	Hunts	e	/	/	/	/	/	/	/
Kilburn Hall (aka? Denby)	w	Brocton	Kilburn Hall, Kilburn, Derby	Derby	e	/	/	/	/	/	/	/
Kimbolton	w	Pattishall	The Stables, Kimbolton Castle, Kimbolton, Hunts	Hunts	e	/	/	/	/	/	/	/
King George V Hospital, Dublin	h		King George V Hospital, Dublin	Ireland	i	/	/	/	/	/	/	/
King George's Hospital	h		King George's Hospital, Stamford Street, London SE1	London	e	/	/	/	/	/	/	/
King's Lynn	w	Pattishall	St James's Hall, King's Lynn, Norfolk	Norfolk	e	/	/	/	/	/	/	06.01.19

Name	Camp	Location	County	Type			Date
Kingsbridge	ad	Dorchester	Kingsbridge, Devon	Devon	e	/	
Kingsbury	w	Dorchester	Kingsbury (no county given - Somerset most likely)	Somerset	e	/	
Kingsdown	w	?	Kingsdown, Sevenoaks, Kent	Kent	e	/	
Kinlochleven	w	Stobs	Kinlochleven, Argyllshire	Argyll	s	/	
Kinmel Park Military Hospital	h		Military Hospital, Kinmel Park, Denbigh, N Wales	Denbigh	w	/	
Kintillo	a	Stobs	Kintillo, Bridge of Ern, Perthshire, Scotland	Perth	s	/	
Knockaloe		KNOCKALOE	Knockaloe, Peel, Isle of Man	IOM	i		
Knutsford	w	Handforth	Knutsford, Cheshire	Cheshire	e	/	
Labroke Hall (aka Southam)	w	Dorchester	Ladbroke Hall, Harbury, Southam, Warwickshire	Warks	e	/	
Lakenham	w	Pattishall	Lakenham Mills, near Norwich, Norfolk	Norfolk	e	/	
Lambourne	a	Dorchester	The Chestnuts, Lambourne, Berkshire	Berks	e		
Lampeter	a	Frongoch	Drill Hall, Lampeter, Cardiganshire, Wales	Cardigan	w	/	
Lancaster Castle	w	Leigh	Lancaster Castle, Lancaster	Lancs	e		
Lancing	w	Pattishall	Lancing, Sussex	Sussex	e	/	
Laneham	a	Brocton	Laneham, Retford, Nottinghamshire	Notts	e	/	
Langley Park (aka Black Park)	a	Feltham	Langley Park, Iver Heath, Buckinghamshire	Bucks	e	/	10.08.18
Langton Priory (aka Guildford)	w	Pattishall	Langton Priory, Guildford, Surrey	Surrey	e	/	
Larkhill	w	Dorchester	Larkhill, Salisbury Plain, Wiltshire	Wilts	e	/	
Lawford Heath	w	Dorchester	Lawford Heath, Rugby, Warwickshire	Warks	e	/	
Leadenham	w	?	Glebe Farm, Leadenham, Lincoln	Lincs	e	/	
Leasowe	w	Handforth	Leasowe Castle, near Birkenhead, Cheshire	Cheshire	e	/	
Ledbury	a	Shrewsbury	42 West Street, Leominster, Herefordshire	Hereford	e	/	
Leicester Hospital	h		No 5 Northern General Hospital, Leicester	Leics	e	/	
Leigh		LEIGH	Leigh, Lancashire	Lancs	e	/	
Leigh Court	w	Dorchester	Leigh Court, Leigh, Worcester	Worcs	e	/	
Leighterton	w	Dorchester	Leighterton, Tetbury, Gloucestershire	Glos	e	/	23.01.19
Leighton Buzzard	w	Pattishall	20 Market Square, Leighton Buzzard, Bedfordshire	Beds	e	/	
Leominster	ad	Shrewsbury	Westbury House, Leominster, Herefordshire	Hereford	e	/	
Lewes	w	Pattishall	North Street, Lewes, Sussex	Sussex	e	/	
Lewisham	o		Lewisham, London SE13	London	e	/	10.12.18
Lewisham Military Hospital	h		Military Hospital, Lewisham, London SE13	London	e	/	
Leystone Farm	a	Stobs	Leystone Farm, Perth, Scotland	Perth	s	/	
Libury Hall	c	LIBURY	Libury Hall, Ware, Hertfordshire	Herts	e	/	
Lincoln Hospital	h		4th Northern General Hospital, Lincoln	Lincs	e	/	
Linton	w	Pattishall	Linton, Cambridgeshire	Cambs	e	/	
Little Balbrogie	w	Stobs	Little Balbrogie, Ardler, (near Coupar Angus), Perthshire	Perth	s	/	
Littleport	w	Pattishall	The Grange, Littleport, Ely, Cambridgeshire	Cambs	e	/	
Liverpool Hospital	h		1st Western General Hospital, Fazakerley, Liverpool	Lancs	e	/	
Llanafon	a	Frongoch	Grogwynion House, Llanafon, Aberystwyth, Cardigan	Cardigan	w	/	
Llanbedr	a	Frongoch	Penyalt Hall, Llanbedr, Merionethshire, N Wales	Merion	w	/	
Llandebie	a	Frongoch	Lime Farm Buildings, Llandebie, Carmarthen, S Wales	Carm	w	/	
Llandebie	w	?	Penyrallt Hall, Llandebie, Carmarthenshire, S Wales	Carm	w	/	
Llandinabo	a	Shrewsbury	42 West Street, Leominster, Herefordshire	Hereford	e	/	

Name	Code	Camp	Address	County	E/W	Ticks	Date
Llanengan	w	?	National School, Llanengan, Abersoch, Carns	Carn	w	/	
Llanerchymedd	a	Frongoch	The Workhouse, Llanerchymedd, Anglesea, N Wales	Anglesey	w	/	
Llanmartin (aka Penycoed Castle)	a	Shrewsbury	Penycoed Castle, Llanmartin, Penhow, Monmouthshire	Monm	w	/	
Llanvihangel	w	?	The Huts, Llanvihangel, Aberegavenny, Mon	Monm	w	/	
London Colney	w	?	Cotlands, London Colney, St Albans, Herts	Herts	e		
Long Ashton (aka Flax Bourton)	ad	Dorchester	The Workhouse, Long Ashton, Bristol	Somerset	e	/	
Long Clawson	a	Brocton	The Hall, Long Clawson, Melton Mowbray, Leics	Leics	e	/	
Long Stratton	w	?	Manor House, Long Stratton, Norfolk	Norfolk	e	/	
Louds Mill	w	?	Louds Mill, Dorset	Dorset	e	/	
Loudwater	w	?	Glen Chess Stables, Loudwater, High Wycombe, Bucks	Bucks	e	/	
Loughborough	ad	Brocton	The Workhouse, Loughborough, Leicestershire	Leics	e	/	
Lynford (West Tofts) (aka Mundford?)	w	?	West Tofts, Mundford, Norfolk	Norfolk	e	/	
Machynlleth	a	Frongoch	Park Common, Machynlleth, Montgomeryshire	Mont	w	/	
Magdalen Camp Military Hospital	h		Military Hospital, Magdalen Camp, Winchester, Hampshire	Hants	e	/	
Maldon	w	Pattishall	Maldon, Essex	Essex	e	/	
Maltreath Marshes	w	?	Maltreath Marshes, Gaerwen, Anglesey	Anglesey	w	/	
Mancetter	w	?	Mancetter, Atherstone, Warwickshire	Warks	e	/	
Manchester Hospital	h		Nell Lane Military Hospital, West Didsbury, Manchester	Lancs	e	/	
Marcham	w	Dorchester	Marcham, Abingdon, Berkshire	Berks	e	/	
Margate	o		Margate, Kent	Kent	e	/	06.01.19
Market Harborough	a	Brocton	Ilston Grange, Market Harborough, Leicestershire	Leics	e	/	
Market Harborough	ad	Brocton	No2 Agricultural Depot, Market Harborough, Leicestershire	Liecs	e	/	
Marks Tey	w	Pattishall	Marks Tey, (near Colchester), Essex	Essex	e	/	
Markshall	w	?	Markshall, Norwich	Norfolk	e	/	
Marshmoor	w	Pattishall	Marshmoor Sidings, North Mimms, Hatfield, Hertfordshire	Herts	e	/	20.03.19
Martlesham	w	Pattishall	Martlesham Heath, Woodbridge, Suffolk	Suffolk	e	/	
Martley (aka Knightwick)	w	Dorchester	Martley, Worcester	Worcs	e	/	
Mayland	w	Pattishall	Mayland, Maldon, Essex	Essex	e	/	
Melchbourne	w	Pattishall	Melchbourne, Sharnbrook, Bedfordshire	Beds	e	/	
Meldreth	w	Pattishall	Meldreth, near Royston, Cambridgeshire	Cambs	e	/	
Middleton Junction	w	?	Middleton Junction, Manchester	Lancs	e	/	12.12.18
Midhurst	w	Pattishall	North Street, Midhurst, Sussex	Sussex	e	/	
Mildenhall	w	Pattishall	Back Row, Mildenhall, Suffolk	Suffolk	e	/	
Mile End Military Hospital	h		Bancroft Road, London E1	London	e	/	
Mill Hill	w	Pattishall	Mill Hill, Hendon, Middlesex	Middx	e	/	
Millbank Hospital	h		Queen Alexandra Hospital, Grosvenor Road, London SW1	London	e	/	
Milldown	w	Dorchester	Blandford, Dorset	Dorset	e	/	
Milnthorpe	a	Leigh	Milnthorpe, Westmorland	Westmor	e		
Monkspath	w	Dorchester	Monkspath, Warwick	Warks	e	/	
Morton	a	Brocton	Morton, Bourne, Lincolnshire	Lincs	e	/	
Morton Fen	w	?	Morton Fen, Morton, Bourne, Lincolnshire	Lincs	e	/	
Mundford (aka Lynford?)	w	Pattishall	West Tofts, Mundford, (near Brandon), Norfolk	Norfolk	e	/	
Napsbury War Hospital	h		Napsbury War Hospital, St Albans, Hertfordshire	Herts	e		

Location		Camp	Description	County				
Narborough	a	Brocton	The Workhouse, Narborough, Leicestershire	Leics	e	/		
Netheravon Aerodrome	cw	Dorchester	The Aerodrome, Netheravon, Wiltshire	Wilts	e	/		16.11.18
Netley Hospital	h		Royal Victoria Hospital, Netley, Hampshire	Hants	e	/		
New Bilton	w	?	New Bilton, Rugby, Warwickshire	Warks	e	/		
Newark House	w	?	Newark House, Hempstead, Gloucestershire	Glos	e	/	18.05.18	
Newcastle Hospital	h		1st Northern General Hospital, Newcastle-upon-Tyne	Northum	e	/		
Newlandside (aka Stanhope)	w	Catterick	Newlandside, Stanhope, Co Durham	Durham	e	/		
Newport Hospital	h		3rd Western General Hospital, Newport, Monmouthshire	Monm	w	/		
Newport Pagnell	w	Pattishall	Headquarters, Westbury House, Newport Pagnell, Bucks	Bucks	e	/		
Newton Abbot	w	Dorchester	The Institute, Newton Abbot, Devon	Devon	e	/		01.03.19
Newtyle	w	?	Newtyle, Forfarshire	Forfar	s	/		
Nocton	a	Brocton	Nocton, Lincoln	Lincs	e	/		
Normanton	w	?	Normanton, Grantham, Lincolnshire	Lincs	e	/		
Normanton	a	Brocton	Normanton, Stamford, Lincolnshire	Rutland	e	/		
Normanton Hall	a	Brocton	Normanton Hall, Hinckley, Leicestershire	Leics	e	/		
North Kilworth	a	Brocton	The Hawthorns, North Kilworth, Rugby, Warks	Leics	e	/		
North Lew	w	Dorchester	Ashbury Court, North Lew, Devon	Devon	e	/		
North Ripon			No 8, North Camp, Ripon, Yorkshire WR	Yorks WR	e	/		
Northallerton	a	Catterick	Northallerton, Yorkshire NR	Yorks NR	e	/		
Northfield (aka Longridge Park)	w	Dorchester	Northfield, Worcestershire	Worcs	e	/		22.01.19
Northiam	w	?	Northiam, Sussex	Sussex	e	/		
Northleach	w	Dorchester	Northleach, Gloucestershire	Glos	e	/		
Northolt	a	Feltham	The Needles, Northolt, Middlesex	Middx	e	/		
Norton Barracks Military Hospital	h		Military Hospital, Norton Barracks, Worcester	Worcs	e	/		
Norton Cuckney	a	Brocton	Norton Cuckney, Mansfield, Nottinghamshire	Notts	e	/		
Ockendon (aka South Okenden)	w	Pattishall	South Ockendon, Romford, Essex	Essex	e	/		
Offchurch Bury	a	Dorchester	Offchurch Bury, Leamington, Warwickshire	Warks	e	/		
Orfordness	w	Pattishall	Orfordness, Suffolk	Suffolk	e	/		
Osbournby	a	Brocton	Osbournby, Sleaford, Lincolnshire	Lincs	e	/		
Ossington	w	?	Hall Stables. Ossington, Newark, Notts	Notts	e	/		
Oswestry		OSWESTRY	Eastern Camp, Park Hall, Oswestry, Salop	Salop	e	/		
Oswestry	w	?	Park Hall Camp, Oswestry, Salop	Salop	e	/		
Oswestry (Officers)	o	OSWESTRY	Officers P/W Camp, Park Hall, Oswestry, Salop	Salop	e	/		
Oswestry, P/W Hospital	h	OSWESTRY	P/W Hospital, Park Hall, Oswestry, Salop	Salop	e	/		
Oswestry, Park Hall Hospital	h	OSWESTRY	Park Hall Hospital, Oswestry, Salop	Salop	e	/		
Oswestry, Western Camp		OSWESTRY	Western Camp, Park Hall, Oswestry, Salop	Salop	e	/		
Otley	a	Catterick	Otley, Yorkshire WR	Yorks WR	e	/		
Oundle	a	Pattishall	Oundle, Northamptonshire	Northants	e	/		
Oxford	h		3rd Southern General Hospital, Oxford	Oxon	e	/		
Oxted	w		Oxted, Surrey	Surrey	e	/		
Panshanger	w	Pattishall	Panshanger, Hertingfordbury, Hertfordshire	Herts	e	/		
Papplewick	a	Brocton	Papplewick, Mansfield, Nottinghamshire	Notts	e	/		
Papworth St Agnes	w	?	The Rectory, Papworth St Agnes, Papworth Everard, Cambs	Cambs	e	/		

Name	Code	Camp	Description	County	Col	Col	Date	Col
Partney	a	Brocton	Partney, Spilsby, Lincolnshire	Lincs	e	/		/
Pateley Bridge	a	Catterick	Pateley Bridge, Harrogate, Yorkshire WR	Yorks WR	e	/		/
Pattishall (formerly Eastcote)		PATTISHALL	Pattishall, near Towcester, Northamptonshire	Northants	e	/		/
Peasmarsh	w	Pattishall	Peasmarsh, Rye, Sussex	Sussex	e	/		/
Penarth	w	Frongoch	Penarth, Glamorgan, S Wales	Glam	w	/		/
Penmaenmawr	w	Frongoch	Penmaenmawr, Carnarvonshire, N Wales	Carn	w	/		/
Pennerley	w	?	Pennerley, Minsterley, Shrewsbury	Salop	e	/		/
Penshurst	w	Pattishall	While House, Bough Beech, Edenbridge, Kent	Kent	e	/		/
Peopleton	w	Dorchester	Peopleton, Pershore, Worcestershire	Worcs	e			/
Perham Down	w	Dorchester	Perham Down, Salisbury Plain, Wiltshire	Wilts	e	/		/
Pershore	ad	Dorchester	Pershore, Worcestershire	Worcs	e	/		/
Pinchbeck Road	ad	Brocton	Pinchbeck Road, Spalding, Lincolnshire	Lincs	e	/		/
Plumtree	ad	Brocton	Plumtree, Nottingham	Notts	e	/		/
Podington	w	Pattishall	Podington, near Wellingborough, Northamptonshire	Northants	e			/
Polmaise (aka Bandeath)	w	?	Polmaise, Bandeath, South Alloa, Stirlingshire	Stirling	s	/	14.12.18	/
Port Clarence	w	Brocton	Port Clarence, Middlesbrough, Yorkshire NR	Durham	e	/		/
Port Talbot	w	Frongoch	Port Talbot, Glamorgan, S Wales	Glam	w	/		/
Portsmouth Hospital	h		5th Southern General Hospital, Portsmouth, Hampshire	Hants	e			/
Potter's Bar	w	Feltham	Potter's Bar, Middlesex	Middx	e	/		/
Potton	w	Pattishall	Potton, Sandy, Bedfordshire	Beds	e			/
Purfleet Military Hospital	h		Military Hospital, Purfleet, Essex	Essex	e	/		/
Raasay	w	Stobs	Raasay, Kyle, Rossshire, Scotland	Inverness	s	/	21.03.19	/
Radford	cw	Dorchester	Radford, near Coventry, Warwickshire	Warks	e	/c		/
Ragdale Hall	a	Brocton	Ragdale Hall, Grimston, Melton Mowbray, Leics	Leics	e	/		/
Rainham	w	Pattishall	Rainham, Essex	Essex	e			/
Ramsbury	w	Dorchester	Barney Farm, Ramsbury, Wiltshire	Wilts	e	/		/
Ramsgate	o		Ramsgate, Kent	Kent	e	/	19.02.18 ??	/
Ranskill	a	Brocton	The Maltings, Ranskill, Bawtry, Yorkshire	Notts	e	/		/
Reading War Hospital	h		War Hospital, Reading, Berkshire	Berks	e			/
Redhill	w	Pattishall	73 London Road, Redhill, Surrey	Surrey	e	/		/
Redmires	o		Redmires, Sheffield, Yorkshire WR	Yorks WR	e	/		/
Retford	a	Brocton	The Workhouse, Retford, Nottinghamshire	Notts	e	/		/
Revesby	w	?	Revesby, Boston, Lincolnshire	Lincs	e	/		/
Rhoose	w	Frongoch	Kemey's Hotel, Rhoose, near Cardiff, S Wales	Glam	w	/		/
Richmond Military Hospital	h		Grove Road, Richmond, Surrey	Surrey	e	/		/
Rickmansworth	w	Pattishall	Rickmansworth, Hertfordshire	Herts	e	/		/
Riding Mill (aka Slaley)	w	Catterick	Slaley PO, Riding Mill, Northumberland	Northum	e			/
Ripon	o		Ripon, Yorks	Yorks WR	e	/		/
Rippingale	a	Brocton	Rippingale, Bourne, Lincolnshire	Lincs	e	/		/
Rippingale Fen	a	Brocton	Rippingale, Bourne, Lincolnshire	Lincs	e	/		/
Robertsbridge	w	Pattishall	Robertsbridge, Sussex	Sussex	e	/		/
Rochford	w	Pattishall	Rochford, Essex	Essex	e	/		/
Rochford	w	Dorchester	Rochford House, Tenbury Wells, Worcestershire	Worcs	e	/		/

Rockfield	Rockfield, Monmouth		Monm	w	w		/
Rockland All Saints	Rockland, Attleborough, Norfolk	Pattishall	Norfolk	e	w	/	/
Romsey	Romsey, Hampshire	Dorchester	Hants	e	w	/	/
Ross-on-Wye	Ross-on-Wye, Herefordshire	Shrewsbury	Hereford	e	w.c	/w	/
Rosyth	Inverkeithing, Rosyth, Fifeshire, Scotland	Stobs	Fife	s	w	/	/
Rothwell	Rothwell, Kettering, Northamptonshire	Pattishall	Northants	e	w	/	/
Rowley	Healyfield, Castleside, near Consett, Co Durham	Catterick	Durham	e	w	/	/
Rowrah	Rowrah, (near Whitehaven), Cumberland	Leigh	Cumb	e	w	/	/
Rumshott	Rumshott Wood, Tubs Hill, Sevenoaks, Kent	Pattishall	Kent	e	w	/	/
Rushden	Rushden House, Rushden, Northamptonshire	Pattishall	Northants	e	w	/	/
Ruthin	Bathafarm Hall, Ruthin, Denbighshire, N Wales	Frongoch	Denbigh	w	a	/	/
Ruthwell	Ironhurst, Ruthwell, Dumfries, Scotland	Stobs	Dumfries	s	w	/	21.02.19
Saffron Walden	The Union, Saffron Walden, Essex	Pattishall	Essex	e	w	/	/
Saint Albans	St Albans, Hertfordshire	Pattishall	Herts	e	w	/	11.11.18
Saint Mellion	Amy Down, St Mellion, Cornwall	?	Cornwall	e	w	/	/
Salford Priors	Salford Priors, Evesham, Worcestershire	?	Warks	e	w	/	/
Saltram	Saltram, Woodford, Plympton, Devon	Dorchester	Devon	e	w	/	/
Sandgate	"Sandgate", Storrington, Sussex	Pattishall	Sussex	e	w	/	/
Sandhill Park	Sandhill Park, near Taunton, Somerset	Dorchester	Somerset	e	w	/	/
Sawley	Sawley, Ripon, Yorkshire WR	Catterick	Yorks WR	e	w	/	/
Seafield (aka Nethy Bridge)	Seafield, Nethy Bridge, Invernessshire	Stobs	Inverness	s	w	/	/
Sealand	Sealand, Chester	?	Flint	w	w.c	/w	/c
Seer Green	Rawlings Farm, Seer Green, Beaconsfield, Bucks	?	Bucks	e	w	/	/
Selby	The Workhouse, Selby, Yorkshire WR	?	Yorks WR	e	w	/	/
Semer	Cosford Workhouse, Semer, Hadleigh, Suffolk	Pattishall	Suffolk	e	a	/	/
Send	Bought on Hall, Send, Surrey	Feltham	Surrey	e	w	/	/
Sheffield Hospital	3rd Northern General Hospital, Sheffield		Yorks WR	e	h	/	/
Shelsley Walsh	Shelsley Walsh, Worcester	Dorchester	Worcs	e	w	/	/
Shepton Mallet	Shepton Mallet, Somerset	Dorchester	Somerset	e	ad	/	/
Shere	Holmbury St. Mary, Shere, Surrey	Pattishall	Surrey	e	w	/	/
Shipmeadow	Shipmeadow Workhouse, Beccles, Suffolk	?	Suffolk	e	w	/	/
Shirehampton	Shirehampton, near Bristol	Dorchester	Glos	e	w	/	/
Shotley	Naval Sick Quarters, Shotley, Ipswich, Suffolk		Suffolk	e	h	/	/
Shotley	HM Training Establishment, Shotley, Ipswich, Suffolk		Suffolk	e		/	/
Shouldham	Shouldham, Downham Market, Norfolk	Pattishall	Norfolk	e	w	/	/
Shrewsbury	Abbey Wood, Shrewsbury	SHREWSBURY	Salop	e		/	18.02.19
Sidbury	Sidbury, Sidmouth, Devon	Dorchester	Devon	e	w	/	/
Sinnington	Sinnington, (near Pickering), Yorkshire NR	Catterick	Yorks NR	e	a	/	/
Skeffington	Skeffington Vale, Leicester	?	Leics	e	w	/	/
Skipton Officers Camp	Skipton, Yorkshire WR		Yorks WR	e	o	/	/
Sleaford	The Union Workhouse, Sleaford, Lincolnshire	Brocton	Lincs	e	w	/	/
Slough	Slough, Buckinghamshire	Feltham	Bucks	e	w	/	/
Snettisham	Snettisham, King's Lynn, Norfolk	?	Norfolk	e	w	/	/

Place	Type	Parent	Description	County	Cat	C1	C2	C3	C4	Date
Soberton	ad	Dorchester	Soberton, Bishop's Waltham, Hampshire	Hants	e			/	/	
Soho Pool	w	Dorchester	Soho Pool, Hookley, Birmingham	Warks	e			/	/	
Somerby Hall	a	Brocton	Somerby Hall Stables, Gainsborough, Lincolnshire	Lincs	e			/	/	
Somerford Hall (aka Brewood)	a	Brocton	Somerford Hall, Brewood, Stafford	Staffs	e			/	/	
Sompting	w	?	Sompting, Worthing	Sussex	e			/	/	
South Brent	ad	Dorchester	Coronation Hall, South Brent, S Devon	Devon	e			/	/	
South Carlton (aka Monks Abbey)	w	?	Monks Abbey, Lincoln	Lincs	e		/	/	/	
South Cleatham	a	Catterick	South Cleatham, Barnard Castle, Co Durham	Durham	e		/	/	/	
South Molton	a	Dorchester	Unicorn Hotel, South Molton, N Devon	Devon	e		/	/	/	
South Ockenden	w	?	South Ockenden, Romford Essex	Essex	e			/	/	
Southampton	t	Brocton	Skating Rink Receiving Depot, Shirley, Southampton	Hants	e		/	/	/	12.02.19
Southampton	ot		Bevois Mount Receiving Depot, Southampton	Hants	e		/	/	/	12.02.19
Southend-on-Sea	o		Southend-on-Sea, Essex	Essex	e			/	/	11.12.18
Southill Park	w	Pattishall	Southill Park, Biggleswade, Bedfordshire	Beds	e			/	/	
Sowerby	w	?	Sowerby, Thirsk, Yorkshire NR	Yorks NR	e			/	/	/
Spalding	t		The Union, Spalding, Lincolnshire	Lincs	e			/	/	
Spettisbury	w	?	Lower Almer Farm, Spettisbury, Blandford, Dorset	Dorset	e		/	/	/	
Sproxton Moor	w	?	Ampleforth College, Malton, Yorks	Yorks NR	e		/	/	/	
Stainby	c.w	Brocton	Stainby, Grantham, Lincolnshire	Lincs	e		/c	/	/	
Stainton Sidings	w	Leigh	Stainton Sidings, Dalton-in-Furness, Lancashire	Lancs	e		/	/	/	
Standon	w	?	New Street Farm, Standon, Ware, Herts	Herts	e			/	/	
Stanford-le-Hope	w	Pattishall	Stanford-le-Hope, Essex	Essex	e			/	/	
Stanley Moor (aka Burbage)	w	Brocton	Stanley Moor, Ladmanlow, Burbage, Buxton, Derbyshire	Derby	e		/	/	/	
Stanstead	w	Pattishall	Oak Hall, Bishop's Stortford, Hertfordshire	Herts	e			/	/	
Starcross	w	Dorchester	Starcross, (near Exeter) Devon	Devon	e			/	/	
Steeple Bumpstead	w	Pattishall	Bower Hall, Steeple Bumpstead, Haverhill, Suffolk	Essex	e			/	/	/
Steyning	w	Pattishall	Steyning, Sussex	Sussex	e			/	/	
Stobs		STOBS	Stobs, Hawick, Roxburgh, Scotland	Rox	s		/	/	/	
Stobs P/W Hospital	h		P/W Hospital, Stobs, Hawick, Roxburgh, Scotland	Rox	s		/	/	/	
Stoke Edith	a	Shrewsbury	42, West Street, Leominster, Herefordshire	Hereford	e			/	/	/
Stoke Green	a	Feltham	Stoke House, Stoke Green, Slough, Bucks	Bucks	e			/	/	
Stone	a	Brocton	Mill Factory, High Street, Stone, Staffordshire	Staffs	e			/	/	
Stoulton	a	Dorchester	Stoulton, Whittington, Worcester	Worcs	e			/	/	
Stow Park	a	Brocton	Stow Park, Morton, Bourne, Lincolnshire	Lincs	e			/	/	
Stowell	a	Dorchester	Stowell, Wincanton, Somerset	Somerset	e			/	/	/
Stratford	o		11 and 13 Water Lane, Stratford, London E15	London	e			/	/	11.12.18
Stratford St Mary	w	?	Stratford St Mary, Colchester, Essex	Essex	e			/	/	/
Stratford-on-Avon	w	Dorchester	Shottery, Stratford-on-Avon, Warwickshire	Warks	e		/	/	/	
Strathord	w	?	Strathord, Perthshire	Perth	s		/	/	/	
Sudbury	a	Brocton	Nestles Factory, Sudbury, Derbyshire	Derby	e			/	/	
Sutton Veny	w.c	Dorchester	Sutton Veny, Warminster, Wiltshire	Wilts	e	/w	/c	/	/	15.09.18
Sutton Veny Military Hospital	h		Sutton Veny Military Hospital, Warminster, Wiltshire	Wilts	e		/	/	/	
Swanage	w	Dorchester	Swanage, Dorset	Dorset	e			/	/	

Tadcaster	a	Catterick	The Workhouse, Tadcaster, Yorkshire WR	Yorks WR	e		/	
Talgarth	a	Frongoch	Tregunter Park, Talgarth, Brecknockshire, Wales	Brecon	w		/	
Taplow Canadian Hospital	h		Canadian Hospital, Taplow, Buckinghamshire	Bucks	e		/	
Tarrylaw	a	Stobs	Tarrylaw Farm, near Balbeggie, Perth, Scotland	Perth	s	/	/	
Taunton (Officers)	o		Sandhill Park Officers Camp, Taunton, Somerset	Somerset	e		/	
Temple Bruer	a	Brocton	Temple Bruer, Navenby, Lincolnshire	Lincs	e		/	
Tempsford	w	Pattishall	Tempsford, Sandy, Bedfordshire	Beds	e		/	
Tendring	w	Pattishall	Tendring, Weeley, Essex	Essex	e	//	/	
Tenterden	ad	Pattishall	Tenterden, Kent	Kent	e	//	/	
Thing Hall	a	Shrewsbury	Thing Hall, Withington, Hereford	Hereford	e		/	
Thirsk	ad	Catterick	The Workhouse, Thirsk, Yorkshire NR	Yorks NR	e	/	/	
Thornbury	w	Dorchester	Thornbury, Bristol	Glos	e		/	
Thornton-le-Moors	w	?	Thornton-le-Morrs, Ince, Cheshire	Cheshire	e		/	
Thorpe Satchville	a	Brocton	No. 113 Agricultural Camp, Thorpe Satchville, Melton Mowbray	Leics	e	//	/	
Thorpe, Norfolk War Hospital	h		The Norfolk War Hospital, Thorpe, Norwich	Norfolk	e	//	/	
Timberland	a	Brocton	The Maltings, Timberland, (near Sleaford), Lincoln	Lincs	e		/	
Tiverton	a	Dorchester	Parkside, Tiverton, Devon	Devon	e	/	/	
Tockwith	a	Catterick	Brogden Old Brewery, Tockwith, York	Yorks WR	e		/	
Toddington	w	Dorchester	Toddington, Winchcombe, Gloucestershire	Glos	e	/	/	
Tonbridge	w	?	The Priory, Bordyke, Tonbridge, Kent	Kent	e		/	
Tooting Military Hospital	h		Church Lane, Tooting, London SW17	London	e		/	
Totnes	w	?	Bridgetown Parish Rooms, Totnes, Devon	Devon	e		/	
Tovil	w	Pattishall	Tovil House, Tovil, Maidstone, Kent	Kent	e	//	/	
Towyn	ad	Frongoch	Neptune Hall, Towyn, Merionethshire, Wales	Merion	w	//	/	
Trawsfynydd	w	Frongoch	Trawsfynydd, Merionethshire, Wales	Merion	w		/	
Turvey	w	Pattishall	Homelands, Turvey, Bedfordshire	Beds	e	//	/	
Tutnall and Cobley	w	Dorchester	Tutnall, Bromsgrove, Worcestershire	Worcs	e		/	
Tuxford	a	Brocton	Tuxford, Nottinghamshire	Notts	e		/	
Twyford	w	Dorchester	Knowl Hill, Twyford, Berkshire	Berks	e		/	
Uckfield	a	Pattishall	The Grange, Uckfield, Sussex	Sussex	e	//	/	
Upavon	w	Dorchester	Upavon, Wiltshire	Wilts	e		/	
Uppingham	w	Brocton	Uppingham, Rutland	Rutland	e	/	/	
Upton	w	?	Upton, Huntingdon	Hunts	e	//	/	
Upton	w	Pattishall	The Vicarage, Upton, Northamptonshire	Northants	e		/	
Upton-on-Severn	a	Dorchester	Holdfast Hall, Upton-on-Severn, Worcestershire	Worcs	e		/	
Upware	w	Pattishall	Upware, Wicken, Cambridgeshire	Cambs	e		/	
Usk	a	Shrewsbury	Ponthycarne House, Usk, Newport, Monmouthshire	Monm	w		/	
Uttoxeter	a	Brocton	Racecourse Buildings, Uttoxeter, Staffordshire	Staffs	e			29.01.19
Waddesdon	w	Pattishall	The Bothy, The Gardens, Waddesdon, Bucks	Bucks	e		/	
Wainfleet	ad	Pattishall	Wainfleet, Lincolnshire	Lincs	e		/	
Wakefield	c.o	WAKEFIELD	Lofthouse Park, Wakefield, Yorkshire WR	Yorks WR	e	/c	/c	/o
Wakerley	w	Pattishall	Wakerley, Stamford, Lincolnshire	Northants	e	/	/	
Walsham-le-Willows	w	Pattishall	Walsham-le-Willows, Bury St Edmunds, Suffolk	Suffolk	e		/	

Place	Type	Camp	Location	County	e/w				
Wandsworth Hospital	h		3rd London General Hospital, Wandsworth, London SW	London	e				/
Wantage	a	Dorchester	Wantage, Berkshire	Berks	e				/
Wareham	w	?	Wareham, Dorset	Dorset	e			/	/
Warmsworth	ad	Catterick	Warmsworth Hall, Doncaster, Yorkshire WR	Yorks WR	e			/	/
Warren Wood	w	Pattishall	Warren Wood, Croxton, Thetford, Norfolk	Norfolk	e				/
Wasdale Head	w	?	Down i Dale, Wasdale Head, Cumberland	Cumb	e		/	/	/
Watlington	a	Dorchester	Brightwell, Watlington, Oxfordshire	Oxon	e			/	/
Wellesbourne	ad	Dorchester	Holly Lodge, Wellesbourne, Warwickshire	Warks	e			/	/
Welshpool	a	Frongoch	The Horse Repository, Welshpool, Montgomery	Mont	w			/	/
Wem	a	Shrewsbury	42 West Street, Leominster, Herefordshire	Salop	e			/	/
Weobley	a	Shrewsbury	The Workhouse, Weobley, Herefordshire	Hereford	e				/
Wereham	w	?	Wereham, Stoke Ferry, Norfolk	Norfolk	e			/	/
West Ham	w	Pattishall	Abbey Mills, Manor Road, West Ham, London E15	London	e			/	/
West Mersea	w	Pattishall	West Mersea, Colchester, Essex	Essex	e			/	/
Weston-on-the-Green	w	Dorchester	Weston-on-the-Green, Bicester, Oxfordshire	Oxon	e	16.01.19		/	/
Wetherby	ad	Catterick	The Brewery, Wetherby, Yorkshire WR	Yorks WR	e			/	/
Weyhill	w	?	Weyhill Fair Ground, Weyhill, Andover, Hampshire	Hants	e		/	/	/
Whitwell	a	Pattishall	Whitwell, Reepham, Norfolk	Norfolk	e		/	/	/
Wigmore	a	Shrewsbury	Wigmore, Kingsland, Herefordshire	Hereford	e			/	/
Wilby	a	Pattishall	Wilby, Eye, Suffolk	Suffolk	e			/	/
Willington	a	Brocton	Willington Hall, Willington, Derbyshire	Derby	e			/	/
Wimborne	w	Dorchester	Little Canford Farm House, Wimborne, Dorset	Dorset	e			/	/
Winchcomb	a	Dorchester	Winchcomb, Gloucestershire	Glos	e			/	/
Winchester	w	?	Morn Hill, Winchester, Hampshire	Hants	e				/
Wingland (aka Sutton Bridge)	w	Brocton	Wingland, Sutton Bridge, Lincolnshire	Lincs	e			/	/
Winwick	w	Pattishall	Winwick, Northamptonshire	Northants	e			/	/
Wisborough Green	w	Pattishall	The Workhouse, Wisborough Green, Billinghurst, Sussex	Sussex	e				/
Withern	a	Brocton	Withern, nr Alford, Lincolnshire	Lincs	e			/	/
Witney	w	Dorchester	Witney, Oxfordshire	Oxon	e			/	/
Witney Aerodrome	w	?	Aerodrome, Witney, Oxfordshire	Oxon	e				/
Woburn	w	Pattishall	Woburn, Bedfordshire	Beds	e		/	/	/
Woking Detention Barracks	p		Detention Barracks, Woking, Surrey	Surrey	e				/
Womenswould	w	Pattishall	Denne Hill Farm, Womenswould, Canterbury, Kent	Kent	e			/	/
Woodborough	a	Brocton	Woodborough, Nottingham	Notts	e			/	/
Woodford	w	?	Woodford Camp, Plympton, Devon	Devon	e				/
Woodham Ferrers	w	Pattishall	Woodham Lodge, Woodham Ferrers, Essex	Essex	e			/	/
Woodstock	w	Dorchester	Drill Hall, Woodstock, Oxfordshire	Oxon	e			/	/
Wookey	a	Dorchester	Wookey, Wells, Somerset	Somerset	e			/	/
Wool	w	?	Wool, Wareham, Dorset	Dorset	e			/	/
Woolwich Hospital	h		Royal Herbert Hospital, Woolwich, London SE	London	e				/
Wootton Bassett	a	Dorchester	Corner House, Wootton Bassett, Wiltshire	Wilts	e			/	/
Worcester	h		Military Hospital, Worcester	Worcs	e			/	/
Worthy Down	w	Dorchester	Worthy Down, Winchester, Hampshire	Hants	e				/

Wrotham	a	Pattishall	Bayldon House, Kingsdown, Wrotham, Sevenoaks, Kent	Kent	e			/
Wrottesley	a	Brocton	Wrottesley Hall, Wrottesley, Codsall, Staffordshire	Staffs	e		/	/
Wymondham	a	Brocton	Wymondham, Leicestershire	Leics	e		/	/
Yarborough	w	?	The Workhouse, Yarborough, Louth, Lincs	Lincs	e			/
Yardley Gobion	w	Pattishall	Yardley Gobion, Stoney Stratford, Buckinghamshire	Northants	e		/	
Yatesbury	w	Dorchester	Yatesbury, Calne, Wiltshire	Wilts	e	/	/	

Escapers

The following list has been extracted from newspapers. In many cases only surnames were given, often mis-spelt and even the places mentioned are sometimes uncertain due to wrong spellings. In many cases the places of capture were not given in the newspapers seen by this author.

Four names have entries in the notes column showing that they succeeded in getting out of the country to Germany or Denmark. The Hungarian 'History of PoWs' records that an un-named German airman arrived back in his country after stealing an aircraft, but no confirmation has been found in the British press concerning this man, or his exploit. However August Junght is recorded as getting away from Frith Hill/Blackdown (see p.93) at about the right date and there is no subsequent report of his recapture or continuing absence from the camp.

Name	rank	escaped from	date, if stated	source	where caught, or re-captured" if not stated	date, if stated	source	notes
Achilles		IoM	21/03/1917	Times 25May17	Wendover		Times 25Feb19	
Agathen, Heinrich		Knockaloe	08/03/1917	Times 10Mar17	re-captured		Times 25May17	
Ahlers A	clerk	Leigh	12/10/1917	Times 15Oct17	west coast of IoM		Times 10Mar17	
Ahrens, Norbert		Stobs		Times 25Aug17	Manchester	15/10/1917	Times 16Oct17	stole boat at Scarborough
Ammerlich, Max	Zepp PO	Dyffryn Aled	04/04/1915	Times 6Apr15	in North Sea		Times 4Sep17	
Andler, Hans	ObLt	Healeyfield, Consett		Times 19Dec17	Llanbedr, nr Harlech	11/04/1915	Times 12Apr15	
Anvoart		Frongoch	13/04/1916	FO383/164	recaptured	15/04/1916	FO383/154	
Arenkens, Wilhelm	Gefreiter	Alexandra Palace	04/07/1915	Times 6Jul15	re-captured	06/07/1915	Times 7Jul15	
Arndt Auguste	schoolteacher	Pattishall	31/08/1917	Times 1Sep17	Denton, Northampton		Times 3Sep17	
Ball, Max F		Boston		Times 16Jan18				
Baringer, Benjamin		Kegworth	05/09/1918	Times 13Sept18	Kneeton, Notts		Times 13Sep18	planned to steal aircraft
Bastoen, Paul		Skipton	30/06/1918	Times 2July18	recaptured		Skipton Herald 5July	
Bauneisher, Louis		Feltham	16/10/1917		re-captured		Times 18Oct17	
Beeib, Leon		Aldershot			re-captured		Times 27Aug19	
Behrendt		Wainfleet	15/10/1919	Times 21Oct19	re-captured		Times 21Oct19	
Benzion A		Liverpool		Times 25Sept17				
Berg (or Borg), Petersen		Dorchester	17/09/1915	Times 18Sep15	West Hartlepool	20/09/1915	Times 21Sep15	
Bergmann, Edwin		Healeyfield, Consett		Times 7Feb18				
Berling, Paul		Kegworth	24/09/1917	Times 26Sep17	Hickling	27/09/1917	Times 29Sep17	
Berschmann, Kurt		Etwell, Derby		Times 16Jan19	recaptured		Times 16Jan19	
Biger, Joseph		Whitehaven		Times 12Aug19				
Birkson		Wool		Times 10Oct18	re-captured		Times 11Oct18	
Birnbacker, Alois		Foxburrow, Chigwell		Times 19Sep18				
Bissa		Foxburrow, Chigwell		Times 19Sep18				
Bleister								
Block	Lt	Sandhill Park	25/08/1917	Times 27Aug17	Toller Down, Dorset shot in attempt		Times 29Aug17	
Bockmeyer		Oldcastle		Times 22Sep16				
Boedt	U Boat officer	Ripon		Times 13Jan19				
Boenicke, Ferdinand	navy	Kegworth	24/09/1917	Times 26Sep17	re-captured		Police Gaz 2Oct17	
Boerner		Kegworth	24/09/1917	Times 26Sep17	re-captured		Times 26Sep17	
Boldt, Ernst		Leigh	12/10/1917	Times 15Oct17	Manchester	15/10/1917	Times 16Oct17	
Boldt, Ernst		Shrewsbury		Times 15Jan17	re-captured		Times 15Jan17	
Bookel P		Brocton			re-captured		Times 8Sep19	
Borbeck, Hans		Bramley		Times 12Sep17	re-captured		Times 13Sep17	
Boumann		Bungay		Times 13Sep18	Lingfield (Redlingfield?)		Times 13Sep18	
Boykreyer, August	seaman	Oldcastle	15/01/1916	Times 17Jan16	Rathowen, W Meath		Times 19Jan16	
Brane, Johann Deidrich	Lt	Stratford reprisal		Times 11Jun18	Walsham, Norfolk		Times 13Jun18	recaptured at Walton-on-the-Naze per Stratford Express
Brevor		Burbage, Buxton		Times 3May19				

Name	Rank/Role	Camp	Date	Location/Status	Source	Date 2	Source 2	Notes
Brinkmann, Heinrich	Unter-Off	Frongoch	13/04/1916	recaptured		15/04/1916	FO383/154	complained to US Embassy
Brinkmann, Wilhelm	sailor	Knockaloe	08/03/1917	west coast of IoM	Times 10Mar17		Times 10Mar17	
Brossmann, William	Lt, army	Colsterdale	21-23/08/1917	near Whitby	Times 24Aug17	28/08/1917	Times 29Aug17	
Bruggmann		Newtown		re-captured			Times 10Aug18	
Brune, William	sailor	Frith Hill		Esher	Times 27Sep16		Times 28Sep16	
Brunte, Herman	sailor	Leigh	24/10/1917	Aughton, Ormskirk	Times 25Oct17	26/10/1917	Leigh Chron 2Nov17	
Buck, Marzlan		Woburn		re-captured	Times 16Aug17		Times 16Aug17	
Buhler, Wilhelm		Kedlington, Suffolk		Swaffham	Times 3Oct17		Times 4Oct17	
Bunte, Herman		Shrewsbury		re-captured	Times 15Jan17		Times 15Jan17	should this be Brunte?
Burchart, Henrich		Flowerdown	24/04/1918		Times 25Apr18			
Burgath		Kington		Prestigne	Times 6Aug18		Times 6Aug18	
Burghagen, Walter	navy	Kegworth	24/09/1917	Hickling	Times 26Sep17	27/09/1917	Times 29Sep17	Burghmann in "Times" 29/9
Burkhardt H F	Eng Lt	Dyffryn Aled	02/06/1918	Llanfynydd, Wrexham	Times 3Jun18		Times 5Jun18	
Burkhardt, Helmuth F		Holyport		Bath, on a train	Times 12Nov17		Times 19Nov17	
Butz, Paul		Catterick		re-captured			Times 8Apr18	
Butz, Paul O	naval PO	Stobs		in North Sea	Times 25Aug17		Times 4Sep17	stole boat at Scarborough
Christlieb, Albert	civilian	Alexandra Palace	12/05/1916	Wapping, trying to board a ship	Times 13May16		Times 17&19May16	
Christoff, Wilhelm		Leighterton		re-captured			Times 14Sep18	
Christopher		Blandford	08/08/1918	re-captured	Times 16Aug18		Times 16Aug18	
Chylangi, Geno		Yate			Times 17Mar17			
Class, Louis		Reading Jail		surrendered in London	Times 5Nov17		Berks Chron 9Nov17	
Clausnidzer Ernst J L		Shrewsbury	16/06/1918	Tipton	Times 19Jun18		Times 19Jun18	
Clentik	Lt	Chelmsford Detn Bks	26/05/1917	Basildon	Times 28May17	28/05/1917	Times 28May17	
Cmentek, Anton		Holyport	07/12/1916	Windsor	Times 9Dec16		Times 9Dec16	
Cullsen, Jens P	sailor	Knockaloe	08/03/1917	west coast of IoM	Times 10Mar17		Times 10Mar17	
Curt, Lamprecht		Larkhill	19/08/1917	re-captured	Times 20Aug17	19/08/1917	Times 20Aug17	
Daga, Jack (aka John Digger)		Corby			Police Gaz 22Jan18			
Dahl W		Abbey Dore		re-captured			Times 8Sep19	
Davidek, Carl		Winchester		recaptured	Times 21Nov18		Times 21Nov18	
Davidsen, George C		Sealand			Police Gaz 22Jan18			
Debborn, Gustav		Winchester	26/03/1918	re-captured	Times 27Mar18		Times 29Mar18	
Definanske		Llanfrothen	10/10/1919	Penrhyndeudraeth	Times Penrhyn police	11/10/1919	Penrhyn police	Dolgellau Archives
Deickman, Hans C	sailor	Oldcastle	14/09/1915	west coast of IoM	Police Gaz 17Sep15		Police Gaz 12Oct15	
Dibbern, Gustav		Corby	21/07/1917	re-captured	Times 23Jul17		Times 28Jul17	
Dickert, Walter	fisherman	Fovant		Lincoln	Times 15Sep17		Times 17Sep17	
Doering		Banbury		re-captured	Times 13Sep18			
Doering		Banbury		re-captured			Times 14Sep18	from railway gang
Dreacher				French ship at Grimsby			Times 20Feb19	
Drescher, Paul		Brocton			Times 18Mar18			
Dreshel, Paul		Retford		re-captured	Police Gaz 7Mar19		Police Gaz 11Mar19	escaped in a railway wagon
Drex, Paul		Doncaster			Times 8Mar19			jumped from moving train

Name	Rank/Occupation	Camp	Date	Location/Status	Reference	Date 2	Reference 2	Notes
Duber, Michael F	planter	Alexandra Palace	19/07/1915	Coles Green	Times 21Jul15	25/07/1915	Times 26Jul15	
Dunker		Upavon		re-captured	Times 13Sep18		Times 13Sep18	
Dusselmann, Walter	naval PO	Stobs			Times 25Aug17		Times 4Sep17	stole boat at Scarborough
Eber, Richard	Sgt Major	Handforth	11/08/1917	re-captured reported & denied	Times 14Aug17		Times 17&25Aug17	still at large Times 31Aug
Ehlen		Stobs	05/09/1917	re-captured	Times 6Sep17		Times 19Sep17	
Ehlerb, Victor		Knockaloe	08/04/1918	Port Erin	Times 11Apr18	13/04/1918	Times 15Apr18	
Ehlers, Gesche L	ship officer	Oldcastle	24/08/1917	re-captured	Times 25Aug17		Times 27Aug17	
Escosuras, Carlos K de la		Reading Jail			Times 5Nov17			alias Diaz. Sought assylum in the Spanish Embassy
Eysoldt, Walter		Alexandra Palace			Police Gaz 11Feb16 re-captured		Times 15Feb16	
Fassien, Arthur L		Shrewsbury	12/02/1918		Times 20Feb18			
Ferol, Hans		Lofthouse		Hull			Times 23Jul19	
Flindt		Newtown		re-captured			Times 10Aug18	
Flink, Josef	Lt	Holyport		Beckenham	Times 27Aug17		Times 29Aug17	intended to steal an aircraft
Fraas		Stobs	05/09/1917	re-captured	Times 6Sep17		Times 19Sep17	
Frank, Earich		Flowerdown	24/04/1918		Times 25Apr18			
Fronnelt		Healeyfield, Consett			Times 19Dec17			
Geblin, Gustav		Stobs	26/10/1915	Hawick Exp 19Oct15 Granton		26/10/1915	Hawick Exp 29Oct15	
Gemest, Herman		Kegworth	24/09/1917	re-captured	Times 26Sep17		Times 26Sep17	
Gevers, Heinrich J A		Sealand, Flint		re-captured	Times 12Nov17		Times 14Nov17	
Gieseck, Herman		Wingland, Sutton Br			Police Gaz 17Sep18			
Gitzen, Wilhelm		Pattishall	31/08/1917	Denton, Northampton	Times 1Sep17		Times 3Sep17	
Glende, Otto		Langport			Times 16Jul19		Times 3Oct19	
Gohmer		Dorchester	02/02/1915	re-captured	Police Gaz 4Feb16		Police Gaz 11Feb16	
Goldberger, Sigmund		Burbage, Leics	25/11/1918	Leicester	Police Gaz 10Dec18		Times 16Dec18	
Graurnam, Karl	seaman	Oldcastle	15/01/1916	Rathowen, W Meath	Times 17Jan16		Times 19Jan16	
Grey, Johann		Bicester	06/06/1918	re-captured	Times 8Jun18		Times 8Jun18	
Griem, Alfons	merch officer	Oldcastle	11/08/1915	Co Cavan	Times 13Aug15	13/08/1915	Times 14Aug15	
Grium, Alfons C M		Sealand, Flint	10/11/1917	re-captured	Times 12Nov17		Times 14Nov17	
Groensky, Albert	sailor	Handforth	11/08/1917	re-captured reported & denied	Times 14Aug17		Times 17&25Aug17	still at large Times 31Aug
Gross, Herman		Knockaloe	23/08/1917	Douglas	Times 28Aug17		Times 8Sep17	
Grote, Freiherr von	naval Lt	Holyport		caught tunnelling	Times 15Mar16			
Grote, Thomas von	Lt, navy	Colsterdale	21-23/08/17	near Whitby	Times 24Aug17	28/08/1917	Times 29Aug17	
Grueber van, Johannes		Catterick	19/08/1918	re-captured	Times 20Aug18		Times 9Oct18	
Gruhle, Otto		Rowley, nr Consett	17/10/1916	Dipton	Times 19Oct16	17/10/1916	Times 19Oct16	
Gruhlen, Otto		Southill, Old Warden	23/06/1917	re-captured	Times 25Jun17		Times 4Jul17	
Gruss, Emil		Tenbury Wells			Police Gaz 20Sep18			reported drowned by other PoWs but may have escaped as no body found.
Gutzehr, Albert		Wellsbourne		re-captured	Times 19Aug18		Times 21Aug18	
Haak, Bernhard	naval CPO	Stobs		in North Sea	Times 25Aug17		Times 4Sep17	stole boat at Scarborough
Habel, W		Farnborough		Pilcot, nr Odiham	Times 4Dec17		Times 7Dec17	
Hanecke, Joseph	L Cpl	Handforth		Bingley	Times 22Aug16		Times 29Aug16	

Name	Rank/Status	Camp	Date	Source 1	Location	Date 2	Source 2	Notes
Harbecker, Wilhelm		Winchester			Portsmouth	23/12/1918	Times 27Dec18	
Harker		Bramley			Silchester		Times 2Aug18	
Harker, Paul H		Wool			re-captured		Times 10Oct18	Times 11Oct18
Harnischmacher		Southminster					Times 12Aug19	
Harris, Frederick	sailor	Knockaloe			west coast of IoM	08/03/1917	Times 10Mar17	Times 10Mar17
Harte, Herman		Pattishall			Denton, Northampton	31/08/1917	Times 1Sep17	Times 3Sep17
Hartmann		Winchester			re-captured		Times 31Jan18	Times 31Jan18
Hauser, Eduard	Lt	Kegworth			re-captured	09/10/1918	Times 10Oct18	Times 14Oct15
Haussner		Stobs			re-captured	05/09/1917	Times 6Sep17	Times 19Sep17
Heidrich, Paul		Wellsbourne			re-captured		Times 19Aug18	Times 21Aug18
Heinrich, Arthur		Larkhill			re-captured	15/05/1917	Times 16May17	
Heinz		Blandford			re-captured	08/08/1918	Times 16Aug18	Times 16Aug18
Heisker, Albert		Wool			re-captured		Times 10Oct18	Times 11Oct18
Heldorf, Hans W von	Lt	Dyffryn Aled			Llandudno	14/08/1915	Times 16Aug15	16/08/1915 Times 17Aug15	submarine rendezvous failed
Helldelder, Lorenz	officer	Ripon					Times 18Mar18	ex Colsterdale? not Ripon
Henneck		Thornbury			re-captured			Times 15Jul18
Henning, Heinrich J G von	CaptLt	Dyffryn Aled			Llandudno	14/08/1915	Times 16Aug15	16/08/1915 Times 17Aug15	submarine rendezvous failed
Henrard, Franz B	Lt	Holyport			re-captured		Times 26Sep17	Times 27Sep17
Henschkel, Franz B	sailor	Leigh			Aughton, Ormskirk	24/10/1917	Times 25Oct17	26/10/1917 Leigh Chron 2Nov17
Heritz, Karl	Lt	Lofthouse			re-captured			Times 1Sep19
Hertzog	2Lt	Sandhill Park			Toller Down, Dorset	25/08/1917	Times 27Aug17	Times 29Aug17
Heubner, Alex		Kings Lynn			re-captured	04/05/1918	Times 6May18	Times 6May18
Heym, Hans		Dorchester			West Hartlepool	17/09/1915	Times 18Sep15	20/09/1915 Times 21Sep15
Heymann, Paul		Glendevon			re-captured			Times 4Oct17
Hiller, Augustus	officer	Ripon			recaptured	16/03/1918	Times 18Mar18	Times 19Mar18	ex Colsterdale? not Ripon
Hitchen, Carl		Winchester					Times 22Dec17		alias Charles Grenfell Frederick Leyton
Hodgson, Edward E	British Citizen	Islington			Bloomsbury		Times 21Nov16	Times 24Nov16
Hoemke		Winchester			re-captured		Times 29May19	Times 5Jun19
Hoffmann, Paul		Bicester			re-captured	06/06/1918	Times 8Jun18	Times 8Jun18
Holling W		Dorchester			re-captured			Times 8Sep19
Homke, Otto		Larkhill			South coast	17/04/1918	Times 6May18	Times 6May18
Homke, Otto		Bramley			barque on Thames		Times 3Sep17	Times 17Sep17
Horn, Arped	Austrian Army	Donington			London	14/07/1917	Times 16Jul17	Times 19Jul17
Horn, Wilhelm		Littock Forest			Nethy Bridge	02/07/1917	Times 4Jul17	05/07/1917 Times 6Jul17
Hornemann, Ernst		Chepstow				07/03/1918	Times 9Mar18	
Hubner, Paul		Woburn			re-captured		Times 28Nov16	Times 29Nov16
Isher, Joseph		IoM			re-captured	21/03/1917	Times 25May17	Times 25May17
Ivan, Walther		Dorchester			Southampton	17/09/1915	Times 18Sep15	Times 18Sep15
Jager		Banbury			re-captured			Times 15Mar19
Jarombet					Wendover			Times 25Feb19	trying to steal a boat

Name	Rank	Location	Date	References	Notes	Additional
Jaworek, Alois		Woburn		re-captured	04/08/1917 Times 6Aug17	
Jemptzin		Brandon			Times 14Feb19	
Jenlar, Carl		Reading Jail			Times 5Nov17	Hemlar, per Berks Chronicle
Jensen, Wilhelm	Naval WO	Frongoch	13/02/1917	Harlech	B.Festiniog police	Dolgellau Archives
Jensen, Wilhelm H	Zepp PO	Stobs		in North Sea	Times 25Aug17	
Jeske		Kington		Prestigne	Times 6Aug18	stole boat at Scarborough
Jockell		Aldershot		re-captured	Times 27Aug19	
Johl	Fahnrich	Handforth	05/05/1916	Gorton	Times 8 May16	
Joksch, Alfred	Bosuns Mate	Stobs	26/10/1915	re-captured	Times 28Oct15	06/05/1916 Times 8 May16
Jottling, Friedrich	waiter	Dorchester			Times 26Oct16	Police Gaz 2Nov15
Jugenfeld, Baron T von		Knockaloe	08/04/1918	Port Erin	Times 11Apr18	Fredrick Gretten per Pol Gaz 13/04/1918 Times 15Apr18
Junght Ernst A	airman	Frith Hill	26/08/1915		Times 31Aug15	
Justus, Heinz E H	Ober Lt	Colsterdale	31/03/1905	on the road to Masham	his own account	dressed as a woman when caught
Justus, Heinz E H	Ober Lt	Lofthouse / train near South Elmshall		surrendered at Cardiff	Times 26Oct18	"escaped dressed as a woman", but per his book this was from the train taking him from Holyport to Lofthouse Times 29Oct18
Kaars, Frank	officer	Ripon	16/03/1918		Times 18Mar18	ex Colsterdale? not Ripon
Kafmer, Wilhelm	stoker	Corby	21/07/1917	Lincoln	Times 23Jul17	Times 28Jul17
Kahn or Cahn	Off-stell	Handforth	05/05/1916	Gorton	Times 8 May16	named Kassner in Police Gaz 24/7 06/05/1916 Times 8 May16
Kalienke, Otto A		Sealand			Police Gaz 22Jan18	
Kampen, van		Middleton, Lancs			Times 14Sep18	
Kamsalar		Burbage, Buxton			Times 3May19	
Kanopka, Karl		Knockaloe		found in camp	Times 15Aug16	Times 17Aug16
Kasper, Wilhelm		Larkhill	15/05/1917		Times 16May17	
Kazakewics, Wojesch		IoM			Times 15May17	(not seen - in early ed)
Kehrhan, Ferdinand	British citizen	Islington			Times 21Nov16	recapture not traced but 13Apr17 he appealed against sentence, so must have been caught
Keilhack, Hans	naval Lt	Donington	17/09/1915	Chatham	Times 20Sep15	23/09/1915 Times 24Sep15
Keilhack, Hans	naval Lt	Holyport		caught tunnelling	Times 1Feb16	
Kella		Tetbury		re-captured		Times 21Aug18
Kempe, Fritz		Bramley		re-captured	Times 12Sep17	Times 13Sep17
Kerst, Arthur		Pattishall	31/08/1917	Denton, Northampton	Times 1Sep17	Times 3Sep17
Killenalt		Banbury			Times 13Sep18	from railway gang
Kirchner Otto R		Shrewsbury	10/06/1915	Welshpool	Times 14Jun15	11/06/1915 Times 14Jun15
Kirst, Arthur		Berkshire ?		Glasgow		Times 27Sep19
Klaiss, Edmund	Lt	Stratford reprisal		Walsham, Norfolk	Times 11Jun18	recaptured at Walton-on-the-Naze per Stratford Express Times 13Jun18
Klapproth, Alfred	merch officer	Lofthouse	28/05/1915		Times 2Jun15	arr Copenhagen, Times 29Jun15
Kleinberg		Catterick		re-captured		Times 17Aug18
Knisig, Gustav		Langport		re-captured	Times 16Jul19	Times 3Oct19
Koch		Notts		Hull		Times 4Jan19

Name		Location	Date	Reference		Status	Notes
Koch, Carl	army	Kegworth	24/09/1917	Times 26Sep17	Police Gaz 2Oct17	re-captured	
Koch, Carl		Kings Lynn	04/05/1918	Times 6May18	Times 6May18	re-captured	
Koch, Julius Reinhard		Frongoch	13/04/1916	FO383/164	FO383/154	recaptured	complained to US Embassy
Kockrich, Gustav		Abram Colliery, Leigh	12/11/1917	Leigh Chron 16Nov1	Leigh Chron 16Nov17	Croston, Preston	
Koehn, Otto	Lt	Dorchester	11/12/1914	Times 14Dec14	Times 14Dec14	Tilbury	The man in the box!
Koening, Otto		Banbury	07/10/1918	Police Gaz 22Oct18	Police Gaz 25Oct18	re-captured	
Koerdt		Banbury			Times 14Sep18	re-captured	
Kohler, Hans		Stanhope	07/05/1917	Times 10May17	Times 10May17	re-captured	
Konig, Karl		Kinlochleven	15/08/1917	Times 16Aug17			
Konrad, Karl		Crawford, Lanark		Times 18Oct17	Times 19Oct17	Carlisle	
Kostknike, Gustav		Woburn	04/07/1917	Times 5Jul17	Times 6Aug17	re-captured	
Kovacs, Michael		Alexandra Palace		Times 7Apr17			
Kraus		Kegworth	24/09/1917	Times 26Sep17	Times 26Sep17	re-captured	
Kraus, Hans		Skipton	30/06/1918	Times 2July18	Craven Herald 5July	re-captured	
Kreuger, Otto		Shrewsbury	12/02/1918	Times 20Feb18	Times 20Feb18	Rotherham	
Kreuz		Oldcastle		Times 22Sep16	Times 22Sep16	re-captured	
Kropke, Heinrich F		Alexandra Palace		Times 28Jun16			
Kuppers, Gotfried		Corby		Times 24Apr17			
Kurt, Adolf		Wellsbourne		Times 19Aug18	Times 21Aug18	re-captured	
Kurt, Thomas K		Wool		Times 10Oct18	Times 11Oct18	re-captured	
Laessig, Max W		Shrewsbury	12/02/1918	Times 20Feb18			
Landoverg, Eric		Kegworth	24/09/1917	Times 26Sep17	Times 26Sep17	re-captured	
Laskus, Hans		Skipton	30/06/1918	Times 2Jul18	Craven Herald 5July	Clitheroe	
Lassen		Lofthouse		Times 24Mar19			
Laue, Franz	Lt	Dyffryn Aled		Times 24Oct18	Times 26Oct18	Caernarvon	
Laue, Franz		Byrnnnyn, Abergele		Police Gaz 8Nov18			
Laue, Fritz	Lt army	Colsterdale	21-23/08/17	Times 24Aug17	28/08/1917 Times 29Aug17	near Whitby	also Lage in "Times" and Laue in "Police Gaz"
Lehe		Retford			Times 29Jan19	re-captured	
Lehmann	Lt	Chelmsford Detn Bks	26/05/1917	Times 28May17	28/05/1917 Times 28May17	Basildon	
Lehmann, Emil		Kegworth	24/09/1917	Times 26Sep17	Times 26Sep17	re-captured	
Leikes, Otto		IoM		Times 1Mar17	Times 2Mar17	re-captured	
Leiss, Fritz		Maldon		Police Gaz 24Sep18			
Leonhardt					Times 27May19	Baldock	
Leroe H M		Lofthouse		Times 12Aug19	Times 12Aug19	re-captured	
Leroi H M	Lt	Lofthouse		Times 21Jul19			
Leschnik, Hans		Totteridge			Times 27Aug19	re-captured	
Lippchutz, Benno		Douglas	23/08/1917	Times 25Aug17			still at large, "Times" 4Sept
Lippchutz, Benno	sailor	Knockaloe		Times 12Aug18			still at large 26Aug
Lobez, Alfons		Bramley	17/09/1917	Times 19Sep17	Times 22Sep17	re-captured	Lober in Police Gaz 18/9
Loepitz, Ernst		Banbury	07/10/1918	Police Gaz 22Oct18	Police Gaz 25Oct18	re-captured	

Name	Occupation	Location	Date	Source	Place	Result	Notes
Loewe, Wilhelm	navy	Kegworth	24/09/1917	Times 26Sep17	Kegworth	re-captured	Police Gaz 2Oct17
Lubben		Mill Hill		Times 15Jul18	Waltham Abbey		Times 15Jul18
Lubke, Paul		?		Times 4Sep17	Perthshire		Times 4Sep17
Lutz, Gustav		Kegworth	24/09/1917	Times 26Sep17	Kegworth	re-captured	Times 26Sep17
Luvke		Banbury				re-captured	Times 15Mar19
Maglic, Konstantin (Petrovitch)		Alexandra Palace		Times 19May16	off Gt Yarmouth 12Jun		The Dandy Hun
Maier, Karl	army	Kegworth	24/09/1917	Times 26Sep17	Hickling		27/09/1917 Times 29Sep17
Mallmann, Joseph	navy	Kegworth	24/09/1917	Times 26Sep17			re-captured not traced
Mandey, Emil	sailor	Handforth	01/11/1917	Times 3Nov17	Stalybridge		Times 10Nov17
Marein		Whitehaven		Times 12Aug19			
Marienfeld, Georg	sailor	Handforth	01/11/1917	Times 3Nov17	Stalybridge		Times 10Nov17
Martinke	sailor	Catterick				re-captured	Times 17Aug18
Mathlesen, Peter	sailor	Frith Hill		Times 27Sep16	Wokingham		Times 29Sep16
Mattias, Heinrich E	Lt, navy	Colsterdale	21-23/08/17	Times 24Aug17	near Whitby		28/08/1917 Times 29Aug17 convicted of treason
McGarry, John	Sein Feiner	Lincoln Jail		Police Gaz 7Feb19			
Meisner		Greenwood		Times 27Aug18	re-captured		Times 28Aug18
Mersdest		Newark		Times 15Oct19			
Michaelski, Karl	sailor	Frith Hill		Times 27Sep16	Wokingham		Times 29Sep16
Michalski, Carl	sailor	Stobs		Times 6Jan16	recaptured		Times 8Jan16 recap ar Newcastleton, per website
Mielitz, O		Farnborough		Times 4Dec17	Pilcot, nr Odiham		Times 7Dec17
Milroy, John	Sein Feiner	Lincoln Jail		Police Gaz 7Feb19			
Moenck, Max		Leighterton		Police Gaz 13Sep18	re-captured		Police Gaz 17Sep18
Mohr, Richard		Frith Hill		Times 27Sep16	Esher		Times 28Sep16
Morlang, Karl	airman	Oldcastle	11/08/1915	Times 13Aug15	Co Cavan		13/08/1915 Times 14Aug15
Muller	merch officer	Upavon			re-captured		Times 14Sep18
Muller, Curt		Reading Jail		Times 5Nov17			Police Gaz 13Nov17
Muller, Heinrich		Pattishall	31/08/1917	Times 1Sep17	Denton, Northampton		Times 3Sep17
Muller, Otto		IoM	21/03/1917	Times 25May17	re-captured		Times 25May17
Muller, von	Capt, navy	Kegworth	24/09/1917	Times 26Sep17	Tollerton		25/09/1917 Times 26Sep17 of SMS Emden
Munchen, Fritz		Mill Hill		Times 22Mar18			
Nassau, Gerhard von		Holyport		Times 12Nov17	Bath, on a train		Times 19Nov17
Naujoch A	labourer	Cove Heights	22/08/1917	Times 24Aug17	Westbrook		Times 28Aug17 named in Police Gazette
Neller, Charles		Reading	03/11/1917	Berks Chron 9Nov17			
Oetter		Foxburrow, Chigwell		Times 19Sep18			
Oezvick, Ludvig	stoker	Knockaloe	08/03/1917	Times 10Mar17	west coast of IoM		Times 10Mar17
Ofall		Stamberd, Brecon		Times 2May19			
Oldenbuttel		Upavon		Times 13Sep18	re-captured		Times 13Sep18
Osterhoff		Stobs	05/09/1917	Times 6Sep17	re-captured		Times 17Sep17
Ottermann, Herman		Corby		Times 24Apr17			
Otto, Wilhelm	sailor	Handforth	01/11/1917	Times 3Nov17	Stalybridge		Times 10Nov17 Times Index gave place as Bearstead
Pachr, Albert		Foxburrow, Chigwell		Times 19Sep18	re-captured		Police Gaz 1Oct18

Surname	Rank	Camp	Date	Location	Reference	Date2	Reference2	Notes
Pelusss			Middleton, Lancs		Times 14Sep18			
Persch, George			Maldon		Police Gaz 24Sep18			
Perus, Karl			Yate		Times 17Mar17			on parole from Knockaloe
Peters, Robert			Oasby, Lincs	16/09/1918	Times 19Sep18			
Petersen			Liverpool		Times 25Sep17			
Petersen			Mill Hill		Times 15Jul18			Times 15Jul18
Petersen W J E	Lt		Dyffryn Aled	02/06/1918	Times 3Jun18		Waltham Abbey	Times 5Jun18
Petrovitch, Stevan (Maglic)			Alexandra Palace		Times 19May16		Llanfynydd, Wrexham	The Dandy Hun
Plessing	Lt		Redmires				off Gt Yarmouth 12Jun	Times 7Feb19
Plushow, Gunter	air officer		Donington	05/07/1915	Times 6Jul15		York	got back to Germany by stowing away on the Flushing boat
Porschke, Herman			Winchester	26/03/1918	Times 27Mar18		re-captured	Times 29Mar18
Potti, Paul			Foxburrow, Chigwell		Times 19Sep18		re-captured	Police Gaz 1Oct18
Pranzon, Arnold			Crawford, Lanark		Times 18Oct17		Carlisle	Times 19Oct17	named Granger in re-capture notice
Prondzynski, Stephan von			Kegworth	24/09/1917	Times 26Sep17		re-captured	Times 26Sep17
Quante J			Abbey Dore				re-captured	Times 8Sep19
Quenel, Rudolf	sailor		Stobs	18/10/1916	Times 21Oct16		re-captured	Times 21Oct16
Radnutz, Max			Glendevon				re-captured	Times 4Oct17
Rastenbolz, John	Sgt Major		Frongoch	13/02/1917	B.Festiniog police	14/02/1917	Harlech	B Festiniog police	Dolgellau Archives
Reighel			Bramley				Newbury	Times 6Sep18
Reil, Heinrich			Fovant		Times 15Sep17		re-captured	Times 17Sep17
Reimer, Walter			Kedlington, Suffolk		Times 3Oct17		Swaffham	Times 4Oct17
Reinsvorss, Helmuth	officer		Ripon		Times 18Mar18		recaptured	Times 19Mar18	named Reinsdorff in recap notice
Reitz, Karl	Lt		Handforth		Times 22Aug16		Bingley	Times 29Aug16
Ren, Herman	sailor		Leigh	19/01/1918	Times 21Jan18	24/01/1918	Gloucestershire	Times 28Jan18	Reu in Times, Ren in local papers
Rew, Herman			Brecon	27-28/11/18			W India Dock	Times 6Dec18
Ries, Friedrich			Dalston Hospital	16/03/1916	Times 17Mar16			
Rohreig, Otto			Douglas	29/07/1917	Times 31Jul17		Ramsey	Times 6Aug17
Ronessler, Fritz W	sailor		Leigh	24/10/1917	Times 25Oct17	26/10/1917	Aughton, Ormskirk	Leigh Chron 2Nov17	Roesser per Times
Rossfer			Hereford				London	Times 23Oct18
Rottman			Southminster		Times 12Aug19			
Routenberg, Hans	navy		Kegworth	24/09/1917	Times 26Sep17		re-captured		but report of re-capture not traced
Ruhlurnd H			Lofthouse		Times 12Aug19			
Russert E			Abbey Dore				re-captured	Times 8Sep19
Saalfeld, Otto			Brocton		Times 20Aug19			
Sabish, Arthur			Penmaenmwar	24/06/1918			re-captured	Times 26Jun18
Sahm, H			Farnborough		Times 4Dec17		Pilcot, nr Odiham	Times 7Dec17
Salamon, Paul			Sealand, Flint		Times 12Nov17		re-captured	Times 14Nov17
Sanders-Leben, Rudolf von	Lt		Dyffryn Aled	04/04/1915	Times 6Apr15	11/04/1915	Llanbedr, nr Harlech	Times 12Apr15
Sandhagen, Conrad			Larkhill	17/04/1918	Times 6May18		South coast	Times 6May18
Sarmkoth			Burbage, Buxton		Times 3May19				trying to steal a boat

Name	Rank/Role	Camp	Date	Location	Reference 1	Date 2	Reference 2	Notes
Scheumann, Paul	Lt	Yatesbury		Hotel in London	Times 18Oct17		Times 18Oct17	from Chippenham per "Times"
Schlander, Carl		Knockaloe	08/04/1918	Port Erin	Times 11Apr18	13/04/1918	Times 15Apr18	
Schloots, Hugo		Bramley			Police Gaz 9Apr18			
Schmidt		Mill Hill		Waltham Abbey	Times 15Jul18		Times 15Jul18	
Schmidt, Emile (aka Revosa)	ship steward	Stratford	29/12/1916		Times 30Dec16			
Schmidt, Franz		Loddington Pitch			Times 4Apr18			
Schmidt, Frederich		Knockaloe	08/04/1918	Port Erin	Times 11Apr18	13/04/1918	Times 15Apr18	
Schmidt, Friedrich K W	soldier	Leigh	30/05/1915	shot dead in the attempt	Times 1Jun15			
Schmidt, Gunther	sailor	Frith Hill		Esher	Times 27Sep16		Times 28Sep16	
Schmidt, Johannes	ship captain	Alexandra Palace	02/09/1915		Police Gaz 7&10Sep15			got back to Germany (Times 5/10)
Schneider		Brocton			Times 7Feb18			
Schneider, Daniel		Kinlochleven	15/08/1917		Times 16Aug17			
Schneider, Rudolf	officer	Ripon	16/03/1918		Times 18Mar18			ex Colsterdale? not Ripon
Schoerner		Bramley		Newbury			Times 6Sep18	
Schonherr, Hans		Frongoch	13/04/1916	recaptured	FO383/164	15/04/1916	FO383/154	
Scholtz, Orbum A von		Holyport		Beckenham	Times 27Aug17		Times 29Aug17	intended to steal an aircraft
Schorling		Kegworth	24/09/1917	re-captured	Times 26Sep17		Times 26Sep17	
Schulte, Wilhelm		Pattishall	31/08/1917	Denton, Northampton	Times 1Sep17		Times 3Sep17	
Schulte, William	sailor	Hatfield	02/06/1918		Times 3Jun18			
Schultz		Pattishall		Wendover			Times 25Feb19	
Schultz, Heinrich		Pattishall		Castlethorpe			Times 11Aug19	
Schultz, Walter H		Stobs	31/08/1917	Denton, Northampton	Times 1Sep17		Times 3Sep17	
Schulz, Emil	army ActOff	Mill Hill		in North Sea	Times 25Aug17		Times 4Sep17	stole boat at Scarborough
Schulze, Paul		Kegworth			Times 22Mar18			
Schwarz		Kegworth	24/09/1917	re-captured	Times 26Sep17		Times 26Sep17	
Schwarz, Carl		Woburn		re-captured	Times 28Nov16		Times 29Nov16	
Schweineher, von, Ernst		Dorchester	02/02/1915	re-captured	Police Gaz 4Feb16		Police Gaz 11Feb16	
Schwenke, Friedrich	soldier	Leigh	10/04/1915	Salford	Times 12Apr15	10/04/1915	Times 12Apr15	
Schwerin KE	Lt	Lofthouse			Times 12Aug19			
Scott, Graeme	British Citizen	Islington		Bloomsbury	Times 21Nov16		Times 24Nov16	
Screinuller	Lt	Oswestry			Times 24Mar19			
Sedel, Wilhelm F		Stanhope	07/05/1917	re-captured	Times 10May17	08/05/1917	Times 10May17	
Seeberger, Carl		Kegworth	24/09/1917	re-captured	Times 26Sep17			Feeburger in "Times" 26/9, report of re-captured not traced
Sens, Bruno		Shrewsbury	16/06/1918	Tipton	Times 19Jun18		Times 19Jun18	
Seyssert, Wilhelm O	farmer	Alexandra Palace	19/07/1915	Coles Green	Times 21Jul15	25/07/1915	Times 26Jul15	
Sherberth, Friedrich		Knockaloe	23/08/1917	Douglas	Times 28Aug17		Times 8Sep17	
Simon		Whitehaven			Times 12Aug19			
Simon, Paul		Oswestry		Harwich			Times 15Dec19	
Skirde, Albert		Staley, Cheshire	22/04/1918	re-captured	Times 25Apr18		Times 25Apr18	
Soffnitza, Paul		Bulphan	04/07/1918	Brentwood	Times 8Jul18		Times 8Jul18	

Name	Rank/Role	Location	Date	Source	Place	Notes
Spindler, Karl	Navy	Donington	14/07/1917	Times 16Jul17	Nottingham	
Spira, Emmanuel		Healeyfield, Consett		Times 7Feb18		
Spraub, Fritz	officer	Ripon		Times 18Mar18		ex Colsterdale? not Ripon planned to steal aircraft
Staclehbauer, Julius		Kegworth	05/09/1918	Times 13Sept18	Kneeton, Notts	
Stander, August		Knockaloe	08/04/1918	Times 11Apr18	Port Erin	13/04/1918 Times 15Apr18
Stansfor, Bertram H		Sealand, Flint		Times 12Nov17	re-captured	14Nov17
Stauffer, Henry B	civilian	Alexandra Palace	19/07/1915	Times 21Jul15	Coles Green	25/07/1915 Times 26Jul15
Stehr, Emil	sailor	Handforth	01/11/1917	Times 3Nov17	Portsmouth	12Nov17
Steht, Emil	PO	Stobs	26/10/1915	Times 28Oct15		
Stein		Bungay		Times 13Sep18	Lingfield (Redlingfield?)	13Sep18
Steinhardt, Ernst J	Lt	Kegworth	09/10/1918	Times 10Oct18	re-captured	14Oct15
Steinmann		Bulford	10/09/1917	Times 12Sep17	re-captured	12Sep17
Stermkops		Lofthouse		Times 24Mar19		
Stoffel, Paul		Knockaloe	08/04/1918	Times 11Apr18	Port Erin	13/04/1918 Times 15Apr18
Stoldt, Heindrich	sailor	Handforth	01/11/1917	Times 3Nov17	Portsmouth	12Nov17
Stoldt, Heindrich	sailor	Leigh	19/01/1918	Times 21Jan18	Grimsby	20/01/1918 Times 28Jan18
Stoll, Hans		Bramley	19/09/1918	Police Gaz 24Sep18	re-captured	Police Gaz 27Sep18
Stoltman, Paul		Banbury			re-captured	Times 4Oct17
Stolzmann, Hans	navy	Kegworth	24/09/1917	Times 26Sep17	Hickling	27/09/1917 Times 29Sep17 Hodzmann in "The Times" 26/9, and Stolymann on 29/9
Storrer Henry		Worthy Down	01/10/1918	Times 3Oct18		
Strang, George von		Douglas		Times 30Jun16	re-captured	Times 1Jul16 tried to swim out to a steamer - attempted suicide after re-capture
Strang, George von		IoM		Times 1Mar17		Times 2Mar17
Strang, George von		Douglas		Times 17Mar17		Times 20Mar17 named von Stringan, 17/3
Strassburger, August		Bramley	17/09/1917	Times 19Sep17	re-captured	Times 22Sep17
Strautmann, Joseph		Dorchester	17/09/1915	Times 18Sep15	Southampton	Times 18Sep15
Surchs, Paul		Sealand, Flint		Times 12Nov17	re-captured	Times 14Nov17
Tarnou		Lewisham	02/07/1918	Times 4Jul18	Farnborough (Kent?)	Times 4Jul18
Tegel, Fritz		Winchester		Times 21Nov18	recaptured	Times 21Nov18
Thelen, Otto	air officer	Donington	17/09/1915	Times 20Sep15	Chatham	23/09/1915 Times 24Sep15
Thelen, Otto		Holyport	07/12/1916	Times 9Dec16	Windsor	Times 9Dec16
Thelen, Otto		Kegworth	24/09/1917	Times 26Sep17	re-captured	Times 26Sep17
Thelen, Otto	air officer	Holyport		Times 1Feb16	caught tunnelling	
Thielman, Karl	Lt	Stratford reprisal		Times 11Jun18	Walsham, Norfolk	Times 13Jun18 re-captured at Walton-on-the-Naze per Stratford Express
Tholens, Herman	CaptLt	Dyffryn Aled	14/08/1915	Times 16Aug15	Llandudno	16/08/1915 Times 17Aug15 submarine rendezvous failed
Thomsen		Kegworth	24/09/1917	Times 26Sep17	re-captured	Times 26Sep17
Treffitz	OberLt z See	Donington	05/07/1915	Times 6Jul15	Millwall Docks	05/07/1915 Times 6Jul15
Trimborne P		Abbey Dore			re-captured	Times 8Sep19
Valera, Edward (Eamon) de	Sein Feiner	Lincoln Jail		Police Gaz 7Feb19		convicted of treason
Valker		Dorchester	17/09/1915	Times 18Sep15		

Name	Role		Location	Date	Source	Outcome	Date2	Source2	Notes
Verendt			Bungay		Times 13Sep18	Lingfield (Redlingfield?)		Times 13Sep18	
Villbrandt, Karl	sailor		Stobs	26/10/1915	Times 28Oct15				
Vincent			Oswestry		Times 8Jan19	re-captured		Times 9Jan19	
Voegler, Heinrich			Isle of Man	31/08/1915	Times 2Sep15	re-captured	01/09/1915	Times 2Sep15	resisted arrest with knife
Voight						Stainby, Grantham		Times 7Jan19	
Voight, Jan			Douglas	29/07/1917	Times 31Jul17	Ramsey		Times 6Aug17	
Voigt			Belmont		Times 13Jan19				
Waldhausen			Oswestry		Times 11Apr19	re-captured		Times 12Mar19	
Wallbaum, Hans			Skipton	30/06/1918	Times 2Jul18	Clitheroe		Craven Herald 5July	
Warcyak			Netley Hospital		Times 8Apr16	re-captured		Times 10Apr16	
Webber			Newark		Times 15Oct19				
Weber, Alous			Pencoed, Mon	26/09/1917	Times 28Sep17	Llanwern, Mon	26/09/1917	Times 28Sep17	
Weigart, August			Lentram	25/03/1918	Times 27Mar18	re-captured		Times 27Mar18	
Weil, Freidrich			Loddington Pitch		Times 4Apr18				
Weiner, Friedrich N	civilian		Lofthouse	28/05/1915	Times 2Jun15				arr Copenhagen, Times 29Jun15
Weingertner, Joseph	sailor		Leigh	19/01/1918	Times 21Jan18	Gloucestershire	24/01/1918	Times 28Jan18	
Werner			Mill Hill			re-captured		Times 7Aug18	
Wertsch, Emile	sailor		Leigh	19/01/1918	Times 21Jan18	Grimsby	20/01/1918	Times 28Jan18	
Wessels			Bulford	10/09/1917	Times 12Sep17	re-captured		Times 12Sep17	
Wetzel, Wilhelm			Eastcote	12/09/1915	Times 14Sep15	Northampton	12/09/1915	Times 14Sep15	
Wigar, George			IoM		Times 1Mar17	re-captured		Times 2Mar17	
Willan H			Abbey Dore			re-captured		Times 8Sep19	
Winkelmann, Max Ernst	Navy		Donington	14/07/1917	Times 16Jul17	Nottingham		Times 17Jul17	
Witz, Franz			Banbury	07/10/1918	Police Gaz 22Oct18	re-captured		Police Gaz 25Oct18	
Witz, Franz			Banbury		Times 31Jan18				
Wrenmann, August			Larkhill	15/05/1917	Times 16May17				
Wrottle			Retford			re-captured		Times 29Jan19	
Wulfs			Brecon	27-28/11/18		W India Dock		Times 6Dec18	
Yarus, Herman			Eastcote	12/09/1915	Times 14Sep15	Northampton	12/09/1915	Times 14Sep15	
Young, Hans			Winchester	23/12/1918	Times 27Dec18	Portsmouth		Times 27Dec18	
Zenmiatin, August T			Sealand, Flint		Times 12Nov17	re-captured		Times 14Nov17	
Zimpel, Bernhardt J			Shrewsbury	10/06/1915	Times 14Jun15	Welshpool	11/06/1915	Times 14Jun15	
Ziolowski, Alexander	sailor		Stobs	18/10/1916	Times 21Oct16	re-captured		Times 21Oct16	
Zoundoch, Hans			Pencoed, Mon	26/09/1917	Times 28Sep17	Llanwern, Mon	26/09/1917	Times 28Sep17	
Zucker, J			Farnborough		Times 4Dec17	Pilcot, nr Odiham		Times 7Dec17	

un-named reports -- some indexed but not seen

not seen	1		Limerick (attempt)		Times 14Sep14	n/a			
	1 sailor		Eastcote		Times 13May15	on a British collier		Times 13May15	after 3 months
	1 Corporal		Frongoch		Times 15Apr16	re-captured		Times 17Apr16	
	3 sailors		Douglas		Times 21Apr15	Kirkstanton		Times 21Apr15	

#	Type	Location	Date	Reference	Outcome/Location	Date	Reference	Notes
3	privates	Frongoch		Times 15Apr16	near Wrexham		Times 17Apr16	
3	sailors	Rutherglen		Times 30Oct16	re-captured		Times 30Oct16	
4	sailors	Knockaloe		Times 15Jan16	Peel Harbour		Times 17Jan16	
2	not seen	Donington		Times 16Oct15				
2		Knockaloe	09/03/1917	Times 12Mar17	re-captured		Times 12Mar17	
	not seen	Woburn		Times 31May17				
2		Stobs		Times 10Aug17	Broughton, Peebles		Times 10Aug17	
					Southall		Times 24Aug17	
1	not seen	Cove Heights		Times 28Aug17	Hook, Hants		Times 28Aug17	jumped from moving train
1		Walton-on-Thames		Times 12Sep17	re-captured		Times 15Sep17	
3		Fovant		Times 15Sep17	Camberley		Times 10Oct17	
	1 soldier and 2 sailors				re-captured		Times 24Oct17	
5		Stobs	17-18/10/1917	Times 19Oct17				
	not seen 3 sailors	Bramley		Times 26Oct17	Birmingham	18/02/1918	Times 20Feb18	to visit pantomime ???
4		Burton-on-Trent	18/02/1918	Times 20Feb18	Orford Ness		Times 6Mar18	
4		Bramley			recapture		Times 15Mar18	
3	not seen 2	Mill Hill		Times 21Mar18				
3		Bramley			Burghfield, Reading	26/04/1918	Times 29Apr18	
4		Beachley	01/04/1918		re-captured		Times 4May18	charged with theft
2		Rothwell, Kettering	05/05/1918		Broughton		Times 8May18	
3		Bramley	27/05/1918		Northfield, B'ham		Times 29May18	
1		Beachley	04/06/1918		Newport		Times 7Jun18	
3		Perham Down		Times 11Jun18				
1		Bramley			re-captured		Times 18Jun18	
1					Weybridge		Times 3Jul18	
2		Kelham	01/07/1918	Times 4Jul18	re-captured		Times 4Jul18	after 3 months on the run
2		Oakhall, Essex		Times 5Sep18	Mersea		Times 5Sep18	stole a boat, but ran aground
3		Badsey			Witney		Times 18Nov18	
3		Inverlaidnan			Inverness		Times 18Nov18	
2		Bovington			Dorchester		Times 23Nov18	
2					Ashwell		Times 31Dec18	
2	Zepp crew L33	Ripon			Hull		Times 13Jan19	
2					Tovil, Maidstone		Times 6Feb19	
2					Southampton		Times 19May19	on a Danish timber vessel
2					Brockenhurst		Times 22May19	
4		Kimbolton			re-captured		Times 5Aug19	
4		Bulford			re-captured		Times 12Aug19	
4		Bromyard?			Breedon		Times 23Aug19	
2		Soberton, Hants		Times 9Oct19	re-captured		Times 11Oct19	
20	officers	Lofthouse		Times 13Nov19	tunnel frustrated			

Bibliography

Anon	"1914, The First Prisoners", in *Yesterday*, No.4 (August 1988), pp6-9, Portsmouth Publishing & Printing, ISSN 0953 6760
Anon	*German Prisoners in Great Britain* (no publisher, no date)
Anon	"Military Occupation of the Doon Valley", in *Scottish Post #112*, Winter 2006
Angus I	"The Imperial German Navy at Scapa Flow" in *Stamps*, March 1985
Abell F	*Prisoners of War in Britain 1756-1815*, OUP, 1914
Allen WJ	*SS "Borodino" M.F.A. No.6: a short account of the work of the Junior Army and Navy Stores Ltd with H.M. Grand Fleet, December 1915 - February 1919*, JA&NS Ltd, London, nd (1919)
Baily L	*Craftsman and Quaker: the story of James T Baily 1876-1957*, Geo Allen & Unwin, London, 1959
Bird JC	*Control of Enemy Alien Civilians in Great Britain 1914-1918*, Garland Pub, New York, 1986, ISBN 0 8240 1910 5
Bennett, A	"Looking Back at Libury Hall" in *Hertfordshire Countryside*, vol.35, No.260, (December 1980), pp40-41
Brodie A, Croom J & Davies JO:	*English Prisons, An Architectural History*, English Heritage, Swindon, 2002, ISBN 1 873592 53 1
Bloch H & Hill G	*Germans in London, No.1, East Ham & West Ham documentary sources 1865-1919*, All Points East, 2000, ISBN 0 9538370 0 9
Brown A	"British Prisoner of War Camp Markings 1914-1918", a series of articles in *Forces Postal History Soc., Newsletter* between Nos.105 and 122, 1970-73, ISSN 9051-7561
Brown M & Meehan P	*Scapa Flow*, Penguin Press, London, 1968
Carnevale-Mauzan M	*Iconographie des camps de prisonniers de guerre pendant la 1re Guerre mondiale*, Philoffset Editions (nd)
Carter FJ	*The Post & Censor & other Marks from Prisoners of War Letters 1914-1919*, 1st ed, privately circulated, c1932, and 3rd edition, NM Russell (ed), Chavril Press, Perth, 1996, ISBN 1 872744 176
–	"Notes on the Prisoners of War Information Bureau: official marks and stationery", in *Philatelic Adviser* No.18, March 1935, pp170-171
–	"Notes on British General Censor Marks for Prisoners of War", in *Philatelic Adviser* No.19, May 1935, p186, and No.21, December 1935, pp222-223
–	"The Marks and Postmarks of Prison Ships in British Waters", in *Philatelic Adviser*, No.21, December 1935, p224
–	"Prisoners-of-War Postmarks 1914-1920", *Philatelic Adviser* No.23, June 1936, pp26-27
Cesarani D & Kushner T:	*The Internment of Aliens in Twentieth Century Britain*, Frank Cass, London, 1993, ISBN 0 7146 4095 6
Clarke K	*Clarke's Camberley at War (1914-1918)*, author, Camberley, 1986, ISBN 0 9509945 1 0
Cohen-Portheim P	*Time Stood Still: my internment in England 1914-1918*, Duckworth, London, 1931
Colley N	"Some observations concerning ....the interned German Fleet, Scapa Flow, 1918-1919", in *Forces Postal History Society Newsletter, No.236* (Summer 1998) ISSN 9051-7561
Cox & Co	*List of British Officers taken prisoner in the various theatres of war between August 1914 and November 1918*, (1919) reprint by The London Stamp Exchange Ltd, London, 1988, ISBN 0 948 13081 4
Cresswell YM	*Living with the Wire: civilian internment in the Isle of Man during two World Wars*, Manx National Heritage, Douglas, IoM, 1994, ISBN 0 901106 35 6
Cunliffe-Lister S	*Days of Yore: a History of Masham and District*, private, Masham, Yorks NR, 1978, ISBN 0 950631 10 8
Dewey PE	*British Agriculture in the First World War*, Routledge, London, 1989
Draper L & P	*The Raasay Iron Mine: where enemies became friends*, authors, Dingwall, Ross-shire, 1990, ISBN 0 9514870 0 0 and Supplemental ed 2003
Drower J	*Good Clean Fun, the story of Britain's first holiday camp*, Arcadia Books, London, 1982, ISBN 0 9508344 0 8
Durnford H, et al	*Tunnelling to Freedom, and other escape narratives from World War I*, Dover Publications Inc, Mineola, NY, 2004, ISBN 0 48643434 6 (originally published as "Escapers All" by J Lane, London, 1932)
Ebelshauser GA	*The Passage: a Tragedy of the First World War*, Griffin Books, Huntingdon, WV, USA, 1984, ISBN 0 9604770 2 0
Felstead ST	*German Spies at Bay*, Hutchinson, London, 1920
Ferguson DM	*The Wrecks of Scapa Flow*, Orkney Press, Stromness, 1985, ISBN 0 907618 065
Field C	*Internment Mail of the Isle of Man*, FJ Field Ltd, Sutton Coldfield, 1989, no ISBN

Fyson R	"The Douglas Camp Shootings of 1914", in *Proc. Isle of Man Natural History and Antiquarian Soc*, vol.XI, No.1 (April 1997-March 1999)
Garner JW	*International Law and the World War*, Longmans Green, London, 1920
Garrett R	*P.O.W.*, David & Charles, Newton Abbot, 1981, ISBN 0 7153 7986 0
German Government	*Deutsche Kriegsgefengene in Feindesland: amtliches material*, Walter de Gruyter & Co, Berlin and Leipzig, nd.
Gillman P & L	*Collar the Lot! How Britain Interned and Expelled its Wartime Refugees*, Quartet Books, London, 1980, ISBN 0 7043 2244 7
Harfield A	*Blandford and the Military*, Dorset Publishing, Sherborne, 1984, ISBN 0 902129 679
Harris, J	*Alexandra Palace, a hidden story*, Tempus Publishing, Stroud, 2005, ISBN 07524 36368
Hayles M & Hedges B	*Around Maidenhead in Old Photographs* (extract supplied by Maidenhead Library)
Heusel FE	*Handforth through the Ages*, Cheshire Libraries & Museums, 1982, ISBN 0 904532 02X
HM Government	
Admiralty	*War Orders, Prisoners of War*, N.L. 48398/15- , 1916, draft in PRO: ADM 1/8446/15
Home Office	"Rules and Regulations for Alton Abbey Concentration Camp" published in *The Messenger* (1915), pp 117-119
–	*List of Prisoner of War Camps in England and Wales with postal and telegraphic addresses*, Home Office, January 1918, plus May 1918 list, plus *Supplementary List*, October 1918 and *Second Supplementary List*, April 1919. PRO: ADM 1/8506/265
–	*Prisoner of War Branch, Home Office, November 1914 - April 1919* (no date) and *Memorandum on P/W work between May and December 1919* (initialled 22.12.19) PRO: HO 45/11025/410118
House of Commons	*Report from the Joint Select Committee on Government Works at Cippenham, together with proceedings, minutes and appendices.* 1919 (131) v.5.
Foreign Office	*Report dated 27 Feb 1915 by Mr JB Jackson on his visits to Internment and Prisoner of War Camps in Great Britain undertaken at the request of the German Government*, PRO: HO 45/10760/269116
–	*Reports of Visits of Inspection made by Officials of the United States Embassy to various Internment Camps in the United Kingdom*, HMSO, Misc No.30 (1916) Cd 8324
POWIB	*List of Places of Internment*, (printed January 1919)
War Office	*Standing Orders and Notices*, issued at Stobs, April 1915
–	*Censorship Regulations for Prisoners of War employed in France*, SS468 (March 1917) and *Amendments to .... ditto ....* (June 1918)
–	*Prisoners of War Companies: Orders and Instructions*, SS457 (February 1918) and *Additions to ..... ditto .....* SS457a, b, c, d & e, (March 1918 - May 1919)
–	*Report on Postal Censorship during the Great War (1914-1919)* War Office paper 63/2/661, March 1920, PRO: DEFE 1/131 ("Farquharson")
–	*Report on the Directorate of Prisoners of War*, War Office paper 1/GEN No/2648. Sprt 1920, PRO: HO 45/11025/68577. ("Belfield")
Hoehling AA	*The Great War at Sea: a History of Naval Action 1914-1918*, Galahad Books, New York, 1985, ISBN 0 88365 207 2
Hopkins T	*Prisoners of War*, Simpkin Marshall, London, 1914
Horn, Pamela	*Rural Life in England in The First World War*, Gill and Macmillan, New York, 1984, ISBN 0 312 69604 3
Horne JM	"The German Connection" in *Transactions of the Hawick Archaeological Society*, 1988
International Committee	of the Red Cross: *Documents publiés a l'occasion de la Guerre de 1914-1915, Rapports ... première série*, Geneva, March 1915 and *Quatorzième série*, Geneva, June 1917
–	*Turkish Prisoners in Egypt*, ICRC, London, 1917
Ibs, Dr H	*Herman J Held: a Kiel scholarly life in the clutches of passing time* (extracts, translated by Claire Sharp held in Wakefield Library)
Jackson R	*The Prisoners 1914-18*, Routledge, London, 1989, ISBN 0 415033 77 2
Jefferies D	"Prisoner of War Camps in Scotland", in *Scottish Post*, Oct/Dec 1992, pp490-491
Kavanagh G	*Museums and the First World War; a social history*, Leicester University Press. London, 1994, ISBN 0 7185 1713 X
Kelly R	*The Mail of Mann: the story of postal services in the Isle of Man*, Manx Associated Publications, Onchan, IoM, 1988, ISBN 1 871142 00 8
Kelsall D	*The Dark Cloud: Stockport in the Great War 1914-1919*, Richardson (Manchester) 1999, ISBN 1 852161 33 7
Killeen KAL	*The Prisoner of War Ships*, author, Newport, Isle of Wight, 1993, no ISBN
Kniveton GN *et al*	*Centenary of the Borough of Douglas 1896-1996* (extract provided by Manx Library)
Kötetben K	*Hadifogoly Magyarok Története*, [The history of Hungarian Prisoners of War] Athenaeum, Budapest, nd

Lauterpacht H	*International Law, a treatise*, 5th edition, 2 vols, Longmans Green, London, 1935/37
Leece JB	"Detention Camps in the Isle of Man 1914-1918 and 1939-1945" in *The Postal History Society Bulletin,* No.143, pp43-45, May-June 1966
McCarthy DJ	*The Prisoner of War in Germany*, 3rd edition, Skeffington, London, (nd)
MacDonagh M	*In London during the Great War: diary of a journalist*, Eyre & Spottiswoode, London, 1935
MacLennan JM	"A Prisoner of War Camp" in *The Army Quarterly*, vol.13, pp368-375
Macpherson WG, Horrocks WH & Beveridge WWO:	*History of the Great War - Medical Services, Hygiene*, Vol.II, HMSO, London, 1923
Maglic K	*The Dandy Hun*, The Bodley Head, London, 1937
Mann K	*London: the German Connection*, KT Publishing, Chilton Polden, Somerset, 1993, ISBN 0 9522380 0 4
Manx National Heritage Library:	*Internment during World Wars 1 & 2 - Select Bibliography*
Manz S	"New Evidence on Stobs Internment Camp 1914-19", in *Transactions of the Hawick Archaeological Society*, 2003
Mark G	*British Censorship of Civil Mails during World War I, 1914-1919*, Stuart Rossiter Trust Fund, Bristol, 2000, ISBN 0 953000 41 9
Moss R & Illingworth I	*Pattishall: a Parish Patchwork*, Millcop, Astcote, Northants, 2000, no ISBN
Moxter H	"German and Austrian Internees at Oldcastle, Co Meath, Ireland, 1914-1918", in *Civil Censorship Study Group Bulletin*, vol.25, No.4 (October 1998)
–	*Censorship of Mail in Ireland*, author, Oberjosbach, Germany, 2003, no ISBN
–	and a number of articles in *The Revealer* between 1993 and 1999
Murray EJ	"Stobs Camp 1903-1959", in *Trans. of the Hawick Archaeological Society*, 1988, pp12-25
Naish, Major TE	"The German Prisoners of War Camp at Jersey during the Great War 1914-1918", in *Bulletin of the Société Jersiaise*, vol.XVI, part III, 1955
Newport W	*Stamps and Postal Hgistory of the Channel Islands*, Heinemann, London, 1972
Noschke R & Rocker R	*An Insight into Civilian Internment in Britain during WWI*, Anglo-German Family History Soc, Maidenhead, Berks, 1998, ISBN 0 9514133 7 6
Olsen P	*Donington Hall: the History of an Ancient Family Seat*, Granta Editions, 1990, ISBN 0 906782 57 0
OMahony S	*Frongoch: University of Revolution*, FDR Teoranta, Killkeney, Ireland, 1987
O Mathuna P	"German P.O.W. Mail between Templemore and Germany 1914 and 1915", in *75 Years of Irish Stamps*, FAI, Belm-Vehrte, Germany, 1997
Over L	*The Royal Hundred of Bray* (extract provided by Maidenhead Library)
Panyani P	*The Enemy in our Midst, Germans in Britain during the First World War*, Berg, Oxford, 1991, ISBN 0 85496 308 1
–	"An Intolerant Act by an Intolerant Society: the Internment of Germans in Britain during the First World War", in Cesarani & Kushner q.v.
Payne F	*A History of Darenth Hospitals*, author, 2000, no ISBN
Picot LtCol HP	*The British Interned in Switzerland*, Edward Arnold, London, 1919
Plüschow G	*My Escape from Donington Hall* (trans: de Chary), Bodley Head, London, 1922
Pochhammer H	*Graf Spees letzte Fahrt*, Koehler, Leipzig, 1926
Potter T	*Reflections of Lancaster* (extract provided by Lancaster Library)
Ritson-Smith L	"The German Officers Prisoners of War Camp, Philiberds, Holyport 1914-1919" in *Berkshire Old and New* No.16, 1999, pp33-46
Rowley RG	*The Book of Skipton*, Barracuda Books, Buckingham, 1983
Roxburgh RF	*The Prisoners of War Information Bureau in London*, Longmans Green, London 1915
Ruge F	*Scapa Flow 1919: the end of the German Fleet* (trans Masters D), Ian Allan, London, 1973
Russell NM (ed)	see Carter FJ, above
Sachsse & Cossman	*Kreigsgefangenen in Skipton*, Reiinhardt, Munich, 1920 (and an anonymous translation of extracts held at Skipton Library)
Sadden J	*Keeping the Home Fires Burning: the story of Portsmouth & Gosport in WWI*, Portsmouth Publishing & Printing (1990) ISBN 1 871182 042
Sargeaunt BE	*The Isle of Man and the Great War*, Brown & Sons, Douglas IoM, 1920
Scott PT	"Captive Labour: The German Companies of the B.E.F., 1916-1920", in *Army Quarterly and Defence Journal*, 110 No.3, 1980
–	"German Prisoners Employed in Britain" in *The Great War 1914-1918*, vol.1, No.4 (August 1989) ISSN 0955-2375
–	"Captive Labour: The German Companies of the B.E.F. 1916-1920", in *The Great War 1914-1918*, vol.2, No.2 (February 1991) ISSN 0955-2375
Smith L	*The German Prisoner of War Camp at Leigh 1914-1919*, Richardson, Manchester, 1986, ISBN 0 907511 98 8

Somerset County	*Minute Books of The Somerset County War Agricultural Committee 1918-1919*, held at Somerset County Record Office, Taunton
Somerville D	"Channel Islands Mail during the First World War", in *Les Iles Normandes*, vol.14, No.3, September 1995 and vol.17, No.1, March 1998
Southerton P	*Reading Gaol by Reading Town*, Berkshire Books, Stroud, 1993, ISBN 0 7509 0296 5
Specht M	*The German Hospital in London and the Community it served 1845 to 1948*, Anglo-German Family History Soc, Cookham, Berks, new ed 1997, ISBN 0 9514133 0 9
Speed RB, III	*Prisoners, Diplomats and the Great War*, (Contributions in Military Studies, No.97), Greenwood Press, New York, 1990, ISBN 0 313 26729 4
Squires A	*Donington Park & the Hastings Connection*, Kairos Press, 1966, ISBN 1 871344 10 7
Stanley Gibbons Ltd	*Channel Islands: Specialised Catalogue of Stamps and Postal History*, 2nd ed, p179, Stanley Gibbons, London, 1983, ISBN 0 85259 052 0
Stielow CH	"The Poorhouse at Islington" in *Die Woche* (date not known)
Stobbs S	"Prisoners of War and Internees Camps in Lancashire, Yorkshire and the Isle of Man during World Wars 1 & 2", in *A Postscript to the Postal Historian*, vol.15, pp40-46, 1965
Thomas AB (comp)	*St Stephen's House: Friends Emergency Work in England 1914-1920*, The Emergency Committee, London, (nd)
Toogood, Rev R	*A History of Bramley*, Bramley Shell Pub., Bramley, Hampshire, ISBN P102 0304 80
Townshend C	*Easter 1916, The Irish Rebellion*, Penguin Books, London, 2006, ISBN 0141 01216 2
Vischer AL	*Barbed Wire Disease, a psychological study of the Prisoner of War*, John Bale Sons & Danielsson, London 1919
von Reuter V-Adm L	*Scapa Flow: the account of the greatest scuttling of all time* (trans. Mudie), Hurst & Blackett, London, 1940
von Rintelen F	*The Dark Invader*, Dickson, London, 1933
Walling J	"Held - Prisoner at Lofthouse Camp" in *Mitteilungsblatt 50*, Dec 1999 (Anglo-German Family Hist Society), ISSN 0954-3457
–	*The Internment and Treatment of German Nationals during the 1st World War*, Riparian Publishing, Great Grimsby, 2005, ISBN 0 9523848 2 5
Walsh PP	*A History of Templemore and its Environs* (extract provided by Tipperary Libraries)
Ward R	"Detention Camps in the Isle of Man", in *The Postal History Society Bulletin*, No.146, pp82-83, Nov-Dec 1966
–	"Ripon / 208 / Yks", *The Philatelic Journal of Great Britain*, vol.82, pp38-43, June 1972
Wathen JG	*Beech and Beyond: from Farm to Village; 1239-1990*, Avon Books, London, 1996, ISBN 1 86033 114 9
Watson VC	"Elizabethville, County Durham", in *Stamp Collecting*, vol.93, p299, 13 Nov 1959
West, Margery	*Island at War*, Western Books, Laxey, IoM, ISBN 0 9511512 0 7
Whitehouse CJ & GP	*A Town for Four Winters, Great War Camps on Cannock Chase*, private, 1983, ISBN 0 902974 03 3
Whitney Dr JT	*Isle of Man: Handbook of stamps and postal history*, 3rd edition, Picton Publishing, Chipenham, Wilts, 1978, ISBN 0 902633 67 8
–	"Isle of Man Camp Mail" in *Stamps Collecting* (in 2 parts) 4 Jan 1979, pp807-811, and 11 Jan 1979, pp913-919
–	"Interned off Southend" in *Stamp Mail*, March 1989, pp10-11
Wilde LA	*A Short History of Margate College 1873-1940*, nd, no ISBN.
Wishart AT	"Prisoner of War Camps in Scotland 1914-1918", in *Germania Posta XV Handbook*
Wood P	"Lofthouse Park" in *Aspects of Wakefield*, ed Taylor K (1998)
–	"The Zivilinternierungslager at Lofthouse Park", in *Aspects of Wakefield*, 3rd edition, ed Taylor K (extracts provided by Wakefield Library)
Woodhouse DG	*Anti-German Sentiment in Kingston upon Hull: the German Community and the First World War*, Kingston-upon-Hull City Record Office, 1990 ISBN 0 904767 24 8
Woolmer R	*Playing Cricket in Holyport Village since 1844* (extract provided by Maidenhead Library)

The Times and many local newspapers quoted in the footnotes and referenced.
The Police Gazette
The National Archives   Many files in the series FO383 and HO45 and others as quoted in footnotes and referenced.

Index

Note that a number of reports of escapes etc only give surnames of the men involved. In other cases different names appeared in different, and sometimes the same, newspapers.

Admiralty	1
Agents, supervising PoWs	3
concern over submarine PoWs	6, 85
Transport Office	1, **2**
Victualling Office	1
Agincourt, Battle (1415)	1
Air raids	10, 175
Aldridge, Capt CP	70
Alexandra Palace	41-**45**
Allpress, Maj EP	117
Aliens Restrictions Act (1914)	9
American War of Independence	2
Ammerlich, Max	198
Andania RMS	**181**
Anderton, LtCol W A I	121
Andler, Ober-Lt Hans	84, 209
Ansley, LtCol J H	131, 133, 155
Arenkens, Gefreiter W	95
Armistice agreements	7
Armstrong, Mr (censor)	96
Armstrong, Capt	106
Armstrong, Capt A P J	137
Army Apprentices School, Chepstow	49
Army Council Instructions (ACIs)	15, 24, 31
Ascania RMS	**178**
Ashbourne, agricultural depot	60
Austrian PoWs	
concentrated at Sandhill Park	167-168
concentrated at Frith Hill	94
Austro-Hungarians refuse to work	44
Aylesbury, female camp	46-47
Bac, Mr	125
Bacon, Lt H H	146
Baden-Powell, Lord	61
Baily, James	126
Baird, William & Co	161
Baldamus, Hauptmann Fritz	151
Ball, Max F	156
Balzer, Mr	125
Bastoen, Paul	120
Bauneisher, Louis	187
Beachley Camp, Chepstow	48-50
Beck, Johann (died)	153
Bedford, Dr D J	119
Beech Abbey, Alton	51, **52**
Beirich A	124
Belfield, Lt Gen Sir Herbert	5
'Belgian Arms, The', Holyport	107
Belgian Refugees	41, 150
Belmont Hospital, Sutton	53-54
Bergmann, Edwin	74
Berschmann, Kurt	120
Beutter, Lt Edmund	156
Bevan, Lt (censor)	96
Bevois Mount, Southampton	191, **192**
Biercher, Johann	212
Blagrove, Colonel H J	132
Bland, Capt FCC, later Major	78
Blandford Camp, Dorset	55
Block, Col	73
Block, Lt	167
Bockmeyer (shot)	148
Boedt (U-boat officer)	165
Boenicke, Ferdinand	120
Boerner	120
Boldt, Ernst	185
Boles, LtCol D F, MP	167
Bölle, Julius	**157**
Bond, LtCol R P, RAMC	67
Books examined by the censors	17
Booton, Walter Henry	185
Borodino SS	**173**
Bowman, LtCol H J	195
Boy Scouts on guard duty	51, 154
Bramley Camp, Nr Basingstoke	56
Brandon, Capt E A	168
Braue, Diedrich	204
Braun, Karl	164
Bremer, Alfred	**156**
Brennan-Whitmore W	96
Bright, Major R G T, CMG	185
Brinkmann, Unteroffizier H	95, 118
British PoWs held abroad	
correspondence of	21
Brixton Prison	209
Brocton Camp, Stafford	57-60
Brossmann, Willi	62
Bruckmann, Pvt, reward for gallantry	76
Brush making	80, 113
Brussels Conference 1874	3
Buchgeister, Karl (shot)	56
Buchholzke, Herr (consul)	175
Budingan, Graf von	142
Bulkeley, Maj H C, later LtCol	74
Bültzingsloewen, Major von	188
Bunte, Herman	185
Burghagen, Walter	120
Burkind, Alfred	151
Burkhardt, Lt HF	86, 108
Burns, Lt	96
Burrows, Major N	193
Busch. Dr zum	66
Butler, LtCol, RAMC	53
Butz, Paul	198
Byrne, Sir W	9, 78
Cahn, Off-Stell	102, 212
Calypso SS	**173**
Camp newspapers	16, 102, 113, 124, **129**
Camp list	217
Canada SS	**182**
Cannock Chase	
German War Cemetery	8, 58
Cantlie, Sir James (British Red Cross)	125
Captain's Letter	**32**
Carpendale, LtCol J M	121

253

Catterick Camp	61
Cawston, Lt Col G	61
Cecil, Lord Robert	6
Censorship	
by Admiralty	3
Circulation of mail for censorship	14, 15
Censorship (contu)	
Defensive aspects	13
Division of correspondence	23
Greeting cards	25
Handling of mail	24
History of	14
Information gained	14
Labels and handstamps	37-40
moved to Cologne	16
Objects of	14
Parcels	24, 27
P/W Branch	**40**
Red Cross mail	23
Registered mail	23
Staff and premises	27, 29, **40**
Testing Department	25
Termination of censorship	28
Transit (non-terminal) mail	27
Chatham Naval Detention Barracks	6
Chelmsford Prison	210
Cholmondeley, Major C H	121
Cholmondleey, Colonel H C	130, 184
Christ's Hospital School	111
Churton, Capt W A V	158
Cippenham - see Slough camp	189-190
Civilian Internment Camps Committee	9
Class (or Cress), Louis	211
Claus, Major	165
Clausnidzer, Ernst J L	185
Cmentek, Lt Anton	108
Cohen-Portheim, P	122, 139, 201
Colsterdale, Masham	62-**64**
Colvin, Col CH	108
Commissioners for taking care of	
sick and wounded seamen	1
Cooke, LtCol E C	164
Cornwallis Road, Islington camp	112
Correspondence of PoWs and Internees	13 et seq
Business letters	20
Free postage	13
restricted in response to	
German rules	13
Inland letters postage paid	17
proportion censored	17
Regulations	31
Restrictions	15, 16
Stationery	33
Statistics	28, 30
Thomas Cook & Son service	24
with Embassies and Legations	17
Concentration Camps (first)	2
Cottell, LtCol AB, RAMC	84
Crimean War	2
Cunningham's Holiday Camp	78
Cupik, Ladislov	**127**
Dalston, German Hospital	65-**66**
Dartford War Hospital	67-**69**
Dartmoor Prison	2
Dauncey, LtColTHE	102

Dawnay, Maj Hon EH	106
de Burgh, Col U G C, CB	201
Defitanske	97
Destitute Aliens Committee	9, 78, 121, 136
name changed 1916	9
Detainees - use of PoW mail facilities	18
Devonport Naval Detention Barracks	6
Die Lisboa SS	188
Dixon, Major J Q	121
Donington Hall Camp	70-**72**
Dorchester, Camp	73–**77**
Douglas Camp, Isle of Man	78-**83**
Druschke H W	123
Ducat-Hammersley, Major HCC	101, 184
Dush, Andrew	169
Dusselmann, Walter	198
Dwyer-Hampton, LtCol B C	152
Dyffryn Aled Camp, North Wales	84-**87**
submarine officers	6
Early camps listed	9
Eastcote camp (aka Pattishall)	154-**157**
East Morton cemetery	188
Eber, Feldwebel Richard	103
Edinburgh Castle	1, 88
Redford Barracks	88
Elve (Dutch ship)	175
Employment of PoW labour proposed	7
first work parties	92
railway work	93
problems for censors	16
Escapers list	235
Escocuras, Carlos Kuhne	211
Exemption / Repatriation Committee	10
Exeter, St Sidwell's School	208
Extra Letter	**32**
Falmouth Workhouse	208
Fassien, Arthur Leo	185
Faulkner, Dr	130
Feltham Camp, Middlesex	89, **91**
Fergusson, Colonel W J S	136
Fictional PoWs	13
Fiennes, Sir James & Sir Roger	1
Finch's Shipyard, Chepstow	48
Firminger, Major R E	146
Fischer, Captain	145
Flink, Lt Joseph	108
Forged banknotes	55, 56
France, employment of PoWs in	7, 74, 213-**216**
Franke, Emile (shot and wounded)	164
Free postage for PoWs and Internees	13
Freemantle, Admiral	170
Freiburg University	140
French Government	
employment of PoWs	213
offer to 'borrow' PoWs	8
Friedrich (an Austrian stowaway)	163
'Friendly Aliens'	10, 11, 89, 90
Frith Hill Camp, Frimley	92-94
Frongoch Camp, Bala	95-**98**
Frossard, Dr E	166, 168
Fyfe Scott, Major H N	121
Gallantry award to PoW	76
Geblin, Gustav	195

Gemest, Herman	120	Henrard, Lt Franz	108
Geneva Conventions 1906 and 1929	3	Herting H	101
Georgevitz, Lt van	119	Hertzog, 2Lt	167
German Hospital, Dalston	65-**66**	Heutz, Josof (trial)	56
German reprisals against British PoWs	6, 7, 13, 21, 146, 213	Hewett, LtCol W S	86
		Heygate-Lambert, Col F A	96, 201
German War Cemeteries	8, 58	Heym, Hans	74
Gernhuber, Benno	93	Hiller, Augustus	165
Gerrard Mr, US Ambassador in Berlin	6	Hitner	140
Gey	125	Hock, Jacob (died)	146
Gitzen, Wilhelm	156	Hodgson Edward,	112
Gladstone, LtCol Sir J	107	Holmes, Mr W M (censor)	123
Glencree, Ireland, German War Graves	8	Holyport Camp	**106-109**
Glossop, Maj B R M	106	Home Office, POW Branch formed	10
Godfrey-Faussett, Maj R F	113	Hood, LtCol W E C	49
Gohmer	74	Hopkins, Father CP	51
Gordon-Cumming, LtCol L S	117	Horn, Arped	71, 86, 210
Gosport, Fort Elson	208	Horsham Camp	**110**-111
Grant, Lt.Col Sir A G	57	Howley, Maj E H, RAMC	57
Grattan, LtCol O'D C	155	Howsin, Miss	46
Grey, Sir Edward, later Viscount	6	Hull - air raid	10
Grey, MajGen W H	48	Hungarian officers	
Grien, Alfons	148	concentrated at Sandhill Park	168
Groensky, Albert	103	delayed repatriation	168
Grota, Thomas von	62	Hunter, LtCol W C	187
Grote, Lt Freiherr von	107	Hutchinson, St John	113
Guthrie, Maj R L, RAMC	53	Hyde Vale, 38, Greenwich	51
Haak, Bernhard	198	Indian Wars	2
Hackney Wick Camp	99-**100**	Invalids - agreement to repatriate	13
Haedler, Hugo (died)	159	Irish prisoners 1916	11, 27, 95
Haig, General Sir Douglas	7, 213	women at Aylesbury	46
Haines, Lt.Col G S	117, 140, 146, 201	Islington Camp	112-**116**
		Iven, Walther	74
Hague Conventions 1899 and 1907	3	*Ivernia* RMS	**174**
Rules	5,13	Jager, Kark (died)	55
Hall, LtCol John	55, 93	Jameson, Sir Starr Bt	5
Halliday, Sir F L	112	Jensen, Wilhelm	97, 198
Hamilton, Col H B H	121	Jersey camp	117-**118**
Hamilton, Col S	111	Jewish internees	80, 102, 113, 208
Hancock, Capt F W	**199**	Johl, Fahnrich-z-S	102, 212
Hancock, Capt G S	181	Johnson, Maj L W, later LtCol	89
Handforth Camp	101-**105**	Johnston, Maj Robert VC	148
Haneche, Gefreiter Joseph	192	Johnstone, Col HA	62
Hanke, Otto	56	Joksch, Alfred	195
Hannar, Judah	201	'Jolly Eight, The'	**50**
Hans, Paul (trial)	56	Jowitt W A, KC	112
Harris, Mr A (purser)	123	Julius, Wilhelm	175
Harrison, Lt	181	Junght, E A	93
Hart, Lt E C M	166	Justus, Heinz H E	62, 108, 141
Harte, Herman	156		
Harvey, Col J H	107	Kaars, Frank	165
Harvey, Sir Paul	5	Kageneck, Graf, SGO	71
Hatton, Mrs	46	Kagerer, Georg (died)	161
Hatton, Major W deB	130	Karch	125
Hauser, Eduard	120	Kaye, Major A B R	121
Heilmann, Paul (drowned)	93	Kegworth camp	119-120
Heinitz, Max (died)	55	Kehrhan, Ferdinand	112, **128**
Heligoland, Battle (1914)	5	Keilbach, Lt Hans	71, 107, 210
Helldorf, Lt H W von	85	Kenner, George	92-93
Hellmich, G'dsman Wilhelm (died)	167	Kenney-Herbert, LtCol A H C	102, 184
Hellselder, Lorenz	165	Kerry, Erwin	99
Hemlar (or Jenlar), Carl	211	Kerst, Arthur	156
Hemmers, Feldwebel-Lt	102	King Edward III	1
Henlle camp	152	King John (of France)	1
Henning, Korvettenkapitan H G von	85	Kirchner O R	184

Kitchener, Lord	10, 213	Maglic, K (aka Petrovitch)	44, 119
Klaiss, Edmund	204	Mahn, Lt (died)	108
Klapproth, Alfred	139	Maier, Karl	120
Klein, Karl (died)	195	Mallett, Sir Louis	95, 184
Kleinert, Mathias	**160**	Mallmann, Joseph	120
Kleist, Major von	188	Mandey, Emil	103
Knox, Mr A (censor)	123	Mannhausen, Lt (died)	108
Knockaloe camp	10, 121-**129**	Margate camp	145
Koanig, Ernst	184	Marienfeld, Georg	103
Kobbellick (shot)	58	Markel, Dr	6
Koch, Carl	120	Markievicz, Constance	46
Koch, J R	95, 118	Marlang, Carl	148
Koch, Richard	**211**	Marshall, Dr Robert	78
Koehn, Otto (man in the box)	73	Mass breakout	120
Kohler, Herr	127	Matthies, H E	62
Kohler O	124	Matuszak, Unteroffizier (died)	108
Koningin Regentes sunk while carrying PoWs	11	Meier, Major	120
		Meiser, Johan (died)	174
Kosher food and kitchens	80, 102, 113	*Melitta*, German steamer	118
Kraus	120	Merry, Captain	137
Kraus, Hans	187	Metcalfe-Smith LtCol B	121
Kreuz	148	Meusel, Fritz (trial)	56
Krueger, Otto	185	Michalski, Carl	195
Kummeth, Richard	164	Midland Agricultural College	119
		Midwood, LtCol H	166, 168
Labour companies in France	213-216	Milbay Prison, Plymouth	1
Laessig, Willi	185	Milldown work camp	55
Lailey, Bernard KC	112	Mobbs, Noel	190
Lake Manitoba SS	**179**	Money of Pows and Internees	
Lancaster Camp	130-131	Camp Purser / Bank	19, 142
Landoverg, Eric	120	Loans between prisoners	20
Laskus, Hans	187	Remittances	19
Lassen 125		Montesquieu, Charles Baron	1
Last PoW to leave Britain	8, 153	Müller, Captain (ex SMS *Emden*)	119, 120
Laue, Franz	86	Muller, Curt	211
Laue, Fritz	62	Müller, E	123
Leeds Pals	62, 63	Müller, Joseph	**157**
Leeman Road camp - see York	206-207	Müller, Heinrich	156
Le Havre	213, 214, **216**	Müller, Willi	136, 137
Lehmann, Lt-z-S Emil	102, 120, 210		
Leigh camp	132-134	Napoleonic Wars	2
Lenders, Dr Theodore	148	Nassau, Lt Gerhard von	108
Letter-sheets introduced	15	National Shipyards	48
German complaint about	15	Netley Hospital	193
Lewisham camp	135	Newbury camp	146-147
Liborius, Carl (died)	103	Newcastle "Concentrate Camp"	208-**209**
Libury Hall	18, 136-138	'New South Wales'	189
Lindsay, LtCol J A H	178	Newspapers produced in camps	16, 102, 113, 124, **129**, **197**, **198**
Liebrock, Oberst,	20		
Little Fernhill Hill camp	152	Nobbs, Lt A, RAMC	179
Lloyd, Major E T	140	Nodin, Major A	121
Loans between prisoners	20	Norman Cross Prison	2
Lofthouse Park camp	139-**144**	Noschke R	44, 200, 201
Loewe, Wilhelm	120	Nunnerley, LtCol P J R, RAMC	71
Longmoor Camp	92		
Low, LtCol F S	140	O'Connell J J	96
Lowry, Edward G	6	O'Halloran, Lt Col M, RAMC	57
Luscombe LtCol G A	44, 201	O'Reilly M W	96
Lusitania sunk - repercussions	10, 80, 92, 101, 122, 131, 154, 195, 200, 201	Ohms, Willi	**199**
		Oldcastle camp	148-**149**
		Olympia camp	150
Lutz, Gustav	120	Oster, Willi (shot)	152
Lutz, Otto	78	Oswestry camps	**151**-153
		Other places of detention	208
MacLeod, Capt K G	161	Otto, Wilhelm	103
Madoc, LtCol H W	78	Owen, Col H O'B	73

Panzera, LtCol F W	121, 137		194, 204
Parish Church Council objects to German graves	108	on PoW correspondence etc	13, 18, 76, 213
		German, against British PoWs	6, 7, 13, 21, 146, 213
Parker, Major W RAMC	152		
Pattishall camp (aka Eastcote)	154-**157**	Reuter, Admiral von	71, 152, 170
Pekukes, Julius (died)	159	Revosa (alias of E Schmidt)	201
Permit to visit	45	Richards, Maj A C, later LtCol	97, 117
Perry, Sir Percival	190	Richwein, Franz	**50**
Perth Prison	2	Rintelen, F von	71
Peters, Dr (of Bala)	97	Riot by prisoners	74, 78, 130
Peters, Dr E A	181, 182	Ripon Camps	165
Petersen, Lt W J E	86	Ritter, Major	85
Peterson, Lt Mathias	209	Robert McAlpine & Sons	189
Peterson W	123	Robertson, Major K S	119
Phryne SS (French ship)	213, **216**	Rocker, Mrs Milly	46
Picot, LtCol F S	71, 119, 120, 152	Rohan, Prince	191
Pleadwell, Dr, US Navy	67	Ronaldson, Col R W H, CB	187
Plessen, Baron	191	Ross, Korvettenkapitan J	71, 191
Plessing, Lt	164	Rouen 213-214	
Pliefke, SergtMaj Karl (shot)	61	Rouse, LtCol A H T	140
Plotke F J	66	Routenberg, Hans	120
Plüschow, Gunter	70, 74, 106	*Royal Edward* SS	**175**
Pochhammer, Korvettenkapitan Hans	106, 107	Royal Victoria Military Hospital	193
Poitiers, Battle (1356)	1	Rücker, Clemens	212
Porchester Castle	1	Ruge, Lt F	170
Port Clarence	57		
POW Information Bureau	5	St Colomb Workhouse	208
Correspondence, treatment of	18, 25	Salthill - see Slough camp	189-190
Handstamps and labels	33-36	Samesch, Brigadier-Colonel	168
Stationery	33	Sampson LtCol Winn	86
Welfare Committees	5	Sanders Leben, Lt HFR von	84
PoWs - first reports	5	Sandhill Park camp	166-**169**
in Empire Countries - censorship	19	Sandwich, Lord	5
Prisoner ploughmen	167	Sankey Committee	96
Privilege camp	80, 93, 125, 139	Sarepta Sisters	65
Prondzynski, Stephan van	120	*Saxonia* RMS	**176**
Privileges suspended	76, 86	Scapa Flow, PoWs ex German Fleet	8, 71, 72, 142, 152, 170-171
Pulley, Maj O C	117		
Queen's Ferry camp	158-**160**	Schlagintweit, Capt Theodore	84
		Schmidt, Emil (alias Revosa)	201
RAF men to take over huts from PoWs	55	Schmidt, Friedrich (shot)	132
Raasay camp	161-162	Schmidt, Johannes	44
Ramsgate camp	163	Schmidt, William (shot)	103
Rastenbolz, Sergt Major John	97	Schneider, Rudolf	165
Rauch, Off-Stell H	61	Scholten, pastor	159
Rauchstadt, Frederick	201	Scholtz, Orbum von	108
Reading Prison	210-**211**	Schönherr H	95
Redford Barracks, Edinburgh	88	Schools used for detention	208
Redmires Camp, Sheffield	164	Schorling	120
Redruth Workhouse	208	Schroder family	65, 136
Rees, Sir John David, MP	5, 137	Schroder, Herman	156
Rehbehn, Mr	125	Schulte, Wilhelm	156
Reinavoss, Helmuth	165	Schultz, Emil	198
Reitz, Lt Karl	102	Schultz, Heinrich	156
Release to neutral country agreed with Germany	11	Schultz, Walter H	156
		Schultze, Major	142
Religious Society of Friends, appeal	9	Schwartz	120
Repatriation		Schweinichen, Fahnrich Ernst von	74, 155, 212
Agreements with Germany		Schwenke, Friedrich	132
invalids, youths and older men	11	Schwyzer, Captain (Swiss)	124
1918 agreement	11	*Scotian* SS	**179**
Committees set up	10, 11	Scott, Graeme	112
Internees from Britain in 1919	11	Screinuller, Lt	151
PoWs from Britain	8	Secret inks	13, 31
Reprisals		Seebag-Montefiore, E	9, 78
camps set up in Britain	7, 135, 145, 163,	Seeberger, Carl	120

Segelken, Captain Friedrich (died)	159
Select Committee on National Expenditure	48
Sens, Bruno	185
Seven Years War (1756-63)	1
Sewing machine manufacture	99
'Sick and Hurt Office, The'	1
Simon, Paul	153
Sissinghurst Castle	1
Sheet music forbidden from post	17
Ships as places of detention	172-**183**
Shirley Skating Rink, Southampton	**192**, 193
Shrewsbury camp	184-186
Skea, Quartermaster Sergeant	161
Skipton camp	187-**188**
Slough camp	189-**190**
Slough Trading Co, (later Slough Estates Ltd)	190
Smuts, General J C	189
Smyth, LtCol WS	94
Sosinka, Paul (died)	161
South African Wars	2
Censorship	3
Southampton transit camps	191-193
Southend-on-Sea camp	194
Spindler, Karl	71
Spraub, Fritz	165
Stachelbauer, Julius	120
Stafford Detention Barracks	61, 212
Standard Shipyard	48
Stehr, Emil	103, 195
Steinhardt, Ernst J	120
Stevens, Mr G G	166
Stobs camp	195-**199**
Stoldt, Heindrich	103
Strang, Georg von	80
Stratford camp	200-**203**
Stratford, officers' reprisal camp	204
Strautmann, Joseph	74
Stelter, Eward (died)	52
Stocker, LtCol W A	117
Stockhurst, Alfred	154
Stoltzmann, Hans	120
Sturgis, LtCol H	165
Submarine crew PoWs	
segregated but policy abandoned	6, 85
Dyffryn Aled - main camp for	85
mail specially handled	16
Swalm, Albert A	178, 179, 193
Swansea, Lutland Street School	208
Swedish diplomats care of PoWs	7, 17
Swiss diplomats care of German PoWs	7, 17
Tarnou, Walter	135
Tarry, Major G G	132
Tax demands on PoWs	99, 102
Taylor, Dr A E	67, 75, 124
Taylor, Major G	121, 178
Teicher, Dr Konrad	151
Telegrams to prisoners	17
Templemore camp, Ireland	205
Thelan, Lt Otto	71, 107, 108, 120, 210
Thermometers made by PoWs	75
Thielmann, Hugo Karl	204
Tholens, Korvettenkapitan H	85, 210

Thomas, Brig E A D'A	121
Thomsen	120
Tirpitz, Lt von	84, 88
Token coinage for PoWs	**4**, 31, 214
Trade Union objections to PoW labour	49, 80, 113, 162
Trefftz, Ober-Lt	70
Truro Workhouse	208
Tunisian SS	**183**
Turner, Col W A T, RAMC	151
Tyrwhitt-Walker, LtCol J	191
Uccusic, August	123
United Alien Relief Societies, appeal	9
United States Embassy	6
UPU Convention, Rome 1906	13
Urania SS	172
Uranium SS	**183**
Valleyfield Prison	2
Versailles, Treaty (1919)	7
Vausch, Kurt	78
Vickers Ltd	99
Villbrandt, Karl	195
Vincent	151
Vischer, Dr A L	124
Voigt, Alfred	53
Volker	74
Waddiington LtCol F G	151
Waldhausen	151
Walker, LtCol R S F	41
Wallbaum, Hans	187
Wallis, Captain	85
War Office	
Directorate of PoWs	5
Expense of PoW and Internee mails	13
Weiner, Frederick	139
Wenzel, Otto (died)	185
Westphalia, Treaty (1648)	1
Wetzel, Wilhelm	155
Wighard, Joseph (died)	52
Wilbraham, Major R J	191, 193
Wilcher R	123
Wilson, J Havelock MP	154
Winkelmann, Max Ernst	71
Woking Detention Barracks	212
Women internees	46
Workhouses used for detention	208
Wright, Major K C	57, 95, 132, 213
Wunderle W	124
Wynne-Edwards, Col T A	158
Yarus, Herman	155
York camps	206-207
Youths in internment	51, 125, 130, 131
Zeppelin - air raids	10, 175
crew PoWs	57
mail specially handled	16
Zimpel, B J	184